ur • Tree • Pond & River • Butterfly & Moth

Dinosaur • Plant • Seashore • Flag • Insect

cient Egypt • Ancient Rome • Crystal & Gem

• Explorer • Dog • Horse • Cinema • Costum

• Amphibian • Elephant • Knight • Mummy

g • Desert • Prehistoric Life • Pyramid • Jungl

ing • Pirate • North American Indian • Africa

py • Religion • Eagle • Witch & Wizard • Spac

Russia • Light • Energy • Electricity • Force &

tronomy • Earth • Life • Evolution • Ecology

ics • Rennaissance • Impressionism • Goya

ctive • Dance • Future • Bird • Rock & Minera

ver • Butterfly & Moth • Sport • Shell • Earl

ashore • Flag • Insect • Money • Fossil • Fish

Rome • Crystal & Gem • Reptile • Invention

se • Cinema • Costume • Boat • Ancient Greec

• Knight • Mummy • Cowboy • Whale • Azte

ife • Pyramid • Jungle • China • Archaeology

rican Indian • Africa • Ocean • Battle • Goril

itch & Wizard • Space Exploration • Shipwrec

ectricity • Force & Motion • Chemistry • Matte

olution • Ecology • Human Body • Medicine

DORLING KINDERSLEY DK EYEWITNESS GUIDES

INDEX

Dorling Kindersley

LONDON, NEW YORK, AUCKLAND, DELHI,
JOHANNESBURG, MUNICH, PARIS and SYDNEY

For a full catalogue, visit

 www.dk.com

Project Editor Ranjana Saklani
Assistant Editor Glenda Fernandes
Senior Editor Scarlett O'Hara
DTP Designers Andrew O'Brien,
Umesh Agarwal, Sunil Sharma, and Ajay Varma
Production Josie Alabaster
Consultant Chris Bernstein

The publisher would like to thank the following for
their kind permission to reproduce their photographs:
American Museum of Natural History: 2br;
Natural History Museum: 3

First published in Great Britain in 1999
by Dorling Kindersley Limited,
9 Henrietta Street, London WC2E 8PS

A CIP catalogue record for this book
is available from the British Library.

ISBN 0 7513 6109 7

Printed by L.E.G.O. in Italy

EYEWITNESS GUIDES

INDEX

Dorling Kindersley

DK EYEWITNESS GUIDES

A–Z

AFRICA 61
AMPHIBIAN 41
ANCIENT EGYPT 23
ANCIENT GREECE 37
ANCIENT ROME 24
ARCHAEOLOGY 56
ARCTIC & ANTARCTIC 57
ARMS & ARMOUR 4
ASTRONOMY 82
AZTEC 47

BATTLE 63
BIBLE LANDS 30
BIRD 1
BOAT 36
BUILDING 58
BUTTERFLY & MOTH 7

CAR 21
CASTLE 49
CAT 29
CHEMISTRY 79
CHINA 55
CINEMA 34
COSTUME 35
COWBOY 45
CRIME & DETECTION 73
CRYSTAL & GEM 25

DANCE 99
DESERT 51
DINOSAUR 13
DOG 32

EAGLE 69
EARLY PEOPLE 10
EARTH 83
ECOLOGY 86
ELECTRICITY 77
ELECTRONICS 90

ELEPHANT 42
ENERGY 76
EVOLUTION 85
EXPLORER 31

FARM 66
FISH 20
FLAG 16
FLYING MACHINE 22
FORCE & MOTION 78
FOSSIL 19
FUTURE 100

GORILLA 64
GOYA 93

HORSE 33
HUMAN BODY 87

IMPRESSIONISM 92
INSECT 17
INVENTION 27

JUNGLE 54

KNIGHT 43

LIFE 84
LIGHT 75

MAMMAL 11
MANET 94
MATTER 80
MEDICINE 88
MEDIEVAL LIFE 65
MONET 95
MONEY 18
MUMMY 44
MUSIC 12

NORTH AMERICAN
INDIAN 60

OCEAN 62

PERSPECTIVE 98
PIRATE 59
PLANT 14
POND & RIVER 6
PREHISTORIC LIFE 52
PYRAMID 53

RELIGION 68
RENAISSANCE 91
REPTILE 26
ROCK & MINERAL 2
RUSSIA 74

SEASHORE 15
SHARK 40
SHELL 9
SHIPWRECK 72
SKELETON 3
SPACE EXPLORATION 71
SPORT 8
SPY 67

TECHNOLOGY 89
TIME & SPACE 81
TRAIN 39
TREE 5

VAN GOGH 96
VIKING 50
VOLCANO 38

WATERCOLOUR 97
WEATHER 28
WHALE 46
WITCH & WIZARD 70
WRITING 48

1–100

1 BIRD
2 ROCK & MINERAL
3 SKELETON
4 ARMS AND ARMOUR
5 TREE
6 POND & RIVER
7 BUTTERFLY & MOTH
8 SPORT
9 SHELL
10 EARLY PEOPLE

11 MAMMAL
12 MUSIC
13 DINOSAUR
14 PLANT
15 SEASHORE
16 FLAG
17 INSECT
18 MONEY
19 FOSSIL
20 FISH

21 CAR
22 FLYING MACHINE
23 ANCIENT EGYPT
24 ANCIENT ROME
25 CRYSTAL & GEM
26 REPTILE
27 INVENTION
28 WEATHER
29 CAT
30 BIBLE LANDS

31 EXPLORER
32 DOG
33 HORSE
34 CINEMA

35 COSTUME
36 BOAT
37 ANCIENT GREECE
38 VOLCANO
39 TRAIN
40 SHARK

41 AMPHIBIAN
42 ELEPHANT
43 KNIGHT
44 MUMMY
45 COWBOY
46 WHALE
47 AZTEC
48 WRITING
49 CASTLE
50 VIKING

51 DESERT
52 PREHISTORIC LIFE
53 PYRAMID
54 JUNGLE
55 CHINA
56 ARCHAEOLOGY
57 ARCTIC & ANTARCTIC
58 BUILDING
59 PIRATE
60 NORTH AMERICAN
INDIAN

61 AFRICA
62 OCEAN
63 BATTLE
64 GORILLA
65 MEDIEVAL LIFE
66 FARM
67 SPY

68 RELIGION
69 EAGLE
70 WITCH & WIZARD
71 SPACE EXPLORATION
72 SHIPWRECK
73 CRIME & DETECTION
74 RUSSIA
75 LIGHT
76 ENERGY
77 ELECTRICITY
78 FORCE & MOTION
79 CHEMISTRY
80 MATTER

81 TIME & SPACE
82 ASTRONOMY
83 EARTH
84 LIFE
85 EVOLUTION
86 ECOLOGY
87 HUMAN BODY
88 MEDICINE
89 TECHNOLOGY
90 ELECTRONICS

91 RENAISSANCE
92 IMPRESSIONISM
93 GOYA
94 MANET
95 MONET
96 VAN GOGH
97 WATERCOLOUR
98 PERSPECTIVE
99 DANCE
100 FUTURE

Future updates and editions will be available online at www.dk.com

SUBJECTS

HISTORY
AFRICA
ARMS & ARMOUR
BATTLE
CASTLE
CHINA
COWBOY
EXPLORER
KNIGHT
MEDIEVAL LIFE
MYTHOLOGY
NORTH AMERICAN
 INDIAN
PIRATE
RUSSIA
SHIPWRECK
VIKING
WITCH & WIZARD

ANCIENT WORLDS
ANCIENT EGYPT
ANCIENT GREECE
ANCIENT ROME
AZTEC
BIBLE LANDS
MUMMY
PYRAMID

THE BEGINNINGS OF LIFE
ARCHAEOLOGY
DINOSAUR
EARLY PEOPLE
PREHISTORIC LIFE

PAINTING
GOYA
IMPRESSIONISM
MANET
MONET

PERSPECTIVE
RENAISSANCE
VAN GOGH
WATERCOLOUR

THE ARTS
CINEMA
COSTUME
DANCE
MUSIC
WRITING

SCIENCE
ASTRONOMY
CHEMISTRY
EARTH
ECOLOGY
ELECTRICITY
ELECTRONICS
ENERGY
EVOLUTION

FORCE & MOTION
HUMAN BODY
LIFE
LIGHT
MATTER
MEDICINE
SKELETON
TECHNOLOGY
TIME & SPACE

TECHNOLOGY
BOAT
CAR
FLYING MACHINE
FUTURE
INVENTION
SPACE EXPLORATION
TRAIN

ANIMALS
AMPHIBIAN
BIRD
BUTTERFLY & MOTH
CAT
DOG

EAGLE
ELEPHANT
FISH
GORILLA
HORSE
INSECT
MAMMAL
REPTILE
SHARK
WHALE

HABITATS
ARCTIC & ANTARCTIC
DESERT
JUNGLE
OCEAN
POND & RIVER
SEASHORE

THE EARTH
CRYSTAL & GEM
FOSSIL
PLANT
ROCK & MINERAL
SHELL

TREE
VOLCANO
WEATHER

THE WORLD AROUND US
BUILDING
CRIME & DETECTION
FARM
FLAG
MONEY
RELIGION
SPORT
SPY

Future updates and editions will be available online at www.dk.com

The Ultimate Reference Tool

THE *EYEWITNESS INDEX* LINKS OVER 100 *Eyewitness Guides* into **a huge multi-volume encyclopedia**. Whether you are researching, fact checking, or browsing, this **detailed index** will guide you to the information you need.

Owning an *Eyewitness Guide* is almost like having **your own private museum**, with **hundreds of incredible exhibits** and a treasure trove of **fascinating information** about each one. The *Eyewitness Index* catalogues your entire collection, allowing you to **retrieve information** about science and technology, history and the natural world, the arts, geography, and earth science. **Cross-references** allow you to connect information between volumes and subject areas for a truly **cross-curricular** approach to research.

With over 8,000 topics, more than 10,000 detailed entries and at least 35,000 incredible images, the *Eyewitness* collection is **a vast library** of information.

Look online at **www.dk.com** for future updates and editions.

Using your *Eyewitness* world of information

music, **MUSIC 12**; **SPACE EXPLORATION 71** 8, 9, 12, 32; **VIKING 50** 50; **WRITING 48** 7, 21, 25
African, **AFRICA 61** 22, 23, 38, 60-61
Aztec, **AZTEC 47** 56-57
Chinese, **CHINA 55** 12, 52-53
Greek, **ANCIENT GREECE 37** 25, 33, 34, 46
in ritual, **MUSIC 12** 20, 50-51, 54, 55
medieval times, **CASTLE 49** 44-45; **MEDIEVAL LIFE 65** 54, 56-57
Russian, **RUSSIA 74** 48, 49
musical instruments, **AFRICA 61** 60-61; **ANCIENT ROME 24** 48, 49; **FORCE & MOTION 78** 48
see also under individual instruments

Main index heading
The index is an alphabetical list of all the subjects in the Eyewitness Guides. *Look for the subject you need to see if it is included as a main heading.*

Sub-heading
When the guides contain a lot of information about a topic, a list of **sub-headings** help you decide which are the most useful pages for you.

Page number
Once you have found the correct Eyewitness Guide, turn to this page to find the information you need.

Cross-reference
Look for a **cross-reference** at the end of the entry. It suggests similar entries you can look up.

Eyewitness Guide *Title*
Each entry gives you the title of the Eyewitness Guide you should look at to find the information you need.

Volume number
In addition to its title, each Eyewitness Guide is numbered from 1 to 100. This is the number of the guide you need to look at.

> 66 Every now and again, in the world of information books, a publishing phenomenon bursts clear of the field with a brilliant new series. 99
> **The Times Educational Supplement**

4 8, 9
EECE 37 25,

HELL 9 53
DESERT 51 10
99 58
PACE
8, 9, 12, 32;
WRITING 48

1 22, 23, 38,

56-57
5 12, 52-53
REECE 37

2 20,

ASTLE 49
Life 65 54,

74 48, 49

24 48, 49;
N 78 48
idual

8, 47, 51, 54
grave goods, **MUMMY 44** 30-31
Greece, **MUMMY 44** 19, 42-43
masks, **MUMMY 44** 18-19
mummification,
ANCIENT EGYPT 23 14-19; **EARLY PEOPLE 10** 39
natural, **MUMMY 44** 8-9, 62-63
Peru, **MUMMY 44** 52-54
royal, **MUMMY 44** 36-37
mummified bodies, **DESERT 51** 13
Mungo, Lake, **PREHISTORIC LIFE 52** 57
murals, **BUILDING 58** 52, 53
murder, **CRIME & DETECTION 73** 22-23, 40, 58
Murdock, William, **ENERGY 76** 55
Murelli, Sister Alvina, **CRIME & DETECTION 73** 26
murex shells, **SHELL 9** 8, 12, 51
Murphy, Eddie, **CINEMA 34** 55
Murray, Mae, **CINEMA 34** 21
Murray Island, **WITCH & WIZARD 70** 56, 57
Mursi peoples, **AFRICA 61** 22
Mursilis I, King, **BIBLE LANDS 30** 50
muscles,
CHEMISTRY 79 8, 31, 41, 51; **ENERGY 76** 8, 14; **HUMAN BODY 87** 11, 13, 20-23; **LIFE 84** 22-23, 24, 25
energy, **ENERGY 76** 6, 15, 53, 57

musk oxen, **ARCTIC & ANTARCTIC 57** 14-15, 40
musketeers, **ARMS & ARMOUR 4** 39
muskets **ARMS & ARMOUR 4** 33, 52; **BATTLE 63** 42, 46, 47, 48; **PIRATE 59** 28, 48
flintlock, **ARMS & ARMOUR 4** 38, 40-41
matchlock, **ARMS & ARMOUR 4** 34, 35, 38-39
Muslims, **CASTLE 49** 16-17, 34-35; **KNIGHT 43** 54, 55; **MEDIEVAL LIFE 65** 7, 28, 44, 45; **WRITING 48** 34-35
see also Islam
muslin, **COSTUME 35** 18, 28, 31
mussels, **FISH 20** 34, 43;
FOSSIL 19 10-11, 26; **OCEAN 62** 20-21, 58-59; **SEASHORE 15** 14, 22, 26, 31
date, **SEASHORE 15** 43
freshwater, **POND & RIVER 6** 52, 53, 59
green, **SEASHORE 15** 27
horse, **SEASHORE 15** 15
mustang, **COWBOY 45** 6-8, 12, 32
mustering, **COWBOY 45** 56-57
Mut, **PYRAMID 53** 52
mutation, **EVOLUTION 85** 51, 52, 53, 54; **FUTURE 100** 51;
LIFE 84 32, 42, 61
mutualism, **ECOLOGY 86** 46
Muybridge, Eadweard, **CAT 29** 19; **IMPRESSIONISM 92** 28, 49; **INVENTION 27** 50, 51; **SKELETON 3** 55

as photographer, **CINEMA 34** 10, 11
mu-yus, **MUSIC 12** 55
Mycenaeans, **ANCIENT GREECE 37** 6, 7, 10, 11; **BIBLE LANDS 30** 16, 17, 40
myopia, **LIGHT 75** 16, 19
myosin, **LIFE 84** 22, 23
myrtle, **FOSSIL 19** 3
mysticism, **WITCH & WIZARD 70** 12, 54, 55, 59
mythology, **CRYSTAL & GEM 25** 60; **RENAISSANCE 91** 32-33, 58; **SPACE EXPLORATION 71** 8
African, **AFRICA 61** 36-37
about monkeys, **GORILLA 64** 58-59

N

Nabopolassar, **BIBLE LANDS 30** 50
nacre, **CRYSTAL & GEM 25** 55
Nadar, **MONET 95** 6, 24
Nahal Hemar, **BIBLE LANDS 30** 34
Nakhimov, Admiral, **RUSSIA 74** 55
nameplates, **TRAIN 39** 54-55
Namib Desert, **DESERT 51** 12, 23, 28, 36
Namibia, **AFRICA 61** 18, 24; **CAT 29** 43
Nandi peoples, **DANCE 99** 15
nanotechnology, **FUTURE 100** 28, 34-35, 54
Napaljarri peoples, **DESERT 51** 12
Napata, **PYRAMID 53** 48
Naples, John, **INVENTION 27** 31
Naples, **ANCIENT GREECE 37** 26, 42; **ANCIENT ROME 24** 36; **CASTLE 49** 28; **VOLCANO 38** 31, 36, 60, 62

Napoleon I, Emperor of France, **HORSE 33** 42; **MUMMY 44** 10-11, 25; **PYRAMID 53** 23; **SHARK 40** 60
Napoleonic Wars, **BATTLE 63** 19, 49, 56, 58; **PIRATE 59** 59
weapons used, **ARMS & ARMOUR 4** 52, 53
Napoleon III, Emperor, **IMPRESSIONISM 92** 6, 18, 48; **MANET 94** 38, 42-43, 44
narwhals, **ARCTIC & ANTARCTIC 57** 46; **MAMMAL 11** 51; **WHALE 46** 10, 23, 36-37
NASA, **FUTURE 100** 10; **SPACE EXPLORATION 71** 19, 35; **TIME & SPACE 81** 44, 61
Natchez, **NORTH AMERICAN INDIAN 60** 24
National Aeronautics and Space Administration, *see* NASA
National Railway Museum, **TRAIN 39** 52
National Security Agency, USA, **SPY 67** 42
Native American peoples, **DESERT 51** 45, 52, 56, 57
Native Americans, **FARM 66** 32
writing, **WRITING 48** 8, 19, 53
NATO, **FUTURE 100** 11; **SPY 67** 39
natural selection, **ECOLOGY 86** 37; **EVOLUTION 85** 36-37, 43, 58; **LIFE 84** 42, 43
adaptation, **EVOLUTION 85** 38, 39, 42
competition, **EVOLUTION 85** 32, 34, 35
Darwin, **EVOLUTION 85** 20, 22, 31, 33
Mendelism, **EVOLUTION 85** 50
naturalism, **RENAISSANCE 91** 6, 18, 20-21
nautiloids, **EVOLUTION 85** 27, 60, 61; **FOSSIL 19** 28
Nautilus, **FOSSIL 19** 28; **SKELETON 3** 25
Navajo peoples, **DESERT 51** 56, 57; **NORTH AMERICAN INDIAN 60** 44, 48-49, 63
navigation, **ARCTIC & ANTARCTIC 57** 14, 55; **BOAT 36** 52; **CHINA 55** 22, 61; **PIRATE 59** 24
in aircraft, **FLYING MACHINE 22** 44-45, 46-47
automatic systems, **SHIPWRECK 72** 42
celestial, **ASTRONOMY 82** 14-15, 19
early, **TIME & SPACE 81** 13, 22

aardvarks, ELEPHANT **42** 12, 13; FOSSIL **19** 54; MAMMAL **11** 8, 51

abacus, CHINA **55** 40; INVENTION **27** 30

abalones, SEASHORE **15** 26

abbesses, MEDIEVAL LIFE **65** 22, 38

abbeys, MEDIEVAL LIFE **65** 38

abbots, MEDIEVAL LIFE **65** 38

Abbott, Bud, CINEMA **34** 54

abdomen, HUMAN BODY **87** 42, 43, 44, 46

Abel, Rudolph, SPY **67** 39

abhinaya, DANCE **99** 20

abominable snowman, GORILLA **64** 59

aboriginal peoples, ARCHAEOLOGY **56** 16, 44, 59, 62; ARMS & ARMOUR **4** 8-9, 56; EARLY PEOPLE **10** 13, 19; FLAG **16** 51

　Australian, COSTUME **35** 7; COWBOY **45** 38, 56

　bark painting, SHARK **40** 47

　beliefs, RELIGION **68** 8, 9

　boomerangs, BATTLE **63** 37

　desert, DESERT **51** 12, 46, 51, 57

　Dreamtime, DANCE **99** 27, 34, 44

　medicine, JUNGLE **54** 43, 57

abracadabra, WITCH & WIZARD **70** 9

Abraham, BIBLE LANDS **30** 10, 28; RELIGION **68** 42, 43

absolute zero, ENERGY **76** 20

Abu Roash, PYRAMID **53** 9

Abu Simbel, AFRICA **61** 10; ANCIENT EGYPT **23** 29

Abusir, PYRAMID **53** 24, 38

Abydos, PYRAMID **53** 29

Abyssinian, CAT **29** 17, 25, 46, 52-53

acacia, ECOLOGY **86** 48; PLANT **14** 36; TREE **5** 28

Académie des Beaux-Arts, MONET **95** 34

Académie Suisse, IMPRESSIONISM **92** 10

Academy Awards, CINEMA **34** 37, 39, 62

acceleration, FORCE & MOTION **78** 24, 30, 34; TIME & SPACE **81** 29, 43

accelerators, FORCE & MOTION **78** 62, 63; MATTER **80** 58, 60, 61

accessories, COSTUME **35** 18-19, 27, 36

accipitrids, EAGLE **69** 11, 13, 16

accordians, MUSIC **12** 17

accumulators, ELECTRICITY **77** 19

acetic acid, CHEMISTRY **79** 17, 42

Achaemenes, BIBLE LANDS **30** 52

Achilles, ANCIENT GREECE **37** 12, 35, 55, 61

Acholi peoples, AFRICA **61** 22

achromatic lens, LIGHT **75** 17, 21, 23

acid lakes, VOLCANO **38** 21, 38

acid rain, CHEMISTRY **79** 6; EARTH **83** 17, 50; ECOLOGY **86** 17; FUTURE **100** 18

acids, CHEMISTRY **79** 42-43, 44, 61

　see also under individual acids

acorns, TREE **5** 14, 20, 41, 51

acrobatics, DANCE **99** 23

acrobats, MEDIEVAL LIFE **65** 20, 54

Acropolis, ANCIENT GREECE **37** 7, 16, 17, 38

acrylic, TECHNOLOGY **89** 27, 29, 51

acteon shells, SHELL **9** 42

actin, LIFE **84** 22, 23

actinopterygians, FISH **20** 9

actors, MEDIEVAL LIFE **65** 54, 58

acupuncture, CHINA **55** 28-29; INVENTION **27** 42; MEDICINE **88** 15, 44-45

Adam of Bremen, VIKING **50** 52

Adams, George, ELECTRICITY **77** 10

Adams, John Couch, ASTRONOMY **82** 56

adaptation, EVOLUTION **85** 36, 38-39, 41; LIFE **84** 38, 43

adders, REPTILE **26** 22, 53

Adelaide, Queen of England, TRAIN **39** 44

Adena, ARCHAEOLOGY **56** 12

Adler, Alfred, MEDICINE **88** 47

adobe, BUILDING **58** 13

Adoree, Renee, CINEMA **34** 20

adrenal glands, HUMAN BODY **87** 39, 40

Adriosaurus, FOSSIL **19** 45

advection fog, WEATHER **28** 48, 49, 56

advertising, WATERCOLOUR **97** 56, 57

adze, ANCIENT EGYPT **23** 42; INVENTION **27** 10, 11; VIKING **50** 43

Aegean Sea, ANCIENT GREECE **37** 6, 8, 23, 31; BIBLE LANDS **30** 13, 22; PIRATE **59** 8-9

Aegina, ANCIENT GREECE **37** 40, 52

Aepyornis, FOSSIL **19** 53

aerobatics, FLYING MACHINE **22** 16, 22, 41, 42

aerodynamics, CAR **21** 32, 33, 35

aerofoil, FLYING MACHINE **22** 30, 31

aeroplanes, FUTURE **100** 8, 55, 59; INVENTION **27** 58, 59

　air brakes, FLYING MACHINE **22** 34, 58

　automatic pilot, FLYING MACHINE **22** 32, 40

　cockpit, FLYING MACHINE **22** 14, 42-43, 59

　controls, FLYING MACHINE **22** 14, 34, 40-41

　engines, FLYING MACHINE **22** 12-13, 28-29, 44

　flight deck, FLYING MACHINE **22** 32, 44-45, 56

　instruments, FLYING MACHINE **22** 42-43, 46-47

　landing, FLYING MACHINE **22** 34, 38-39

　navigation, FLYING MACHINE **22** 44-45, 46-47

　windscreen, FLYING MACHINE **22** 42, 43

　wings, FLYING MACHINE **22** 20-21, 26-27

　see also under individual planes

Aertex, COSTUME **35** 55

Aesculapius, ANCIENT ROME **24** 54, 55

Aesop, AMPHIBIAN **41** 59

Afghan hounds, DOG **32** 46, 48

Afghan Wars, BATTLE **63** 43

Africa, AFRICA **61**;

　EARLY PEOPLE **10** 6-7, 14-15, 28-29; WEATHER **28** 6, 38

　in Bible, BIBLE LANDS **30** 33, 40

　body decoration, AFRICA **61** 28-29, 62

　cats, CAT **29** 6, 10, 11, 32

　clothes, AFRICA **61** 24-27, 45

　colonization, AFRICA **61** 7

　crops, AFRICA **61** 15, 16, 17, 18

　currency, AFRICA **61** 49; MONEY **18** 47, 54, 55, 63

　dances, AFRICA **61** 22, 62-63; DANCE **99** 19, 32, 37, 58

　　costumes, DANCE **99** 29

　　religious, DANCE **99** 35

　flags, FLAG **16** 18, 54-55

　government, traditional, AFRICA **61** 30-31

　invasions, ANCIENT ROME **24** 7, 25

　jungles, JUNGLE **54** 40-41

　masks, DANCE **99** 32, 58-59

north, EXPLORER **31** 6, 8, 11, 18, 22

religion, AFRICA **61** 32-35; RELIGION **68** 14-17

volcanoes, VOLCANO **38** 10, 24, 50

western, EXPLORER **31** 6, 21, 49

witches, WITCH & WIZARD **70** 27-32, 40-43

African wildcat, CAT **29** 39, 44-45

African-Americans, COWBOY **45** 18; FLAG **16** 25

afterlife, ANCIENT EGYPT **23** 14, 15, 16-19

Agamemnon, King, ANCIENT GREECE **37** 10, 11, 12, 39

Agaristid moth, BUTTERFLY & MOTH **7** 49

Agassiz, Louis, EARTH **83** 18, 30; FOSSIL **19** 15

agate, ROCK & MINERAL **2** 52, 53, 60, 61; CRYSTAL & GEM **25** 33, 56, 58, 59; VOLCANO **38** 38, 39

Agerup, VIKING **50** 31

Aggersborg, VIKING **50** 22

Agincourt, battle of, CASTLE **49** 10; KNIGHT **43** 30, 32

agnathans, FISH **20** 9

agora, ANCIENT GREECE **37** 16, 25, 32, 52

Agricola, CHEMISTRY **79** 12

agriculture, ECOLOGY **86** 58, 59, 60, 62; FUTURE **100** 27, 38, 39; RUSSIA **74** 16, 17, 35, 38

　land reclamation, ECOLOGY **86** 16

　pests, ECOLOGY **86** 61

　productivity, ECOLOGY **86** 8

　soil erosion, ECOLOGY **86** 22

　see also farming

Agrippa, BIBLE LANDS **30** 40

Ahab, King, BIBLE LANDS **30** 20, 24

ahimsa, RELIGION **68** 36, 37

ahosi, AFRICA **61** 42

Ahura Mazda, RELIGION **68** 40, 41

Ain Ghazal, BIBLE LANDS **30** 9, 24, 42

air, FORCE & MOTION **78** 44, 45; WEATHER **28** 15, 51, 52

Air Force, FLAG **16** 47

air traffic control, FUTURE **100** 24, 25

air-conditioning, FUTURE **100** 19

aircraft, ENERGY **76** 30, 31; TECHNOLOGY **89** 6-7, 33, 37; WEATHER **28** 13, 44

　in battle, BATTLE **63** 25

　engines, FORCE & MOTION **78** 41

airliners, **FLYING MACHINE 22** 32-33, 34-35

airships, **FLYING MACHINE 22** 9, 56-57

Airy, Sir George Biddle, **ASTRONOMY 82** 27

Ajax, **ANCIENT GREECE 37** 35, 61

Akhenaten, **ANCIENT EGYPT 23** 10

Akhmatova, Anna, **RUSSIA 74** 44

Aksum, **PYRAMID 53** 48

Al Mu'tasim, Caliph, **BUILDING 58** 12

Alalakh, **BIBLE LANDS 30** 24, 44

alarms, **CRIME & DETECTION 73** 16, 39

Alaska,
ARCTIC & ANTARCTIC 57 50;
RUSSIA 74 23;
SHIPWRECK 72 30, 31;
VOLCANO 38 11, 35, 46, 57
whales, **WHALE 46** 43, 49, 58, 63

Alba, Duchess of, **GOYA 93** 26-27, 36

albatrosses,
ARCTIC & ANTARCTIC 57 22, 23, 26-27; **BIRD 1** 51;
SKELETON 3 50

Albert, Lake, **EXPLORER 31** 47

Alberti, Leon Battista,
PERSPECTIVE 98 12-14, 23, 26; **RENAISSANCE 91** 28, 30, 32; **WEATHER 28** 43

albite, **CRYSTAL & GEM 25** 6, 16

Albucasis of Cordoba, **MEDICINE 88** 20

Alcatraz,
CRIME & DETECTION 73 12, 13, 57

Alcazar, **CASTLE 49** 16

alchemists, **MATTER 80** 11, 46;
WITCH & WIZARD 70 10, 12-15

alchemy, **CHEMISTRY 79** 12-13, 27, 35

Alcock, John, **FLYING MACHINE 22** 32, 42

alcohol, **CHEMISTRY 79** 7, 59, 61

Alder moth, **BUTTERFLY & MOTH 7** 52

alders, **POND & RIVER 6** 19, 20; **TREE 5** 32, 40, 41

Aldrin, Buzz, **SPACE EXPLORATION 71** 19, 23

Aleppo, **BIBLE LANDS 30** 14

Alesia, **ANCIENT ROME 24** 12

Aleutian Islands, **VOLCANO 38** 11

Alexander I, Tsar of Russia, **RUSSIA 74** 23, 24

Alexander II, Tsar of Russia, **CRYSTAL & GEM 25** 35, 47; **RUSSIA 74** 17, 21, 42

Alexander III, Tsar of Russia, **RUSSIA 74** 21, 31

Alexander the Great,
ARCHAEOLOGY 56 42;
BATTLE 63 44;
EXPLORER 31 10;
HORSE 33 33, 42

Alexander, William, **WATERCOLOUR 97** 26, 27

Alexandra, Empress of Russia, **RUSSIA 74** 21, 30

Alexandria,
ANCIENT GREECE 37 62, 63;
BIBLE LANDS 30 41, 54;
MEDICINE 88 17;
MUMMY 44 29
coins, **BIBLE LANDS 30** 39
empire, **BIBLE LANDS 30** 54
Hellenistic Age,
ANCIENT GREECE 37 7, 46, 62-63; **PIRATE 59** 9; **SPY 67** 9;
ELEPHANT 42 46
library, **WRITING 48** 62

alexandrites,
CRYSTAL & GEM 25 6, 47

Alfa Romeo, **CAR 21** 18

Alfred the Great, King,
MEDIEVAL LIFE 65 6;
VIKING 50 38

algae, **EARTH 83** 10, 11;
EVOLUTION 85 26, 56, 61;
OCEAN 62 20, 22, 24;
SEASHORE 15 12, 36
grades and types, **LIFE 84** 49, 50, 52
non-flowering plants,
PLANT 14 6, 7, 46
single cell, **PREHISTORIC LIFE 52** 6-7, 12-13, 52

Algeria, **AFRICA 61** 27;
MONET 95 6; **PIRATE 59** 14-15, 59

Alhambra, **CASTLE 49** 17

Ali, **RELIGION 68** 59

Alice in Wonderland, **WRITING 48** 55

Alice Springs, Australia, **VOLCANO 38** 35

alkaline batteries, **ELECTRICITY 77** 18

alkalis,
CHEMISTRY 79 8, 44-45, 58

Allah, **RELIGION 68** 54, 55, 57

alleles, **LIFE 84** 40, 41, 43

alligator snapping turtles, **SHELL 9** 57

alligators, **REPTILE 26** 16, 21, 35, 56

Allosaurus, **PREHISTORIC LIFE 52** 34-35

alloys, **CHEMISTRY 79** 11, 15, 24;
MATTER 80 6, 14, 16;
TECHNOLOGY 89 14-15
aluminium,
TECHNOLOGY 89 43
brass, **MATTER 80** 12, 13, 17
bronze, **MATTER 80** 16, 17

gold, **TECHNOLOGY 89** 30
magnesium,
TECHNOLOGY 89 42
steel, **TECHNOLOGY 89** 10, 14
zinc, **TECHNOLOGY 89** 12

Alma-Tadema, Sir Lawrence,
ANCIENT GREECE 37 30, 42;
ANCIENT ROME 24 39

Almodovar, Pedro, **CINEMA 34** 55

almsgiving, **RELIGION 68** 58

alpenhorns, **MUSIC 12** 21

Alpha, space station, **SPACE EXPLORATION 71** 58-59

alphabet, **EARLY PEOPLE 10** 40;
VIKING 50 59; **WRITING 48** 14-19

Alphege, Archbishop, **VIKING 50** 17

Alps, **ANCIENT ROME 24** 7;
EARTH 83 46, 48, 58

Altamira, **ARCHAEOLOGY 56** 57;
EARLY PEOPLE 10 24, 25

alternating current,
ELECTRICITY 77 25, 40, 41, 55; **ELECTRONICS 90** 23, 28, 37, 38; **ENERGY 76** 33
distribution of,
ELECTRICITY 77 44

alternators, **ELECTRICITY 77** 40

Althing, **VIKING 50** 20, 28, 29

altins, **MONEY 18** 40

alula, **BIRD 1** 8, 10

aluminium,
CRYSTAL & GEM 25 32, 37, 42, 49; **EARTH 83** 20;
MATTER 80 14, 16, 23
alloys, **TECHNOLOGY 89** 43, 15, 58
light metal, **CHEMISTRY 79** 24
mineral,
ROCK & MINERAL 2 56;
CHEMISTRY 79 18, 24

Alvarado, Pedro de, **EXPLORER 31** 30

alveoli, **HUMAN BODY 87** 26, 27

Amanishakheto, Queen, **PYRAMID 53** 52-53

Amaterasu Omikami, **RELIGION 68** 34

Amathus, **BIBLE LANDS 30** 38

Amazon lily, **JUNGLE 54** 31

Amazon River, **CAT 29** 34-35, 37;
WHALE 46 33, 44, 63
basin, **JUNGLE 54** 30-31, 62

amazonite, **CRYSTAL & GEM 25** 32

amber, **DESERT 51** 57;
ELECTRICITY 77 6, 8, 14, 21;
RUSSIA 74 14, 29;
VIKING 50 27, 46, 49;
TREE 5 23
gems, **CRYSTAL & GEM 25** 54;
ROCK & MINERAL 2 14
fossils, **FOSSIL 19** 6, 20;
INSECT 17 10; **PREHISTORIC LIFE 52** 52

ambulances, **MEDICINE 88** 58-59

Amenemhat I, Pharaoh, **PYRAMID 53** 40

Amenemhat III, Pharaoh, **PYRAMID 53** 40, 42, 43

Amenhotep I, Pharaoh, **MUMMY 44** 37

Amenhotep II, Pharaoh, **MUMMY 44** 37

Amenhotep III, Pharaoh, **ANCIENT EGYPT 23** 44;
MUMMY 44 33, 37;
PYRAMID 53 33

America, **CAT 29** 49, 57;
EXPLORER 31 22-23, 33;
FLAG 16 54-55; **VIKING 50** 6, 21, 24; **WEATHER 28** 61
American Revolution, **SPY 67** 30
Civil War, **BATTLE 63** 33, 50, 51, 60
football, **SPORT 8** 10-13
native peoples,
ARCHAEOLOGY 56 9, 29, 62;
BATTLE 63 17, 36, 53, 56;
COWBOY 45 19, 40-42, 48-49; **DANCE 99** 18, 33, 39, 43
railroad, **TRAIN 39** 18-19
War of Independence, **ARMS & ARMOUR 4** 41
weather, **WEATHER 28** 7, 33, 42, 54
"west", **ARMS & ARMOUR 4** 60-61
see also Central America, North America, South America, United States

America's Cup, **BOAT 36** 60

American Christian flag, **FLAG 16** 25

American Legion flag, **FLAG 16** 24

American Saddlebreds, **COWBOY 45** 8-9

American Standardbreds, **HORSE 33** 60

Ames Jr., Adelbert, **PERSPECTIVE 98** 58, 59

Ames, Aldrich, **SPY 67** 34

amethyst,
ROCK & MINERAL 2 55, 61;
CRYSTAL & GEM 25 19, 32, 58, 60

amino acids, **LIFE 84** 36, 37, 55, 56; **MATTER 80** 43

Amish, **HORSE 33** 56

ammeters, **ELECTRICITY 77** 22, 24, 25; **ENERGY 76** 36, 43

ammonia, **CHEMISTRY 79** 32, 42, 43, 48; **MATTER 80** 36, 42
Solvay process,
CHEMISTRY 79 62, 63

ammonites,
ARCTIC & ANTARCTIC 57 10;
ROCK & MINERAL 2 20, 39;
SHELL 9 38; **SKELETON 3** 13

evolution, EVOLUTION 85 9, 26, 27, 61
fossils, FOSSIL 19 6, 28-29, 63
prehistoric, PREHISTORIC LIFE 52 16, 39, 53, 61
ammunition, BATTLE 63 26, 30, 42
amniotic fluid, HUMAN BODY 87 45, 46
amoeba, LIFE 84 13, 22, 28, 32
Amorites, BIBLE LANDS 30 50
Ampère, André-Marie, ELECTRICITY 77 26-27; LIGHT 75 42
amperes, ELECTRICITY 77 24, 25, 42
amphibians, AMPHIBIAN 41 6-7, 8-9; DESERT 51 26; FISH 20 6, 12; LIFE 84 22, 53; SKELETON 3 20, 21
colonization of land, FOSSIL 19 12, 13, 42-43
evolution, PREHISTORIC LIFE 52 7, 24-25
"age of fish", EVOLUTION 85 60, 61
reproduction, PREHISTORIC LIFE 52 52
see also frogs, newts, salamanders, toads
amphibole, CRYSTAL & GEM 25 38
amphitheatres, ANCIENT ROME 24 25, 28, 32, 60
amphorae, ARCHAEOLOGY 56 49-51; PIRATE 59 11; SHIPWRECK 72 50, 55, 57
Greek, Ancient, ANCIENT GREECE 37 48, 49
Roman, ANCIENT ROME 24 45, 60
amplification, ELECTRONICS 90 8, 28-31, 36; FORCE & MOTION 78 48, 49; INVENTION 27 52
amplifiers, ELECTRONICS 90 30-31; ELECTRICITY 77 34, 53, 61, 63; MUSIC 12 58
amplitude, FORCE & MOTION 78 48, 49, 50
ampulae of Lorenzini, SHARK 40 19, 29, 43
amputation, MEDICINE 88 26, 54
amulets, ANCIENT EGYPT 23 12, 24, 28; DESERT 51 52, 53, 55, 56; EARLY PEOPLE 10 36, 37
mummies, MUMMY 44 12, 16, 20-21
Viking, VIKING 50 18, 37
witchcraft, WITCH & WIZARD 70 28-31, 54
Amun, PYRAMID 53 26, 52, 53
Amun-Re, ANCIENT EGYPT 23 24, 28

Amundsen, Roald, ARCTIC & ANTARCTIC 57 20, 52, 54-55; EXPLORER 31 40, 54; FLAG 16 42
anacondas, GORILLA 64 16; REPTILE 26 40
anaemia, MEDICINE 88 31
anaesthesia, INVENTION 27 42, 43; MEDICINE 88 26, 48-49, 50; TECHNOLOGY 89 56
anal fin, SHARK 40 6-7, 40-42
Analects, The, RELIGION 68 30
Anatolia, BIBLE LANDS 30 13, 16, 30, 38
anatomy, MEDICINE 88 17, 24
Anatosaurus, DINOSAUR 13 28
ancestors, AFRICA 61 32, 36, 37, 40; ARCHAEOLOGY 56 42-43
early humans, dating of, ARCHAEOLOGY 56 55
earliest skeleton, ARCHAEOLOGY 56 6
worship, WITCH & WIZARD 70 41, 56, 57
Anchiterium, HORSE 33 9
anchor and chain, SHIPWRECK 72 42
Anchorage, Alaska, VOLCANO 38 57
anchors, BOAT 36 35, 43, 51; VIKING 50 24
Ancient Romans, see Romans, Ancient
Andalucian horses, COWBOY 45 7, 12-13
andalusite, CRYSTAL & GEM 25 49
Anders, William, EXPLORER 31 59
Andersen, Hans Christian, SHIPWRECK 72 59
Andes, EARTH 83 47
mummies, MUMMY 44 52
André, Major John, SPY 67 30
Andrea Doria, SHIPWRECK 72 9
Andrée, Salomon, ARCTIC & ANTARCTIC 57 52
Andrew, St., FLAG 16 47; RUSSIA 74 9
Andronicus, WEATHER 28 42
anemometers, WEATHER 28 12, 43, 62
anemones, OCEAN 62 24, 28-29, 31; SEASHORE 15 36-37, 38, 48
angel shark, SHARK 40 6, 17-18, 36-39
angelfish, FISH 20 15, 16, 20
Angelico, Fra, RENAISSANCE 91 24
angels, RELIGION 68 49, 51; TIME & SPACE 81 10, 11, 26, 40

angiosperms, FOSSIL 19 13, 38
anglerfish, FISH 20 20, 21
Angleton, James Jesus, SPY 67 50
Anglo-Saxon peoples, ARCHAEOLOGY 56 11, 27, 43; BUILDING 58 46; WRITING 48 24
arms, ARMS & ARMOUR 4 14
costume, COSTUME 35 12-13
Angola, AFRICA 61 16-17, 24, 60
angular crabs, SHELL 9 38
angwantibo, GORILLA 64 12
animals, AZTEC 47 60, 61; TREE 5 19, 50-52; VIKING 50 36-37, 38; WITCH & WIZARD 70 36-39, 54
African, AFRICA 61 6, 10, 16
classification, LIFE 84 49, 50, 52-53
endangered, JUNGLE 54 62
as food, AFRICA 61 18-19
illegal trade, CRIME & DETECTION 73 28
mummies, MUMMY 44 6, 9, 44-47
nocturnal, JUNGLE 54 28-29
predators, JUNGLE 54 46-47
primitive breeds, ARCHAEOLOGY 56 59
remains, ARCHAEOLOGY 56 30-31, 44-47
Roman, ANCIENT ROME 24 22, 32
Russian, RUSSIA 74 10, 11, 13, 53
sacred, RELIGION 68 20-21, 44, 51
skins, EARLY PEOPLE 10 18, 20, 32, 61
as symbols, ANCIENT EGYPT 23 60-61
in amulets, WITCH & WIZARD 70 28-31
warm-blooded, LIFE 84 26, 49, 53
see also under individual animals
animation, CINEMA 34 45, 50-53
ankh, ANCIENT EGYPT 23 13; WITCH & WIZARD 70 20
ankoku butoh, DANCE 99 43
Anlamani, PYRAMID 53 50
Anna, Empress of Russia, RUSSIA 74 28, 57
Anning, Mary, FOSSIL 19 46
anodes, ELECTRICITY 77 18, 19, 3
in cathode ray tubes, ELECTRICITY 77 54, 55, 62, 63
ant lions, INSECT 17 40
Antarctic Ocean, ARCTIC & ANTARCTIC 57 12-13; WEATHER 28 16, 20, 61; WHALE 46 10, 14, 48, 61

birds, ARCTIC & ANTARCTIC 57 22-23, 24
explorers, ARCTIC & ANTARCTIC 57 54-55
ice sheet, ARCTIC & ANTARCTIC 57 11
Antarctic Treaty, ARCTIC & ANTARCTIC 57 62, 63
Antarctica, ARCTIC & ANTARCTIC 57; EARTH 83 18, 19, 36, 55; ECOLOGY 86 16, 24; EXPLORER 31 34, 44, 54-55; VOLCANO 38 11, 35
anteaters, JUNGLE 54 12; MAMMAL 11 8, 51; SKELETON 3 31
antelopes, DESERT 51 46; MAMMAL 11 10, 58; SKELETON 3 31, 53
antennae, INSECT 17 7, 12, 16-17; LIFE 84 24, 44, 48
mechanical, SPY 67 23, 44, 45, 49
anthracite, ROCK & MINERAL 2 7, 37
anthropoids, GORILLA 64 6
Anthus, ANCIENT ROME 24 23
Antibes, MONET 95 39
antibiotics, MEDICINE 88 42, 50; TECHNOLOGY 89 56, 60
anticyclones, WEATHER 28 14
Antioch, CASTLE 49 34
Antiochus IV, BIBLE LANDS 30 54
Antipater, BIBLE LANDS 30 56
antiques, fake, ARCHAEOLOGY 56 55, 56-57
antisepsis, MEDICINE 88 48-49, 50, 54
antiseptics, INVENTION 27 43
Antisitia, ANCIENT ROME 24 23
anti-war dances, DANCE 99 18, 38
antlers, ARCTIC & ANTARCTIC 57 15, 34, 35, 38; MAMMAL 11 14, 26, 62-63; VIKING 50 36, 59
Antonello da Messina, PERSPECTIVE 98 6
Antoniadi, Eugène, ASTRONOMY 82 44, 48
Antonius Pius, ANCIENT ROME 24 9
Antony, Mark, BIBLE LANDS 30 56
ants, DESERT 51 22; INSECT 17 21, 39, 56-57; JUNGLE 54 36-37; PLANT 14 36
Antwerp Academy, VAN GOGH 96 24, 26-27
Anubis, ANCIENT EGYPT 23 14, 19; DOG 32 15, 24, 25, 34; MUMMY 44 10, 21, 27, 44; PYRAMID 53 45

Anzani, Alessandro,
FLYING MACHINE 22 15
engine, FLYING MACHINE 22
15, 22, 28, 29
aorta, HUMAN BODY 87 24,
29, 39, 40
blood, HUMAN BODY 87
27, 31
Apache peoples,
NORTH AMERICAN
INDIAN 60 8, 44, 48-50;
ARMS & ARMOUR 4 51
apatite, CRYSTAL & GEM 25
9, 19
Apatosaurus, DINOSAUR 13 12,
43, 62; FOSSIL 19 48, 49
Apd ar-Rahman I,
BUILDING 58 33
apes, FOSSIL 19 55, 58;
JUNGLE 54 44-45;
MAMMAL 11 8, 14;
PREHISTORIC LIFE 52
54-55, 56
brains,
GORILLA 64 6, 8, 36, 50
defences, GORILLA 64 34-35
early, EARLY PEOPLE 10 6, 7
great, GORILLA 64 8-9, 36-37
human similarities,
EARLY PEOPLE 10 6-7;
GORILLA 64 6, 8-9, 60-61
knuckle-walking,
GORILLA 64 9
language, GORILLA 64 36, 37
lesser, GORILLA 64 30-31
Aphrodite, ANCIENT
GREECE 37 20, 31, 60, 62;
ANCIENT ROME 24 6;
BIBLE LANDS 30 25, 55
Aphrodite butterflies,
BUTTERFLY & MOTH 7 28
Apocrypha, BIBLE LANDS 30 58
Apollinaire, Guillaume,
WRITING 48 44, 49
Apollo butterflies,
BUTTERFLY & MOTH 7 30
Apollo mission,
ASTRONOMY 82 34, 41;
SPACE EXPLORATION 71 12,
18-19, 34
Apollo, sun god,
ANCIENT GREECE 37 21, 24,
25, 32; ANCIENT ROME 24
49; DANCE 99 37
Apollonius,
WITCH & WIZARD 70 12
apostles,
RELIGION 68 50, 52, 53
apothecaries, MEDICINE 88
40-41
Appaloosa, COWBOY 45 19
appendix,
HUMAN BODY 87 37
Appenzell, DOG 32 44
apples, FARM 66 38, 39;
TREE 5 32, 35, 38, 39
appliances, ELECTRICITY 77 46

domestic, ELECTRICITY 77
48-49; TECHNOLOGY 89
40-41, 52
aqche, MONEY 18 40
aqualungs, SHIPWRECK 72 46
aquamarines,
CRYSTAL & GEM 25 38, 39,
56, 61
aquariums, SEASHORE 15 18, 35
aqueducts, ANCIENT ROME 24
26, 27; CASTLE 49 35
aquifers, DESERT 51 14;
EARTH 83 15
Arab horses, HORSE 33 38-39, 42
Arabia, BIBLE LANDS 30 38
Arabian Desert, DESERT 51 7, 9,
12, 21
Arabic language,
RELIGION 68 54, 57, 58;
WRITING 48 7, 18, 34-35
kufic script, WRITING 48 8
Arabs, BATTLE 63 7;
EXPLORER 31 9, 18-20, 29, 46
medicine, MEDICINE 88
20-21
arachnids, DESERT 51 24-25;
INSECT 17 9
Aradus, BIBLE LANDS 30 22
Arago, François, LIGHT 75 48
Aragon, FLAG 16 36
aragonite, CRYSTAL & GEM 25 23
Aramaean kingdoms,
BIBLE LANDS 30 22, 44
Arapaho, DANCE 99 18
arawana, FISH 20 37, 44
Arbuckle, "Fatty", CINEMA 34
54, 55
arc lamps, CINEMA 34 16, 17,
19, 32; LIGHT 75 52
archaeology,
ARCHAEOLOGY 56 48, 54, 56;
EARLY PEOPLE 10 62-63;
MUMMY 44 11, 17, 36, 38
conservation,
ARCHAEOLOGY 56 34-35,
38-41
experimental,
ARCHAEOLOGY 56 58-59
industrial,
ARCHAEOLOGY 56 50, 60-61
marine, ARCHAEOLOGY 56
32-33; OCEAN 62 54-55
Archaeopteris, FOSSIL 19 37
Archaeopteryx, BIRD 1 6;
FOSSIL 19 37, 52, 53
Archaeosigillaria, FOSSIL 19 36
archbishops,
MEDIEVAL LIFE 65 8, 10, 30
Archduke butterflies,
BUTTERFLY & MOTH 7 22
Archelaus, BIBLE LANDS 30
39, 54
Archelon, FOSSIL 19 44
Archer, A.,
ANCIENT GREECE 37 17
Archer, Frederick Scott,
INVENTION 27 41

archerfish, FISH 20 36
archers, ARMS & ARMOUR 4 15,
18, 20, 21; KNIGHT 43
30-31, 32
archery, SPORT 8 52-53
arches, BUILDING 58 32-33,
46, 61
Archimedes,
FORCE & MOTION 78 12, 24,
43; INVENTION 27 8, 9, 24
levers,
FORCE & MOTION 78 16
Principle, FORCE &
MOTION 78 14-15, 24
pulleys, FORCE &
MOTION 78 18, 19
screw, BOAT 36 38; FORCE &
MOTION 78 12-13;
FOSSIL 19 24
spiral, FORCE & MOTION 78 55
architects, BUILDING 58 6, 7
architecture,
AZTEC 47 16-17, 18-19;
BUILDING 58 32, 39, 42, 49;
PERSPECTIVE 98 40-41
drawings, WATERCOLOUR 97
9, 57
Gothic, BUILDING 58 33, 34,
36, 59
Islamic,
ARCHAEOLOGY 56 18-19;
BUILDING 58 36, 46, 58, 61
orders, BUILDING 58
ornamentation,
BUILDING 58 58-61
perspective,
PERSPECTIVE 98 10-11, 14-15
Renaissance, BUILDING 58 32,
39, 42, 49
Rococo, BUILDING 58 46
Romanesque, BUILDING 58
33, 59
Russian, RUSSIA 74 16,
26-29, 36
see also building
archosaurs, PREHISTORIC
LIFE 52 33, 40
Arctic,
ARCTIC & ANTARCTIC 57;
EARTH 83 18; ECOLOGY 86
16, 28, 29, 31; WEATHER 28
16, 20
birds, ARCTIC &
ANTARCTIC 57 14-15, 20-21
clothes, ARCTIC &
ANTARCTIC 57 49, 50, 56-57
dolphins, WHALE 46 10
explorers, ARCTIC &
ANTARCTIC 57 52-53;
EXPLORER 31 50-53
mummies, MUMMY 44 7, 9
native peoples,
ARCTIC & ANTARCTIC 57 48,
49, 50-51
seals, WHALE 46 14
shipwrecks, SHIPWRECK 72
11, 38

walruses, WHALE 46 42
whales, WHALE 46 7, 42
Arctic Ocean, ARCTIC &
ANTARCTIC 57 8, 12
Arctiid moths, BUTTERFLY &
MOTH 7 16, 53, 56
Arena Chapel,
RENAISSANCE 91 8-9
Argenteuil, MONET 95 12,
20-23, 26
Argentina,
CAT 29 40-41; DANCE 99 55;
FLAG 16 55
Argo, SHIPWRECK 72 28
argon, TECHNOLOGY 89 41, 59
argonauts, SHELL 9 19
Argyle diamonds, CRYSTAL &
GEM 25 25, 59
Argyll, CAR 21 59
Ariane rocket,
ASTRONOMY 82 35;
SPACE EXPLORATION 71 12,
14-15, 35
Aristarchus, ANCIENT
GREECE 37 58;
ASTRONOMY 82 11
Aristophanes,
ASTRONOMY 82 22
Aristotle, ENERGY 76 15, 16;
HUMAN BODY 87 6, 8, 9, 10;
MATTER 80 8; VOLCANO 38
52; WHALE 46 6
on elements,
FORCE & MOTION 78 6,
24, 26
philosophy, ANCIENT
GREECE 37 46, 47
Arjuna, RELIGION 68 20, 23
Arkwright, Richard,
INVENTION 27 37
Arles, VAN GOGH 96 42-45,
49, 52
Arliss, George, CINEMA 34 62
armadillos, SKELETON 3 30, 50;
DINOSAUR 13 32, 33;
EVOLUTION 85 23, 24;
MAMMAL 11 8, 27, 29
Armenia, RUSSIA 74 12, 22
Armero, Colombia,
VOLCANO 38 56, 58
armies,
ANCIENT EGYPT 23 36-37;
MEDIEVAL LIFE 65 9, 22, 24
armillary sphere,
ASTRONOMY 82 11, 15, 26
Armitage, Edward A.,
ANCIENT ROME 24 46
armour, ARMS & ARMOUR 4;
AFRICA 61 44-45, 46-47;
BATTLE 63 11, 38, 44;
CASTLE 49 30, 34, 36
ancient, ANCIENT GREECE 37
10, 54-55
cavalry,
ANCIENT ROME 24 13
gladiators, ANCIENT
ROME 24 30-31, 33

legionaries, ANCIENT ROME **24** 10-11
armourers, CASTLE **49** 60; KNIGHT **43** 16-17, 34
Indian, ARMS & ARMOUR **4** 32-33
knights, ARMS & ARMOUR **4** 24-25, 26-27; KNIGHT **43**
early, KNIGHT **43** 12-13
jousts, ARMS & ARMOUR **4** 30-31; KNIGHT **43** 45
making, KNIGHT **43** 16-17
wearing, KNIGHT **43** 28-29
medieval, MEDIEVAL LIFE **65** 7, 25, 28-29
Armstrong, Edwin, ELECTRONICS **90** 48
Armstrong, Louis, MUSIC **12** 23
Armstrong, Neil, ASTRONOMY **82** 34; EXPLORER **31** 58; FUTURE **100** 10; SPACE EXPLORATION **71** 19, 23
Armstrong Siddeley FLYING MACHINE **22** 49
Arnold, Benedict, SPY **67** 30
aromatherapy, MEDICINE **88** 44; TECHNOLOGY **89** 47
Arrieta, Dr., GOYA **93** 46-47
arrowheads, POND & RIVER **6** 14, 20
arrows, ANCIENT EGYPT **23** 37, 44; ARMS & ARMOUR **4** 3, 10, 21; CASTLE **49**, 13, 16, 26; DESERT **51** 46; JUNGLE **54** 34; SPORT **8** 53
early, EARLY PEOPLE **10** 13, 26, 27, 28
longbow, ARMS & ARMOUR **4** 18-21
North American Indian, ARMS & ARMOUR **4** 63
poisoned, ARMS & ARMOUR **4** 9
Viking, VIKING **50** 12, 14, 20
see also archery, bows
arson, CRIME & DETECTION **73** 30, 31, 47
art, RUSSIA **74** 46-47
Africa, AFRICA **61** 10, 11
desert, DESERT **51** 47, 60-61
early, EARLY PEOPLE **10** 22, 23, 24-25
Gothic, RENAISSANCE **91** 6, 16-17
Japan, MANET **94** 36-37, 40, 56; MONET **95** 22, 36, 37, 43, 61; VAN GOGH **96** 31, 36-37, 47
pop, PERSPECTIVE **98** 60-61
Romantic period, PERSPECTIVE **98** 46-47
Roman, ANCIENT ROME **24** 6, 25, 36, 42
see also Impressionism, Perspective, Watercolour and under individual artists

Art, Nouveau, BUILDING **58** 44, 56, 59; WATERCOLOUR **97** 44
Artemis, ANCIENT GREECE **37** 20, 21, 27, 62; ANCIENT ROME **24** 63
arteries, HUMAN BODY **87** 22, 28-31, 60; LIFE **84** 15, 27
arthropods, FOSSIL **19** 30-31; LIFE **84** 24, 30, 49, 53; PREHISTORIC LIFE **52** 7, 14, 20-23, 27; SHELL **9** 22
Arthur, King, ARMS & ARMOUR **4** 16; KNIGHT **43** 41; WITCH & WIZARD **70** 17
artificial limbs, MEDICINE **88** 54-55
artificial organs, FUTURE **100** 40, 41, 59
artificial selection, ECOLOGY **86** 58; EVOLUTION **85** 30-31
artillery, BATTLE **63** 26, 34-35, 50; CASTLE **49** 24
aryballos, ANCIENT GREECE **37** 7, 14, 15, 49
Asama, Japan, VOLCANO **38** 34
Asante peoples, DANCE **99** 15, 37
gold, AFRICA **61** 54, 56-57
kingdom, AFRICA **61** 10, 30, 43
asbestos, CRYSTAL & GEM **25** 33
asceticism, RELIGION **68** 36, 51
Asclepiades, ANCIENT GREECE **37** 58, 59
asepsis, MEDICINE **88** 48-49, 50, 54
ash trees, TREE **5** 16, 22, 25, 29
Ashkelon, BIBLE LANDS **30** 20
Ashton, Frederick, DANCE **99** 33, 40, 56
Ashurnasirpal II, BIBLE LANDS **30** 49
Asia Minor, ANCIENT GREECE **37** 27, 35, 52, 62
Asia, ANCIENT GREECE **37** 54, 63; ARCTIC & ANTARCTIC **57** 8, 34, 48; EXPLORER **31** 10-12, 16-18
central, ARCHAEOLOGY **56** 29-31, 49; RUSSIA **74** 12, 22, 36, 59
south-east, JUNGLE **54** 48, 57, 60
Asimov, Isaac, FUTURE **100** 8, 44
Asklepios, ANCIENT ROME **24** 54, 55
asparagus, PLANT **14** 34
Aspelta, PYRAMID **53** 50
aspirin, CRYSTAL & GEM **25** 62

Assam, WEATHER **28** 39
assassinations, CRIME & DETECTION **73** 58
assassins, SPY **67** 28, 30, 36, 40
asses, HORSE **33** 12, 16-17; MAMMAL **11** 10
wild, DESERT **51** 34
assignats, MONEY **18** 31, 37
Assisi, VOLCANO **38** 7
Assyria, BIBLE LANDS **30** 23, 28, 33, 38; FLAG **16** 8; PIRATE **59** 8
battles, BATTLE **63** 7; BIBLE LANDS **30** 46-47
Empire, EXPLORER **31** 7
medicine, MEDICINE **88** 8-9
Astaire, Fred, CINEMA **34** 57; DANCE **99** 54
Astarte, BIBLE LANDS **30** 24-25, 48, 55
asteroids, ASTRONOMY **82** 36, 49, 58; FOSSIL **19** 32; FUTURE **100** 56, 59; ROCK & MINERAL **2** 41; TIME & SPACE **81** 15
Aston, F. W., MATTER **80** 52
astrolabes, PIRATE **59** 24; SHIPWRECK **72** 22, 32, 33
astrology, WITCH & WIZARD **70** 15, 50, 54, 58
astronauts, FUTURE **100** 10, 11, 14, 38; SPACE EXPLORATION **71** 10, 17, 36-37
at work, SPACE EXPLORATION **71** 30-31
deaths, SPACE EXPLORATION **71** 34-35
in space, SPACE EXPLORATION **71** 28-29
tests, SPACE EXPLORATION **71** 40
training, SPACE EXPLORATION **71** 24-25
astronomy, ASTRONOMY **82**; INVENTION **27** 34; MEDIEVAL LIFE **65** 45; SPACE EXPLORATION **71** 52-53
Astyages, King, BIBLE LANDS **30** 52
Aswan, PYRAMID **53** 32, 43
Aswan Dam, ANCIENT EGYPT **23** 8; MUMMY **44** 10
Athena, ANCIENT GREECE **37** 21, 23, 25, 44; ANCIENT ROME **24** 50
athenosphere, VOLCANO **38** 13
Athens, ANCIENT GREECE **37** 7, 16-19, 38
athletics, SPORT **8** 38-41
Atlantic Ocean, ARCTIC & ANTARCTIC **57** 8; EARTH **83** 30, 34, 36, 48; SHIPWRECK **72** 28; VIKING **50** 11

crossings, FLYING MACHINE **22** 9, 32, 42
weather, VOLCANO **38** 11; WEATHER **28** 6, 7, 61
voyages, EXPLORER **31** 12-13, 30, 48, 57
Atlantis, lost city, OCEAN **62** 55
Atlas moths, BUTTERFLY & MOTH **7** 47
atmosphere, EARTH **83** 10-11; ECOLOGY **86** 8, 52, 60; SPACE EXPLORATION **71** 10, 11; WEATHER **28** 6, 58, 60
atmospheric pressure, WEATHER **28** 18
eruptions, VOLCANO **38** 6, 14, 16, 34
gases, EARTH **83** 6, 7, 19
life-sustaining, ASTRONOMY **82** 37, 42-43
weathering, EARTH **83** 50, 51
and winds, WEATHER **28** 33, 42, 44, 52
atom bomb, TIME & SPACE **81** 37; ENERGY **76** 47; FUTURE **100** 8, 10
atomic clock, TIME & SPACE **81** 37, 44, 56
atomic energy, TECHNOLOGY **89** 59, 63
atomic theory, CHEMISTRY **79** 16-17, 20
atoms, EARTH **83** 20, 23, 25, 29; ENERGY **76** 20, 43, 46; FORCE & MOTION **78** 43, 55, 62; MATTER **80** 7, 12, 35, 56; TECHNOLOGY **89** 9, 12, 15, 17
collision, FORCE & MOTION **78** 63
as conductors, ELECTRICITY **77** 20
in crystals, CRYSTAL & GEM **25** 14-15, 20, 21
as electrons, ELECTRONICS **90** 26, 36, 55
in electromagnetic waves, LIGHT **75** 42-43
forces, TECHNOLOGY **89** 20, 21
and heat, MATTER **80** 30, 38
and light, LIGHT **75** 6, 8, 42-43
and molecules, MATTER **80** 36-37
motion, ENERGY **76** 36, 44, 45, 48
in particle accelerators, ELECTRICITY **77** 12, 30-31
periodic tables, CHEMISTRY **79** 22-23
quantum theory, TIME & SPACE **81** 36, 52, 53
splitting, MATTER **80** 54-55
strings, TIME & SPACE **81** 58, 59
structure, FORCE & MOTION **78** 62; MATTER **80** 34, 48-49, 50

atrium, architecture, **Ancient Rome 24** 22, 24, 25, 27

atrium, heart, **Human Body 87** 6, 27, 28-29

Atterdag, Valdemar, **Flag 16** 40

Attila the Hun, **Ancient Rome 24** 63

Auburn, **Car 21** 22, 23

Audubon, John James, **Dog 32** 29; **Explorer 31** 45, 62

Auenbrugger, Leopold, **Medicine 88** 28-29

augers, **Shell 9** 43

augite, **Crystal & Gem 25** 14

Auguste, Jules-Robert, **Watercolour 97** 54

Augustine, St., **Medieval Life 65** 39

Augustine volcano, Alaska, **Volcano 38** 7

Augustus, Emperor, **Ancient Rome 24** 8, 18, 50, 52; **Bible Lands 30** 54, 56

auks, **Arctic & Antarctic 57** 10, 20

aureus, **Money 18** 36

auriculotherapy, **Medicine 88** 45

aurochs, **Archaeology 56** 26, 44-45

auroras, **Arctic & Antarctic 57** 7; **Astronomy 82** 39, 43; **Light 75** 6

aurora australis, **Weather 28** 58
aurora borealis, **Weather 28** 58

auscultation, **medicine 88** 29

Austin, **Car 21** 24-25, 30-31, 62

Australasia, **Cat 29** 10, 40

Australia, **Explorer 31** 34-39, 49, 56; **Volcano 38** 35; **Weather 28** 44, 49, 55
aboriginal peoples,
creation myth, **Dance 99** 27, 34; **Witch & Wizard 70** 56
clothes, **Costume 35** 7
cowboys, **Cowboy 45** 56
currency, **Money 18** 50, 51, 63
dolphinaria, **Whale 46** 57
flags, **Flag 16** 50-51
monsoon, **Weather 28** 38
rainforests, **Jungle 54** 44, 56-57
witchcraft, **Witch & Wizard 70** 56-57
tectonic plates, **Volcano 38** 11

Australopithecus, **Fossil 19** 58, 59

Austria, **Battle 63** 55; **Flag 16** 32-33; **Money 18** 32, 34, 62

Austro-Prussian War, **Battle 63** 20

automobiles, *see* cars

autotrophs, **Energy 76** 52, 53

Autry, Gene, **Cowboy 45** 60

Auvers, **Van Gogh 96** 39, 58, 59, 60

avalanches, **Weather 28** 41

avatars, **Religion 68** 18, 20, 23

Avelignese horse, **Horse 33** 51

Avery, Henry, **Pirate 59** 34, 37, 47

Avicenna of Persia, **Medicine 88** 21, 24; **Medieval Life 65** 45

avocets, **Bird 1** 33, 39

Avogadro, Amadeo, **Chemistry 79** 16, 17; **Matter 80** 37

Avro Vulcan bomber, **Flying Machine 22** 39

Awdry, Reverend, **Train 39** 61

awls, **Early People 10** 32

axes, **Ancient Egypt 23** 36, 42; **Archaeology 56** 8, 45, 50; **Castle 49** 53, 59; **Mummy 44** 56
African, **Africa 61** 44, 46
Aztec, **Aztec 47** 13, 26, 59
battle-axes, **Arms & Armour 4** 23; **Battle 63** 38-39
Chinese, **China 55** 10, 11, 15
early, **Early People 10** 12, 30, 47, 55
Indian, **Arms & Armour 4** 23, 32
pirates, **Pirate 59** 12, 29, 33
Stone Age, **Arms & Armour 4** 6, 7
types, **Arms & Armour 4** 9, 22-23; **Knight 43** 7, 18-19
Viking, **Arms & Armour 4** 15; **Viking 50** 7, 15, 21, 23

axinite, **Crystal & Gem 25** 48

axis, **Astronomy 82** 12, 13, 38, 42
Saturn, **Astronomy 82** 52
Uranus, **Astronomy 82** 54

axles, **Force & Motion 78** 7, 10-11, 39
gyroscope, **Force & Motion 78** 56
machine, **Force & Motion 78** 22
steam driven, **Force & Motion 78** 21

axolotl, **Fossil 19** 42

Axumites, **Pyramid 53** 48

aye-ayes, **Gorilla 64** 10, 11

Ayurvedic medicine, **Medicine 88** 10, 14

Azande peoples, **Africa 61** 46, 49, 52

Azerbaijan, **Russia 74** 12, 22

azimuth, **Astronomy 82** 60
horizon ring, **Astronomy 82** 26

Azores, **Whale 46** 38, 49

Aztec peoples, **Aztec 47** 6-7, 8; **Early People 10** 58; **Explorer 31** 30-33, 62; **Jungle 54** 58, 60; **Pirate 59** 20-21
architecture, **Aztec 47** 16-17, 18-19
entertainment, **Aztec 47** 56-57, 58-59
family life, **Aztec 47** 20-21, 22-23
farming, **Aztec 47** 12-13
food, **Aztec 47** 24-25, 60, 61
jewellery, **Aztec 47** 51, 52, 53
markets, **Aztec 47** 14, 26, 27, 39
mummies, **Aztec 47** 19, 34-35, 54
pyramids, **Pyramid 53** 6, 54, 60-61
religion, **Aztec 47** 30-33
sacrifices, human, **Aztec 47** 8, 30, 36-37
Spanish conquest, **Aztec 47** 62
weapons, **Arms & Armour 4** 22

azurite, **Rock & Mineral 2** 33, 45; **Crystal & Gem 25** 16, 24

Baal, **Bible Lands 30** 24

Babbage, Charles, **Electronics 90** 9; **Force & Motion 78** 23; **Invention 27** 62

Babel, Tower of, **Bible Lands 30** 10, 50; **Building 58** 39

babies, **Human Body 87** 16, 17, 44-47

Babington, Anthony, **Spy 67** 25

baboons, **Gorilla 64** 22, 32; **Mammal 11** 16, 44; **Skeleton 3** 31
hamadryas, **Gorilla 64** 26, 27, 58
olive, **Gorilla 64** 22, 27

Babylon, **Ancient Greece 37** 58, 63; **Astronomy 82** 8-9, 26, 48; **Bible Lands 30** 10, 50, 53
medicine, **Medicine 88** 8-9, 12
people, **Bible Lands 30** 20, 50-52

bacchante, **Dance 99** 54

Bacchus, **Ancient Rome 24** 24, 51, 53, 56

backbones, **Human Body 87** 14-15, 58
intervertebral discs, **Human Body 87** 14, 19, 42
spine, **Skeleton 3** 20, 38-41, 63
human, **Medicine 88** 24, 45
see also vertebrae

Backer, Harriet, **Impressionism 92** 61

backstaffs, **Pirate 59** 25

Bacon, Roger, **Astronomy 82** 22

Bacon, Sir Francis, **Earth 83** 34; **Matter 80** 11

bacteria, **Ecology 86** 14, 19, 36, 40; **Evolution 85** 48, 56, 61; **Life 84** 12, 20, 21, 24; **Mummy 44** 8, 14, 59
classification, **Life 84** 50
disease, **Life 84** 28, 29, 58
DNA, **Life 84** 34, 61
fossil, **Evolution 85** 26, 55, 60
nitrogen cycle, **Ecology 86** 20, 21
ocean, **Ocean 62** 46-47, 60
sewage treatment, **Ecology 86** 15
viruses, **Life 84** 58, 59

Bad Boy, Chief, **Writing 48** 8

Baden-Powell, Robert, **Spy 67** 24

Badge-flag, **Flag 16** 10

badgers, **Mammal 11** 40, 59, 61; **Skeleton 3** 14, 30; **Tree 5** 18, 19

badges, **Battle 63** 16-17 **Castle 49** 31, 37, 44; **Crime & Detection 73** 11, 32, 34

badminton, **Sport 8** 35

Baekeland, Leo, **Chemistry 79** 53, 55; **Invention 27** 60; **Matter 80** 44; **Technology 89** 27

Baffin Island, **Explorer 31** 40

bagatelle, **Sport 8** 63

Baghdad, **Viking 50** 6, 18

B

Bagiun peoples, **AFRICA 61** 18
Baglivi, Giorgio,
    HUMAN BODY 87 20
bagpipes, **MEDIEVAL LIFE 65** 57;
    MUSIC 12 16
Baikal, Lake, **RUSSIA 74** 10, 39
bail, **CRIME & DETECTION 73** 15
baileys, **CASTLE 49** 8, 9, 36
bailiffs, **MEDIEVAL LIFE 65** 15, 17
Baird, John Logie,
    ELECTRICITY 77 62;
    FUTURE 100 9
Bakelite,
    CHEMISTRY 79 53, 54, 55, 57;
    ELECTRICITY 77 21
Baker, Ezekiel, **BATTLE 63** 43
Baker, Samuel, **EXPLORER 31** 47
Bakewell, John, **FARM 66** 7
Bakst, Leon, **RUSSIA 74** 48
Balaclava, battle of,
    BATTLE 63 16
balances, **INVENTION 27** 16, 23
Balanchine, George,
    DANCE 99 17, 56
Balanocidaris, **FOSSIL 19** 17
balconies,
    BUILDING 58 56-57, 62
bald uakaris, **GORILLA 64** 16
Baldishol, **VIKING 50** 13
baldric, **COSTUME 35** 27, 29
Balinese dance,
    DANCE 99 11, 33
ball bearings, **FORCE &**
    MOTION 78 39
Ball on Shipboard,
    FLAG 16 17
ballet, **DANCE 99** 12-13, 20,
    21, 44
    American classical,
        DANCE 99 56
    costumes, **DANCE 99** 30, 31
    folk, **DANCE 99** 42
    footwear, **DANCE 99** 24-25
    modern, **DANCE 99** 45, 26
    positions, **DANCE 99** 12-13, 45
    Russian, **DANCE 99** 30, 45, 56;
        RUSSIA 74 48, 49, 53
    shoes, **DANCE 99** 24-25
ballistics, **CRIME &**
    DETECTION 73 42, 43, 46;
    FORCE & MOTION 78
    26-27, 57
balloons, **ARCTIC &**
    ANTARCTIC 57 52;
    BATTLE 63 24, 25;
    WEATHER 28 6, 12, 13, 50
    hot air,
        FORCE & MOTION 78 15
ballroom dancing,
    DANCE 99 48, 49, 54
balsam, **MUMMY 44** 7
Baltic Sea, **VIKING 50** 6, 26;
    WHALE 46 59
Baltic States, **RUSSIA 74** 12,
    22, 59
Baltimore, **PIRATE 59** 53
Baltimore orioles, **BIRD 1** 48, 52

Baluchis, **DESERT 51** 40, 41
bamboo, **JUNGLE 54** 14; **TREE 5** 7
    paper, **WRITING 48** 22, 31
bamboo sharks, **SHARK 40** 6, 33
Bambuku peoples,
    AFRICA 61 35
Bamileke peoples, **AFRICA 61** 59
bandicoots, **MAMMAL 11** 8, 54
Bandit Queen, **CRIME &**
    DETECTION 73 56
Bangladesh, **CAT 29** 31
banking, **MEDIEVAL LIFE 65** 6, 47
banknotes, *see* notes
banks, earthen,
    BUILDING 58 12
Banks, Sir Joseph,
    ELECTRICITY 77 17,
    EXPLORER 31 35, 49, 51
banks,
    MONEY 18 16, 18, 21, 37
banners, **MEDIEVAL LIFE 65** 24
Bannister, Roger,
    FUTURE 100 10
Bannockburn, battle of,
    BATTLE 63 39
Banting, Frederick, **HUMAN**
    BODY 87 41; **MEDICINE 88** 43
banyans, **TREE 5** 6, 13
baobabs, **TREE 5** 37, 43
baptism, **RELIGION 68** 48, 51, 52
Bar Mitzvah, **RELIGION 68** 44, 45
Bara, Theda, **CINEMA 34** 20
Baragwanathia, **FOSSIL 19** 36
Barb, **COWBOY 45** 6
Barbari, Jacopo de',
    RENAISSANCE 91 58, 60
barbarians, **KNIGHT 43** 6
Barbarossa brothers,
    PIRATE 59 14
Barbary Coast, **PIRATE 59** 7,
    14-17, 59
Barbary macaques,
    GORILLA 64 58
barbels,
    SHARK 40 7-8, 19, 38-39
barbeled hound sharks,
    SHARK 40 6
Barbera peoples, **AFRICA 61** 31
Barbera, Joe, **CINEMA 34** 50
barber-surgeons,
    MEDICINE 88 27
barbicans, **CASTLE 49** 15, 28
barbs, **BIRD 1** 20, 21, 26, 29
barbules, **BIRD 1** 21
Bardeen, John,
    ELECTRONICS 90 38
Barents, Willem,
    ARCTIC & ANTARCTIC 57 6;
    EXPLORER 31 40
barges, **BOAT 36** 21, 24, 33, 34
bark, **WRITING 48** 32
Barker, Thomas, **WEATHER 28** 61
barley, **FARM 66** 6, 21, 22, 28
Barlow, Peter,
    ELECTRICITY 77 38
barn owls, **ANCIENT EGYPT 23**
    35; **BIRD 1** 12, 24, 42

barnacles, **OCEAN 62** 27, 55, 58;
    SEASHORE 15 12, 44;
    SHELL 9 9, 25, 40, 49;
    SHIPWRECK 72 56
    as fossils, **FOSSIL 19** 30, 31
    goose, **OCEAN 62** 38
    as parasites,
        ARCTIC & ANTARCTIC 57 46;
        SHARK 40 26
Barnard, Christian,
    FUTURE 100 10
barns, **BUILDING 58** 10, 24;
    FARM 66 20, 23, 41-43;
    MEDIEVAL LIFE 65 12, 13
    beehive, **BUILDING 58** 12
barometers,
    FLYING MACHINE 22 9;
    WEATHER 28 11, 14, 33, 62
Baroncelli, Marquis,
    COWBOY 45 52-53
barques, **BOAT 36** 6;
    PIRATE 59 23
barracuda, **FISH 20** 35;
    OCEAN 62 28
Bar-rakib, **BIBLE LANDS 30** 40
barre, **DANCE 99** 12, 53
Barrie, J.M., **PIRATE 59** 61
Barry, James, **VOLCANO 38** 8
Bart, Jean, **PIRATE 59** 51
barter, **ANCIENT EGYPT 23** 40;
    AZTEC 47 26;
    EARLY PEOPLE 10 56;
    MONEY 18 8-9, 21, 48
Barth, Heinrich, **DESERT 51** 62
Baryonyx walkeri, **FOSSIL 19** 50, 51
baryte bronite,
    CRYSTAL & GEM 25 24
basalt, **ARCHAEOLOGY 56** 13;
    CRYSTAL & GEM 25 9, 32;
    EARTH 83 7, 22, 25, 32;
    PYRAMID 53 32;
    SEASHORE 15 9
    volcanic rocks,
        ROCK & MINERAL 2 8,
        17, 19; **VOLCANO 38** 8
Basch, Samuel von,
    INVENTION 27 43
baseball, **SPORT 8** 22-25
bases, **CHEMISTRY 79** 42-43,
    44, 61
basinets, **CASTLE 49** 30
basketball, **SPORT 8** 20
baskets, **ANCIENT EGYPT 23** 47;
    ARCHAEOLOGY 56 28;
    MUMMY 44 23
basking sharks, **FISH 20** 10, 61;
    SHARK 40 6-7, 24, 34-35
Basques, **FLAG 16** 37
Bass, George,
    SHIPWRECK 72 13, 49
bassoons, **MUSIC 12** 9, 13
Bastet, **ANCIENT EGYPT 23** 24, 25
Batavian Republic, **FLAG 16** 30
Bates, Henry, **EXPLORER 31**
    48-49; **JUNGLE 54** 51, 61
baths, Roman,
    ANCIENT ROME 24 27, 38, 39

batons, **BATTLE 63** 17
bats, animals, **EVOLUTION 85**
    22, 38, 42; **FOSSIL 19** 52,
    54, 56; **JUNGLE 54** 27, 28;
    SKELETON 3 16, 50
    desert, **DESERT 51** 18
    echo-location,
        ECOLOGY 86 36-37
    fishing, **JUNGLE 54** 33
    flying mammals,
        MAMMAL 11 18-19
    pollination, **JUNGLE 54** 24
    shelters, **JUNGLE 54** 36
bats, sports, **SPORT 8** 25,
    26-29, 34
    baseball, **SPORT 8** 25
    cricket, **SPORT 8** 26-29
    table tennis, **SPORT 8** 34
battalions, **BATTLE 63** 14-15
batteries, **ENERGY 76** 23, 38, 42;
    FUTURE 100 52;
    INVENTION 27 52, 53
    alkaline, **ELECTRICITY 77** 18
    in cars, **CAR 21** 30, 50, 51
    in communication,
        TECHNOLOGY 89 49
    development of,
        ELECTRICITY 77 16-19, 20
    first, **ELECTRICITY 77** 31
    invention of,
        INVENTION 27 38-39
battering rams, **CASTLE 49** 24
battle-axes, **BATTLE 63** 38-39
battlements, **KNIGHT 43** 23, 24
battles, **BATTLE 63**
    Agincourt, **KNIGHT 43** 30, 32
    Balaclava, **BATTLE 63** 16
    Bannockburn, **BATTLE 63** 39
    Chang Ping, **CHINA 55** 14
    Crécy, **BATTLE 63** 36, 37, 63;
        KNIGHT 43 30, 32
    Fleurus, **BATTLE 63** 25
    Fort Wagner, **BATTLE 63** 51
    Hastings, **KNIGHT 43** 8-9
    Hegelbord, **BATTLE 63** 42
    Inkerman, **BATTLE 63** 61, 62
    Little Big Horn,
        BATTLE 63 53
    Poitiers, **BATTLE 63** 7, 36, 63;
        KNIGHT 43 32
    Waterloo, **BATTLE 63** 19, 27,
        49, 56
Batu, **RUSSIA 74** 8, 9
Batutta, Ibn, **EXPLORER 31** 19
Baudelaire, Charles,
    IMPRESSIONISM 92 8, 9;
    MANET 94 12, 15, 16, 18;
    MONET 95 13
bauxite, **CHEMISTRY 79** 18, 25, 47;
    ROCK & MINERAL 2 13, 56
bay colour, **HORSE 33** 38-40
Bayeu, Francisco,
    GOYA 93 8-9, 16-17
Bayeux Tapestry,
    BOAT 36 17; **CASTLE 49** 8, 9;
    PERSPECTIVE 98 9;
    VIKING 50 10, 35, 38, 43

bayonets, **ARMS & ARMOUR 4**
40-41, 48, 51; **BATTLE 63** 42,
43, 47
Bazille Frédéric,
IMPRESSIONISM 92 10-11, 12,
16; **MONET 95** 10, 11, 14, 16
The Improvised Ambulance,
MONET 95 11
Self-portrait with Palette,
MONET 95 15
beach fleas, **INSECT 17** 9
beach hose, **SHIPWRECK 72** 31
beachcombing, **SEASHORE 15**
58-61
beacons, **SHIPWRECK 72** 34, 36
beads, **COSTUME 35** 6, 18, 57, 58
beagles, **DOG 32** 16, 17, 41, 49
bearded ark shells, **SHELL 9** 46
bearings, **INVENTION 27** 12, 13
bears, **ARCTIC & ANTARCTIC 57**
8, 32-33; **MAMMAL 11** 9, 49,
50; **VIKING 50** 36;
EVOLUTION 85 39
Beatles, **MUSIC 12** 60
Beaton, Sir Cecil, **CINEMA 34** 37
Beatty, Warren, **CINEMA 34** 59
Beauchamp, Pierre,
DANCE 99 45
Beaufort, Sir Francis,
WEATHER 28 43
Beaufort Scale, **WEATHER 28** 43
Beaumont, William,
HUMAN BODY 87 37
beavers, **MAMMAL 11** 9, 20, 29,
50; **POND & RIVER 6** 37;
SKELETON 3 52
Becchi, Antonio, **BOAT 36** 7
Becket, Thomas, **CASTLE 49** 23;
MEDIEVAL LIFE 65 42
Beckmann, Max,
PERSPECTIVE 98 50-51
Becquerel, Antoine,
MATTER 80 46
bedbugs, **INSECT 17** 36, 61
Bede, St., **MEDIEVAL LIFE 65** 36
bedeguars, **INSECT 17** 43
Bedouin peoples, **DESERT 51** 9,
43, 58-59, 60
beds, **VIKING 50** 9, 32
Beebe, Prof. W., **SHARK 40** 55
beech trees, **TREE 5** 14-15,
22, 25
Beeckman, Daniel,
GORILLA 64 38
beehives, **BUILDING 58** 12
Beerbohm, Sir Max,
WATERCOLOUR 97 31
bees, **FARM 66** 16, 39;
INSECT 17 38, 46, 58-59;
JUNGLE 54 25
anatomy, **INSECT 17** 6
beetles, **DESERT 51** 22, 23, 25;
EVOLUTION 85 21, 43, 49;
INSECT 17 22-23, 30-31;
JUNGLE 54 13, 23, 54;
LIFE 84 39, 48, 49
skeleton, **SKELETON 3** 22

water, **POND & RIVER 6** 9, 17,
50-51
beetroot stone, **FOSSIL 19** 24
beganna, **MUSIC 12** 34
Beigh, Ulugh,
ASTRONOMY 82 10
Beijing, **CHINA 55** 54, 60, 62, 63
Beit Dagin, **BIBLE LANDS 30** 45
Belarus, **RUSSIA 74** 12, 23, 59
belemnites, **FOSSIL 19** 17, 21,
29, 46; **SKELETON 3** 13
Belemnoteuthis, **FOSSIL 19** 21
Belgian Draught horses,
HORSE 33 50
Belgium, **FLAG 16** 30-31;
MONEY 18 19, 34, 35, 62
Belize, **PYRAMID 53** 54, 56
Bell, Alexander Graham,
kite design,
FLYING MACHINE 22 11
telephone, **ELECTRONICS 90**
25, 38, 42; **ENERGY 76** 39;
INVENTION 27 44;
TECHNOLOGY 89 49
Bell, Chichester,
INVENTION 27 47
Bell Jet-Ranger, **FLYING
MACHINE 22** 50-51, 52-53
Belle-Ile, **MONET 95** 38, 39
Bellerophon, **ANCIENT
GREECE 37** 23
Bellini, Giovanni,
RENAISSANCE 91 34, 44,
45, 46
Bellini, Jacopo, **PERSPECTIVE 98**
21; **RENAISSANCE 91** 26
bells, **MUSIC 12** 54
church, **VIKING 50** 63
belts, **COSTUME 35** 13, 27, 36;
COWBOY 45 23, 49, 61;
SPORT 8 44, 49
beluga sturgeons, **FISH 20** 42
Belzoni, Giovanni,
PYRAMID 53 22
Ben Hur, **ANCIENT ROME 24** 34
Bene-Amer peoples,
AFRICA 61 14
Benedict, St.,
MEDIEVAL LIFE 65 36, 37
Benedictine order,
MEDIEVAL LIFE 65 36-38
Benesh, Joan, **DANCE 99** 57
Benesh, Rudolf, **DANCE 99** 57
Beni Hasan, **BIBLE LANDS 30**
11, 45
Benin, Ancient, **AFRICA 61** 6, 49
bronzes, **AFRICA 61** 55;
ARCHAEOLOGY 56 62
royalty, **AFRICA 61** 32, 42, 54
Bennett, Bill, **FLYING
MACHINE 22** 62
Bennie, George, **TRAIN 39** 59
Bent pyramid, **PYRAMID 53**
14, 15
Bentham, Jeremy,
MUMMY 44 62
Benthosuchus, **FOSSIL 19** 43

Bentley, **CAR 21** 18, 19
Bentley, W.A., **WEATHER 28** 40
Benz, **CAR 21** 6, 7, 12, 42
Benz, Karl, **CAR 21** 6;
ENERGY 76 30;
INVENTION 27 48
benzene, **CHEMISTRY 79** 48, 49,
52, 53
Berber peoples,
AFRICA 61 23, 27
Bergman, Ingrid, **CINEMA 34** 27
Beringer, Johann, **FOSSIL 19** 7
Berkeley, Busby, **CINEMA 34** 57;
DANCE 99 51
Berlin Wall, **SPY 67** 38, 39
Berliner, Emile,
INVENTION 27 47
Bermuda Triangle,
OCEAN 62 55
Bern, **FLAG 16** 32, 33
Bernard, Claude, **ENERGY 76** 52;
HUMAN BODY 87 34;
LIFE 84 26
Bernard, St.,
MEDIEVAL LIFE 65 36
Bernoulli, Daniel, **FORCE &
MOTION 78** 45
Bernstein, Leonard,
DANCE 99 14
berries, **TREE 5** 38-39
Berry, Charlotte de,
PIRATE 59 33
Berry, Duke of, **CASTLE 49** 14,
15, 22; **RENAISSANCE 91** 16
berserkir, **VIKING 50** 14
Bertillon, Alphonse, **CRIME &
DETECTION 73** 50, 53
beryl, **CRYSTAL & GEM 25** 13,
15, 38-39; **ROCK &
MINERAL 2** 45, 46, 50
Berzelius, Jons Jakob,
CHEMISTRY 79 59
Besnier, **FLYING MACHINE 22** 6
Bessemer, Henry,
MATTER 80 16
Besson, Luc, **WHALE 46** 55
Best, Charles, **HUMAN BODY 87**
41; **MEDICINE 88** 43;
TECHNOLOGY 89 60
Beth Shan, **BIBLE LANDS 30** 12,
43, 62
Bethe, Hans, **ENERGY 76** 48;
MATTER 80 57
Bethlehem, **BIBLE LANDS 30** 57;
RELIGION 68 49
Bhagavad Gita, **RELIGION 68** 20,
21, 23
Bhutan Glory butterfly,
BUTTERFLY & MOTH 7 31
Bible, **BIBLE LANDS 30**;
EVOLUTION 85 14, 16;
MEDIEVAL LIFE 65 30;
RELIGION 68 48, 50-53
the Ark, **SHIPWRECK 72** 58
Book of Ezra,
BIBLE LANDS 30 52

Book of Genesis, **BIBLE
LANDS 30** 10, 50
Book of Nehemiah,
BIBLE LANDS 30 58, 60, 61
Book of Numbers,
BIBLE LANDS 30 26
creation story,
EVOLUTION 85 6
the flood, **EVOLUTION 85** 10
Gutenburg,
MEDIEVAL LIFE 65 62;
WRITING 48 43
Jewish, **RELIGION 68** 43-45
medieval drama,
MEDIEVAL LIFE 65 58, 59
New Testament, **BIBLE
LANDS 30** 58, 60, 61
Old Testament, **BIBLE
LANDS 30** 7, 28, 58, 61
Psalter, **WRITING 48** 24, 25
scribes, **MEDIEVAL LIFE 65** 40
St. Luke's Gospel,
BIBLE LANDS 30 59
Wycliffe's,
BIBLE LANDS 30 61
Bichon Frise, **DOG 32** 59
bicycles, **DESERT 51** 62;
FORCE & MOTION 78 11, 21,
38, 57; **INVENTION 27** 12;
TECHNOLOGY 89 21, 29, 33
biers, **MUMMY 44** 14, 16
Big Bang theory,
ENERGY 76 62-63;
MATTER 80 60, 62, 63;
SPACE EXPLORATION 71 52;
TIME & SPACE 81 8, 39,
60-61
Big Blue, **WHALE 46** 55
Big-root Borer moth,
BUTTERFLY & MOTH 7 48
bilberry, **TREE 5** 53
Bilbibin, Ivan, **WRITING 48** 48
bilge pumps, **SHIPWRECK 72** 42
billiards, **SPORT 8** 62
Billings, Joseph, **RUSSIA 74** 23
bills, **MONEY 18** 13, 28, 29
bills of exchange,
MONEY 18 20, 21
Billy the Kid, **COWBOY 45** 45;
CRIME & DETECTION 73 14
bin, **MUSIC 12** 40
binary fission, **LIFE 84** 32, 50
binoculars, **BATTLE 63** 25;
INVENTION 27 29;
LIGHT 75 55
biodegradable products,
FUTURE 100 54, 55
biodiversity, **ECOLOGY 86** 28,
54, 57; **ELEPHANT 42** 60
biological control,
ECOLOGY 86 30, 61, 63
bioluminescence, **SHELL 9** 54
biomass, **ECOLOGY 86** 10, 40
biopsy, **MEDICINE 88** 52
biosphere, **ECOLOGY 86** 7, 16,
18, 62
reserves, **JUNGLE 54** 63

biotechnology, **TECHNOLOGY 89** 44, 60-61
birches, **POND & RIVER 6** 19; **TREE 5** 23-25, 41
birchir reedfish, **FISH 20** 9
bird-eating spiders, **SKELETON 3** 23
birds, **BIRD 1**;
  EVOLUTION 85 23, 25, 41, 47;
  JUNGLE 54 22, 25;
  LIFE 84 26, 31, 49, 53;
  PLANT 14 24, 26, 27;
  TREE 5 20, 21, 38, 39
  Antarctic, **ARCTIC & ANTARCTIC 57** 22-23, 24
  Arctic, **ARCTIC & ANTARCTIC 57** 14-15, 20-21
  beaks, **BIRD 1** 35, 36-37, 59
  claws, **BIRD 1** 7, 32
  desert, **DESERT 51** 10, 16, 30-31
  eggs, **BIRD 1** 54-55, 56-57
  evolution, **BIRD 1** 6; **EVOLUTION 85** 42, 45, 62
  feathers, **BIRD 1** 20-22, 26, 63
  flightless, **BIRD 1** 17, 32
  fossils, **FOSSIL 19** 21, 47, 52, 53; **PREHISTORIC LIFE 52** 28, 33, 42-43
  on land, **BIRD 1** 52, 53
  nests, **BIRD 1** 44-45, 48-49; **JUNGLE 54** 36-37; **TREE 5** 51
  as pollinators, **PLANT 14** 24
  predators, **ARCTIC & ANTARCTIC 57** 24-25
  senses, **BIRD 1** 34-35
  skeletons, **SKELETON 3** 18-19, 30, 50
  tails, **BIRD 1** 18-19, 22, 27
  on water, **BIRD 1** 50-51; **OCEAN 62** 28-29, 40, 62; **SEASHORE 15** 52-53, 54-55
  wings, **BIRD 1** 10, 11
  see also under individual birds
birds of paradise, **BIRD 1** 18, 28, 29; **JUNGLE 54** 54, 56
birefringence, **CRYSTAL & GEM 25** 18
biremes, **BOAT 36** 20
Biro, Joseph and Georg, **INVENTION 27** 19
Biro, Ladislao, **TECHNOLOGY 89** 39
birth rate, **FUTURE 100** 16
birthstones, **CRYSTAL & GEM 25** 61
Biscay, Bay of, **SHIPWRECK 72** 21
bishops, **MEDIEVAL LIFE 65** 7, 9, 31, 54
Bismarck, Chancellor, **FLAG 16** 28
bismuth, **CRYSTAL & GEM 25** 26
bits, **COWBOY 45** 16-17
bitterlings, **FISH 20** 43

bitterns, **POND & RIVER 6** 31
bivalves, **FOSSIL 19** 15, 26, 32, 63; **SEASHORE 15** 26-27, 42-43
biwa, **MUSIC 12** 37
Bjørn Jarnsmiða, **VIKING 50** 16
Black, Harold S., **ELECTRONICS 90** 30, 31
Black, Joseph, **CHEMISTRY 79** 28, 60; **ENERGY 76** 20, 21; **MATTER 80** 23
Black Bess, **HORSE 33** 46
"Black Chamber", **SPY 67** 27
Black Death, **MEDIEVAL LIFE 65** 7, 10, 60, 61
black desert, **DESERT 51** 8
black goby, **FISH 20** 40
Black Hawk, **NORTH AMERICAN INDIAN 60** 23
black holes, **ASTRONOMY 82** 7, 60-61, 63; **FORCE & MOTION 78** 61; **MATTER 80** 63; **TIME & SPACE 81** 61, 62-63
  geometry, **TIME & SPACE 81** 40
  relativity, **TIME & SPACE 81** 45, 46-47
black markets, **CRIME & DETECTION 73** 8
Black Prince, **CRYSTAL & GEM 25** 46
Black pyramid, **PYRAMID 53** 42
Black Sea, **ANCIENT GREECE 37** 7, 14, 23; **EXPLORER 31** 10
Black Stone, **RELIGION 68** 54, 55
Blackbeard, **PIRATE 59** 30-31, 35, 58
blackberries, **SEASHORE 15** 13
Blackbird, **SPY 67** 52, 53
blackbirds, **BIRD 1** 37, 42, 47, 53; **SKELETON 3** 30
blackbucks, **MAMMAL 11** 26; **SKELETON 3** 53
blackcaps, **BIRD 1** 39
Blackfeet peoples, **NORTH AMERICAN INDIAN 60** 10-11, 28, 34
  sun dance, **NORTH AMERICAN INDIAN 60** 36-37
blackflies, **INSECT 17** 15
Blackfoot, **DANCE 99** 18
blackmail, **SPY 67** 10, 14, 40, 41
blacksmiths, **TECHNOLOGY 89** 12, 13, 17, 44; **VIKING 50** 15
blackthorns, **TREE 5** 35, 39
bladders, **BOAT 36** 9; **HUMAN BODY 87** 38-39, 43, 46
blades, **SPORT 8** 50
Blake, William, **CAT 29** 30; **PERSPECTIVE 98** 46; **WATERCOLOUR 97** 42, 43

Blanc, Mel, **CINEMA 34** 51
Blashford-Snell, John, **JUNGLE 54** 61
blastoids, **FOSSIL 19** 33
Blaue Reiter, Der, **WATERCOLOUR 97** 58
Blaxland, John, **EXPLORER 31** 38
blende, **CRYSTAL & GEM 25** 48, 49
blenny, **FISH 20** 32
Blériot, Louis, **EXPLORER 31** 57; **FLYING MACHINE 22** 18, 28, 29, 40
  Type XI aircraft, **FLYING MACHINE 22** 14-15, 22
Bligh, William, **JUNGLE 54** 60
blind shark, **SHARK 40** 6
blizzards, **WEATHER 28** 40
blood, **CRIME & DETECTION 73** 41, 42, 44, 47; **HUMAN BODY 87** 7, 13, 24; **INSECT 17** 6; **LIFE 84** 16, 26, 27
  clotting, **LIFE 84** 27, 61
  circulation, **HUMAN BODY 87** 26, 28-33, 40; **MEDICINE 88** 24-25, 30, 37, 60
  immune system, **LIFE 84** 29
Blood, Captain, **PIRATE 59** 63
blood pressure, **MEDICINE 88** 28, 38, 61
blood stream, **LIFE 84** 9, 29, 32
blood transfusion, **MEDICINE 88** 25, 50, 57, 58
blood vessels, **HUMAN BODY 87** 20, 21, 30-31; **LIFE 84** 15
  see also cells, blood
bloodhounds, **DOG 32** 13, 16, 35, 48
blood-letting, **MEDICINE 88** 22, 26
bloomers, **COSTUME 35** 24, 34, 37, 43
blotters, **WRITING 48** 56
blouses, **COSTUME 35** 9, 50
blowflies, **INSECT 17** 21
blow-holes, **SEASHORE 15** 8
blubber, **ARCTIC & ANTARCTIC 57** 32, 42, 44, 46
Blue Ensign, **FLAG 16** 16
Blue Heeler, **COWBOY 45** 57
blue john, **CRYSTAL & GEM 25** 51
Blue Peter, **FLAG 16** 16
Blue Riband, **BOAT 36** 54, 55
blue shark, **FISH 20** 19, 30, 58; **SHARK 40** 18, 20, 22
blue tits, **BIRD 1** 52, 58-59, 60
"Blue Train", **TRAIN 39** 42
Bluebeard, **BOAT 36** 29
bluebottles, **INSECT 17** 32
blue-ringed angelfish, **FISH 20** 17
Blundell, James, **MEDICINE 88** 25

blunderbusses, **ARMS & ARMOUR 4** 48-49
Blunt, Anthony, **SPY 67** 57
Blunt, Charles F., **WEATHER 28** 27
boa constrictors, **GORILLA 64** 16; **REPTILE 26** 40-41
boar, **ANCIENT ROME 24** 14, 53, 58
Boardman, Chris, **FUTURE 100** 55
boas, feather, **COSTUME 35** 51
boas, snakes, **REPTILE 26** 11, 20
  constrictor, **GORILLA 64** 16; **REPTILE 26** 40-41
  Pacific Island, **REPTILE 26** 63
  South American tree, **REPTILE 26** 54-55
boat burials, **VIKING 50** 8, 12
boaters, **COSTUME 35** 46
boathooks, **SHIPWRECK 72** 42
boats, **BOAT 36**; **EARLY PEOPLE 10** 20, 21; **KNIGHT 43** 8, 45
  early, Egypt, **ANCIENT EGYPT 23** 38-39; **PYRAMID 53** 28-29;
  canal, **BOAT 36** 34, 35
  China, **CHINA 55** 38-39, 60-61
  construction, **BOAT 36** 17, 18-19
  fire-fighting, **BOAT 36** 52
  funerary, **ANCIENT EGYPT 23** 19
  inland, **BOAT 36** 34-35
  power, **BOAT 36** 7
  reed, **BOAT 36** 21
  river, **BOAT 36** 21, 36, 38
  sail, **BOAT 36** 7, 14, 60
  whaling, **WHALE 46** 46, 47, 48, 50
bobbies, **CRIME & DETECTION 73** 10, 32
Boccaccio, Giovanni, **RENAISSANCE 91** 8, 13
Boccioni, Umberto, **PERSPECTIVE 98** 54-55
Bode's Law, **ASTRONOMY 82** 54
Bodhisattvas, **CHINA 55** 27
Bodiam castle, **CASTLE 49** 28
body, **HUMAN BODY 87**
body decoration, **AFRICA 61** 28-29, 62; **DESERT 51** 48, 52, 53, 56; **EARLY PEOPLE 10** 34, 35
body temperature, **LIFE 84** 18, 26, 58
Boeings, 247 D, **FLYING MACHINE 22** 32-33
  747, **FLYING MACHINE 22** 9, 35
  747-400, **FLYING MACHINE 22** 45
Boer War, **BATTLE 63** 57, 59, 60; **SPY 67** 31

Boerhaave, Hermann,
    MEDICINE 88 26
Boethius,
    ANCIENT GREECE 37 58
"bog man", Pete Marsh,
    CRIME & DETECTION 73 9
Bogart, Humphrey,
    CINEMA 34 27
Boggs, J.S.G., **CRIME &**
    DETECTION 73 59
bogies, **TRAIN 39** 15, 19, 22, 23
Bogman, **ARCHAEOLOGY 56** 36
Bogong moths, **BUTTERFLY &**
    MOTH 7 51
Bohlin, Edward H.,
    COWBOY 45 9, 15
Bohr, Niels, **MATTER 80** 50, 51
Bohun, Sir Henry de,
    BATTLE 63 39
boilers, **TRAIN 39** 14, 15, 22, 23
boiling point, **MATTER 80** 22, 23
boleadoras, **COWBOY 45** 48-49
Boleyn, Anne, **WITCH &**
    WIZARD 70 14
Bolivia, **CAT 29** 41;
    MONEY 18 38
    Bolivian tape dance,
    DANCE 99 47
Bolsheviks, **RUSSIA 74** 30-31, 42
    Red Army, **RUSSIA 74** 32-33
Boltzmann, Ludwig,
    MATTER 80 39
bombard, **MUSIC 12** 16
bomber planes,
    FLYING MACHINE 22 20, 24,
    39, 42
bombs, **BATTLE 63** 32, 34; **CRIME**
    & DETECTION 73 27, 52, 54,
    55; **SPY 67** 38, 42, 53-55
Bonaparte, Napoleon, *see*
    Napolean I, Emperor of
    France
Bond, James,
    SPY 67 9, 12, 56, 59
bonds, chemical,
    CHEMISTRY 79 20, 25, 48, 49
bones,
    ARCTIC & ANTARCTIC 57 45,
    46; **HUMAN BODY 87** 14-17,
    30, 40; **MAMMAL 11** 50-51,
    58-59; **SKELETON 3** 58-59,
    62-63
    in archaeology,
    ARCHAEOLOGY 56 14, 24, 26,
    44-45
    fractures, **SKELETON 3** 61-62
    marrow, **HUMAN BODY 87** 33
    in toolmaking,
    EARLY PEOPLE 10 18, 21, 32, 33
bonnets, **COSTUME 35** 44,
    46, 60
Bonnie and Clyde, **CRIME &**
    DETECTION 73 57
Bonny, Anne, **PIRATE 59** 32,
    35, 63
bonobos, **GORILLA 64** 9, 33,
    56-57

intelligence, **GORILLA 64** 36
Bonpland, Aimé, **JUNGLE 54** 60
bonytongues, **FISH 20** 45
Book of Hours, **WRITING 48** 24
Book of Kings, **WRITING 48** 35
Book of the Dead,
    ARCHAEOLOGY 56 40-41;
    MUMMY 44 12-13, 14;
    PYRAMID 53 22, 29, 44, 50;
    WRITING 48 48
    Egyptian, **ANCIENT EGYPT 23**
    18, 19; **RELIGION 68** 11
    Tibetan, **RELIGION 68** 28, 29
books, **PIRATE 59** 60-61;
    SHIPWRECK 72 13, 58, 59;
    WITCH & WIZARD 70 16-18,
    25; **WRITING 48**
    binding, **WRITING 48** 46-47, 61
    Chinese, **CHINA 55** 16, 24-25
    early materials, **WRITING 48**
    30-33
    illustrated, **MEDIEVAL LIFE 65**
    40, 41, 62; **WATERCOLOUR 97**
    44-45; **WRITING 48** 48-49
    making, **WRITING 48** 46-47
    medieval, **MEDIEVAL LIFE 65**
    40, 41, 62
    on-line, **FUTURE 100** 28, 30
    paperback, **WRITING 48** 61
    pop-up, **WRITING 48** 54-55
    selling, **WRITING 48** 60-61
    spy, **SPY 67** 9, 56, 58, 59
Boole, George,
    ELECTRONICS 90 50
boomerangs,
    ARMS & ARMOUR 4 8-9;
    BATTLE 63 37; **DESERT 51** 46;
    FLAG 16 50
booms, **BOAT 36** 15, 32, 33, 62
Booth, Hubert Cecil,
    FUTURE 100 8
boots,
    ARCTIC & ANTARCTIC 57 50,
    56, 57;
    COSTUME 35 24-25, 51, 58;
    COWBOY 45 22-27, 52-53;
    SPORT 8 14, 17, 20, 24
booty, **PIRATE 59** 9, 21, 36-37
Bordeaux, **GOYA 93** 58, 60, 61
Bordighera, **MONET 95** 38, 39
Borelli, Giovanni,
    SHIPWRECK 72 44
Borneo, **JUNGLE 54** 34, 38, 48;
    WITCH & WIZARD 70 52
Borobudur, **RELIGION 68** 8
borzois, **DOG 32** 15, 46-48
Bosch, Hieronymus, **GOYA 93**
    31; **RENAISSANCE 91** 42
Bossard, Frank, **SPY 67** 50
"Boston Strangler", the,
    CRIME & DETECTION 73 52
Botany Bay, **EXPLORER 31** 38
Botswana, **AFRICA 61** 12-13, 18,
    46; **MONEY 18** 17, 63
Botticelli, Sandro, **OCEAN 62** 16;
    RENAISSANCE 91 6, 7, 32-33;
    WATERCOLOUR 97 47, 49

bottle-nosed dolphins,
    FISH 20 7
Boudin, Eugène,
    IMPRESSIONISM 92 12, 13, 19;
    MONET 95 6, 16-17, 24
Bourbon dynasty, **FLAG 16** 26
Bourne, Matthew, **DANCE 99** 41
bournonite,
    CRYSTAL & GEM 25 10
Bouts, Dieric,
    RENAISSANCE 91 34
Bouvier's crabs, **SHELL 9** 46
bouzouki, **MUSIC 12** 37
bow ties, **COSTUME 35** 37
bowenite,
    CRYSTAL & GEM 25 51
bowerbirds, **JUNGLE 54** 37
bowfins, **FISH 20** 9, 41
Bowie, Colonel James,
    COWBOY 45 38
Bowie, David, **SPACE**
    EXPLORATION 71 9
bowling, **SPORT 8** 56-57
bowls, Hansa, **CASTLE 49** 43
Bowman, William, **HUMAN**
    BODY 87 38
bows, **BOAT 36** 7, 32, 33, 48, 49;
    EARLY PEOPLE 10 26, 28, 29;
    SPORT 8 52
    and arrows, **AFRICA 61** 19;
    BATTLE 63 36-37; **DESERT 51** 46
    Inuit, **NORTH AMERICAN**
    INDIAN 60 60
    crossbows, **ARMS &**
    ARMOUR 4 18-21
    longbows, **ARMS &**
    ARMOUR 4 18-21
    North American Indian,
    ARMS & ARMOUR 4 62-63
    short bows, **ARMS &**
    ARMOUR 4 8, 9, 19
bowsprits, **BOAT 36** 25, 27, 41;
    PIRATE 59 30
box brooches, **VIKING 50** 48
box fishes, **SKELETON 3** 24
Boxer Rebellion, **CHINA 55** 63
boxers, dogs, **DOG 32** 44, 45;
    SKELETON 3 30
boxing, **SPORT 8** 46
Boyce, George Price,
    WATERCOLOUR 97 46
Boyd, Belle, **SPY 67** 30
Boyle, Robert, **HUMAN BODY 87**
    24; **MATTER 80** 26, 39
bracelets,
    ANCIENT EGYPT 23 56;
    COSTUME 35 13, 18; **EARLY**
    PEOPLE 10 45, 46, 49
braces, roofs, **BUILDING 58** 24
brachiation,
    GORILLA 64 30, 31
brachiopods, **FOSSIL 19** 9, 17,
    25, 63; **SHELL 9** 39, 51, 60
Brachiosaurus, **DINOSAUR 13** 12;
    FOSSIL 19 49
Bracquemond, Marie,
    IMPRESSIONISM 92 44

bradawl, **ANCIENT EGYPT 23** 43
Bradley, James,
    ASTRONOMY 82 42
Braer, **SHIPWRECK 72** 30
Brahe, Tycho, **ASTRONOMY 82**
    18, 19, 26
Brahma, Hindu god,
    RELIGION 68 18
Brahms, Johannes, **DANCE 99** 17
Braille, Louis,
    HUMAN BODY 87 50
braille, **WRITING 48** 7
brain coral, **SHELL 9** 51, 53
brain, **FUTURE 100** 32-33;
    HUMAN BODY 87 15, 23,
    58-63; **MUMMY 44** 14, 15;
    SKELETON 3 6, 26
    evolution, **EARLY PEOPLE 10** 7,
    11, 19
    growth, **HUMAN BODY 87** 48
    perception,
    of colour, **LIGHT 75** 30,
    32-33, 40
    of images, **LIGHT 75** 12,
    18, 26
    senses, **HUMAN BODY 87** 52,
    54, 56, 57
brakes, **FORCE & MOTION 78** 22,
    30, 36, 38
    air, **FLYING MACHINE 22** 34, 58
    car, **CAR 21** 9, 38, 56, 57
    disc, **CAR 21** 33, 38, 39, 57
    fluid, **CAR 21** 39
    hand, **CAR 21** 13, 17, 18
    hydraulic, **CAR 21** 23, 57
    pedal, **CAR 21** 38
    power, **CAR 21** 29
    trains, **TRAIN 39** 8, 9, 15, 26
Bramah, Joseph, **MATTER 80** 18
Bramante, Donato,
    RENAISSANCE 91 29, 50, 51, 59
Bramantino,
    RENAISSANCE 91 29
bramble shark, **SHARK 40** 6-7
Branagh, Kenneth,
    CINEMA 34 37, 47
Brancacci, Felice,
    RENAISSANCE 91 18
Brand, Max, **COWBOY 45** 61
Brando, Marlon, **CINEMA 34** 35
Braque, Georges,
    PERSPECTIVE 98 52, 53;
    WATERCOLOUR 97 60
brass, **TECHNOLOGY 89** 10, 30
brass, musical instruments,
    MUSIC 12 8, 9
    early, **MUSIC 12** 20-21
    see also under individual
    instruments
brass bands,
    MUSIC 12 22, 24, 25
brassières, **COSTUME 35** 54-55
Braun, Ferdinand,
    INVENTION 27 56
Braun, Wernher von, **SPACE**
    EXPLORATION 71 15
Brazil nuts, **TREE 5** 42

Brazil, FLAG 16 55;
MONEY 18 38, 62;
VOLCANO 38 39;
WEATHER 28 61
Braziliano, Rock,
PIRATE 59 27
bread, ANCIENT EGYPT 23 48;
FARM 66 28, 29; MUMMY 44
31; VIKING 50 34
early, EARLY PEOPLE 10 31
in middle ages, MEDIEVAL
LIFE 65 18, 20, 21
breastbones, HUMAN BODY 87
15, 17, 24, 25
breastplates, ARMS &
ARMOUR 4 25, 26, 33, 39
breathing, HUMAN BODY 87 7,
24-27, 33
breeches, COSTUME 35 21, 23,
26, 32
breeding, FISH 20 23, 40, 41,
42, 52
Breteuil, Gabrielle de,
ENERGY 76 16
Breton, Adela, AZTEC 47 49
brewing,
TECHNOLOGY 89 44, 60
Brewster, David,
PERSPECTIVE 98 45
bricks, ANCIENT EGYPT 23 46;
PYRAMID 53 33, 40;
ROCK & MINERAL 2 15, 35;
TECHNOLOGY 89 20, 22
brickmaking,
BUILDING 58 13
uses, BUILDING 58 12, 14-15
bridal dress,
COSTUME 35 44-45
bridges, BATTLE 63 54, 55;
CASTLE 49 29; FORCE &
MOTION 78 43, 48, 49;
SHIPWRECK 72 33, 42;
railway bridges, TRAIN 39
20-21, 22, 23
bridles, COWBOY 45 9, 12, 16,
26, 27; HORSE 33 30-31
brig, BOAT 36 26, 27
Brighton, WHALE 46 63
brills, FISH 20 25
Brimstone butterflies,
BUTTERFLY & MOTH 7 58
Bristol Fighters, FLYING
MACHINE 22 18-21
Bristol School, art,
WATERCOLOUR 97 41
Britain, ANCIENT GREECE 37 7,
39; MUMMY 44 9, 58, 59
army, BATTLE 63 48, 58-59
ranks, BATTLE 63 16-17,
61, 63
weapons, BATTLE 63 39,
43, 51
currency, MONEY 18 46-47
early, MONEY 18 24-25
dance, DANCE 99 43
ballet, DANCE 99 50
Morris, DANCE 99 19

explorers,
early, EXPLORER 31 13, 34,
36, 40
naturalists, EXPLORER 31 49
flag, FLAG 16 46-47
Navy, SHIPWRECK 72 18, 20, 24
Roman, ANCIENT ROME 24
38, 53; ARCHAEOLOGY 56
48-49, 58-59, 63
acquisition of,
ANCIENT ROME 24 7, 12
"Roman peace" in,
ANCIENT ROME 24 14,
15, 17
Van Gogh in,
VAN GOGH 96 8-10
Viking invasions, VIKING 50 7
religion, VIKING 50 63
trade, VIKING 50 26
weather, WEATHER 28 48, 61
witches, WITCH &
WIZARD 70 32, 33, 36
British Columbia, MONEY 18
49; WHALE 46 35
British Library, WRITING 48
43, 63
British Museum, London,
ANCIENT GREECE 37 6, 17
British Rail, TRAIN 39 40, 41,
52, 54
brittlestars, FOSSIL 19 18, 19, 32;
SEASHORE 15 10, 40
broadsides, WRITING 48 49
broadswords, ARMS &
ARMOUR 4 17, 43, 44-45;
BATTLE 63 40, 41
Broca, Pierre,
HUMAN BODY 87 60, 61
brocades, COSTUME 35 15, 17,
24, 30
bronchi,
HUMAN BODY 87 24, 26
Bronston, Samuel,
CINEMA 34 39
Brontosaurus, DINOSAUR 13 62
bronze, AFRICA 61 54-55;
ARCHAEOLOGY 56 8, 20, 50;
INVENTION 27 10, 11;
TECHNOLOGY 89 14, 16, 30
bronze age,
EARLY PEOPLE 10 42, 43
Chinese, CHINA 55 11, 56
jewellery, EARLY PEOPLE 10
44, 45, 49
Viking, VIKING 50 46
metalworking,
INVENTION 27 14, 15
Roman, ANCIENT ROME 24
60, 61
sculptures, ancient,
ARCHAEOLOGY 56 62
tools, ancient,
ARCHAEOLOGY 56 36, 37, 49;
EARLY PEOPLE 10 43, 44, 47, 49
Viking, VIKING 50 42
vessels, EARLY PEOPLE 10
50, 53

weapons, ARMS & ARMOUR 4
10-11; EARLY PEOPLE 10 43,
46, 47, 55
Bronze Age,
ANCIENT GREECE 37 7, 8,
10, 50; ARCHAEOLOGY 56 16,
36-37; EARLY PEOPLE 10 31,
41, 44, 46
weapons,
ARMS & ARMOUR 4 10-11
Bronzino, Agnolo,
RENAISSANCE 91 61
brooches,
COSTUME 35 12, 13, 18, 40;
EARLY PEOPLE 10 48;
VIKING 50 9, 48-49, 55
Brown, Arthur, FLYING
MACHINE 22 32, 42
Brown, Robert, MATTER 80 38
Brown butterflies, BUTTERFLY &
MOTH 7 28
Brown China-mark moths,
BUTTERFLY & MOTH 7 56, 57
brown crabs, SHELL 9 9
Brown repeater,
ELECTRICITY 77 59
Brücke, Die,
WATERCOLOUR 97 58
Brueghel, Pieter,
WATERCOLOUR 97 38
brumbies, HORSE 33 36
Brunel, Isambard Kingdom,
BOAT 36 47; TRAIN 39 21
Brunelleschi, Filippo,
PERSPECTIVE 98 6, 12, 14;
RENAISSANCE 91 12, 18, 28
Bruni, Lionardo,
RENAISSANCE 91 26
Brunton, Winifred,
MUMMY 44 50; PYRAMID 53
39, 42, 43, 51
brushes,
ANCIENT EGYPT 23 33;
WATERCOLOUR 97 6, 23, 62;
WRITING 48 10, 12
Brussel, Dr. James, CRIME &
DETECTION 73 52
Brynhild, the Valkyrie,
VIKING 50 30, 57
bryozoans, FOSSIL 19 18, 19, 24
bubble shells, SHELL 9 14, 42
bubbles, LIGHT 75 36, 39
bubonic plague, MEDICINE 88
22-23
buccaneers, PIRATE 59 6,
26-27, 30
Bucephalus, HORSE 33 33
Buchanan, Nat, COWBOY 45 56
buckets, VIKING 50 26, 56
sacred,
ANCIENT EGYPT 23 30
buckeyes, TREE 5 29
buckhounds, DOG 32 40
buckies, SHELL 9 34
Buckland, William, FOSSIL 19 50
buckles, COSTUME 35 13, 15, 18,
25, 27; VIKING 50 29

Buddha, CHINA 55 27, 56;
MUMMY 44 7, 62;
RELIGION 68 26, 35;
WRITING 48 33
Siddharth, RELIGION 68
24-25, 27, 30
Buddhism, ARCHAEOLOGY 56
16-17, 51; CHINA 55 25,
26-27, 54; DANCE 99 9, 33;
RELIGION 68 24-27
in Tibet, RELIGION 68 28-29
Budding, Edwin, FORCE &
MOTION 78 20
budgerigars, BIRD 1 25, 27
buds, PLANT 14 14, 17, 38;
TREE 5 24-25
flower,
PLANT 14 9, 12, 16, 18
Budyonny, Marshal,
RUSSIA 74 33
Buehrig, Gordon, CAR 21 23
Buff Tip moths, BUTTERFLY &
MOTH 7 43
Buffalo Bill, see Cody, Buffalo
Bill
Buffalo Bird Woman,
NORTH AMERICAN
INDIAN 60 33
buffalo dance,
DANCE 99 18
buffaloes, COWBOY 45 30, 40,
45; FARM 66 30, 47;
MAMMAL 11 60; NORTH
AMERICAN INDIAN 60 28,
32, 37
bugaku, DANCE 99 30, 36, 43
Bugatti, CAR 21 18, 19, 63
Bugatti, Ettore, CAR 21 19, 63
bugging, CRIME &
DETECTION 73 38;
SPY 67 16-19, 48
in business, SPY 67 44-45
detection, SPY 67 49
bugles, MUSIC 12 24
bugs, INSECT 17 8, 36-37, 60
Buick, CAR 21 62
buildings, ARCHAEOLOGY 56
52-53, 58-59; BUILDING 58;
TECHNOLOGY 89 22-23, 53
Art Nouveau, BUILDING 58
44, 56, 59
Baroque, BUILDING 58 59
dummy, PYRAMID 53 12, 13
high-rise, FUTURE 100 22-23
early materials,
brick, ARCHAEOLOGY 56
8, 53
stone, ARCHAEOLOGY 56
52-53
wattle and daub,
ARCHAEOLOGY 56 58, 63
wood, ARCHAEOLOGY 56 8,
29, 37, 50
pre-fabricated, FUTURE 100
18, 20
underground remains,
ARCHAEOLOGY 56 10-11

bulbs, light, ELECTRICITY 77 19, 43, 46, 47
bulbs, plants, PLANT 14 11, 12, 33
bulkheads, BOAT 36 47
bull huss, SHARK 40 63
bull shark, SHARK 40 22, 48
bulldogs, DOG 32 39, 44, 45, 54
bullets, ARMS & ARMOUR 4 46, 56, 57, 59; BATTLE 63 42, 46; CRIME & DETECTION 73 42, 57
bullet-proof, TECHNOLOGY 89 28
bullhead sharks, FISH 20 42, 54
Bullimore, Tony, SHIPWRECK 72 39
bulls, COWBOY 45 6, 30-31, 52-55
fighting, COWBOY 45 13, 54
riding, COWBOY 45 62-63
bumblebees, INSECT 17 38, 42, 59
Bunsen, Robert, ASTRONOMY 82 31; CHEMISTRY 79 19, 31, 59; MATTER 80 31
Bunsen burner, MATTER 80 30, 31, 32
buntings, BIRD 1 52
buoyancy, FORCE & MOTION 78 14, 15, 42; SHARK 40 7, 10, 14
buoyancy control device, SHIPWRECK 72 46
buoys, FLAG 16 19; OCEAN 62 13; SHIPWRECK 72 10, 11, 35; WEATHER 28 12
burgee, FLAG 16 6
Burgess, Guy, SPY 67 35, 57
Burgess shale, FOSSIL 19 20
burglary, CRIME & DETECTION 73 16, 17, 37, 43
burials, ANCIENT EGYPT 23 19; ARCHAEOLOGY 56 7, 11, 26, 31

C

Caan, James, CINEMA 34 43
cabaca, MUSIC 12 56
cabane, COWBOY 45 28, 52-53
cabbages, PLANT 14 55
cabochons, CRYSTAL & GEM 25 32, 44, 47, 58
Cabot, John, EXPLORER 31 40, 63
cacti, AZTEC 47 25, 39; DESERT 51 18, 19, 20-21, 36; PLANT 14 36, 52-53, 59
caddies, SPORT 8 60
caddisflies, BUTTERFLY & MOTH 7 7
Cadillac, CAR 21 28, 29, 30, 50
Caernarvon, Lord, ANCIENT EGYPT 23 23
Caesar, Julius, ELEPHANT 42 46; ANCIENT ROME 24 7, 12, 51; PIRATE 59 10; SPY 67 20
and Herod, BIBLE LANDS 30 56
Caesar, Sir Julius, WRITING 48 62
caftan, COSTUME 35 59
Cagney, James, CINEMA 34 59
Cai Lun, WRITING 48 22
Caillebotte, Gustave, IMPRESSIONISM 92 30-31, 58, 61; MONET 95 21
biography, IMPRESSIONISM 92 62
The Man at the Window, IMPRESSIONISM 92 6
Paris, a Rainy Day, IMPRESSIONISM 92 31
Le Pont de l'Europe, IMPRESSIONISM 92 33
Caillié, René, DESERT 51 62
Cainotherium, FOSSIL 19 54
Cairo, AFRICA 61 7; ANCIENT EGYPT 23 63; PYRAMID 53 20, 21
cakewalk, DANCE 99 58
Calabar bean, JUNGLE 54 43
calabash, DESERT 51 47
Calais, CASTLE 49 27
Calamity Jane, COWBOY 45 59
calappa crabs, SHELL 9 43
calcites, CRYSTAL & GEM 25 9, 11, 13, 23; PREHISTORIC LIFE 52 6, 16; ROCK & MINERAL 2 17, 22-23, 24
calcium carbonate, CHEMISTRY 79 38, 44, 45, 49; EARTH 83 27

calcium, CHEMISTRY 79 18, 22, 44, 53; CRYSTAL & GEM 25 22, 45, 54, 55; EARTH 83 15, 20; MATTER 80 36, 37
calculators, ELECTRONICS 90 8, 9, 53, 63; INVENTION 27 30, 31, 62; SPY 67 19
calculus, TIME & SPACE 81 6, 29
Caledonian peoples, ANCIENT ROME 24 14
calendar stone, EARLY PEOPLE 10 58
calendars, TIME & SPACE 81 9, 27
calf roping, COWBOY 45 34, 59, 62-63
Calgary Stampede, COWBOY 45 62
Calicut, EXPLORER 31 20
California, EXPLORER 31 44; VOLCANO 38 49, 61; WHALE 46 57 63
Californian blind gobies, FISH 20 24
Caligula, ANCIENT ROME 24 8
calipers, BATTLE 63 28; INVENTION 27 17
calligraphy, Chinese, CHINA 55 30-31, 32; WRITING 48 6, 10-11
Islamic, WRITING 48 7, 34-35, 53
Russian, WRITING 48 53
western, WRITING 48 7, 27, 28, 51
calories, ENERGY 76 36, 52, 53
calorimeter, ENERGY 76 20, 21, 53, 55
calotype, INVENTION 27 40
Calvert, Edward, WATERCOLOUR 97 43
Calvo, Marco Fabio, RENAISSANCE 91 50
Calymene, FOSSIL 19 30
cam, TECHNOLOGY 89 33, 36
Camarasaurus, DINOSAUR 13 19, 62
Camargo, Marie, DANCE 99 45
Camargue, COWBOY 45 6, 13, 52-53, 55
Cambodia, DANCE 99 10
Cambrian period, EVOLUTION 85 26, 46, 47, 60
Cambridge Flag, FLAG 16 24
camels, AFRICA 61 23, 48; DESERT 51 40-41, 42, 46; FARM 66 13; MAMMAL 11 10, 58
Bactrian, DESERT 51 38-39, 43
dromedary, DESERT 51 37, 61
camel-spiders, DESERT 51 24
cameo, COSTUME 35 19, 40
Camera Lucida, PERSPECTIVE 98 45

camera obscura, CINEMA 34 6; PERSPECTIVE 98 34, 35,42-43; WATERCOLOUR 97 41
cameras, FUTURE 100 8, 13, 43; INVENTION 27 40, 41, 51, 62; LIGHT 75 24-25, 26, 27; TECHNOLOGY 89 33
digital, FUTURE 100 35, 53
emitron, ELECTRONICS 90 27
lens, LIGHT 75 24-25, 37
movie, CINEMA 34 13, 14-15, 19
pinhole, SPY 67 13
spy, SPY 67 14-15, 48, 51
concealed, CRIME & DETECTION 73 38; SPY 67 28
microdot, SPY 67 23
multi-spectral, SPY 67 52
surveillance, FUTURE 100 14, 42
television, TECHNOLOGY 89 55, 57
video, FUTURE 100 14, 43; SPY 67 45
Cameroon, AFRICA 61 38, 59, 60; VOLCANO 38 20; FLAG 16 18, 19
camisole, COSTUME 35 54
Camm, Sidney, FLYING MACHINE 22 24
camouflage, ARCTIC & ANTARCTIC 57 16, 40; SEASHORE 15 34-35, 50-51; SHARK 40 8, 38-39; SPY 67 23, 52, 57
mimicry by animals, JUNGLE 54 50-51
Campbell, John, INVENTION 27 35
Campbell, Malcolm, CAR 21 58
camshafts, CAR 21 42, 44, 45
can can, DANCE 99 58
can opener, INVENTION 27 6
Canaan, BIBLE LANDS 30 20, 25, 28, 39; RELIGION 68 42
art, BIBLE LANDS 30 36, 38, 42-43
gods, BIBLE LANDS 30 24-25, 37, 55
Canada, ARCTIC & ANTARCTIC 57 8, 34, 50, 61; CAT 29 36, 58; EXPLORER 31 42; WHALE 46 15, 37, 58
currency, MONEY 18 48, 49, 62
Canadian National Railway, TRAIN 39 63
flag, FLAG 16 14, 48-49
weather, WEATHER 28 40, 56
Canaletto, INVENTION 27 40; PERSPECTIVE 98 42-43
canals, CHINA 55 38-39
Canary Wharf Tower, PYRAMID 53 63
candles, INVENTION 27 20, 21, 22; TECHNOLOGY 89 41

Canes Venatici, **ASTRONOMY 82** 62

Cang Jie, **CHINA 55** 30; **WRITING 48** 10

Canidae, **DOG 32** 6, 20, 34

cannibalism, **AZTEC 47** 37

Canning jewel, **CRYSTAL & GEM 25** 55

Cannizzaro, Stanislao, **MATTER 80** 37

cannons, **BOAT 36** 20, 28; **CASTLE 49** 36, 62; **SHIPWRECK 72** 14, 18, 24

  in battle, **BATTLE 63** 26-27, 29, 32

  pirates', **PIRATE 59** 7, 23, 28-29

canoe shells, **SHELL 9** 42

canoes, **AFRICA 61** 18; **AZTEC 47** 14; **BOAT 36** 16, 33; **NORTH AMERICAN INDIAN 60** 12-13, 53

  bark, **BOAT 36** 12-13

  dugouts, **BOAT 36** 14-15

cans, **TECHNOLOGY 89** 14, 62, 46-47

Canterbury Tales, **CASTLE 49** 46; **KNIGHT 43** 11, 53

Canton, **CHINA 55** 62

Cantor, Eddie, **CINEMA 34** 23

canvas shoes, **COSTUME 35** 24

caps, **COSTUME 35** 28, 36, 38

capacitors, **ELECTRICITY 77** 9, 12, 13, 62; **ELECTRONICS 90** 18, 20-21, 33

  filter, **ELECTRONICS 90** 34, 43

  memory, **ELECTRONICS 90** 56, 57

  power supply, **ELECTRONICS 90** 31

  radio, **ELECTRONICS 90** 22, 52

  tuning, **ELECTRONICS 90** 53

  variable, **ELECTRONICS 90** 34, 52, 53

Cape Churchill, **ARCTIC & ANTARCTIC 57** 32

Cape Dorset, **ARCTIC & ANTARCTIC 57** 21, 24

Cape Evans, **ARCTIC & ANTARCTIC 57** 54, 55

Cape Horn, **EXPLORER 31** 24

Cape of Good Hope, **EXPLORER 31** 20-21, 24

capercaillies, **BIRD 1** 38

capes, **COSTUME 35** 20, 27

capillaries, **HUMAN BODY 87** 26, 27, 30-33; **LIFE 84** 27, 28

capitals, **BUILDING 58** 32, 58

Capitoline Hill, **ANCIENT ROME 24** 10, 17, 50

Capone, Al, **CRIME & DETECTION 73** 13, 24, 25

caps, **COSTUME 35** 28, 36, 38, 46

capstans, **FORCE & MOTION 78** 10, 11

capstones, **PYRAMID 53** 43, 44-45

Captorhinus, **DINOSAUR 13** 56

Capuchin monkeys, **GORILLA 64** 16, 17, 20-21

Capuchin monks, **MUMMY 44** 60-61

caracal, **DESERT 51** 34

Caradosso, **RENAISSANCE 91** 51

Caraka, **MEDICINE 88** 14

carapaces, **SHELL 9** 9, 28, 30, 45, 51

carats, **CRYSTAL & GEM 25** 52, 56

Caravaggio, **BIBLE LANDS 30** 30

caravans, **AFRICA 61** 48; **DESERT 51** 38, 47

carbines, **ARMS & ARMOUR 4** 41; **BATTLE 63** 10, 48, 51

carbohydrates, **CHEMISTRY 79** 34, 49, 50; **ECOLOGY 86** 9, 14, 18

carbolic acid, **MEDICINE 88** 48

carbon, **CHEMISTRY 79** 11, 30, 40, 41; **CRYSTAL & GEM 25** 14, 34; **MATTER 80** 16, 35, 50; **ROCK & MINERAL 2** 24, 41, 48

  arc, **INVENTION 27** 50

    lamps, **ELECTRICITY 77** 37, 42, 43, 48

  atoms, **CHEMISTRY 79** 27

  compounds, **CHEMISTRY 79** 48-49, 50, 60; **MATTER 80** 27, 40-41

  carbonates, **ROCK & MINERAL 2** 43

  cycle, **ECOLOGY 86** 18-19; **JUNGLE 54** 62; **MATTER 80** 42

  fibre composites, **TECHNOLOGY 89** 28-29

    lamps, **TECHNOLOGY 89** 41

  role in life process, **LIFE 84** 7, 27

carbon dioxide, **CHEMISTRY 79** 29, 31, 48, 49; **ECOLOGY 86** 9, 18, 19, 63; **ENERGY 76** 52, 56; **MATTER 80** 7, 20, 26; **WEATHER 28** 6

  in air, **MATTER 80** 29, 34; **EARTH 83** 10

  atmosphere, **ASTRONOMY 82** 42-43

  gas, **MATTER 80** 28

  molecules, **MATTER 80** 37

  photosynthesis, **ENERGY 76** 50, 51

  on planets, **ASTRONOMY 82** 46-47, 48-49

  and plants, **MATTER 80** 21, 42

  in rainwater, **EARTH 83** 17

  in rocks, **EARTH 83** 21

  and trees, **WEATHER 28** 61

carbon disulphide, **CHEMISTRY 79** 53

carbon fibres, **FUTURE 100** 54, 55

  fire extinguishers, **CHEMISTRY 79** 7

  gas, **CHEMISTRY 79** 28, 32, 36, 37

  importance of, **CHEMISTRY 79** 34, 35, 50, 51; **LIFE 84** 8-9; **MATTER 80** 63

  photosynthesis, **LIFE 84** 16-17

  respiration, **LIFE 84** 15, 18-19

carbon granules, **ELECTRICITY 77** 59

carbon monoxide, **CHEMISTRY 79** 36, 37

Carboniferous period, **EVOLUTION 85** 61

carbonization, **ARCHAEOLOGY 56** 6, 28-29, 44, 46

carborundum, **CRYSTAL & GEM 25** 27

Carcharadon, **FOSSIL 19** 34

Cardano, Girolamo, **CINEMA 34** 6

careening, **PIRATE 59** 44-45

Carew, Sir George, **SHIPWRECK 72** 18, 19

Caribbean, region, **DANCE 99** 11, 54; **VOLCANO 38** 32, 51; **WEATHER 28** 7

Caribbean Sea, **PIRATE 59** 30-31, 38-39

caribou, **ARCTIC & ANTARCTIC 57** 38-39, 40, 50

Carlisle, Anthony, **ELECTRICITY 77** 32

Carlson, Chester, **ELECTRICITY 77** 14

Carnarvon, Lord, **MUMMY 44** 38, 40

carnelian, **CRYSTAL & GEM 25** 33, 58, 61

carnivals, **DANCE 99** 10, 49

carnivores, **ECOLOGY 86** 12, 42, 48, 51; **MAMMAL 11** 9, 50, 58, 63; **POND & RIVER 6** 10, 12; **SKELETON 3** 35, 41

Caroline, of Brunswick, **WITCH & WIZARD 70** 15

Carolingian Empire, **VIKING 50** 37, 48

Carothers, Wallace, **FUTURE 100** 9

carpenters, **BUILDING 58** 7, 8-9, 24; **VIKING 50** 42, 43

carpet sharks, **FISH 20** 19, 58; **SHARK 40** 6

carps, **FISH 20** 6, 8, 9, 15; **POND & RIVER 6** 12, 13, 24-25; **SKELETON 3** 20

carrier pigeons, **BATTLE 63** 52; **SPY 67** 20, 21

carrier shells, **SHELL 9** 40

carrion, **EAGLE 69** 8, 28, 35, 42

Carroll, Lewis, **AMPHIBIAN 41** 42; **ELECTRONICS 90** 51; **WHALE 46** 42; **WRITING 48** 55

carrots, **PLANT 14** 13, 21, 55

cars, **CAR 21**; **FORCE & MOTION 78** 20, 22, 38; **INVENTION 12** 27, 48; **TECHNOLOGY 89** 30, 42-43, 53

  axle, **CAR 21** 9, 38, 52, 53

  body, **CAR 21** 16, 24, 32-35

  boot, **CAR 21** 8, 25, 26, 29

  carburettor, **CAR 21** 19, 39, 48, 49

  chassis, **CAR 21** 13, 16, 26, 36

  clutch, **CAR 21** 9, 38, 42, 52

  engine, **CAR 21** 6-7, 9, 42-47

  exhaust, **CAR 21** 38, 39, 44-45

  futuristic, **FUTURE 100** 25-27, 54

  gears, **CAR 21** 39, 52, 53

  ignition, **CAR 21** 13, 45, 50, 51

  lights, **CAR 21** 20-21, 41, 50

  racing, **CAR 21** 18-19, 32, 33

  solar, **FUTURE 100** 18

  sports, **CAR 21** 18, 23, 26, 27

  steering, **CAR 21** 7, 9, 38, 56-57

  see also brakes, wheels, *and under individual cars*

Carson, Kit, **COWBOY 45** 47

Carson, Rachel, **ECOLOGY 86** 61

Cartagena, **PIRATE 59** 23

Carter, Howard, **ANCIENT EGYPT 23** 23; **ARCHAEOLOGY 56** 11; **MUMMY 44** 29, 37, 38-39

Carthage, **ANCIENT ROME 24** 6, 7, 60; **BIBLE LANDS 30** 23; **EXPLORER 31** 6

Carthusian order, **MEDIEVAL LIFE 65** 36, 39

Cartier, Jacques, **EXPLORER 31** 42

cartilage, **HUMAN BODY 87** 16, 25, 49

  discs, **HUMAN BODY 87** 14, 19, 42

  fishes, **FISH 20** 8, 35, 54, 59

  shark, **SHARK 40** 6-8, 10-12, 32

cartoons, **CINEMA 34** 50-53; **RUSSIA 74** 34, 42, 51

cartouches, **PYRAMID 53** 18, 34

cartridges, **ARMS & ARMOUR 4** 56, 59, 60, 61; **BATTLE 63** 30, 42, 48

carts, **FARM 66** 8, 21, 35, 43; **HORSE 33** 46-47, 54-55

carvings, **BUILDING 58** 18-19, 54-55; **EARLY PEOPLE 10** 21, 24, 59; **WRITING 48** 7, 17

cascadura, **FISH 20** 10

Case, **CAR 21** 63

casinos, **CRIME & DETECTION 73** 27

Casler, Herman, **CINEMA 34** 11

Caspian Sea, **CAT 29** 57; **VOLCANO 38** 50

Cassatt, Mary, **IMPRESSIONISM 92** 43, 45, 56-57; **MONET 95** 59

  biography, **IMPRESSIONISM 92** 62

  and Degas, **IMPRESSIONISM 92** 51, 55

  Five O'Clock Tea, **IMPRESSIONISM 92** 44

Two Young Women in a Loge, IMPRESSIONISM **92** 51

cassettes, FUTURE **100** 10, 52

cassia, ANCIENT EGYPT **23** 41

Cassidy, Butch, CRIME & DETECTION **73** 56

Cassini, Giovanni, ASTRONOMY **82** 28, 50, 52; TIME & SPACE **81** 33

Cassini space probes, SPACE EXPLORATION **71** 44, 45

cassocks, COSTUME **35** 29

Castagno, Andrea del, RENAISSANCE **91** 23

castanets, DANCE **99** 15, 17; MUSIC **12** 56

castellan, CASTLE **49** 48

Castiglione, Baldassare, RENAISSANCE **91** 48

Castile, FLAG **16** 36, 37

castles, BUILDING **58** 34, 36, 37, 39; CASTLE **49** 6-7; KNIGHT **43** 22-23; MEDIEVAL LIFE **65** 14, 25
concentric, CASTLE **49** 12-13
construction, CASTLE **49** 56-57
as defence, KNIGHT **43** 24-25
early, CASTLE **49** 8-9
France, CASTLE **49** 14-15
Germany, CASTLE **49** 18-21
as home, KNIGHT **43** 34-35
Japan, CASTLE **49** 36-37
Spain, CASTLE **49** 16-17

Castniid moths, BUTTERFLY & MOTH **7** 45, 56

castor-oil, PLANT **14** 58

Castro, Fidel, RUSSIA **74** 37; SPY **67** 36, 43

casts, FOSSIL **19** 6, 26

CAT scan, MEDICINE **88** 38-39; MUMMY **44** 51

cat shark, SHARK **40** 6, 12, 20-21

cat's-eyes, CRYSTAL & GEM **25** 45, 47, 49

catacombs, MUMMY **44** 60-61

Catal Huyuk, Turkey, FARM **66** 6; VOLCANO **38** 6

catalpa, TREE **5** 27, 37

catalysts, CHEMISTRY **79** 7, 36-39, 44, 63
enzymes, CHEMISTRY **79** 34, 35, 50
plastics, CHEMISTRY **79** 56, 57

catalytic converters, CHEMISTRY **79** 36-37; FUTURE **100** 11

catamarans, BOAT **36** 63

catapults, ANCIENT ROME **24** 12; CASTLE **49** 25; KNIGHT **43** 26-27

catastrophe theory, EVOLUTION **85** 16-17, 28

caterpillars, ARCTIC & ANTARCTIC **57** 19; BUTTERFLY & MOTH **7** 8, 14-15; INSECT **17** 20-21, 34, 35; JUNGLE **54** 23, 50

birth, BUTTERFLY & MOTH **7** 12-13
exotic, BUTTERFLY & MOTH **7** 16-19

catfish, FISH **20** 15, 19, 28, 30

cathedrals, BUILDING **58** 33, 34, 50; KNIGHT **43** 9; MEDIEVAL LIFE **65** 6, 32-34, 41
Basel, MEDIEVAL LIFE **65** 43
Canterbury, MEDIEVAL LIFE **65** 38, 39, 42
Chartres, MEDIEVAL LIFE **65** 35, 40
Nôtre Dame, MEDIEVAL LIFE **65** 54
Santiago de Compostela, MEDIEVAL LIFE **65** 42, 43

Catherine, the Great, RUSSIA **74** 20, 21, 24, 25

Catherwood, Frederick, PYRAMID **53** 59

catheters, MEDICINE **88** 52

cathodes, CHEMISTRY **79** 27, 46, 47; ELECTRICITY **77** 18, 19, 32, 33

cathode rays, ELECTRICITY **77** 54-55; ELECTRONICS **90** 27; INVENTION **27** 56, 57; MATTER **80** 48, 49
tube, ELECTRONICS **90** 26, 33, 39, 44, 57; ELECTRICITY **77** 54, 55, 62, 63
television, ELECTRICITY **77** 62, 63

Catlin, George, HORSE **33** 57

cats, ANCIENT EGYPT **23** 60, 61; CAT **29**; SKELETON **3** 16, 32, 58
brains, CAT **29** 13, 14-15, 25
claws, CAT **29** 15, 27, 41-42
communication, CAT **29** 20, 26, 29, 32
cubs, CAT **29** 24-25, 32, 43
domestic, MAMMAL **11** 9, 59, 60-61
birth, MAMMAL **11** 34-35
grooming, CAT **29** 50, 62-63; MAMMAL **11** 46-47
growth, MAMMAL **11** 38-39
kittens, CAT **29** 24-25, 61; MAMMAL **11** 36-37
play, MAMMAL **11** 42-43
Egyptian mau, CAT **29** 46
extinction, CAT **29** 8, 40-41
hunting, CAT **29** 11, 18, 22-23
legends, CAT **29** 48-49
mummies, MUMMY **44** 42, 46-47
pedigrees, CAT **29** 50, 51, 52-57
senses, CAT **29** 16-17, 20-22
tabby cats, CAT **29** 45, 55, 60
whiskers, CAT **29** 6, 15, 16-17
wildcats, CAT **29** 10, 39, 44-45
see also under individual cats

catshark, FISH **20** 59

cattle, AFRICA **61** 16, 18, 43; DESERT **51** 42, 43, 50; FARM **66** 44-49; MAMMAL **11** 10, 35; VIKING **50** 38
Aberdeen Angus, COWBOY **45** 30-31, 33
branding of, COWBOY **45** 52, 55, 63
charms, AFRICA **61** 36
early, ARCHAEOLOGY **56** 45
Herefords, COWBOY **45** 30-31, 33
Longhorns, COWBOY **45** 25, 28, 30, 38
medieval farm, CASTLE **49** 54
Shorthorns, COWBOY **45** 30-31, 56
skeletons, SKELETON **3** 44, 47, 57, 61
stampedes, COWBOY **45** 40

"Cattle Annie", COWBOY **45** 58

cattle stations, COWBOY **45** 28-29, 56, 58

cattle trails, COWBOY **45** 24, 36, 38-39, 42
dangers, COWBOY **45** 40-41

Caturus, FOSSIL **19** 35

Caucasus, RUSSIA **74** 12, 15, 22, 59

cauldrons, CASTLE **49** 40; PIRATE **59** 43; VIKING **50** 35

cautery, MEDICINE **88** 26, 51
irons, MEDICINE **88** 8, 22

cavaliers, COSTUME **35** 26

cavalry, BATTLE **63** 19, 25, 44, 52; HORSE **33** 42-43, 57; SPORT **8** 51
African, AFRICA **61** 44-45
cavalrymen, BATTLE **63** 13, 46, 47
heavy, BATTLE **63** 10-11, 41, 45
Roman, ANCIENT ROME **24** 12, 13

cave dwellings, DESERT **51** 45

cave paintings, ARCHAEOLOGY **56** 16, 57, 62-63; EARLY PEOPLE **10** 22, 24, 27; ROCK & MINERAL **2** 32; WATERCOLOUR **97** 6

Cavelier, Robert, EXPLORER **31** 43

Cavendish, Henry, CHEMISTRY **79** 29; ELECTRICITY **77** 20; FORCE & MOTION **78** 35

Cavendish, Thomas, PIRATE **59** 23

caves, limestone, ROCK & MINERAL **2** 22-23

caviar, RUSSIA **74** 14, 15

Caviglia, Giovanni, PYRAMID **53** 27

Caxton, William, WRITING **48** 40, 42

Cayley, Sir George, FLYING MACHINE **22** 10, 52

CD-ROMS, FUTURE **100** 25

cedars, TREE **5** 30, 31, 44

ceilings, BUILDING **58** 52, 59

Celadus, ANCIENT ROME **24** 30

celestial spheres, ASTRONOMY **82** 12-13, 26, 42

"Céline", SPY **67** 57

cellos, MUSIC **12** 30, 31

cells, biological, CHEMISTRY **79** 50, 51; HUMAN BODY **87** 12-13, 44
basic structure, LIFE **84** 10-11
blood, HUMAN BODY **87** 17, 27, 32-33, 48; LIFE **84** 50
red blood cells, LIFE **84** 11, 14, 27, 29
white blood cells, LIFE **84** 27, 28, 34
division, HUMAN BODY **87** 44, 48, 50
DNA, LIFE **84** 36, 37
metabolism, LIFE **84** 7, 9, 18, 27
nerve, HUMAN BODY **87** 59, 60, 63
nucleus, HUMAN BODY **87** 21, 59
organisms, LIFE **84** 14-15, 50, 52
multicellular organisms, LIFE **84** 14-15, 50, 52
single-celled organisms, LIFE **84** 12-13, 32, 50
origin, LIFE **84** 56-57
sensory, HUMAN BODY **87** 52, 54-55, 57
sex, LIFE **84** 41, 42
study of, LIFE **84** 15
wall, LIFE **84** 8, 10, 11, 13

cells, electrical, ELECTRICITY **77** 16, 18, 19, 20

cellular pathology, MEDICINE **88** 30

celluloid, INVENTION **27** 41, 50, 60

cellulose, CHEMISTRY **79** 50, 53, 54, 55; ECOLOGY **86** 14, 15; LIFE **84** 8, 10, 17

Celsus, Cornelius, MEDICINE **88** 18

Celtic peoples, ARMS & ARMOUR **4** 10-11; EARLY PEOPLE **10** 45, 48, 52-53; WITCH & WIZARD **70** 17, 59

cement, ROCK & MINERAL **2** 35; TECHNOLOGY **89** 20-21, 24

cemeteries, BATTLE **63** 63

Cennini, Cennino, RENAISSANCE **91** 22

Cenozoic era, EVOLUTION **85** 47, 61, 62

centaur, HORSE **33** 22

centimes, MONEY **18** 30, 31, 55, 58

centipedes, **Insect 17** 9; **Jungle 54** 35
Central America, **Early People 10** 40, 58-59; **Explorer 31** 23, 33, 42; **Jungle 54** 22-23, 58, 60, 62
pyramids, Aztec, **Pyramid 53** 60-61
Mayan, **Pyramid 53** 56-57, 58-59
Mexican, **Pyramid 53** 54-55
Central Pacific Railroad, **Train 39** 18
centreboards, **Boat 36** 23, 35, 63
centrifugal force, **Force & Motion 78** 52-53; **Time & Space 81** 47
centripetal force, **Force & Motion 78** 52-53
cents, **Money 18** 28, 48, 49, 54
centurions, **Ancient Rome 24** 10, 14
century plants, **Desert 51** 18
cephalaspids, **Fossil 19** 34
Cephalaspis, **Fish 20** 12, 13
cephalopods, **Fossil 19** 26, 28-29; **Ocean 62** 32, 37; **Shell 9** 8, 18, 19, 38
Cepheids, **Astronomy 82** 60, 62
ceramics, **China 55** 56, 58; **Electricity 77** 21, 47; **Technology 89** 62
Cerberus, **Dog 32** 44
cereals, **Archaeology 56** 6, 28, 46, 59; **Early People 10** 30-31, 54, 58; **Farm 66** 6, 14, 28, 30
cerebellum, **Human Body 87** 57, 60-62
cerebrum, **Human Body 87** 57, 59, 60-63
Cervantes, Miguel de, **Horse 33** 42; **Knight 43** 63
cervix, **Human Body 87** 43, 44, 45, 46
Cesalpino, Andrea, **Human Body 87** 28
Cespedes, Pablo de, **Perspective 98** 35
Cessna, 172E Skyhawks, **Flying Machine 22** 27
cesspits, **Archaeology 56** 6, 10-11, 46
Cestius, Caius, **Pyramid 53** 62
Ceylon, **Money 18** 35
Cézanne, Paul, **Impressionism 92** 10, 12, 16; **Monet 95** 24, 48, 59; **Perspective 98** 52; **Van Gogh 96** 58
Auvers, Panoramic View, **Impressionism 92** 35
The Bay of Marseilles, **Impressionism 92** 59

The Plate of Apples, **Impressionism 92** 45
watercolours, **Watercolour 97** 52-53, 55, 60
Chad, **Africa 61** 8
Chadwick, James, **Matter 80** 47, 52, 53
chaffinches, **Bird 1** 12, 36, 46, 52
Chagall, Marc, **Russia 74** 46
Chaillu, Paul du, **Gorilla 64** 50, 62
chain gangs, **Pirate 59** 39
chain mail, **Arms & Armour 4** 14, 15, 24, 33; **Costume 35** 12; **Viking 50** 13, 15
chalcedony, **Crystal & Gem 25** 32, 33
chalcopyrite, **Crystal & Gem 25** 20, 24
Chaldean dynasty, **Bible Lands 30** 50-51
chalets, **Building 58** 6
chalices, **Knight 43** 52
chalk, **Rock & Mineral 2** 15, 20, 32; **Seashore 15** 10-11, 63
Challenger, HMS, **Earth 83** 30-31, 38; **Ocean 62** 11, 45, 52; **Shark 40** 54-55
Challenger Space Shuttle, **Astronomy 82** 34
Chalmers, **Car 21** 62
chamber pots, **Knight 43** 35
Chamberlen, Dr. William, **Medicine 88** 27
chameleons, **Desert 51** 28; **Jungle 54** 50-51; **Reptile 26** 12, 16, 39; **Skeleton 3** 20
African, **Reptile 26** 20
Jackson's, **Reptile 26** 29
"Champagne Spy", **Spy 67** 58
Champollion, Jean-François, **Ancient Egypt 23** 35; **Mummy 44** 11; **Pyramid 53** 46; **Writing 48** 12
Chancay peoples, **Aztec 47** 11; **Mummy 44** 52, 54
Chandler, Raymond, **Crime & Detection 73** 37
Chandrasekhar, S., **Time & Space 81** 45
Chang Ping, battle of, **China 55** 14
Changjiang, **Whale 46** 63
Channel Isles, **Money 18** 46, 62
Channel Tunnel, **Train 39** 21, 63
chap hooks, **Cowboy 45** 24-25
chaparejos, leather, **Cowboy 45** 26-27
batwing, **Cowboy 45** 7, 18-19, 26-27
shotgun, **Cowboy 45** 23, 26
woollies, **Cowboy 45** 19, 26

chapels, **Castle 49** 21, 22-23; **Knight 43** 23
chaplains, **Castle 49** 22
Chaplin, Charlie, **Boat 36** 57; **Cinema 34** 21, 54, 55
Chappé, Claude, **Shipwreck 72** 37
chaps, **Costume 35** 39
Charchevenikova, Manya, **Dance 99** 53
charcoal, **Rock & Mineral 2** 32
Chardin, J.B., **Manet 94** 30, 32, 34
chariots, **Battle 63** 7; **China 55** 14, 15; **Horse 33** 22, 26, 48, 58
ancient, **Ancient Egypt 23** 36; **Ancient Greece 37** 25, 54
racing, **Ancient Rome 24** 6, 21, 34
Charlemagne, Emperor, **Castle 49** 8; **Horse 33** 32; **Knight 43** 6; **Medieval Life 65** 6, 35
Charles I, King of England, **Witch & Wizard 70** 15
Charles III, King of Spain, **Goya 93** 10, 11, 20, 45
Charles IV, King of Spain, **Goya 93** 11, 14, 21, 34
Charles V, King of Spain, **Battle 63** 45
Charles, Jacques, **Flying Machine 22** 8
Charles the Bald, **Viking 50** 16
charleston, **Dance 99** 58, 59
Charleton, Joan, **Watercolour 97** 45
charms, **Africa 61** 36, 37, 42, 43; **Early People 10** 24, 28, 37, 45
sacred, **North American Indian 60** 13, 41, 58
witchcraft, **Witch & Wizard 70** 28-31, 43
Charnley, John, **Medicine 88** 55
Charpentier, Georges, **Impressionism 92** 42
charts, **Pirate 59** 24, 27; **Shipwreck 72** 32
plotter, **Shipwreck 72** 42
chassis, **Car 21** 13, 16, 26, 36
châteaux, **Building 58** 15, 38, 42
defence, **Building 58** 37
French Renaissance, **Building 58** 40, 49
chatelaine, **Costume 35** 38
chatoyancy, **Crystal & Gem 25** 33
Chatterton, Thomas, **Crime & Detection 73** 20
Chaucer, Geoffrey, **Castle 49** 46; **Horse 33** 47; **Knight 43** 11, 53; **Writing 48** 40, 42

Checker, Chubby, **Dance 99** 59
checks, **Costume 35** 41, 57
cheese, **Farm 66** 40, 45, 46, 54
cheetahs, **Cat 29** 11, 15, 42-43; **Desert 51** 34
Chekhov, Anton, **Russia 74** 44, 45
chemise, **Costume 35** 42
chemistry, **Chemistry 79**
chemical bonds, **Matter 80** 36, 43, 50, 51
chemical energy, **Energy 76** 20, 50, 52
chemical reactions, **Chemistry 79** 38-39,40-41; **Matter 80** 11, 20, 28, 30
chemotherapy, **Medicine 88** 42
Cheng Ho, **Explorer 31** 17
chequered flag, **Flag 16** 23
cheques, **Money 18** 58, 59
Cherokee peoples, **North American Indian 60** 17, 26
alphabet, **Writing 48** 19
cherry trees, **Tree 5** 23, 26, 34, 38, 46
Chesapeake Bay, **Pirate 59** 53
Cheselden, Dr. William, **Medicine 88** 27
chess, **Castle 49** 17; **China 55** 50; **Knight 43** 34, 36
chestnuts, **Tree 5** 29, 35, 40, 46
chests, **Pirate 59** 36, 37
Chevreul, Eugène, **Impressionism 92** 20-21, 22, 59
Chevrolet, **Car 21** 18
Cheyenne peoples, **North American Indian 60** 8, 30, 33
Chicago, **Crime & Detection 73** 24, 25, 58
Chichén Itzá, **Pyramid 53** 6, 56, 57
chickens, **Farm 66** 58, 59, 61-63
chicks, **Bird 1** 56-59
chicory, **Plant 14** 54
Chihuahuan Desert, **Desert 51** 6, 16, 21, 30
childhood, **Ancient Rome 24** 20, 21; **Castle 49** 46
Chile, **Dance 99** 14
mummies, **Mummy 44** 52, 55
Chilkat peoples, **North American Indian 60** 56-57
Chillon, castle, **Castle 49** 32; **Flag 16** 32
chimaeras, rabbitfish, **Fish 20** 9, 20, 54
chimeras, ratfish, **Shark 40** 7-8, 13
chimes, **Music 12** 54
chimneys, **Building 58** 40-41; **Train 39** 15, 18, 23, 54

chimpanzees, GORILLA 64 9, 50-53; JUNGLE 54 44-45; MAMMAL 11 7, 40-41, 49
babies, GORILLA 64 51, 61
bones, SKELETON 3 35, 44, 49, 55
communication, GORILLA 64 32
defences, GORILLA 64 34, 35
food, GORILLA 64 51, 52, 53
fossils, FOSSIL 19 58
"Ham", the space-chimp, GORILLA 64 61
intelligence, GORILLA 64 36-37, 50
skills, GORILLA 64 54-55
Chimu peoples, AZTEC 47 10, 11, 18
China Sea, PIRATE 59 33, 54-55
China, BATTLE 63 16, 18; CHINA 55; EXPLORER 31 9, 22, 30; SHIPWRECK 72 16, 17, 33
ancient, ARCHAEOLOGY 56 14, 51, 56; EARLY PEOPLE 10 15, 40, 54-55
architecture, BUILDING 58 27, 42, 58, 60; CHINA 55 38, 40-41, 54
arts, CHINA 55 32-33, 56-57; PERSPECTIVE 98 29
dances, DANCE 99 25, 26, 28, 38
empire, CHINA 55 6-9, 62-63
families, CHINA 55 42-43
farming, CHINA 55 34-37
festivals, CHINA 55 50-51
flags, FLAG 16 9, 15, 58-59
food, CHINA 55 44-45
Great Wall, EARLY PEOPLE 10 54, 55
inventions, CHINA 55 22-23
magic, WITCH & WIZARD 70 54, 55
medicine, CHINA 55 28-29; MEDICINE 88 12, 14-15
money, EARLY PEOPLE 10 56; MONEY 18 7, 12, 21, 52-53
mummies, MUMMY 44 63
religion, CHINA 55 10, 26-27, 43; RELIGION 68 32-33
rockets, SPACE EXPLORATION 71 14
Silk Road, EXPLORER 31 16-19
space, SPACE EXPLORATION 71 12
trade, CHINA 55 40, 58-59, 62-63
writing, CHINA 55 11, 12, 30-31; EARLY PEOPLE 10 41
see also Chinese language, Confucianism, and under individual dynasties
chinchillas, CAT 29 58; MAMMAL 11 9, 45
Chinese language, WRITING 48 10-11, 31

Chinese Liberation Army, FLAG 16 59
Ching Shih, PIRATE 59 33
Ching Yih, PIRATE 59 54-55
Ching-Chi-ling, PIRATE 59 54
Chinook, wind, WEATHER 28 42, 54
chipmunks, MAMMAL 11 9, 48
Chippewa peoples, NORTH AMERICAN INDIAN 60 22, 30
Chirico, Giorgio de, PERSPECTIVE 98 56-57
Chirodipterus, FOSSIL 19 35
chiropractic, MEDICINE 88 45
chisels, ARCHAEOLOGY 56 50; CASTLE 49 56, 59
Chisholm, Jesse, COWBOY 45 39
chitons, FOSSIL 19 26, 27
chivalry, KNIGHT 43 39, 40-41
chlorine, CHEMISTRY 79 20, 23, 26, 27
chlorophyll, ECOLOGY 86 8, 9; LIGHT 75 50; PLANT 14 14, 15
chloroplast, LIFE 84 10, 11, 16, 57
Choctaw peoples, NORTH AMERICAN INDIAN 60 25-26
Chokwe peoples, AFRICA 61 58, 63
cholera, MEDICINE 88 34, 62, 63
chondrichthians, FISH 20 9
chondrosteans, FISH 20 9
chopsticks, CHINA 55 44
choreography, DANCE 99 28, 52, 56, 57
Chrétien, Jean-Loup, SPACE EXPLORATION 71 12
Christ, see Jesus Christ
Christianity, AFRICA 61 32, 33, 36; ANCIENT EGYPT 23 63; RELIGION 68 48-51; VIKING 50 16, 61, 62-63
Christians, ANCIENT ROME 24 50, 56, 62, 63
Christmas, MEDIEVAL LIFE 65 14, 54, 58; RELIGION 68 48, 49
the Church, RELIGION 68 52-53
medieval, MEDIEVAL LIFE 65 13, 30-31, 34
Christians, see Christianity
Christie, Agatha, TRAIN 39 31
Christie, Julie, CINEMA 34 56
Christmas, MEDIEVAL LIFE 65 14, 54, 58; RELIGION 68 48, 49
chromatography, CHEMISTRY 79 15, 60; MATTER 80 26
chromium, MATTER 80 30-31; TECHNOLOGY 89 7, 14, 15
chromosomes, EVOLUTION 85 51, 52; LIFE 84 34, 36, 38, 40

human, LIFE 84 60, 61
chromosphere, ASTRONOMY 82 31, 38, 39
chronometers, SHIPWRECK 72 33; TECHNOLOGY 89 31; TIME & SPACE 81 23, 56
chrysalises, BUTTERFLY & MOTH 7 20-21, 22-23; INSECT 17 24-25, 34-35
chrysanthemums, CHINA 55 55; FLAG 16 15
Chrysaugine moths, BUTTERFLY & MOTH 7 47
chuck wagons, COWBOY 45 36-37
Chui Apoo, PIRATE 59 54
Church, the, RELIGION 68 52-53
medieval, MEDIEVAL LIFE 65 13, 30-31, 34
religious plays, MEDIEVAL LIFE 65 58-59
churches, BUILDING 58 25, 34; RUSSIA 74 19, 27, 34
doorways, BUILDING 58 47
Gothic, BUILDING 58 36, 59
stained glass, BUILDING 58 50-51
see also cathedrals
Churchill, Cape, ARCTIC & ANTARCTIC 57 32
Churchill, Sir Winston, FLAG 16 11; GORILLA 64 58
CIA, SPY 67 36, 42-43, 51
cicada, INSECT 17 12, 36
cichlids, FISH 20 17, 19, 44, 45
cider, FARM 66 39
Cierva C-30, FLYING MACHINE 22 48-49
Cigoli, Lodovico, PERSPECTIVE 98 27, 44
cinchonas, TREE 5 22
cinema, CINEMA 34; LIGHT 75 26, 27
cinematic, CINEMA 34 34-35, 42
halls, CINEMA 34 24-25
3-D, FUTURE 100 48, 49, 59
see also films
cinematography, CINEMA 34 16; INVENTION 27 50-51
cinnamon, TREE 5 23
ciphers, SPY 67 24-25, 35, 42
Circe, WITCH & WIZARD 70 16
circuit, ELECTRONICS 90 16, 22-23, 30, 40
board, ELECTRONICS 90 55, 57
see also integrated circuit
circulation, HUMAN BODY 87 26, 28-33, 40
circumferentors, INVENTION 27 35
circus, ELEPHANT 42 50-51; HORSE 33 39, 58
Circus Maximus, ANCIENT ROME 24 35
cistanche, DESERT 51 19

Cistercian order, MEDIEVAL LIFE 65 36, 37, 38
cities, FUTURE 100 22-23, 58, 59
citizens, ANCIENT ROME 24 8, 10, 15, 16
citric acid, CHEMISTRY 79 9, 42-43
citrine, CRYSTAL & GEM 25 18, 32, 37, 58
Citroen, CAR 21 55
civets, CAT 29 45
Clair, René, CINEMA 34 57
clairvoyance, WITCH & WIZARD 70 54
clams, FOSSIL 19 9, 26; OCEAN 62 17, 24, 58-59; SEASHORE 15 26, 27, 42; SHELL 9 16, 17, 34, 50
Clantons, COWBOY 45 43
Clare, St, MEDIEVAL LIFE 65 37
clarinets, MUSIC 12 9, 12, 13
clarion bells, CAR 21 10
Clark, Dr. Eugenie, SHARK 40 51
Clark, William, EXPLORER 31 42, 45, 63
Clarke, Arthur C, FUTURE 100 8, 10, 44; SPACE EXPLORATION 71 9
Clarke, Edward, ELECTRICITY 77 36
Clarke, Samuel, FOSSIL 19 47
Classical Period, ANCIENT GREECE 37 7, 16, 42
Claudius, Emperor, ANCIENT ROME 24 8, 30; ARCHAEOLOGY 56 57
Clausewitz, Carl von, BATTLE 63 6
clay, BUILDING 58 12-13, 26; EARTH 83 27, 53; ROCK & MINERAL 2 11, 21, 32, 43; TECHNOLOGY 89 6, 8, 16
boulders, EARTH 83 26, 59
tablets, WRITING 48 9
claystone, ROCK & MINERAL 2 9, 11
cleaners, FISH 20 46, 47
clear-wing butterflies, BUTTERFLY & MOTH 7 57
clear-wing moths, BUTTERFLY & MOTH 7 52
cleavage, CRYSTAL & GEM 25 15, 18, 42
Clemenceau, Georges, MONET 95 45, 58, 60-61
Clements, Frederic E., ECOLOGY 86 34, 36
Cleopatra, ANCIENT EGYPT 23 62; MUMMY 44 43
clergy, CASTLE 49 22-23
clerks, WRITING 48 56
Cleveland Bay, HORSE 33 38, 54
clicking sticks, DESERT 51 12

climate, EARTH 83 12-13, 33, 60;
EVOLUTION 85 17, 38, 60, 63;
OCEAN 62 12-13, 26;
WEATHER 28 16, 55, 60, 61
change, ARCHAEOLOGY 56
46-47; ECOLOGY 86 34, 35,
37; PREHISTORIC LIFE 52
6-9, 60
cold and hot deserts,
DESERT 51 6, 10
climbing perches, FISH 20 32
clingfish, FISH 20 21;
SEASHORE 15 35
clippers, BOAT 36 40, 41
Clive, Lady, ELEPHANT 42 46
cloaks, ANCIENT GREECE 37 40,
42, 43; COSTUME 35 7, 12,
13, 21; CHINA 55 22
clocks, FORCE & MOTION 78 22,
25, 46;
INVENTION 27 12, 22-23;
TIME & SPACE 81 6,
16-19, 56
atomic, FORCE &
MOTION 78 59
body, TIME & SPACE 81 20
gravity, TIME & SPACE 81
39, 44
mechanism,
TECHNOLOGY 89 32
pendulum, FORCE &
MOTION 78 47
relativity, TIME & SPACE 81
34-35, 36, 56
cloning, FUTURE 100 37
cloth, INVENTION 27 36, 37;
WRITING 48 31, 33
clothes, ARCHAEOLOGY 56 9,
30-31, 34, 41; COSTUME 35;
DESERT 51 48-55
Ice Age, EARLY PEOPLE 10 18,
32-33
Iron Age, EARLY PEOPLE 10 48
medieval,
bailiff's, MEDIEVAL
LIFE 65 15
guildmaster's, MEDIEVAL
LIFE 65 51
monk's, MEDIEVAL
LIFE 65 37
peasant's
MEDIEVAL LIFE 65 11, 15
soldier's,
MEDIEVAL LIFE 65 28-29
womens', MEDIEVAL
LIFE 65 23
clouded yellow butterflies,
BUTTERFLY & MOTH 7 26, 31
cloudless sulphur butterflies,
BUTTERFLY & MOTH 7 4, 7,
22, 50
clouds, WEATHER 28 19,
24-25, 59
classification, WEATHER 28
26-27, 28-29
patterns, WEATHER 28 7, 12
see also rain

clover, FARM 66 14, 16
clown loach, FISH 20 16
clown triggerfish, FISH 20 17
clownfish, FISH 20 46, 47;
SEASHORE 15 49
clubmosses, FOSSIL 19 36, 37
clubs, ARMS & ARMOUR 4 8, 63;
SPORT 8 58
Cluniacs, MEDIEVAL LIFE 65 36
Cluny, France,
ARCHAEOLOGY 56 53
clutch, FORCE & MOTION 78 20,
22, 23
Clydesdale, HORSE 33 42
Cnut the Great, VIKING 50 48,
59, 63
coachwhip plant, DESERT 51 18
coal, CHEMISTRY 79 49, 50;
EVOLUTION 85 11, 16, 44;
PLANT 14 6;
PREHISTORIC LIFE 52 7,
26-27
forest swamps, FOSSIL 19
37, 40
fossil fuel, ENERGY 76 52,
54, 55
in trains, TRAIN 39 19, 26
coal-wagons, TRAIN 39 8,
9, 27
steam trains, TRAIN 39 10,
11, 14, 15
types, ROCK & MINERAL 2 7,
36-37
coal gas, ENERGY 76 34, 54, 55
coaltar, CHEMISTRY 79 52-53, 63
coastguard, WEATHER 28 34
coasts, OCEAN 62 14-15, 18;
WEATHER 28 56
wrecks,
SHIPWRECK 72 31, 32, 42
coat-of-arms, ARMS &
ARMOUR 4 30; BATTLE 63 18;
CASTLE 49 14, 31, 38;
KNIGHT 43 48-49
Russian, RUSSIA 74 9, 11,
21, 28
coat-of-plates, CASTLE 49 30, 63
coats, COSTUME 35 26, 29,
32, 33
frock coats, COSTUME 35 39,
41, 50
cobalt, CRYSTAL & GEM 25 17
cobras, JUNGLE 54 35;
REPTILE 26 58-59
cocaine, MEDICINE 88 13, 50;
PLANT 14 59
cochlea, HUMAN BODY 87 54-55
cockatiels, BIRD 1 24
cockatoos, DESERT 51 30
Cockcroft-Walton generator,
ELECTRICITY 77 12
Cockerell, Christopher,
FUTURE 100 10
cockles, POND & RIVER 6 52, 53,
59; SEASHORE 15 26, 42, 59,
62; SHELL 9 34, 35, 60;
SKELETON 3 24, 25, 43

cockpits, FLYING MACHINE 22
14, 42-43, 59
cockroaches, DESERT 51 22;
DINOSAUR 13 59;
FOSSIL 19 60; INSECT 17 8,
10, 23, 41
cocoa, AZTEC 47 24, 27;
JUNGLE 54 58
coconut crabs, SHELL 9 58
coconuts, SEASHORE 15 58;
TREE 5 13, 42, 43
Cocteau, Jean, CAT 29 56
cod, FISH 20 10, 11, 20, 27;
OCEAN 62 26, 57;
SKELETON 3 20
codes, SPY 67 24-25, 42, 48
breaking, SPY 67 26, 27
letters, SPY 67 40, 41
messages, SPY 67 23, 32
sheet, SPY 67 24, 32
see also Morse code
codex, BIBLE LANDS 30 58-59
codpiece, COSTUME 35 16
Cody, Buffalo Bill
ARMS & ARMOUR 4 60;
COWBOY 45 11, 47, 61;
HORSE 33 56
Coehoorn, Menno van,
BATTLE 63 32
coelacanth, FISH 20 9, 12, 13,
14; FOSSIL 19 60, 61
Coelophysis, DINOSAUR 13 50, 51
coelurosaurs,
DINOSAUR 13 24
coevolution, INSECT 17 11
coffee, DESERT 51 47
Coffin, Owen,
SHIPWRECK 72 38
coffins, AFRICA 61 41
mummy cases, MUMMY 44
10, 22, 23-27
coherer, ELECTRICITY 77 57;
ELECTRONICS 90 25
Cohn, Harry, CINEMA 34 21
coins, SHIPWRECK 72 8, 54, 55;
VIKING 50 8, 18, 26;
WITCH & WIZARD 70 30,
37, 54
ancient, ARCHAEOLOGY 56 14,
26, 57
Chinese, CHINA 55 58; EARLY
PEOPLE 10 56, 57
collections, MONEY 18 60, 61
commemorative, MONEY 18
31, 49, 55
Greek symbols, ANCIENT
GREECE 37 19, 23, 52, 63
Lydian, MONEY 18 10
money, MONEY 18 24, 25
minting, MONEY 18 14,
15, 32
owls, MONEY 18 20, 22
Roman, ANCIENT ROME 24 8,
15, 16, 52, 60;
MONEY 18 10, 36, 38, 40
Colchester,
ANCIENT ROME 24 43

cold fronts, RUSSIA 74 36, 37;
WEATHER 28 34, 36, 56, 57
Cold War, SPY 67 38-39,
54, 57
Coleoptera, INSECT 17 8
Coleridge, Major H. F.,
SPY 67 31
Coleridge, Samuel Taylor,
ARCTIC & ANTARCTIC 57 26
collar bone, HUMAN BODY 87
15; SKELETON 3 62
collared peccary, SKELETON 3 52
collars, COSTUME 35 26, 27, 57;
MUMMY 44 11, 19, 26, 32;
SPORT 8 45
collective farming,
RUSSIA 74 13, 34, 35, 47
collectors, WRITING 48 60-61
collies, DOG 32 42, 43, 47;
SKELETON 3 30
Collins, Michael, SPACE
EXPLORATION 71 19
colobus monkeys,
GORILLA 64 22, 24, 53
Colomb, Admiral Philip,
SHIPWRECK 72 37
Colombia, MUMMY 44 52;
VOLCANO 38 56, 58
colonization, ECOLOGY 86 26,
34-35, 52
Colorado, River, CAT 29 37;
DESERT 51 11;
EXPLORER 31 44
colorimeters,
TECHNOLOGY 89 50
Colosseum,
ANCIENT ROME 24 17, 28,
29, 32
Colossus, SPY 67 26
colour, PERSPECTIVE 98 9, 11, 28;
TECHNOLOGY 89 50-51
and light, LIGHT 75 28-31,
38-39
primary, LIGHT 75 30-31,
32-33
secondary, LIGHT 75 30, 32
separation, LIGHT 75 17
subtraction, LIGHT 75
32-33, 47
colours, BATTLE 63 18-19, 56
regimental, FLAG 16 12, 42
symbolic, FLAG 16 14-15
Colt, Samuel, COWBOY 45 47;
TECHNOLOGY 89 39
Colt revolvers, ARMS &
ARMOUR 4 58, 59, 60-61
Columbia, MONEY 18 23
Columbia River, EXPLORER 31 45
Columbus, Christopher,
EARTH 83 34; HORSE 33 56;
MEDIEVAL LIFE 65 63;
TIME & SPACE 81 10, 12
"Age of Exploration",
EXPLORER 31 22-24, 30, 63
columns, BUILDING 58 32, 33,
48, 49
combat, KNIGHT 43 10, 46-47

early, BATTLE 63 44-45
combine harvesters, TECHNOLOGY 89 45
combs, EARLY PEOPLE 10 32, 34, 35; VIKING 50 31, 36, 59
combustion, CHEMISTRY 79 30-31
comets, ASTRONOMY 82 29, 58; SPACE EXPLORATION 71 42, 44; TIME & SPACE 81 15, 25, 28, 29
comics, SPACE EXPLORATION 71 9, 36
commissars, RUSSIA 74 33
common blue butterflies, BUTTERFLY & MOTH 7 28
common bluebottles, BUTTERFLY & MOTH 7 23, 26
common glider butterflies, BUTTERFLY & MOTH 7 29
common sailer butterflies, BUTTERFLY & MOTH 7 18-19, 23
common sergeant butterflies, BUTTERFLY & MOTH 7 23
communication, ENERGY 76 38-39, 41; ELECTRONICS 90 6, 15, 48-49; SHIPWRECK 72 36, 37, 44; TECHNOLOGY 89 48-49
electrical, ELECTRONICS 90 11, 24-25
fibre-optic, ELECTRONICS 90 62, 63
global, FUTURE 100 11-15
mechanical, ELECTRONICS 90 8, 9
satellite, ELECTRONICS 90 13
communion, RELIGION 68 50, 52
communism, RUSSIA 74 34, 37, 42, 43
hammer and sickle, FLAG 16 14, 35, 57
see also Communist Manifesto, Communist Party, October Revolution
Communist Manifesto, RUSSIA 74 32
Communist Party, RUSSIA 74 30-32, 34, 43
communists, SPY 67 35, 36, 50
commutators, ELECTRICITY 77 36, 37, 39, 40
compact discs, ELECTRONICS 90 47; FUTURE 100 11, 35, 52, 59; TECHNOLOGY 89 26, 58
companies, military, BATTLE 63 14-15
compasses, ARCTIC & ANTARCTIC 57 55; BATTLE 63 24; CHINA 55 22, 61; DESERT 51 62; PIRATE 59 25

distance measurement, INVENTION 27 34, 35
navigation, BOAT 36 52, 53; SHIPWRECK 72 32, 33
in World War II, SPY 67 13, 20, 21
compositors, INVENTION 27 27
compounds, chemical, CHEMISTRY 79 20-21; MATTER 80 6, 26-27, 34
electrolysis, MATTER 80 50
isotopes, MATTER 80 52
uranium, MATTER 80 55
compounds, domestic, AFRICA 61 8, 16-17
compression, TECHNOLOGY 89 20-21, 25, 28
Compsognathus, FOSSIL 19 52
computers, ELECTRONICS 90 6, 15, 30, 32; MONEY 18 6, 20, 21, 58; SHIPWRECK 72 42, 50; SPY 67 46, 47, 51, 53; TECHNOLOGY 89 45, 49, 54-55
in cars, CAR 21 35; FUTURE 100 24-26
chips, ELECTRONICS 90 39, 51, 54-55; FUTURE 100 32
data, ELECTRONICS 90 47
design, TECHNOLOGY 89 15, 38, 53
in detection, CRIME & DETECTION 73 51
digital signals, ELECTRONICS 90 46
images, FUTURE 100 15, 33, 34, 35
invention of, INVENTION 27 62, 63
memory, ELECTRONICS 90 56
microprocessors, ELECTRONICS 90 58, 59
in movies, CINEMA 34 42, 50, 52
in music, MUSIC 12 62, 63
palmtops, FUTURE 100 52
personal, ELECTRONICS 90 55, 57; FUTURE 100 12
programs, ELECTRONICS 90 22
reconstruction by, ARCHAEOLOGY 56 53
supercomputers, ELECTRONICS 90 59
virtual reality, FUTURE 100 48-49
con men, CRIME & DETECTION 73 18, 19
concave lens, LIGHT 75 16, 17, 20
conche, SEASHORE 15 26; SHELL 9 34, 37, 39, 51
Concorde, FLYING MACHINE 22 36-37; FUTURE 100 11, 26, 27
Concoryphe, FOSSIL 19 30
concrete, BUILDING 58 12, 32
concretion, FOSSIL 19 9, 35; ROCK & MINERAL 2 9

condensation, ENERGY 76 28, 29; WEATHER 28 22, 24, 48, 49
condensers, ELECTRICITY 77 12; LIGHT 75 15, 26
condors, EAGLE 69 12, 17, 58
Andean, EAGLE 69 10, 31, 34
Californian, EAGLE 69 34, 39
conduction, ENERGY 76 36
conductivity, CHEMISTRY 79 27, 46
conductors, electricity, CHEMISTRY 79 21, 24, 26; ELECTRICITY 77 10, 18, 20-21
cones, TREE 5 10, 11, 32, 44-45; VOLCANO 38 16, 22, 40
coneshells, SEASHORE 15 26, 27, 49
Confederate flag, FLAG 16 24
Confessore, Alphonse, CRIME & DETECTION 73 19
Confucianism, CHINA 55 14, 18, 26-27; RELIGION 68 30-31
Confucius, CHINA 55 12-13, 42, 52; RELIGION 68 30-32
conger eels, FISH 20 48, 49
conglomerate, ROCK & MINERAL 2 21, 31
Congo, AFRICA 61 32, 35, 39, 47; FLAG 16 15
conifers, DINOSAUR 13 11, 14, 23, 26; FOSSIL 19 37, 38, 39; PLANT 14 6, 7; TREE 5 10-11, 18, 23
needles, TREE 5 30-31, 53
Coniopteris, FOSSIL 19 37
conkers, TREE 5 35, 40
Conklin, Chester, CINEMA 34 55
Connemara ponies, HORSE 33 38
conquistadors, AZTEC 47 62; PYRAMID 53 54, 60
conscription, BATTLE 63 8
conservation, ECOLOGY 86 29, 36, 63
Constable, John, WATERCOLOUR 97 32, 38, 39
Constantine, Emperor, ANCIENT ROME 24 62
Constantinople, ANCIENT ROME 24 34, 62; ARCHAEOLOGY 56 14; CASTLE 49 62; VIKING 50 6, 18, 26, 29
Byzantium, MEDIEVAL LIFE 65 6, 34
crusades, KNIGHT 43 54-55
fall of, MEDIEVAL LIFE 65 63
constellations, ASTRONOMY 82 15, 61, 62, 63
names, ASTRONOMY 82 6, 7, 10
zodiac signs, ASTRONOMY 82 16, 17
consuls, ANCIENT ROME 24 6
contact lenses, FUTURE 100 54

continental drift, EARTH 83 34-35, 36; FOSSIL 19 12-13, 56; VOLCANO 38 10
continents, PREHISTORIC LIFE 52 6-10
contraceptive pill, MEDICINE 88 42
conures, sun, JUNGLE 54 10
convection, ENERGY 76 36, 49
convents, MEDIEVAL LIFE 65 22, 38, 41
converters, ELECTRONICS 90 47, 58
convex lens, LIGHT 75 16-17, 20
Cook, Captain James, ARCTIC & ANTARCTIC 57 7; ASTRONOMY 82 46; BOAT 36 26; EXPLORER 31 29, 34-37, 49, 51
Cook Islands, EXPLORER 31 15
Cooke, William, ELECTRICITY 77 56
cooking, VIKING 50 34-35
utensils, DESERT 51 47
see also kitchens
Cooper, James F., SHIPWRECK 72 25; SPY 67 58
Cooper's Creek, DESERT 51 62
coordinates, ASTRONOMY 82 12-13, 14-15, 27
Coote, Sir Eyre, BATTLE 63 58
coots, BIRD 1 33, 41, 44
copal, DESERT 51 57
Cope, Edward Drinker, FOSSIL 19 50
Copernicus, Nicolaus, ASTRONOMY 82 18, 19, 20; FORCE & MOTION 78 25, 33
copper, ARCHAEOLOGY 56 8, 40, 50-51; AZTEC 47 50, 54; EARTH 83 21; INVENTION 27 14, 39, 44, 63
alloy, CHEMISTRY 79 11, 15, 24
battery, CHEMISTRY 79 46
chemical reactions, CHEMISTRY 79 6, 7, 34, 38
Copper Measure, TECHNOLOGY 89 30
crystals, CRYSTAL & GEM 25 23
early, TECHNOLOGY 89 12, 14, 17
isolation, CHEMISTRY 79 24, 25, 47
ore, CRYSTAL & GEM 25 24; ROCK & MINERAL 2 56
salts, CHEMISTRY 79 44-45
wire, CHEMISTRY 79 24, 47
copper sulphate, CHEMISTRY 79 14, 17, 38, 47
crystals, CHEMISTRY 79 15, 44, 45, 49
copper sulphide, CHEMISTRY 79 47, 58

coppices, ARCHAEOLOGY 56 39, 47, 58
coprolites, ARCHAEOLOGY 56 29, 45
coracles, BOAT 36 10, 11, 21
coracoid, SKELETON 3 53
coral, ARCTIC & ANTARCTIC 57 12, 13; FOSSIL 19 22-23, 32, 63; OCEAN 62 7, 10, 62-63; PREHISTORIC LIFE 52 6, 16-17, 19, 52
cup coral, SEASHORE 15 36, 37
dead man's fingers, SEASHORE 15 58
reef, ECOLOGY 86 35, 46-47, 50; FISH 20 35, 36, 38, 50; SHELL 9 27, 40, 50-53; SHIPWRECK 72 10, 47
coralweed, SEASHORE 15 19, 33
Cord, CAR 21 2
cordierite, CRYSTAL & GEM 25 48, 60
Cordoba, ARCHAEOLOGY 56 18-19
Corinth, ANCIENT GREECE 37 6, 14, 27, 41
Coriolis Effect, WEATHER 28 7, 35, 42
cork, TREE 5 22, 47
Cormeau, Yvonne "Annette", SPY 67 24, 32, 33, 56
cormorants, ARCTIC & ANTARCTIC 57 23; BIRD 1 40; SEASHORE 15 53, 54, 55
corn, FARM 66 8, 20-29, 32
cornbuntings, BIRD 1 52
cornea, LIGHT 75 18, 19
cornets, MUSIC 12 9, 22, 23
cornices, BUILDING 58 53
Cornish rex, CAT 29 58
Cornu, Paul, FUTURE 100 8
corona, ASTRONOMY 82 38-39
coronary arteries, HUMAN BODY 87 29
Corot, Camille, IMPRESSIONISM 92 11, 13, 28, 29; MONET 95 10, 25
The Leaning Tree Trunk, MONET 95 10
corrosion, CHEMISTRY 79 38, 46, 47
salts, CHEMISTRY 79 44, 53
corsairs, PIRATE 59 6, 7, 29, 56
Barbary, PIRATE 59 14-15
French, PIRATE 59 50-51
Malta, PIRATE 59 16-17
corsets, COSTUME 35 42, 50, 54-55
Cortés, Hernándo, AZTEC 47 62, 63; COWBOY 45 9; EXPLORER 31 30-31; HORSE 33 34
Corti, Alfonso, HUMAN BODY 87 55
corundum, CRYSTAL & GEM 25 17, 36-37, 59, 62; ROCK & MINERAL 2 45, 49, 51

cosmetics, ANCIENT EGYPT 23 58-59; ANCIENT ROME 24 18
Cosimo, Piero di, ANCIENT GREECE 37 22
cosmos, TIME & SPACE 81 48, 49
Cosmos, St., MEDICINE 88 23
Cossacks, BATTLE 63 20, 48; RUSSIA 74 12, 16, 22, 23, 44
Costello, Frank, CRIME & DETECTION 73 25
Costello, Lou, CINEMA 34 54
costumes, CINEMA 34 36-37, 42, 44; COSTUME 35
Cote d'Azur, MONET 95 38, 39
cotton, COSTUME 35 9, 38-39
cottongrass, POND & RIVER 6 10
Coubertin, Baron Pierre de, ANCIENT GREECE 37 45
Coucy-le-Chateau, CASTLE 49 57
cougars, CAT 29 10, 36
Coulomb, Charles Augustin de, ENERGY 76 23; FORCE & MOTION 78 39
coulombs, ELECTRICITY 77 25
counterfeiting, CRIME & DETECTION 73 20, 21
counterparts, FOSSIL 19 20, 35
Courbet, Gustave, MANET 94 20, 22, 24-25; MONET 95 8, 12, 13, 25, 40; VAN GOGH 96 22
The Cliff at Etretat after the Storm, MONET 95 40
court dances, DANCE 99 21-23, 33, 36-37
courts,
feudal, MEDIEVAL LIFE 65 9, 22, 26-27
law, CRIME & DETECTION 73 12, 13, 15
sports, SPORT 8 30-31, 35, 36
courtship dance, DANCE 99 39
Cousteau, Jacques, EXPLORER 31 61; SHIPWRECK 72 46; WHALE 46 60
Couture, Thomas, MANET 94 10-11, 13, 38
couture, COSTUME 35 40, 62
covelline, CRYSTAL & GEM 25 24
coverts, BIRD 1 10-11
cowboys, COWBOY 45; HORSE 33 35, 56-57
American, COWBOY 45 16-19, 22-23, 26-27
charros, COWBOY 45 7-9
gardians, COWBOY 45 6, 28, 52-53, 59
gauchos, COWBOY 45 48-49
vaqueros, COWBOY 45 11
cowgirls, COWBOY 45 32-33, 61-62

legendary, COWBOY 45 58-59
cowrie shells,
ANCIENT EGYPT 23 56-57; SHELL 9 13, 18, 50, 51
European, SEASHORE 15 27, 32
serpent's head, SEASHORE 15 26
cows, see cattle
Coxwell, Robert, WEATHER 28 6
coydogs, DOG 32 25
coyotes, DOG 32 18, 19, 24, 25
crabs, DINOSAUR 13 58, 60; FOSSIL 19 19, 30, 31; INSECT 17 9; JUNGLE 54 33; SKELETON 3 24, 25
DNA, EVOLUTION 85 54
freshwater, POND & RIVER 6 58, 61
hermit, OCEAN 62 30-31; SHELL 9 33, 61
king, SHELL 9 39
pearl, SHELL 9 53
saltwater, OCEAN 62 17, 21, 26-27; SEASHORE 15 44-45, 48, 51
shells of, SHELL 9 9, 22, 24-27
shore, SHELL 9 40, 47
spider, SHELL 9 25, 45, 55
crafts, AFRICA 61 52-53; ANCIENT GREECE 37 7, 23, 52-53; CHINA 55 56-57
craftsmen, MEDIEVAL LIFE 65 48, 49, 51
Cranach, Lucas the Elder, RENAISSANCE 91 43, 60
cranes, mechanical, INVENTION 27 24
cranes, sandhill, ARCTIC & ANTARCTIC 57 20
cranks, FORCE & MOTION 78 22, 23
craters, VOLCANO 38 14, 38, 44, 45
cravats, COSTUME 35 29, 32, 37, 41
crawfish, SEASHORE 15 44, 46
crayfish, POND & RIVER 6 54; SHELL 9 22, 24, 56
crayons, VAN GOGH 96 26; WRITING 48 50
cream, FARM 66 44, 46
Crécy, battle of, BATTLE 63 36, 37, 63; KNIGHT 43 30, 32
credit cards, FUTURE 100 10; TECHNOLOGY 89 58
cremation, RELIGION 68 26, 29; EARLY PEOPLE 10 38
crenellations, CASTLE 49 13, 16
crêpe, COSTUME 35 45
crêpe-soled shoes, COSTUME 35 57
crests, KNIGHT 43 12
Cretaceous Period, DINOSAUR 13 56, 59, 60, 61; EVOLUTION 85 61, 62

Crete, ANCIENT GREECE 37 8-9, 10, 50; VOLCANO 38 39; WRITING 48 10
Creuse Valley, MONET 95 38
Crick, Francis, EVOLUTION 85 52, 54; MATTER 80 42, 43
cricket, SPORT 8 26
crickets, INSECT 17 12, 16-17, 20
desert, DESERT 51 24
crime, CRIME & DETECTION 73; MEDIEVAL LIFE 65 9, 24, 26
criminal "types", CRIME & DETECTION 73 52-53
Crimea, RUSSIA 74 9
Crimean War, BATTLE 63 15, 20, 21, 61; RUSSIA 74 23, 55
Florence Nightingale, BATTLE 63 60
"Thin Red Line", BATTLE 63 16
crinoids, FOSSIL 19 12, 32, 33
crinolines, COSTUME 35 40, 41, 42-43
Criollo, COWBOY 45 8, 11-12
Crippen, Dr., CRIME & DETECTION 73 22
Crivelli, Carlo, PERSPECTIVE 98 22-23; RENAISSANCE 91 24
crocodiles, FOSSIL 19 43, 45, 48, 51; JUNGLE 54 32, 46-47; MUMMY 44 44-45; SKELETON 3 33, 46, 53
classification, REPTILE 26 11-12
evolution, DINOSAUR 13 7, 32, 57, 58
family, REPTILE 26 34-35
Crompton, Samuel, INVENTION 27 37
Cromwell, Oliver, BATTLE 63 46
Cromwell, Thomas, SPY 67 40
Crookes, Sir William, CHEMISTRY 79 19, 32, 33; ELECTRICITY 77 54; INVENTION 27 56; MATTER 80 33, 46, 48, 49
Crookes' radiometer, ENERGY 76 27
crops, DESERT 51 15; ECOLOGY 86 29, 30, 58, 61; PLANT 14 54-55
growing, FARM 66 14-17
protecting, FARM 66 18-19
croquet, SPORT 8 61
Crosby, Bing, CINEMA 34 46
crossbills, BIRD 1 19
crossbows,
ARMS & ARMOUR 4 18-21; CASTLE 49 25, 26, 27; KNIGHT 43 32, 50-51, 60; SPORT 8 53
Cross, the, KNIGHT 43 53, 57; RELIGION 68 48, 50, 51, 53
see also crucifixion
Crossley, CAR 21 63
cross-staffs, PIRATE 59 24-25

Crown Jewels,
CRYSTAL & GEM **25** 35,
46, 53; RUSSIA **74** 20, 24
crowns, RUSSIA **74** 14, 18, 20, 24
crows, BIRD **1** 6-7, 32, 34, 42;
SKELETON **3** 19
crucifix, RELIGION **68** 51
crucifixion, RELIGION **68** 48, 50,
51, 53
cruets, KNIGHT **43** 34
Cruikshank, George, ANCIENT
GREECE **37** 56; ARCTIC &
ANTARCTIC **57** 52;
DOG **32** 38;
WATERCOLOUR **97** 44
Crusades, BATTLE **63** 37, 56;
CASTLE **49** 34-35; KNIGHT **43**
54-55; MEDIEVAL LIFE **65** 7,
28, 45, 56
Crusoe, Robinson, PIRATE **59** 49
crustaceans, FISH **20** 7, 35;
FOSSIL **19** 20, 28, 31;
OCEAN **62** 18, 30, 38, 58;
SEASHORE **15** 28, 32,
44-47; SKELETON **3** 24-25
shells, SHELL **9** 7, 9, 55, 58
cryptanalysts, SPY **67** 25-27
crystal balls, WITCH &
WIZARD **70** 14, 37
gazing,
CRYSTAL & GEM **25** 61
healing,
CRYSTAL & GEM **25** 31
Crystal Palace,
CRYSTAL & GEM **25** 7
crystal sets, CRYSTAL &
GEM **25** 62
crystalline spheres,
ASTRONOMY **82** 12-13
crystallography, CRYSTAL &
GEM **25** 13, 14
crystals, CHEMISTRY **79** 15, 16,
17, 44; CRYSTAL & GEM **25**
13, 21, 22, 62; ELECTRONICS
90 38, 57; MATTER **80** 14-15,
30-31; ROCK & MINERAL **2**
6, 44-47
analysis, EARTH **83** 21, 23
atomic structure, CRYSTAL &
GEM **25** 14-15, 17, 18, 21
formation, EARTH **83** 24,
25, 28
growth, CRYSTAL & GEM **25**
20-21, 26, 27
metal, TECHNOLOGY **89** 12, 15
rare, CRYSTAL & GEM **25** 48-49
sulphur, VOLCANO **38** 36, 37
synthetic, CRYSTAL & GEM **25**
26-27, 56, 57
uses, CRYSTAL & GEM **25**
28-29, 30, 31, 63
Cuba, RUSSIA **74** 36, 37
Cuban hock, FISH **20** 17
Cuban land snails, SHELL **9** 15
Cubism, DANCE **99** 30;
PERSPECTIVE **98** 52-53;
WATERCOLOUR **97** 60

cubits, PYRAMID **53** 30;
TIME & SPACE **81** 11, 54
cuckoo spit, INSECT **17** 36
cuckoos, BIRD **1** 34, 53
Cuerdale Hoard, VIKING **50** 49
cuffs, COSTUME **35** 18, 29, 30, 31
Cugnot, Nicholas, TRAIN **39** 10
Cuir, John de, CINEMA **34** 39
cuirasses, BATTLE **63** 10, 27
Culkin, Macaulay,
CINEMA **34** 62
Culpeper, Edmund,
MATTER **80** 10
Culpeper, Nicholas,
MEDICINE **88** 40
cuneiform, WRITING **48** 9
Cunningham, Allan,
EXPLORER **31** 50
Cunningham, Merce,
DANCE **99** 57
Cupid, ANCIENT ROME **24** 24
curach, BOAT **36** 10
curare, JUNGLE **54** 34
Curie, Jacques, CRYSTAL &
GEM **25** 31
Curie, Marie, MATTER **80** 46;
HUMAN BODY **87** 13
Curie, Pierre,
CRYSTAL & GEM **25** 31;
ELECTRICITY **77** 53;
EVOLUTION **85** 29;
MATTER **80** 46
curlews, BIRD **1** 25, 33, 36, 42
currency, *see under individual
currencies*
current, electric,
ENERGY **76** 23, 24, 41, 51
alternating, ELECTRICITY **77**
25, 40, 41, 55;
ELECTRONICS **90** 23, 28, 37,
38; ENERGY **76** 33
direct, ELECTRICITY **77** 12, 25,
37, 40; ENERGY **76** 32, 33
meter, ENERGY **76** 36, 43, 53
currents, ocean, OCEAN **62** 12,
38; SEASHORE **15** 6, 58
Custer, General,
BATTLE **63** 53;
NORTH AMERICAN INDIAN **60**
30-31
custody, CRIME &
DETECTION **73** 15
customs, CRIME &
DETECTION **73** 28, 29, 54
cutlasses, PIRATE **59** 27, 28-29, 32
cuttlebones, SHELL **9** 19
cuttlefishes, SHELL **9** 18, 19
Cuvier, Georges,
EVOLUTION **85** 15, 16, 18, 28;
FOSSIL **19** 14, 15
cyanobacteria, LIFE **84** 12, 50,
57; PREHISTORIC LIFE **52** 12
Cyaxares, BIBLE LANDS **30** 52
Cybele, ANCIENT ROME **24**, 51, 52
cycads, DINOSAUR **13** 10, 11,
14, 26; FOSSIL **19** 38;
JUNGLE **54** 8

cyclones, WEATHER **28** 15, 38, 44
cymbals, ANCIENT EGYPT **23** 50;
DANCE **99** 15; MUSIC **12** 6,
48, 49, 57
crash, MUSIC **12** 52
ride, MUSIC **12** 52-53
cypresses, TREE **5** 10, 32, 44
swamp, TREE **5** 18, 31
Cyprus, ANCIENT GREECE **37**
10, 20, 52, 63; BATTLE **63** 6;
BIBLE LANDS **30** 38, 52, 53;
VOLCANO **38** 25
Cyril, St., RUSSIA **74** 19, 42;
WRITING **48** 19
Cyrillic alphabet,
RUSSIA **74** 42; WRITING **48**
19, 53
cytosine, LIFE **84** 34, 35, 61
czardas, DANCE **99** 42
Czechoslovakia, FLAG **16** 57;
MONEY **18** 32, 62

D

daalder, MONEY **18** 35
dabs, FISH **20** 25, 27
dace, FISH **20** 52
dachas, RUSSIA **74** 53-55
dachshunds, DOG **32** 12, 17,
48, 49
Dadd, Richard,
WATERCOLOUR **97** 43
Daedalus,
ANCIENT GREECE **37** 23
da Gama, Vasco, *see* Gama,
Vasco da
daggers, ARMS & ARMOUR **4**
11, 12, 22-23; BATTLE **63** 38,
39; KNIGHT **43** 19;
PIRATE **59** 29, 36
African, AFRICA **61** 47, 56
early, EARLY PEOPLE **10** 52, 60
Egyptian,
ANCIENT EGYPT **23** 37
Indian, ARMS & ARMOUR **4**
32, 34, 50-51

Japanese,
ARMS & ARMOUR **4** 36
parrying,
ARMS & ARMOUR **4** 43-44
Daguerre, Louis Jacques,
INVENTION **27** 40;
IMPRESSIONISM **92** 28;
LIGHT **75** 24, 25
Dahshur, PYRAMID **53** 14, 40,
42, 47
Dai, Lady, MUMMY **44** 63
Daimler, CAR **21** 9
Daimler, Gottlieb,
INVENTION **27** 48
dairies, FARM **66** 46, 47
Dakota peoples, Sioux,
NORTH AMERICAN
INDIAN **60** 30-31, 63
"massacre at wounded
knee", NORTH AMERICAN
INDIAN **60** 34
medicine, NORTH AMERICAN
INDIAN **60** 11
sun dance, NORTH AMERICAN
INDIAN **60** 36-37
Dalai Lama,
RELIGION **68** 28, 29
dalers, MONEY **18** 18, 20, 43, 45
Dalí, Salvador,
PERSPECTIVE **98** 58
dally, COWBOY **45** 35
Dalmanites, FOSSIL **19** 30
Dalmatians, DOG **32** 19, 20,
21, 55
Dalton, Emmett, COWBOY **45** 45
Dalton, John, CHEMISTRY **79** 16;
CRYSTAL & GEM **25** 14;
TIME & SPACE **81** 58
damask, COSTUME **35** 17
damselfishes, FISH **20** 46
Damian, St., MEDICINE **88** 23
dampers, CAR **21** 38, 39, 54, 55
danburite,
CRYSTAL & GEM **25** 48
dance, AFRICA **61** 22, 62-63;
DANCE **99**; NORTH
AMERICAN INDIAN **60** 36, 37;
WITCH & WIZARD **70** 40, 41,
47, 53
court, DANCE **99** 21-23, 36-37
dragon, DANCE **99** 38
fan, DANCE **99** 46
folk, DANCE **99** 8, 9, 47, 49
limbo, DANCE **99** 11
maypole, DANCE **99** 47
modern, DANCE **99** 8, 45,
51, 59
street, DANCE **99** 50
see also under individual dances
dandelions, PLANT **14** 30-31
Danevirke, VIKING **50** 23
Danfrie, Philippe,
INVENTION **27** 35
Daniell, John Frederic,
INVENTION **27** 38;
ELECTRICITY **77** 19
Daniels, Virginia, CINEMA **34** 20

Dante, RENAISSANCE 91 8, 13
Dapedium, FISH 20 13
Daphne, ANCIENT GREECE 37 21
darabuka, MUSIC 12 50
d'Arcy, Chevalier,
 CINEMA 34 8
Darius I, BIBLE LANDS 30 52
Dark Ages,
 ANCIENT GREECE 37 7, 10,
 12, 14;
 ARMS & ARMOUR 4 14-15;
 MEDIEVAL LIFE 65 6
Dark Star, SPY 67 52, 53
Darling, Grace,
 SHIPWRECK 72 34
Darwin, Charles,
 ARCHAEOLOGY 56 6, 20;
 EARLY PEOPLE 10 23;
 EVOLUTION 85 19, 20-21,
 22, 48; FISH 20 62;
 GORILLA 64 8;
 REPTILE 26 30;
 TIME & SPACE 81 24
 adaptation, EVOLUTION 85 24,
 39, 42
 artificial selection,
 EVOLUTION 85 30
 atoll theory, OCEAN 62 23
 as explorer,
 JUNGLE 54 60, 61
 human evolution,
 EVOLUTION 85 58
 natural selection,
 EVOLUTION 85 28, 34,
 35, 36, 37;
 LIFE 84 42, 43, 55;
 species, EVOLUTION 85 40
Darwinism, EVOLUTION 85
 43, 50
databases, FUTURE 100 52
dates, TREE 5 43
dating techniques,
 ARCHAEOLOGY 56 54-55
 see also radiocarbon dating,
 thermoluminescence
Daubigny, Charles-François,
 IMPRESSIONISM 92 12, 13, 34;
 MONET 95 10, 20, 24, 25
Daumier, Honoré,
 WATERCOLOUR 97 30, 31
Davenport, Thomas,
 ELECTRICITY 77 38
David, King,
 BIBLE LANDS 30 20, 44, 46, 61;
 RELIGION 68 43, 49
Davis, Bette, CINEMA 34 27
Davis, J.P.,
 WATERCOLOUR 97 34
Davis, John, SHIPWRECK 72 32
Davy, Sir Humphry,
 CHEMISTRY 79 25, 46, 58;
 ELECTRICITY 77 3, 19, 32, 37;
 MATTER 80 32
Dawson, Charles, EARLY
 PEOPLE 10 10
Dayak peoples,
 GORILLA 64 58

De Brazza monkeys,
 GORILLA 64 25
de Dion, Bouton,
 CAR 21 8-9, 10
De Forest, Lee,
 ELECTRICITY 77 55, 61;
 TECHNOLOGY 89 54
de Gaulle, Charles,
 FLAG 16 27
de L'Isle, Romé, CRYSTAL &
 GEM 25 12
de Laurentiis, Dino,
 CINEMA 34 28
Dead Sea, BIBLE LANDS 30 6,
 31, 57, 58
Dead Sea Scrolls,
 BIBLE LANDS 30 58, 60
"Deadwood Dick",
 COWBOY 45 18
dealfish, FISH 20 25, 48
Dean, James,
 CINEMA 34 63
Deane, Charles,
 SHIPWRECK 72 14
Deane, John,
 SHIPWRECK 72 14
death sentence, CRIME &
 DETECTION 73 12
Death Valley, DESERT 51 8
 definition, DESERT 51 6
death-head hawk-moths,
 BUTTERFLY & MOTH 7
 14-15, 43
decapods, SHELL 9 24
decathlon, SPORT 8 41
deciduous trees, TREE 5 6, 8,
 46, 53
decks, BOAT 36 41, 49, 62
 gun, BOAT 36 28
 poop, BOAT 36 48
 quarter, BOAT 36 52
deck-seat lifeboat,
 SHIPWRECK 72 3
Declaration of Paris,
 PIRATE 59 58
decomposition,
 ECOLOGY 86 18, 52;
 MATTER 80 12
 decomposers, ECOLOGY 86
 14-15, 27
decompression chambers,
 SHIPWRECK 72 48
decorations, BATTLE 63 58-59
Dee, John,
 CRYSTAL & GEM 25 61
Deep Star, OCEAN 62 53
deer, MAMMAL 11 10, 26, 62, 63;
 SKELETON 3 31, 46, 58
deerhounds, DOG 32 38
defectors, SPY 67 34, 50
defibrillators, MEDICINE 88 59
deflection coils,
 ELECTRICITY 77 62
Defoe, Daniel, PIRATE 59 49;
 SHIPWRECK 72 58
deforestation, GORILLA 64 63;
 JUNGLE 54 62-63

Degas, Edgar, ANCIENT GREECE
 37 56; IMPRESSIONISM 92 6,
 50, 55, 56;
 MANET 94 12, 27, 46, 57;
 MONET 95 24, 48, 59;
 VAN GOGH 96 33, 36
 L' Absinthe,
 IMPRESSIONISM 92 25
 biography,
 IMPRESSIONISM 92 62
 Café Singer,
 IMPRESSIONISM 92 24
 dancers' paintings,
 IMPRESSIONISM 92 51, 52-53
 horses' paintings,
 IMPRESSIONISM 92 48-49
 Japanese influence,
 PERSPECTIVE 98 49
 The Millinery Shop,
 IMPRESSIONISM 92 7
 photography, influence of,
 IMPRESSIONISM 92 28
 sculptures,
 IMPRESSIONISM 92 28,
 52, 58
 Self-portrait,
 IMPRESSIONISM 92 11
Deighton, Len, SPY 67 58
Deinonychus, DINOSAUR 13 19,
 42, 43
Deinosuchus, FOSSIL 19 45
Deir el-Bahri,
 PYRAMID 53 35, 41
Deir el Medina,
 ANCIENT EGYPT 23 23
Dejean, Maurice, SPY 67 10
Pollaiuolo, Antonio del,
 ANCIENT GREECE 37 21
Delacroix, Eugène,
 IMPRESSIONISM 92 16, 20;
 MANET 94 8-9, 15;
 MONET 95 35;
 VAN GOGH 96 26, 52-53
 watercolours,
 WATERCOLOUR 97 29, 50
Delage, CAR 21 18
Delauney-Belville, CAR 21 12
Della Robbia, Luca,
 RENAISSANCE 91 15
Delos, PIRATE 59 10
Delphi Oracle, ANCIENT
 GREECE 37 19, 24, 25, 44;
 WITCH & WIZARD 70 21
delphinula shells, SHELL 9
 12, 54
deluge, WEATHER 28 38, 50
demand valve, SHIPWRECK 72
 45, 46
Demeter, ANCIENT GREECE 37
 20, 24, 26, 50, 60
democracy,
 ANCIENT GREECE 37 7, 18
demons, RELIGION 68 20, 21, 22,
 28; WITCH & WIZARD 70
 52-55
demotic script, WRITING 48 12
Dendera, ANCIENT EGYPT 23 28

Denali National Park, ARCTIC
 & ANTARCTIC 57 9
denarii, MONEY 18 36
dendrites, CRYSTAL & GEM 25
 7, 23, 53
dendrochronology,
 ARCHAEOLOGY 56 29, 31,
 37, 54
Denmark, BUILDING 58 22, 29;
 FLAG 16 40-41, 42; MONEY
 18 42, 43, 62; MUMMY 44
 9, 58
density, ASTRONOMY 82 21, 36,
 45, 52; EARTH 83 16, 40,
 41, 30
d'Eon, Chevalier, SPY 67 28, 29
deoxyribonucelic acid,
 see DNA
Depardieu, Gérard,
 CINEMA 34 47, 56
Deperdussin, FLYING MACHINE
 22 22, 38, 42
depressions, WEATHER 28 15,
 32, 33, 35
Dermaptera, INSECT 17 8
Derringer, Henry, ARMS &
 ARMOUR 4 61
Derringer pistols, ARMS &
 ARMOUR 4 57, 61
dervishes, FLAG 16 19
Descartes, René,
 LIGHT 75 18, 29
desert hare,
 ANCIENT EGYPT 23 45
desert islands, PIRATE 59 48-49
desert lilies, DESERT 51 16
desert rats, FLAG 16 15
desert roses,
 crystal, DESERT 51 9
 plant, DESERT 51 20
desert veil, DESERT 51 54
desertification, ECOLOGY 86
 40, 63
deserts, EARTH 83 34, 55;
 ECOLOGY 86 7, 8, 40-41;
 ROCK & MINERAL 2 11, 12
 African, AFRICA 61 6, 27, 48
 animals in, DESERT 51 36-39
 conditions, ECOLOGY 86 24,
 29, 48
 Egyptian,
 ANCIENT EGYPT 23 8
 hunters, EARLY PEOPLE 10
 28-29
 vegetation in, DESERT 51
 16-17
Desperate Dan, COWBOY 45 36
detectives, CRIME &
 DETECTION 73 11, 22, 36-39
detergents, TECHNOLOGY 89 40
detonate, CAR 21 48
detritivores, ECOLOGY 86 14-15
 estuary, ECOLOGY 86 50, 51
 shoreline, ECOLOGY 86 25, 42
Devanagari script,
 WRITING 48 32
Devi, Rukmini, DANCE 99 54

devil, **WITCH & WIZARD 70** 16, 22, 39
  dancers, **WITCH & WIZARD 70** 46
  worship, **WITCH & WIZARD 70** 13
Devil's Golf Course, **DESERT 51** 8
Devil's toenail, **FOSSIL 19** 16
Devon rex, **CAT 29** 58
Devonian period, **EVOLUTION 85** 60, 61
dew, **DESERT 51** 19, 22, 23; **WEATHER 28** 22, 23, 48
Dewar, James, **ENERGY 76** 26
dharma, **RELIGION 68** 26, 27
dholes, **DOG 32** 18, 19, 26, 27
dhows, **ANCIENT EGYPT 23** 38; **BOAT 36** 25
diabetes, **MEDICINE 88** 29, 42, 43, 61
diadem, **ANCIENT EGYPT 23** 56
Diaghilev, Sergei, **DANCE 99** 45, 56
Diamond Sutra, **CHINA 55** 25; **WRITING 48** 42
diamonds, **CHEMISTRY 79** 27, 48; **CRYSTAL & GEM 25** 18, 25, 34; **ROCK & MINERAL 2** 48, 49, 50, 60; **RUSSIA 74** 14, 24
  in earth, **EARTH 83** 40
  hardness, **MATTER 80** 13, 40, 41
  famous, **CRYSTAL & GEM 25** 35, 46, 58
  reflection, **LIGHT 75** 13, 28
  speed of light, **LIGHT 75** 61
  substitutes, **CRYSTAL & GEM 25** 27, 29, 57
  uses, **CRYSTAL & GEM 25** 28-29, 62, 63
Diana, goddess of hunt, **DOG 32** 41
diaphragm, **HUMAN BODY 87** 7, 21, 24, 25
diatoms, **SKELETON 3** 22
Diaz, Bartolomeu, **EXPLORER 31** 2, 63
Díaz, Bernal, **PIRATE 59** 22
dibbler, **FARM 66** 37
Dickens, Charles, **CRIME & DETECTION 73** 8, 54; **VAN GOGH 96** 8, 15, 44
Dickson, William, **CINEMA 34** 12, 14
Dicranurus, **FOSSIL 19** 30
didelphids, **FOSSIL 19** 61
didjeridu, **DESERT 51** 61
Dieppe, **MONET 95** 38, 39
dies, **TECHNOLOGY 89** 11, 13
diesel, **BOAT 36** 45; **TRAIN 39** 40-41, 52, 53
Diesel, Dr. Rudolph, **TRAIN 39** 40

diet, **DESERT 51** 25, 46-47; **ECOLOGY 86** 6, 38, 45
Dietrich, Marlene, **CINEMA 34** 27
diffraction, **LIGHT 75** 36-37, 44-45
diffusion, **LIFE 84** 20
digestive system, **HUMAN BODY 87** 7, 38, 40
  digestion, **HUMAN BODY 87** 34-37, 41, 61
digital electronics, **ELECTRONICS 90** 46-47, 50, 60
  display, **ELECTRONICS 90** 45
  processor, **ELECTRONICS 90** 58
digitalis, **MEDICINE 88** 7
Diictodon, **DINOSAUR 13** 35
Dillinger, John, **CRIME & DETECTION 73** 16, 17
dilruba, **MUSIC 12** 41
DiMaggio, Joe, **SPORT 8** 22
dimensions, **TIME & SPACE 81** 6-7, 26, 59
  fourth, **TIME & SPACE 81** 34-35, 38, 58
dinghies, **BOAT 36** 62-63
dingos, **DOG 32** 36, 37
Dinictis, **CAT 29** 9
Dinka peoples, **AFRICA 61** 13, 18, 46, 49; **DANCE 99** 8
dinosaurs, **DINOSAUR 13** 6-7, 8-9; **EVOLUTION 85** 15, 18-19, 45; **PREHISTORIC LIFE 52** 32-33, 52, 53; **REPTILE 26** 8
  baby, **DINOSAUR 13** 44-45, 46-47
  bones, **DINOSAUR 13** 12, 16-17, 34-35; **SKELETON 3** 12, 51, 58
  carnivores, **DINOSAUR 13** 23, 33, 36, 38
  claws, **DINOSAUR 13** 42-43
  defence, **DINOSAUR 13** 20-21, 30, 33
  extinction, **DINOSAUR 13** 6, 48-49, 60; **EVOLUTION 85** 46, 47, 62; **PREHISTORIC LIFE 52** 61
  fossils, **FOSSIL 19** 6, 46, 48-51
  herbivores, **DINOSAUR 13** 10, 21, 23, 36
  nests, **DINOSAUR 13** 44-45, 46
  Ornithischians, **PREHISTORIC LIFE 52** 36-37
  plated, **DINOSAUR 13** 20, 21, 34-35
  Saurischians, **PREHISTORIC LIFE 52** 34-35
  tails, **DINOSAUR 13** 18-21
  teeth, **DINOSAUR 13** 23, 24-25, 26
  see also under individual dinosaurs
diocese, **MEDIEVAL LIFE 65** 9, 31; **INVENTION 27** 52

Diocletian, **ANCIENT ROME 24** 62
diodes, **ELECTRICITY 77** 63; **ELECTRONICS 90** 28, 38, 39, 53
  light-emitting, **ELECTRONICS 90** 16, 44
  silicon, **ELECTRONICS 90** 37
Dionysus, **ANCIENT GREECE 37** 20, 25, 46, 60; **ANCIENT ROME 24** 51; **PIRATE 59** 9; **WITCH & WIZARD 70** 21
Dioscorides, Pedanius, **MEDICINE 88** 19, 21
Diplocaulus, **FOSSIL 19** 42
Diplocynodon, **FOSSIL 19** 45
Diplodocus, **DINOSAUR 13** 14-15, 16-19; **PREHISTORIC LIFE 52** 32-33, 35
diplomats, **SPY 67** 11, 29, 40
dipnoi, **FISH 20** 9
dippers, **POND & RIVER 6** 54
Diprotodon, **FOSSIL 19** 56-57
Diptera, **INSECT 17** 8
dire wolf, **DOG 32** 8
direct current, **ELECTRICITY 77** 12, 25, 37, 40; **ELECTRONICS 90** 23, 28, 37, 38
Dir-Zamet, **BIBLE LANDS 30** 6
disco, **DANCE 99** 51, 59
Discoglossus, **FOSSIL 19** 42
discus fish, **FISH 20** 45
discus, **SPORT 8** 41
diseases, **ECOLOGY 86** 59; **LIFE 84** 12, 50; **MUMMY 44** 11, 48-51, 56
  ancient, **ANCIENT ROME 24** 54, 56; **ARCHAEOLOGY 56** 42-43, 46-47; **AZTEC 47** 38, 39
  bacteria, **LIFE 84** 28-29
  Black Death, **ECOLOGY 86** 63
  future treatments, **FUTURE 100** 36-37, 40-41
disguises, **SPY 67** 28, 29, 33
disks, **ELECTRONICS 90** 6, 62, 57
  display, **ELECTRONICS 90** 45
  integrated circuit, **ELECTRONICS 90** 52, 53
  microchip, **ELECTRONICS 90** 51, 55
  radio, **ELECTRONICS 90** 29, 39
  telephone, **ELECTRONICS 90** 7
Disney, Walt, **CINEMA 34** 13, 50
distillation, **CHEMISTRY 79** 7, 12, 13
  fractional, **CHEMISTRY 79** 15, 52-53
distorsio shells, **SHELL 9** 12
distress rockets, **SHIPWRECK 72** 37
ditches, **ARCHAEOLOGY 56** 12
Divali, **RELIGION 68** 18, 37

divers, black-throated, **ARCTIC & ANTARCTIC 57** 21
divers, **OCEAN 62** 48-49, 53, 61; **SHIPWRECK 72** 9, 13, 44-47
dividers, **PIRATE 59** 24-25; **WRITING 48** 17
diving suit, **SHIPWRECK 72** 14, 47, 48, 49
Dixon, Reginald, **CINEMA 34** 24
Dixon, Waynman, **PYRAMID 53** 46
Djehutyhotep, **PYRAMID 53** 46
Djoser, **ANCIENT EGYPT 23** 20; **PYRAMID 53** 7, 10-13, 42
Dmitry, Prince of Russia, **RUSSIA 74** 9, 20
DNA, **CHEMISTRY 79** 51; **ECOLOGY 86** 20; **FUTURE 100** 34-37, 38; **MATTER 80** 42-43; **TECHNOLOGY 89** 60
  evolution, **LIFE 84** 42
  genetic engineering, **LIFE 84** 60, 61
  genetic code, **EVOLUTION 85** 52-53, 55
  identification by, **CRIME & DETECTION 73** 22, 44-46
  mutation, **EVOLUTION 85** 32
  organelles, **LIFE 84** 57
  origin, **EVOLUTION 85** 56, 57
  structure of, **LIFE 84** 11, 34-37
Dobermann Pinschers, **DOG 32** 45, 59
docking, **SPACE EXPLORATION 71** 12, 13, 18, 37
docks, **BOAT 36** 50-51
doctors, **ANCIENT ROME 24** 54, 55
dodos, **BIRD 1** 6; **PREHISTORIC LIFE 52** 61
Dodwell, Christina, **DESERT 51** 63
dog-cockle pearls, **SHELL 9** 37
dogfish, **FISH 20** 28, 43, 54, 60; **FOSSIL 19** 19, 35; **SEASHORE 15** 25, 61; **SKELETON 3** 21
Dogon peoples, **AFRICA 61** 9, 34, 63
dogs, **ARCTIC & ANTARCTIC 57** 51, 58, 59; **COWBOY 45** 40, 57; **DOG 32** 8-9, 10-11; **MAMMAL 11** 16, 36, 42, 43
  bones, **SKELETON 3** 16, 30, 36, 61
  cross-breeds, **DOG 32** 38, 53, 60, 61
  desert, **DESERT 51** 42, 43
  domestic, **DOG 32** 34-37, 48, 56, 58
  evolution, **EVOLUTION 85** 30, 31, 32
  food, **DOG 32** 20, 62, 63
  guard, **DOG 32** 34, 45, 56, 60

hunting, **Dog 32** 34, 41, 50-52
police, **Crime & Detection 73** 54, 55
prairie, **Mammal 11** 56
puppies, **Dog 32** 20-21, 61, 62
shepherd, **Dog 32** 42, 43, 55, 56
toy, **Dog 32** 9, 58, 59
wild, **Dog 32** 18, 26, 27, 32
see also under individual breeds
dogwoods, **Tree 5** 37
Dolce, Ludovico, **Renaissance 91** 46
dolerite, **Earth 83** 51; **Pyramid 53** 34
dollars, **Money 18** 52, 53, 57, 58
dolls, **Africa 61** 23; **Mummy 44** 54; **Witch & Wizard 70** 32, 44, 52-55
Dolly, the cloned sheep, **Future 100** 37
dolphins, **Mammal 11** 10, 12, 42, 51; **Ocean 62** 26-27, 36-37; **Skeleton 3** 41, 51; **Whale 46** 10, 23
bottlenose, **Whale 46** 7, 32-33, 54, 63
dolphinaria, **Whale 46** 57, 63
evolution, **Evolution 85** 22, 23
fossils, **Fossil 19** 46, 47
domes, **Building 58** 36
Domitian, Emperor, **Bible Lands 30** 55
Don Quixote, **Arms & Armour 4** 31; **Horse 33** 42; **Knight 43** 63
Don, **Cowboy 45** 13
Donatello, **Perspective 98** 13; **Renaissance 91** 15, 26
Doni, Angelo, **Renaissance 91** 55
donjons, **Castle 49** 10; **Knight 43** 22
donkeys, **Evolution 85** 41, 48; **Farm 66** 8, 46; **Horse 33** 7, 12, 24-25; **Skeleton 3** 33
Donkin, **Invention 27** 6
Donna, Jorge, **Dance 99** 55
doorbells, **Electricity 77** 30
doors, **Building 58** 46-47, 54, 55
Doppler, Christian, **Light 75** 63
Doppler Effect, **Astronomy 82** 23, 61
Doré, Gustave, **Bible Lands 30** 33
dormice, **Mammal 11** 9, 53, 62
Dorset, **Ancient Rome 24** 13

Dorset, Cape, **Arctic & Antarctic 57** 21, 24
dory, **Boat 36** 43
Dostoevsky, Fyodor, **Russia 74** 44
dot moths, **Butterfly & Moth 7** 49
double agents, **Spy 67** 28, 29, 34, 35
doublets, **Costume 35** 16, 20, 21, 23
doubloons, **Money 18** 24, 38; **Pirate 59** 22, 36
Douglass, A.E., **Archaeology 56** 29
douroucoulis, **Gorilla 64** 16
doves, **Bird 1** 38
dowry bags, **Desert 51** 55
drachmas, **Money 18** 40, 41, 63
drag rider, **Cowboy 45** 40
Dragomiroff, General, **Flag 16** 56
dragon dance, **Dance 99** 38
dragon flags, **Flag 16** 58, 59
dragonets, **Fish 20** 17, 41
dragonflies, **Evolution 85** 11, 49; **Fossil 19** 20, 52, 60; **Insect 17** 11, 14, 46, 49; **Pond & River 6** 17, 48, 49
dragons, **China 55** 16-17, 51; **Reptile 26** 6, 29
dragoons, **Battle 63** 10, 48, 53
drainpipes, trousers, **Costume 35** 57
drainpipes, water, **Building 58** 28
Drake, Sir Francis, **Pirate 59** 18, 22; **Life 84** 62; **Sport 8** 56
drawbridges, **Castle 49** 28, 29
drawers, **Costume 35** 35, 41, 42, 50, 60
drawings, **Building 58** 6, 18
Dreadnought, HMS, **Ocean 62** 51
dresses, **Costume 35** 8, 10, 16, 17, 18
Dressler, Marie, **Cinema 34** 62
drill, military, **Battle 63** 12-15, 40, 45
drills, mechanical, **Invention 27** 8-9, 10, 42
dripstones, **Building 58** 46, 48
drivers, **Train 39** 15, 41, 50
and signals, **Train 39** 33, 34, 35, 49
drogues, **Shipwreck 72** 43
droneflies, **Pond & River 6** 50
drought, **Future 100** 9, 38
drovers, **Cowboy 45** 18, 56-57
drug trafficking, **Spy 67** 51, 54
drugs, **Chemistry 79** 6, 10, 52, 53; **Crime & Detection 73** 26, 28, 29, 54; **Medicine 88** 7, 42-43; **Plant 14** 58, 59
natural, **Medicine 88** 12-13, 40-41

druids, **Witch & Wizard 70** 58, 59
drum kits, **Music 12** 52-53
drumfish, **Fish 20** 19
drums, **Castle 49** 45; **Dance 99** 14, 15, 22, 38; **Medieval Life 65** 56, 57; **Music 12** 48, 50-51, 52-53; **Pirate 59** 22
African, **Africa 61** 61, 63
bass, **Music 12** 53, 57, 60
Chinese, **China 55** 40, 53
snare, **Music 12** 52, 57
of war, **Battle 63** 53
Drusilla, **Ancient Rome 24** 9
"dry" cells, **Electricity 77** 18
Dryosaurus, **Dinosaur 13** 59
DTP, desktop publishing, **Future 100** 11
du Chaillu, Paul, **Gorilla 64** 50, 62
dubbing, **Cinema 34** 47
Dublin, **Viking 50** 7, 17, 26
ducats, **Money 18** 32, 34, 36, 44
Duccio di Buoninsegna, **Perspective 98** 8; **Renaissance 91** 10
duck-billed platypus, **Reptile 26** 37
ducks, **Bird 1** 15, 25, 33, 37; **Farm 66** 59-61; **Pond & River 6** 18, 28, 29, 59; **Skeleton 3** 18, 30
Arctic, **Arctic & Antarctic 57** 20, 21
duckweeds, **Pond & River 6** 6, 9, 13, 44
dudes, **Cowboy 45** 60
dudley bugs, **Fossil 19** 30
duels, **Sport 8** 56; **Viking 50** 28
pistols, **Arms & Armour 4** 46-47
swords, **Arms & Armour 4** 42-45
Duesenberg, J., **Car 21** 18
Dufy, Raoul, **Writing 48** 49
dugongs, sea cows, **Mammal 11** 11; **Ocean 62** 16, 28; **Skeleton 3** 17; **Whale 46** 6, 7, 44-45
Duguay-Trouin, René, **Pirate 59** 7, 19, 50
Duke, Charles, **Space Exploration 71** 23
Dukes, Paul, **Spy 67** 29
Dulles, Allen, **Spy 67** 58
Dülmen ponies, **Horse 33** 36
Dulwich Gallery, London, **Watercolour 97** 9
Dumas, Alexander, **Spy 67** 58
dumb-bells, **Sport 8** 43, 45
dumortierite, **Crystal & Gem 25** 22
dumps, **Money 18** 50
dun colour, **Horse 33** 41

Dunant, Henry, **Battle 63** 60
Dunaway, Faye, **Cinema 34** 59
Duncan, Isadora, **Dance 99** 42
dunes, sand, **Desert 51** 12-13
dungeons, **Castle 49** 32
Dunham, Katherine, **Dance 99** 54
Dunlop, **Car 21** 58, 59
Dunne, John William, **Time & Space 81** 38
dunnocks, **Bird 1** 53
duodenum, **Human Body 87** 36, 37, 41
Dupont, **Crime & Detection 73** 53
Durand-Ruel, Paul, **Impressionism 92** 7, 42-43, 60
Dürer, Albrecht, **Dog 32** 6; **Perspective 98** 26-27, 35, 44; **Renaissance 91** 40-41; **Whale 46** 42
mythological drawings, **Renaissance 91** 27, 43
on proportion, **Renaissance 91** 30
Self-portrait, **Renaissance 91** 7
watercolours, **Watercolour 97** 15, 16-17, 24
Duret, Théodore, **Manet 94** 14, 20, 44, 52
Durga, **Religion 68** 20
Duryea brothers, **Car 21** 8
Dushara, **Bible Lands 30** 25
Dushara, **Fish 20** 41
dwarf gourami, **Fish 20** 41
dwarf pygmy goby, **Fish 20** 6
Dyce, William, **Bible Lands 30** 46
dyes, **Africa 61** 20, 28; **Chemistry 79** 15, 42, 59, 61; **Early People 10** 32, 33; **Technology 89** 50-51
clothes, **Costume 35** 9, 11, 13, 23
man-made, **Light 75** 33
organic, **Chemistry 79** 10
synthetic, **Chemistry 79** 52, 53, 62
dynamite, **Chemistry 79** 36, 62
dynamos, **Electricity 77** 36, 37, 38, 42; **Energy 76** 24, 25, 30, 32
Dzerzhinsky, Felix, **Russia 74** 36

eagle owls, **BIRD 1** 25
eagle rays, **FISH 20** 54
eagles, **ARCTIC & ANTARCTIC 57**
24-25; **BIRD 1** 32, 52, 53;
EAGLE 69 42-43; **JUNGLE 54**
11, 46
breeding, **EAGLE 69** 47, 56, 59
chicks, **EAGLE 69** 12-15, 41, 45
on emblems, **EAGLE 69** 36, 42;
FLAG 16 8, 28
extinction, **EAGLE 69** 37, 47,
56-57
flight, **EAGLE 69** 16-19, 56-58
mating, **EAGLE 69** 12, 18,
19, 31
migration, **EAGLE 69** 18,
56, 57
senses, **EAGLE 69** 30-31
skeletons, **EAGLE 69** 22, 32, 33
talons, **EAGLE 69** 9, 24, 25, 36
worship of, **EAGLE 69** 52, 53
types of,
African fish,
EAGLE 69 25, 31
African hawk, **EAGLE 69** 42
bald, **EAGLE 69** 13, 18, 29, 36
golden, **EAGLE 69** 14,
22-24, 43
harpy, **EAGLE 69** 42, 59
martial, **EAGLE 69** 14, 24, 42
sea eagle, **EAGLE 69** 27, 36,
37, 57
snake, **EAGLE 69** 15, 42, 43
tawny, **EAGLE 69** 9, 16,
19, 42
Earhart, Amelia,
EXPLORER 31 56
Earl, Harley, **CAR 21** 28
Earp, Virgil, **COWBOY 45** 42
Earp, Wyatt, **COWBOY 45** 43
earphones, **FUTURE 100** 52
ears, **HUMAN BODY 87** 15,
22, 58
hearing, **HUMAN BODY 87** 52,
54-55, 61
Earth, **ASTRONOMY 82** 37, 40,
42-43; **EARTH 83**; **FORCE &
MOTION 78** 32, 33, 41, 59;
VOLCANO 38 8, 9, 12, 22
atmosphere, **FORCE &
MOTION 78** 38, 55
core, **EARTH 83** 6-7, 40-41;
ROCK & MINERAL 2 6
crust, **EARTH 83** 6, 7, 32, 40;
ROCK & MINERAL 2 6, 10

gravity, **FORCE & MOTION 78**
34, 35, 47
life, **EARTH 83** 11, 52-53, 62-63
mantle,**EARTH 83** 7, 39, 40-41;
ROCK & MINERAL 2 6, 10
motion, **FORCE &
MOTION 78** 28, 29, 53, 58
rotation, **FORCE &
MOTION 78** 27, 47, 54
earth, in building,
BUILDING 58 12-13, 44
earthquakes, **ARCHAEOLOGY 56**
6, 10; **EARTH 83** 40, 42-43,
49; **FUTURE 100** 22, 51;
OCEAN 62 45
aftershocks, **VOLCANO 38** 46,
55, 59
Armenia, **VOLCANO 38** 5, 9
China **CHINA 55** 22, 41
Guadeloupe, **VOLCANO 38** 51
Japan, **VOLCANO 38** 11
Naples, **VOLCANO 38** 57
San Francisco, **VOLCANO 38** 7
Scotland, **VOLCANO 38** 50
seismography, **VOLCANO 38**
48, 49, 50, 52-55
shockwaves, **VOLCANO 38**
50, 51
tectonics, **EARTH 83** 36, 37, 47
Yugoslavia, **VOLCANO 38** 46
earthworms, **INSECT 17** 9
earwigs, **INSECT 17** 8, 10, 26, 41
East Africa, **EXPLORER 31** 8,
17-18, 46
East Anglia, **VIKING 50** 17
East India Company,
FLAG 16 17
East Indiamen, **PIRATE 59** 19,
46, 47, 51
Easter, **MEDIEVAL LIFE 65** 54, 58;
RELIGION 68 48
Easter eggs, **RUSSIA 74** 25, 55
Eastman, George, **CINEMA 34**
12; **INVENTION 27** 41, 60;
LIGHT 75 27
Eastwood, Clint, **COWBOY 45** 60
Eaton, Charley, **CRIME &
DETECTION 73** 20
ebony, **ANCIENT EGYPT 23** 41
eccentric orbits,
ASTRONOMY 82 18, 37, 58
ECG, **ELECTRICITY 77** 7, 51;
ELECTRONICS 90 7;
MEDICINE 88 7, 38
echidnas, **DESERT 51** 34;
MAMMAL 11 8, 25, 31, 51
Echinocaris, **FOSSIL 19** 30
echinoderms, **FOSSIL 19**
32-33; **OCEAN 62** 10, 19, 25;
SEASHORE 15 40-41, 43;
SHELL 9 9, 20, 54
Echinodon, **DINOSAUR 13** 26
echinoids, **FOSSIL 19** 13, 32,
33, 63
echo-sounder,
SHIPWRECK 72 42
Eckert, John, **FUTURE 100** 10

eclipses, **ASTRONOMY 82** 13, 31,
39, 40; **LIGHT 75** 10, 61, 63;
TIME & SPACE 81 26, 27,
42, 43
ecliptic, **ASTRONOMY 82** 8, 11,
13, 17
eclogite, **CRYSTAL & GEM 25** 8
Ecole des Beaux-Arts,
IMPRESSIONISM 92 11
ecology, **ELEPHANT 42** 60-61;
ECOLOGY 86 6-7;
POND & RIVER 6 12, 34
"consumers", **ECOLOGY 86**
10, 11, 27, 58
diversity, **ECOLOGY 86** 36, 54,
56-57
energy, **ECOLOGY 86** 10-11, 12
equilibrium, **ECOLOGY 86**
32-33
human, **ECOLOGY 86** 58-59,
60-61
"producers", **ECOLOGY 86**
8-9, 10, 11, 15
resources, **ECOLOGY 86** 26,
27, 32
Ecuador, **MUMMY 44** 52
Eddington, Arthur, **FORCE &
MOTION 78** 60
Eden, *see* Garden of Eden
Edfu temple, **PYRAMID 53** 31
Edison, Thomas, **CINEMA 34** 12,
14, 16, 23;
ELECTRONICS 90 25, 28;
ENERGY 76 33; 2;
TECHNOLOGY 89 41
light bulb,
ELECTRICITY 77 41, 43,
46, 47; **LIGHT 75** 52
telegraphy,
ELECTRICITY 77 54, 55, 58
telephone,
INVENTION 27 44, 45, 46
Edison Company,
ELECTRICITY 77 44
Edison-Swan light bulbs,
ELECTRICITY 77 47
editing,
CINEMA 34 29, 30, 48, 49
Edmontosaurus,
DINOSAUR 13 27;
FOSSIL 19 48
Edmund, King,
VIKING 50 7, 17
education, medieval,
MEDIEVAL LIFE 65 30, 41, 62
Edward I, King of England,
CASTLE 49 7, 12, 13;
MEDIEVAL LIFE 65 27
Edward III, King of England,
CASTLE 49 27;
MEDIEVAL LIFE 65 47
Edward IV, King of England,
CASTLE 49 32
Edward V, King of England,
CASTLE 49 32
Edward VII, King of England,
TRAIN 39 45

Edward the Black Prince,
England, **BATTLE 63** 63
Edwardian era, **COSTUME 35**
48-49
eels, **FISH 20** 28, 29, 48, 49;
OCEAN 62 10, 38, 42;
POND & RIVER 6 22, 24;
SEASHORE 15 34
effigies, **WITCH & WIZARD 70**
15, 43, 47
egg shells, marine, **SHELL 9** 13
eggs, **BIRD 1** 54-55, 56-57;
FARM 66 7, 58-61, 63;
LIFE 84 11, 30, 31, 53
butterflies and moths,
BUTTERFLY & MOTH 7 8,
11-12
in humans, **HUMAN BODY 87**
42, 43, 44
sexual reproduction,
LIFE 84 39
egrets, **BIRD 1** 21
Egypt, Ancient,
ANCIENT EGYPT 23; **ANCIENT
GREECE 37** 7, 14, 58, 63;
ANCIENT ROME 24 19, 21;
BATTLE 63 7, 59; **EARLY
PEOPLE 10** 47
archaeological discoveries,
ARCHAEOLOGY 56 15, 16
army, **ANCIENT EGYPT 23**
36-37
art, **PERSPECTIVE 98** 8
Book of the Dead, **MUMMY 44**
12-13, 14
buildings, **BUILDING 58** 13,
16, 18, 57
clothes, **ANCIENT EGYPT 23**
54-55; **COSTUME 35** 8, 9,
36, 60
coins, **MONEY 18** 54, 55, 63
early expeditions to,
EXPLORER 31 8-9
farming,
FARM 66 6, 12, 28, 29
food,
ANCIENT EGYPT 23 48-49
games, **ANCIENT EGYPT 23**
52-53
gods, **RELIGION 68** 10-11
government,
ANCIENT EGYPT 23 9, 12-13,
32; **PYRAMID 53** 8
houses, **ANCIENT EGYPT 23**
46, 47
magic,
WITCH & WIZARD 70 20, 26,
29, 58
medicine, **MEDICINE 88** 8,
12, 37
Middle Kingdom,
PYRAMID 53 6, 8, 40-41
mummies, **MUMMY 44** 10-11
music,
ANCIENT EGYPT 23 50-51
New Kingdom, **PYRAMID 53**
6, 44

Old Kingdom, PYRAMID **53** 6, 8, 39, 40

pyramids, PYRAMID **53**

Ramses (Ramesses II), MUMMY **44** 28, 36, 41, 50

religion, ANCIENT EGYPT **23** 24-25, 28-29

sacred cats, MUMMY **44** 46-47; CAT **29** 46-47

scripts, WRITING **48** 12-13

Sphinx, BIBLE LANDS **30** 25

trade, ANCIENT EGYPT **23** 40-41; ARCHAEOLOGY **56** 51

Tutankhamun, MUMMY **44** 7, 29, 38-39

writing, EARLY PEOPLE **10** 41

Ehrlich, Paul, MEDICINE **88** 42

Einstein, Albert,
ASTRONOMY **82** 38, 63; FORCE & MOTION **78** 58-59, 60, 62; FUTURE **100** 8; MATTER **80** 38, 55

black holes, TIME & SPACE **81** 46, 48

general theory of relativity, TIME & SPACE **81** 36, 42-45

mass and energy, ENERGY **76** 44-45

nuclear bomb, ENERGY **76** 47

special theory of relativity, TIME & SPACE **81** 34-37, 42

speed of light, LIGHT **75** 61, 62, 63

Eisenstein, Sergei, CINEMA **34** 19, 49; RUSSIA **74** 43

El, BIBLE LANDS **30** 24

El Castillo, PYRAMID **53** 56, 57

El Lahun, PYRAMID **53** 40, 42

El Lisht, PYRAMID **53** 8, 40

El Ninó, OCEAN **62** 12

El Salvador, PYRAMID **53** 56

El Tajín, PYRAMID **53** 55

Elam, BIBLE LANDS **30** 50

elasmobranchs, FISH **20** 9

elastic, COSTUME **35** 35, 54, 55

Eleanor, Queen, WITCH & WIZARD **70** 17

Electra, ANCIENT GREECE **37** 39

electric chair, CRIME & DETECTION **73** 22

electric eels, FISH **20** 48, 49

electric field, MATTER **80** 15, 48, 49, 52

electric instruments, MUSIC **12** 58-59, 60-61

electric trains, ELECTRICITY **77** 38, 39; TRAIN **39** 38-39

electrical appliances, FUTURE **100** 8-11, 29

electricity, CHEMISTRY **79** 20-21, 46-47; ELECTRICITY **77**; LIGHT **75** 42, 50, 56; MATTER **80** 49, 50, 60

current, FORCE & MOTION **78** 40, 49, 62; MATTER **80** 16, 17, 32

as energy, ENERGY **76** 22, 24, 32-33; FORCE & MOTION **78** 40, 41, 51

fluid theory, ENERGY **76** 18-19

in future, FUTURE **100** 19, 20, 56

at home, ELECTRICITY **77** 46, 47, 48-49

invention of, INVENTION **27** 39, 53, 54-55

lights, ELECTRICITY **77** 19, 36, 43; LIGHT **75** 52-53

meters, ELECTRICITY **77** 46

photoelectric effect, ENERGY **76** 42

rays, ELECTRICITY **77** 7, 17

symbols, ELECTRICITY **77** 25

electrocardiograph, *see* ECG

electrodes, ELECTRICITY **77** 18, 19, 51, 63

electrodynamics, ELECTRICITY **77** 27

electrolysis, CHEMISTRY **79** 25, 26, 27; ELECTRICITY **77** 19, 32; MATTER **80** 32, 49, 50, 51

electrolytes, CHEMISTRY **79** 46, 47; ELECTRICITY **77** 18, 33

electromagnetism, ELECTRICITY **77** 27, 28-31, 57; ENERGY **76** 22-23, 32, 46; FORCE & MOTION **78** 51, 58, 62, 63; TIME & SPACE **81** 32-33, 52, 59

force, MATTER **80** 60-61

induction, ELECTRICITY **77** 34-35, 40, 58

radiation, ASTRONOMY **82** 32, 60; ENERGY **76** 39, 40-43
absorption, ENERGY **76** 27
Big Bang, ENERGY **76** 62
microwaves, ENERGY **76** 35
nuclear energy, ENERGY **76** 46
spectrum, CRYSTAL & GEM **25** 15, 16, 19; LIGHT **75** 40-44; TIME & SPACE **81** 56, 61

waves, ELECTRICITY **77** 60-61; ELECTRONICS **90** 12-15; INVENTION **27** 52

electromagnets, ENERGY **76** 24, 25, 38, 39

electrometers, ARCTIC & ANTARCTIC **57** 54

electron microscopes, FUTURE **100** 34, 35

electronics, ELECTRONICS **90**; TECHNOLOGY **89** 32, 42, 54-55

digital, ELECTRONICS **90** 46-47, 50, 60

electronic,
currency, FUTURE **100** 59
mail, FUTURE **100** 12, 29, 52
musical instruments, MUSIC **12** 62-63
newspapers, FUTURE **100** 59

pets, FUTURE **100** 31

sensors, FUTURE **100** 42

electrons, ELECTRICITY **77** 20, 55, 62, 63; ENERGY **76** 46; FORCE & MOTION **78** 55, 62; MATTER **80** 62, 63; TIME & SPACE **81** 52, 57, 58, 60

in atoms, MATTER **80** 48-49, 52, 53

and light, LIGHT **75** 43, 44-45, 51

orbits, MATTER **80** 50, 51, 56

oscilloscope, ELECTRONICS **90** 33

particle accelerator, ENERGY **76** 45

photoelectric effect, ENERGY **76** 42, 43

and photons, MATTER **80** 59, 60

radiation, MATTER **80** 46-47

transistor, ELECTRONICS **90** 38, 39

uses, ELECTRONICS **90** 28-29

electroplating, CHEMISTRY **79** 46; ELECTRICITY **77** 32, 33, 36, 42

electroscopes, ELECTRICITY **77** 11, 21

electrostatic charge, ELECTRICITY **77** 10, 12, 16

uses, ELECTRICITY **77** 14-15

electrotherapy, MEDICINE **88** 19, 36, 46

electrums, ANCIENT GREECE **37** 52; MONEY **18** 10

elements, CHEMISTRY **79** 16, 18-19, 50; EARTH **83** 20-21; ELECTRONICS **90** 37; MATTER **80** 16, 20, 26, 62; TIME & SPACE **81** 58

compounds, CHEMISTRY **79** 20, 34

discovery, MATTER **80** 32-33, 34

electrolysis, CHEMISTRY **79** 46, 47; MATTER **80** 50

Hydrogen, ASTRONOMY **82** 37

metals, CHEMISTRY **79** 24, 25

periodic table, CHEMISTRY **79** 21, 22-23

symbols, CHEMISTRY **79** 59

theory of, MATTER **80** 8, 9

elephant birds, BIRD **1** 54, 55; FOSSIL **19** 53

elephant snails, SHELL **9** 15

elephants, ELEPHANT **42**; EVOLUTION **85** 8, 15, 54; JUNGLE **54** 40; MAMMAL **11** 28, 45, 59, 61

African, AFRICA **61** 19, 30; ELEPHANT **42** 7, 51, 56

in Ancient Rome, ANCIENT ROME **24** 7, 25, 32

Asian, ELEPHANT **42** 6, 38, 51, 53

bones of, SKELETON **3** 36-37

bulls, ELEPHANT **42** 32-33, 38, 39

communicating, ELEPHANT **42** 34-35, 59

cows, ELEPHANT **42** 7, 30-31, 59

ears, ELEPHANT **42** 7, 29, 31, 35

evolution, EVOLUTION **85** 44, 62

extinction, ELEPHANT **42** 8-11, 56

habitats, ELEPHANT **42** 6, 24, 25, 27

intelligence, ELEPHANT **42** 6, 40-41, 50

prehistoric, PREHISTORIC LIFE **52** 9, 48-49

reproduction, ELEPHANT **42** 36-37

trunk, ELEPHANT **42** 18-19, 27, 34-35

worship of, ELEPHANT **42** 48-49

see also mammoths, ivory

elephant-snout fish, FISH **20** 20, 34

Eleusis, ANCIENT GREECE **37** 6

elevations, BUILDING **58** 6

elevators, FLYING MACHINE **22** 20, 40, 57, 59

Elgin, Lord, ANCIENT GREECE **37** 17

Elijah, BIBLE LANDS **30** 24

Eliot, George, VAN GOGH **96** 8, 44

Eliot, T. S., CAT **29** 54

Elizabeth I, Queen of England, EXPLORER **31** 25, 40; KNIGHT **43** 41; PIRATE **59** 18-19; SPY **67** 25, 28, 41; WITCH & WIZARD **70** 14

handwriting, WRITING **48** 52

royal carriage, HORSE **33** 46

Elizabeth II, Queen of England, HORSE **33** 42

Elizabeth, Empress of Russia, RUSSIA **74** 21, 24, 28, 29

elks, ARCTIC & ANTARCTIC **57** 34; SKELETON **3** 31

elliptical orbits, ASTRONOMY **82** 18, 34, 37, 58

Ellms, Charles, PIRATE **59** 7, 61

Elma the robot, FUTURE **100** 44-47

Elton, Charles, ECOLOGY **86** 26, 29, 30

elytra, INSECT **17** 6, 8, 12, 22

Emaeus, BIBLE LANDS **30** 30

embalming,
ANCIENT EGYPT **23** 16-17
embosser, WRITING **48** 57
embrasures, CASTLE **49** 26
embryo, LIFE **84** 30, 31;
PLANT **14** 10, 26
emeralds, CRYSTAL & GEM **25**
26, 38-39, 60;
ROCK & MINERAL **2** 50, 60
emery, CRYSTAL & GEM **25** 37
Empedocles,
TIME & SPACE **81** 58
Empire State Building,
ROCK & MINERAL **2** 36
"Empire State Express",
TRAIN **39** 47
emus, BIRD **1** 55
En Gedi, BIBLE LANDS **30** 33
enchantresses, WITCH &
WIZARD **70** 8, 18
endangered species, ECOLOGY
86 24, 63; SEASHORE **15** 56
endocrine system, see
hormones
endoscopes, INVENTION **27** 43;
LIGHT **75** 54;
MEDICINE **88** 28, 52-53;
TECHNOLOGY **89** 57
endosperms, PLANT **14** 10, 26
endurance racing, HORSE **33**
59-60
enemas, MEDICINE **88** 37
energy, ELECTRICITY **77** 4, 36,
39, 42; ENERGY **76** 6-7;
FORCE & MOTION **78** 40-41,
50-51; MATTER **80** 54, 55, 57,
58; TIME & SPACE **81** 23,
30-31, 54
alternative, ENERGY **76**
48, 58-59;
FUTURE **100** 13, 16, 18, 22
chemical, ENERGY **76**
20, 50, 52;
FORCE & MOTION **78** 40,
41, 62
conservation of, FORCE &
MOTION **78** 40
electrical,
ENERGY **76** 32, 36, 60
forms, MATTER **80** 6, 61
kinetic, ENERGY **76** 12, 15,
16-17
Law of Conservation of,
ENERGY **76** 22, 24-25, 26
light, ENERGY **76** 42-43
mass, ENERGY **76** 16,
44-45, 48
measurement of,
ENERGY **76** 36-37
mechanical, ENERGY **76** 8-9,
12, 13, 32
potential, ENERGY **76** 12,
14-15, 16
waves, FORCE & MOTION **78**
49, 50, 51
wind, ENERGY **76** 6, 7,
12-13, 30

engineering, military,
BATTLE **63** 54-55
engines, ENERGY **76** 30-31,
32-33; FORCE & MOTION **78**
19, 41, 42; SPACE
EXPLORATION **71** 14;
TECHNOLOGY **89** 15, 36-37
car, CAR **21** 9, 42-47
invention of, INVENTION **27**
33, 48, 49
jet, TECHNOLOGY **89** 7, 14,
15, 53; FLYING MACHINE **22**
34-35, 36-37
motor, BOAT **36** 48
motorcycle,
FORCE & MOTION **78** 23
rocket,
FORCE & MOTION **78** 31
rooms, BOAT **36** 52
train, TRAIN **39** 10, 40, 41,46
turboprop, FUTURE **100** 27
see also steam engines
England, EXPLORER **31** 13, 34,
36, 40; MUMMY **44** 9, 58, 59;
VIKING **50** 7, 26, 63;
VOLCANO **38** 16, 47, 54
climate, WEATHER **28** 61
flags of, FLAG **16** 46-47
and Van Gogh,
VAN GOGH **96** 8-10
see also Britain
England, Edward, PIRATE **59** 49
English Channel,
SHIPWRECK **72** 10
crossings,
FLYING MACHINE **22** 7,
14-15, 28
English National Ballet
Company, DANCE **99** 53
engraving,
EARLY PEOPLE **10** 25
entertainment,
AFRICA **61** 22-23;
CASTLE **49** 38, 44-45
medieval, MEDIEVAL LIFE **65**
26, 54, 56, 58
Entlebuch, DOG **32** 44
entrechats, DANCE **99** 45
entropy, TIME & SPACE **81** 30-31
envelopes, WRITING **48** 56
environment,
ARCHAEOLOGY **56** 46-47;
FUTURE **100** 16-19
early landscape,
ARCHAEOLOGY **56** 12-13,
44-47
environment-friendly future,
FUTURE **100** 18-19
enzymes,
CHEMISTRY **79** 34, 35, 37, 50;
HUMAN BODY **87** 13, 35, 36;
LIFE **84** 7, 20, 55, 59;
PLANT **14** 43
replication, LIFE **84** 35, 37
Eocene period, CAT **29** 8;
MAMMAL **11** 12, 14
Eohippus, HORSE **33** 8

épée, SPORT **8** 51
Ephemeroptera, INSECT **17** 8
Ephesus, ANCIENT GREECE **37**
14, 27, 52, 62
epicentre, VOLCANO **38** 49,
50, 51
epicycles, ASTRONOMY **82** 11,
18, 19
Epidauros, ANCIENT GREECE **37**
38, 58
epidemiology, MEDICINE **88** 62
epidermis, HUMAN BODY **87** 33,
50, 51
epidote, CRYSTAL & GEM **25** 11
epiglottis, HUMAN BODY **87** 24,
25, 57
epinetron,
ANCIENT GREECE **37** 31
epiphytes, JUNGLE **54** 8, 10,
13, 18-19, 36; PLANT **14** 38,
46, 47
epoxy resin, TECHNOLOGY **89**
18, 27
Epte River, MONET **95** 36, 43
Equidae, HORSE **33** 6, 8, 10, 12
equilibrium, FORCE &
MOTION **78** 42
equinoxes, ASTRONOMY **82** 8, 11
Equisetum, FOSSIL **19** 37
Equus, HORSE **33** 6, 8-9, 20-21, 24
Erasistratus, MEDICINE **88** 17
Erasmus, RENAISSANCE **91** 6
Erechtheion, ANCIENT
GREECE **37** 27
Ericsson, John, BOAT **36** 38
Ericsson, Leif, BOAT **36** 17;
EXPLORER **31** 12
Erik the Red, VIKING **50** 20,
21, 24
ermine, ARCTIC &
ANTARCTIC **57** 36
Eros, ANCIENT GREECE **37** 20,
22, 62
erosion, EARTH **83** 54-55;
EVOLUTION **85** 16, 29;
ROCK & MINERAL **2** 12-13;
SEASHORE **15** 8-11, 42, 59
glacier, EARTH **83** 58, 59
mountains, EARTH **83** 24, 28,
46-47
weathering, EARTH **83** 50
Eryops, FOSSIL **19** 43
erythrite, CRYSTAL & GEM **25** 17
Escher, M.C., PERSPECTIVE **98**
58, 59
escudos, MONEY **18** 38, 63
Eskdalemuir, Scotland,
VOLCANO **38** 50
Eskimo dogs, DOG **32** 56, 57
Eskimos, see Inuit peoples
espionage, see spies
Essenes, BIBLE LANDS **30** 58
essential oils, CHEMISTRY **79** 9,
12, 13
Essex Emerald moth,
BUTTERFLY & MOTH **7** 58
Essex, SHIPWRECK **72** 38

Este, Lionello d',
RENAISSANCE **91** 33
estuaries, ECOLOGY **86** 50-51;
SEASHORE **15** 14, 18, 20
Ethelred, King, VIKING **50** 17
Ethiopia, AFRICA **61** 10, 22,
33, 36; FLAG **16** 34, 54;
WEATHER **28** 18
Etretat, MONET **95** 38, 40-41
Etruscan peoples,
ANCIENT ROME **24** 6;
ARCHAEOLOGY **56** 20-21;
BUILDING **58** 27
alphabet, WRITING **48** 15, 16
eucalyptus, PLANT **14** 34;
TREE **5** 12, 13, 22
Eucharist, RELIGION **68** 50
Euchromiid moths, BUTTERFLY
& MOTH **7** 45, 48
Euclid, LIGHT **75** 12;
PERSPECTIVE **98** 35;
RENAISSANCE **91** 31; TIME &
SPACE **81** 26
Euclidian geometry, TIME &
SPACE **81** 26-27, 40, 41
Eugènie, Empress,
MANET **94** 18
Eugomphodus, FOSSIL **19** 34
Euoplocephalus, DINOSAUR **13**
20, 21
Euparkeria, DINOSAUR **13** 7
Euphrates, River,
BIBLE LANDS **30** 33, 50
Eupterotid moths, BUTTERFLY
& MOTH **7** 46
Eureka Stockade Flag,
FLAG **16** 50
Euripides, ANCIENT GREECE **37**
38; WRITING **48** 6
Euro Space Center,
SPACE EXPLORATION **71**
24, 29
Europe, ARCTIC &
ANTARCTIC **57** 8, 34;
EXPLORER **31** 10, 12-13, 16;
WEATHER **28** 6, 11, 53, 60
early,
art, EARLY PEOPLE **10** 24-25
Bronze Age, EARLY
PEOPLE **10** 42, 46-47
Ice Age, EARLY PEOPLE **10**
14, 18-19
Iron Age,
EARLY PEOPLE **10** 50-51
European Economic
Community,
MONEY **18** 14, 15, 31
European Space Agency,
SPACE EXPLORATION **71** 15,
40, 44, 58
Eurypholis, FISH **20** 13
eurypterids, FOSSIL **19** 31
Eustace the Monk,
PIRATE **59** 12
Eustace, St.,
MEDIEVAL LIFE **65** 43
Eusthenopteron, FISH **20** 13

eutrophication, ECOLOGY 86 21, 54

Evans, Cape, ARCTIC & ANTARCTIC 57 54, 55

Evans, Oliver, ENERGY 76 29; TRAIN 39 11

evaporation, CHEMISTRY 79 7, 9, 14, 15; ENERGY 76 12, 36

Everest, Mt., FUTURE 100 10

evergreens, PLANT 14 35; TREE 5 10

evolution, CAT 29 8, 26; EARLY PEOPLE 10 23; ECOLOGY 86 36-37; EVOLUTION 85; LIFE 84 6, 20, 42-43, 46

of birds, EVOLUTION 85 42, 45, 62

classification, LIFE 84 48, 49

creation, EVOLUTION 85 6-7, 14, 16, 17

death, LIFE 84 7

DNA, LIFE 84 36

of elephants, EVOLUTION 85 44, 62

of fish, EVOLUTION 85 61, 62

of horses, HORSE 33 8-9

of insects, EVOLUTION 85 26, 43, 49, 61

parallel evolution, FOSSIL 19 57

of primates, GORILLA 64 8-9

reproduction, LIFE 84 32

trees, EVOLUTION 85 48-49, 54

see also Darwin, extinction, fossils and under geological periods and species

excavation, ARCHAEOLOGY 56 20-21, 22-24, 63; EARLY PEOPLE 10 62, 66

underwater, ARCHAEOLOGY 56 32-33

excretory system, HUMAN BODY 87 38-39, 42

executions, CRIME & DETECTION 73 8, 52, 56; PIRATE 59 56-57

exhibitions, WATERCOLOUR 97 38-39, 50

Exmoor pony, HORSE 33 20

Exodus, BIBLE LANDS 30 12, 13, 26, 63; RELIGION 68 42, 47

exorcism, WITCH & WIZARD 70 50, 55

exoskeletons, FOSSIL 19 30; SKELETON 3 22-25

explorers, AFRICA 61 6; DESERT 51 62-63; EXPLORERS 31; JUNGLE 54 60-61; WATERCOLOUR 97 26-27

Antarctic, ARCTIC & ANTARCTIC 57 54-55

Arctic, ARCTIC & ANTARCTIC 57 52-53

travelling necessities, ARCTIC & ANTARCTIC 57 56-58

Vikings as, VIKING 50 20-21, 24

explosives, CRIME & DETECTION 73 54

Expressionism, WATERCOLOUR 97 58-59, 60

Exquemeling, Alexander, PIRATE 59 61

extinction, CAT 29 8, 11, 40-41; EVOLUTION 85 14-15, 49, 63; PREHISTORIC LIFE 52 7, 60-61

catastrophe theory, EVOLUTION 85 16

geological periods, EVOLUTION 85 17

mass extinction, EVOLUTION 85 46, 47, 61

extortion, CRIME & DETECTION 73 26; PIRATE 59 54

Exxon Valdez, SHIPWRECK 72 30, 31

Eyck, Jan van, PERSPECTIVE 98 11, 56; RENAISSANCE 91 7, 20

eye lens, LIGHT 75 18, 19

Eye of Horus, PYRAMID 53 28, 52

eyes, HUMAN BODY 87 52-53, 61; LIGHT 75 16, 18, 40, 42

compound, LIGHT 75 19, 54

nerves, HUMAN BODY 87 58-59, 63

optics, PERSPECTIVE 98 6, 62

simple, INSECT 17 7, 9, 14

socket, HUMAN BODY 87 15, 53

Ezion Geber, BIBLE LANDS 30 40

F

Fabergé, Peter Carl, AMPHIBIAN 41 51; CRYSTAL & GEM 25 51; RUSSIA 74 25

Fabriano, Gentile da, RENAISSANCE 91 17

Fabricius, Hieronymus, MEDICINE 88 24

fabrics, COSTUME 35 14, 15, 16; EARLY PEOPLE 10 32-33

Fabris, Pietro, VOLCANO 38 31, 39

Fabritius, Carel, PERSPECTIVE 98 38, 39

factories, TECHNOLOGY 89 34-35

Fairbanks, Douglas, CINEMA 34 21

fairs, MEDIEVAL LIFE 65 54

Fairey-Reed, FLYING MACHINE 22 25, 31

fairy tales, RUSSIA 74 11, 50, 53; WITCH & WIZARD 70 18, 19, 50, 52

falconry, CASTLE 49 44; EAGLE 69 40, 52-55; KNIGHT 43 49, 50

falcons, ARCTIC & ANTARCTIC 57 24; BIRD 1 32, 42; DESERT 51 30; EAGLE 69 46-47

African pygmy, EAGLE 69 12, 58

forest, EAGLE 69 11, 27, 46, 59

gyrfalcon, EAGLE 69 16, 46, 58

lanner, EAGLE 69 11, 46, 47

merlin, EAGLE 69 9, 21

peregrine, EAGLE 69 14, 15, 54, 58

pygmy, EAGLE 69 11, 46, 58

rare, EAGLE 69 46, 59

saker, EAGLE 69 24, 30, 46

as symbols, MUMMY 44 21, 25, 27, 43

Falkland Islands, ARCTIC & ANTARCTIC 57 18, 19

Fallopius, Gabriele, HUMAN BODY 87 43, 55

false prickly crabs, SHELL 9 26

famines, ANCIENT EGYPT 23 8; FUTURE 100 9, 38; MEDIEVAL LIFE 65 60

fan-paintings, WATERCOLOUR 97 7, 19, 50

fans, CHINA 55 46; COSTUME 35 19, 27, 39, 49

Fantin-Latour, Henri, IMPRESSIONISM 92 9, 16; MANET 94 15, 53

Faraday, Michael, CINEMA 34 8; ELECTRONICS 90 10, 11, 18, 24; MATTER 80 50, 51; TIME & SPACE 81 32

electricity, CHEMISTRY 79 46, 49; INVENTION 27 54; ELECTRICITY 77 40

electrolysis, ELECTRICITY 77 32

electromagnetism, ELECTRICITY 77 34, 36, 37, 38

energy conservation, ENERGY 76 22, 23, 24, 32

farads, ELECTRICITY 77 13, 25

Farey, John, FORCE & MOTION 78 33; PERSPECTIVE 98 44

farming, NORTH AMERICAN INDIAN 60 8-9, 16-17; AFRICA 61 16, 18; CHINA 55 34-37; HORSE 33 6-7, 50-51

ancient, ARCHAEOLOGY 56 28, 44-47, 58-59, 62; AZTEC 47 12-13

development of, TECHNOLOGY 89 7, 44-45

early, FARM 66 6, 7

equipment, FARM 66 10, 11, 13

Egyptian, MUMMY 44 32-33

genetic engineering, FARM 66 28, 62, 63

harvesting, FARM 66 20-21, 26-27

hoeing, FARM 66 16, 17

instruments, EARLY PEOPLE 10 30-31, 50, 54

medieval, CASTLE 49 52-53; FARM 66 56; MEDIEVAL LIFE 65 7, 8, 10, 12

organic, FARM 66 58, 60, 62-63

reaping, FARM 66 20, 25-27, 31

Roman, ANCIENT ROME 24 58, 59; ARCHAEOLOGY 56 58-59

sowing, FARM 66 12, 14, 16-18

threshing, FARM 66 20, 22-25, 27

Viking, VIKING 50 38-39

see also collective farming

Faroe Islands, VIKING 50 20; WHALE 46 62

Farr, Sheriff Edward, CRIME & DETECTION 73 13

farthingale, COSTUME 35 22, 23, 42, 54

farthings, MONEY 18 46

fasces, ANCIENT ROME 24 16

fashion houses, COSTUME 35 40

Father Christmas, ARCTIC & ANTARCTIC 57 38

Fatima, RELIGION 68 59

fats, CHEMISTRY 79 7, 40, 41, 49

faults, EARTH 83 39, 43, 48, 49; VOLCANO 38 13, 60, 61

Faustus, WITCH & WIZARD 70 16

Fauvism, WATERCOLOUR 97 58

Favier, Jean-Jacques, SPACE EXPLORATION 71 30, 39

fax machines, ELECTRONICS 90 25, 61, 62; FUTURE 100 12; TECHNOLOGY 89 48-49

FBI, CRIME & DETECTION 73 15, 22, 24, 58; SPY 67 40-42, 45, 55

feasts, MEDIEVAL LIFE 65 14, 21, 26, 54; VIKING 50 34, 50

feathers, ARCTIC & ANTARCTIC 57 14, 20, 21; LIFE 84 26, 53; SEASHORE 15 60-61; SKELETON 3 18

Fécamp, MONET 95 38, 39

Federation Flag, **Flag 16** 50

feldspar, **Crystal & Gem 25** 8, 9, 16, 17, 30, 45; **Earth 83** 20, 23, 25, 27; **Rock & Mineral 2** 8, 16-17, 24, 42

Felidae, **Cat 29** 6, 40

Felis catus, **Cat 29** 10, 44

Felis leo, **Cat 29** 10

Felis silvestris, **Cat 29** 10, 44, 46

felt, **Archaeology 56** 29, 31; **Costume 35** 21

femur, thigh bone, **Human Body 87** 15, 17, 18, 19; **Skeleton 3** 54-55, 56-57

fencing, **Arms & Armour 4** 42-45; **Sport 8** 50-51

fens, **Money 18** 53, 63

Ferdinand VII, King of Spain, **Goya 93** 42-43, 44-45; **Explorer 31** 22-23

Ferlini, Giuseppe, **Pyramid 53** 52

fermentation, **Chemistry 79** 7

Fermi, Enrico, **Energy 76** 46; **Matter 80** 54

ferns, **Dinosaur 13** 10, 11, 27; **Jungle 54** 14, 18, 21, 56; **Pond & River 6** 54, 55; **Tree 5** 21, 48, 53

fossilized, **Fossil 19** 36, 37

Feronia, **Ancient Rome 24** 22

ferrade, **Cowboy 45** 31, 55

Ferranti, Sebastian, **Electricity 77** 44

Ferrari **Car 21** 26, 32-33, 63

ferrets, **Skeleton 3** 41

ferries, **Boat 36** 16

fertilisers, **Ecology 86** 20, 47, 54, 60; **Farm 66** 34, 41, 48, 63

fertilization, **Ecology 86** 7, 47; **Evolution 85** 41, 50, 51; **Life 84** 38, 39, 42

festa cichlid, **Fish 20** 19

festivals, **Dance 99** 11, 19, 32, 36

fetishes, **Witch & Wizard 70** 40-43

fetters, **Pirate 59** 39

feudal system, **Knight 43** 6; **Medieval Life 65** 7, 8-9

Feynman, Richard, **Matter 80** 59; **Time & Space 81** 51, 52

Fiat, **Car 21** 30, 34, 63

fibre optics, **Electronics 90** 62, 63; **Future 100** 13; **Light 75** 54, 55; **Medicine 88** 52-53

fibreglass, **Technology 89** 29

fibrolite, **Crystal & Gem 25** 49

fibulas, **Skeleton 3** 54-55, 56-57

fichu, **Costume 35** 31

fiddler crabs, **Shell 9** 24

fiddles, **Medieval Life 65** 56; **Music 12** 28, 41

fiefs, **Medieval Life 65** 8

field events, **Sport 8** 41

Fielding, Sir Henry, **Crime & Detection 73** 10

F.I.F.A. world cup, **Sport 8** 6

fig shells, **Shell 9** 12

fighter planes, **Flying Machine 22** 19

figs, **Jungle 54** 27, 56

figureheads, **Boat 36** 32-33; **Pirate 59** 51

figworts, **Pond & River 6** 10, 14, 18

Fiji, **Explorer 31** 15, 34-35; **Witch & Wizard 70** 56

filament, **Light 75** 32, 52

filament bulbs, **Electricity 77** 47

filefish, **Fish 20** 51

Fille mal gardée, La, **Dance 99** 40, 41

film, **Cinema 34** 12-13; **Invention 27** 41, 50, 51, 60; **Technology 89** 14, 26-27

holographic, **Light 75** 58, 59

photographic, **Light 75** 25, 27, 43

films, **Cinema 34**; **Perspective 98** 51, 58; **Shipwreck 72** 59; **Space Exploration 71** 9, 12, 55

adventure, **Cinema 34** 58-59

comic, **Cinema 34** 54-55

festivals, **Cinema 34** 62-63

horror, **Cinema 34** 60-61

musicals, **Cinema 34** 56-57

on pirates, **Pirate 59** 6, 62-63

science fiction, **Cinema 34** 60-61

silent, **Cinema 34** 18-19, 22, 46

spy, **Spy 67** 9, 58, 59

technicolor, **Cinema 34** 26-27

three-dimensional, **Cinema 34** 13, 61

on witches, **Witch & Wizard 70** 18, 47

Filomarino, Ascanio, **Volcano 38** 53

filters, **Electronics 90** 7, 23, 34-35, 43

filtration, **Chemistry 79** 14, 35

fin rays, **Fish 20** 27, 30, 31, 32

finches, **Bird 1** 12, 33, 36, 38

fingerprints, **Crime & Detection 73** 36, 40-42, 53; **Future 100** 31, 45; **Mummy 44** 49, 58

classification of, **Crime & Detection 73** 45

dusting, **Crime & Detection 73** 44, 45

Finland, **Flag 16** 44-45; **Money 18** 44, 45, 62

fins, **Flying Machine 22** 27, 59; **Shark 40** 6, 11, 13, 40; **Skeleton 3** 20, 51

shark-fin soup, **Shark 40** 61

Fiocre, Eugenie, **Dance 99** 40

fiords, **Earth 83** 59

Fiorelli, Giuseppe, **Archaeology 56** 28; **Volcano 38** 28, 29

fire, **Ancient Egypt 23** 47; **Energy 76** 10-11, 28, 29; **Invention 27** 10, 14, 20, 21

firemen, **Train 39** 15, 50

heat, **Energy 76** 20, 45

making, **Early People 10** 14, 15, 16-17

sacred, **Religion 68** 40, 41

fire escapes, **Building 58** 38

fire fountains, **Volcano 38** 18, 22, 23, 42

fire thorns, **Desert 51** 18

firearms, *see* guns

Firebird, The, **Dance 99** 20

fireflies, **Jungle 54** 28

fireplaces, **Building 58** 40-41, 54, 55; **Castle 49** 10, 20, 38

firs, **Tree 5** 30, 44

fish, **Early People 10** 9, 26; **Fish 20**; **Jungle 54** 16, 17; **Life 84** 22, 24, 53; **Russia 74** 10, 13-15, 54

breeding, **Fish 20** 23, 40, 41, 42

camouflage, **Fish 20** 16, 17, 20, 21

caviar, **Russia 74** 14, 15

electricity in, **Fish 20** 49, 57

evolution, **Evolution 85** 17, 42, 61, 62

eyes, **Fish 20** 7, 52, 58

feeding, **Fish 20** 34-35, 36-37

fins, **Fish 20** 28-29, 30-31

fossils, **Fossil 19** 24, 28, 34-35; **Seashore 15** 8, 47, 10-11

freshwater, **Pond & River 6** 22-23

gills, **Fish 20** 8-9

prehistoric, **Dinosaur 13** 58, 60; **Prehistoric Life 52** 18-19, 20, 21

saltwater, **Ocean 62** 41-43; **Seashore 15** 22, 30, 34-35

skeletons, **Seashore 15** 58, 59, 60-61; **Skeleton 3** 12, 20-21, 30

see also fishing, *and under individual fish*

Fisher, Carrie, **Cinema 34** 35

fishing, **Africa 61** 18; **China 55** 39; **North American Indian 60** 12, 19, 42, 52; **Ocean 62** 56-58, 62

boats, **Boat 36** 15, 16, 17, 42-45

early, **Ancient Egypt 23** 38, 45; **Ancient Greece 37** 50, 52, 53

equipment, **Archaeology 56** 44

Inuit, **North American Indian 60** 60-61

nets, **Boat 36** 44

fishnet tights, **Costume 35** 59

fission, **Time & Space 81** 37

Fitzwalter, Robert, **Knight 43** 36

Fizeau, Armand, **Light 75** 60, 61, 63

Flag Fen, **Archaeology 56** 36-37

flags, **Flag 16** 6-7, 60-63; **Pirate 59** 34-35, 41, 55

flagships, **Boat 36** 56

flamenco, **Dance 99** 16, 17

flames, **Matter 80** 30-31, 32, 56

flamingoes, **Bird 1** 25, 36; **Skeleton 3** 32

Flamsteed, John, **Astronomy 82** 28

flappers, **Costume 35** 53

flared trousers, **Costume 35** 59

flatfishes, **Fish 20** 24, 25, 26, 27

flatworms, **Pond & River 6** 13, 20, 57

flax, **Ancient Egypt 23** 54, 55; **Costume 35** 7, 8

fleas, **Insect 17** 24, 40

Fleming, Alexander, **Future 100** 9; **Medicine 88** 42

Fleming, Ian, **Spy 67** 9, 12, 56-59

Fleming, John Ambrose, **Electronics 90** 28

Fleming's tube, **Electricity 77** 55, 63

fleur-de-lys, **Knight 43** 48

Fleurus, battle of, **Battle 63** 25

flies, **Evolution 85** 41, 49, 51; **Insect 17** 8, 15, 32-33

flight, **Invention 27** 58-59

Flinders, Matthew, **Explorer 31** 38-39

Flinders Petrie, W. M., **Pyramid 53** 14, 18

flint, **Archaeology 56** 24, 32, 50; **Building 58** 16; **Invention 27** 10, 11,18, 21; **Rock & Mineral 2** 15, 20, 21; **Technology 89** 10

flintworking, **Early People 10** 12, 13

mining, **Archaeology 56** 50

tools, **Early People 10** 18, 19, 27, 32; **Rock & Mineral 2** 28-29

weapons, **Arms & Armour 4** 6, 10; **Early People 10** 19, 26, 27

flintlocks, **Pirate 59** 28, 33

Flipper, **Whale 46** 10, 54

flippers, **Skeleton 3** 51

floats, **Boat 36** 6, 15, 43; **Flying Machine 22** 25, 38

flogging, **PIRATE 59** 39, 41

floods, **EVOLUTION 85** 10-11, 14, 16; **WEATHER 28** 31, 38

floors, **BUILDING 58** 44-45

plans, **BUILDING 58** 6

floppy discs, **FUTURE 100** 11

Florence, **PERSPECTIVE 98** 12; **RENAISSANCE 91** 12-13

Florey, Howard, **MEDICINE 88** 42

Florida, **EXPLORER 31** 32; **WHALE 46** 44

florins, **MONEY 18** 32, 36, 47, 51

flour, **FARM 66** 28, 30

flourescence, **CRYSTAL & GEM 25** 17

flowering plants, **FOSSIL 19** 13, 36, 38-39

flowers, **ARCTIC & ANTARCTIC 57** 9, 18; **CHINA 55** 54-55; **JUNGLE 54** 6, 24-25; **LIFE 84** 33, 38, 39, 41; **PLANT 14** 6, 7, 12-13

anthers, **PLANT 14** 9, 17, 19, 23

buds, **PLANT 14** 14, 17, 38

complex, **PLANT 14** 18-19

composite, **PLANT 14** 21, 30

petals, **PLANT 14** 9, 12, 20

sepals, **PLANT 14** 9, 12, 19, 26

simple, **PLANT 14** 16-17

stamens, **PLANT 14** 16, 17, 27

see also under individual flowers

Floyer, John, **MEDICINE 88** 28, 29

fluid theory, **ENERGY 76** 18-19, 44

fluorescence, **ENERGY 76** 43; **LIGHT 75** 45

fluorescent lights, **ELECTRICITY 77** 47, 62

fluorine, **CHEMISTRY 79** 26, 27, 33, 34, 40

fluorites, **CRYSTAL & GEM 25** 18, 21, 42, 57; **ROCK & MINERAL 2** 49

flutes, **ANCIENT EGYPT 23** 51; **AZTEC 47** 56, 57; **MUSIC 12** 6, 9, 10-11; **VIKING 50** 50

flycatchers, **BIRD 1** 22, 60

flying fishes, **FISH 20** 31

flying foxes, **SKELETON 3** 50

flying machines, **FLYING MACHINE 22**; **TECHNOLOGY 89** 6-7

"Flying Scotsman", **TRAIN 39** 13

flying squads, **CRIME & DETECTION 73** 55

flying squirrels, **MAMMAL 11** 29

flywheel, **TECHNOLOGY 89** 36

FM, **ELECTRONICS 90** 34, 48, 49, 53

foals, **HORSE 33** 10-11, 14-15

fob, **COSTUME 35** 40

focal length, **LIGHT 75** 16, 19, 20, 22

fo'c'sle, **BOAT 36** 49

fodder, **FARM 66** 34-36, 45, 59

fog, **DESERT 51** 6, 19; **SHIPWRECK 72** 10; **WEATHER 28** 23, 48-49, 56

foghorns, **BOAT 36** 58; **SHIPWRECK 72** 34, 36

Fokine, Mikhail, **RUSSIA 74** 48

Fokker Triplane, **FLYING MACHINE 22** 18

folk dances, **DANCE 99** 8, 9, 47, 49

folk music, **MUSIC 12** 10, 12, 16

Russia, **MUSIC 12** 37

Scandinavia, **MUSIC 12** 28

Spain, **MUSIC 12** 42, 56

Fontainebleau, Forest of, **MONET 95** 10

fontanelles, **SKELETON 3** 28

fontanges, **COSTUME 35** 28

food, **ANCIENT ROME 24** 44, 45, 46, 47; **ECOLOGY 86** 30, 31; **ENERGY 76** 14, 25, 50, 51; **TECHNOLOGY 89** 46-47, 50; **VIKING 50** 34-35

canning, **INVENTION 27** 6

as currency, **EARLY PEOPLE 10** 56

dehydrated, **FUTURE 100** 38

energy, **ENERGY 76** 6, 52-53

medieval, **MEDIEVAL LIFE 65** 18-21, 54

prehistoric, **EARLY PEOPLE 10** 8-9, 26, 28

food chain, **AFRICA 61** 14-15, 18-19; **ARCTIC & ANTARCTIC 57** 47, 63; **ECOLOGY 86** 12, 38, 39, 42; **LIFE 84** 20, 21

foodweb, **ECOLOGY 86** 13, 38, 58

primitive, **EARLY PEOPLE 10** 8-9, 10, 26; 28

in seas, **OCEAN 62** 26-29

food mixer, **INVENTION 27** 54, 55

foot rule, **TIME & SPACE 81** 11, 54

football, **CHINA 55** 50

footprints, **FOSSIL 19** 6, 58; **PREHISTORIC LIFE 52** 10, 34, 55, 62

footwear, **COSTUME 35** 24-25

foraminifers, **FOSSIL 19** 41; **SHELL 9** 44

Forbidden City, **CHINA 55** 20, 63

force, **FORCE & MOTION 78**; **MATTER 80** 60-61; **TECHNOLOGY 89** 20-21, 22, 32; **TIME & SPACE 81** 17, 19, 32

atomic, **TIME & SPACE 81** 59

centrifugal, **TIME & SPACE 81** 47; **FORCE & MOTION 78** 52-53

centripetal, **FORCE & MOTION 78** 52-53

equal and opposite, **FORCE & MOTION 30**, 31, 37

gravity, **TIME & SPACE 81** 28-29, 42

forceps, **MEDICINE 88** 8, 19, 25, 27

Ford, **CAR 21** 16, 24, 29, 54

Ford, Harrison, **CINEMA 34** 33, 59

Ford, Henry, **CAR 21** 16, 17; **TECHNOLOGY 89** 34, 42

Ford, John, **CINEMA 34** 58

forecastles, **PIRATE 59** 20, 29

forensic science, **CHEMISTRY 79** 6, 43; **CRIME & DETECTION 73** 40-41, 42-44

forests, **DINOSAUR 13** 10, 11, 14; **ECOLOGY 86** 8, 17, 23, 34; **ELEPHANT 42** 7, 29; **RUSSIA 74** 11, 14, 15

canopy, **JUNGLE 54** 12-13

coniferous, **ECOLOGY 86** 44-45, 52

deciduous, **ECOLOGY 86** 44-45, 63

destruction, **ECOLOGY 86** 44, 56

floor, **JUNGLE 54** 14-15

rainforests, **ECOLOGY 86** 56-57; **JUNGLE 54** 6-7

African, **JUNGLE 54** 40

Australasian, **JUNGLE 54** 56-57

South American, **JUNGLE 54** 30-31

temperate, **ECOLOGY 86** 7, 8, 44-45

types, **JUNGLE 54** 8-9

see also deforestation

forgeries, **CRIME & DETECTION 73** 20, 21, 59; **MONEY 18** 16, 17, 18, 19; **SPY 67** 56

forget-me-nots, **POND & RIVER 6** 15

Forrest, Earle, **COWBOY 45** 61

Forsyth, Frederick, **SPY 67** 58

Fort Wagner, battle of, **BATTLE 63** 51

fortifications, **BATTLE 63** 32, 54-55

forts, **ANCIENT ROME 24** 12, 14; **KNIGHT 43** 22; **VIKING 50** 22-23

fortune-telling, **CHINA 55** 51; **WITCH & WIZARD 70** 36, 37, 50, 55; **WRITING 48** 11

forum, **ANCIENT ROME 24** 17

Fossey, Dr. Dian, **GORILLA 64** 46, 60

fossil fuels, **ECOLOGY 86** 17, 19, 59, 60; **ENERGY 76** 50, 54-55, 57; **FUTURE 100** 16-19, 24; **OCEAN 62** 60-61; **RUSSIA 74** 14, 15

alternatives, **ENERGY 76** 6, 12, 58, 60

carbon cycle, **CHEMISTRY 79** 50, 51

fossilization, **CRYSTAL & GEM 25** 41, 54

fossils, **ECOLOGY 86** 24, 37; **FOSSIL 19**; **LIFE 84** 12, 13, 42; **MATTER 80** 28, 40; **TIME & SPACE 81** 21, 24

dogs, **DOG 32** 8, 9

early mammals, **MAMMAL 11** 12-15, 50

evidence, **EVOLUTION 85** 26-27, 55, 60

fish, **FISH 20** 9, 12, 13, 56

geological periods, **EVOLUTION 85** 16, 17, 60-63

intermediates, **EVOLUTION 85** 42, 44-45, 46

mythical creatures, **EVOLUTION 85** 8, 9

in oceans, **ARCTIC & ANTARCTIC 57** 10; **OCEAN 62** 6-7

prehistoric, **PREHISTORIC LIFE 52** 62-63

in rocks, **EARTH 83** 19,62-63; **ROCK & MINERAL 2** 14, 34, 38-39

skeletons, **SKELETON 3** 12-13

whales, **WHALE 46** 8, 9

Foster, Jodie, **CRIME & DETECTION 73** 58

Foucault, Léon, **FORCE & MOTION 78** 47, 56; **LIGHT 75** 60, 61

foundations, **PYRAMID 53** 30, 31, 50

foundries, **WRITING 48** 37

Fouquet, Jean, **BUILDING 58** 19; **RENAISSANCE 91** 28

frame, **BUILDING 58** 10, 14, 62

Four Temperaments, The, **DANCE 99** 17

Fourier, Joseph, **ELECTRONICS 90** 14, 15

fourth dimension, **TIME & SPACE 81** 6, 34-35, 58

foustanella, **DANCE 99** 46

Fowler, John, **FARM 66** 12; **FORCE & MOTION 78** 40

fox, **DESERT 51** 34, 36, 37; **DOG 32** 14, 16-18, 28-29; **MAMMAL 11** 24, 29, 42, 53

Arctic, **ARCTIC & ANTARCTIC 57** 16-17, 52; **DOG 32** 30; **MAMMAL 11** 21

desert, **DOG 32** 31

skeletons, **SKELETON 3** 40, 52

tracks, **MAMMAL 11** 61, 63

zorros, **DOG 32** 32, 33

foxgloves, **PLANT 14** 59

foxhounds, **DOG 32** 48

fractional distillation, **CHEMISTRY 79** 15, 32, 52-53

fractures, **SKELETON 3** 61

Fragonard, Jean-Honoré, **IMPRESSIONISM 92** 47

frames, **BUILDING 58** 10, 14, 62
France, **ANCIENT ROME 24** 26, 37, 50, 63;
    EXPLORER 31 11, 43;
    WEATHER 28 42; **WITCH & WIZARD 70** 13, 15, 39
    architecture,
        buildings, **BUILDING 58** 23-25, 27, 50
        châteaux, **BUILDING 58** 15, 38, 40, 49
    battles, **BATTLE 63** 42, 48, 58
        armour, **BATTLE 63** 27
        sappers, **BATTLE 63** 54-55
        weapons, **BATTLE 63** 30, 37, 43
    castles, **CASTLE 49** 14-15
    corsairs, **PIRATE 59** 50-51
    fashions, **COSTUME 35** 14, 26, 28, 31
    flags, **FLAG 16** 7, 18, 26-27
    money, **MONEY 18** 30, 31, 54
    Resistance, World War II, **SPY 67** 56, 57
Francis of Assisi, St., **MEDIEVAL LIFE 65** 37
Franciscan order, **MEDIEVAL LIFE 65** 37
François I, King of France, **BUILDING 58** 38;
    RENAISSANCE 91 47, 61
Franco-Prussian War, **BATTLE 63** 10, 29, 31, 50;
    IMPRESSIONISM 92 16, 17;
    MANET 94 43-45
Frankenstein, **WITCH & WIZARD 70** 18
frankincense, **ANCIENT EGYPT 23** 41
Franklin, Benjamin, **EARTH 83** 30; **ELECTRICITY 77** 7, 8;
    ENERGY 76 19;
    INVENTION 27 38;
    LIGHT 75 16
Franklin, Sir John, **ARCTIC & ANTARCTIC 57** 8, 52, 53;
    EXPLORER 31 40-41
Franklin, Rosalind, **EVOLUTION 85** 52; **LIFE 84** 35
Franks, **KNIGHT 43** 6;
    MEDIEVAL LIFE 65 6
Franks, Bobby, **CRIME & DETECTION 73** 23
Franzén, Anders, **SHIPWRECK 72** 27
Fraser-Smith, C., **SPY 67** 12, 59
fraud, **CRIME & DETECTION 73** 18, 19, 31, 59
Fraunhofer, Josef von, **ASTRONOMY 82** 30, 32;
    LIGHT 75 44, 45
Frederick I, Holy Roman Emperor, **MEDIEVAL LIFE 65** 7
Frederick II, Holy Roman Emperor, **KNIGHT 43** 50;
    MEDIEVAL LIFE 65 26

Frederick the Great, **BATTLE 63** 12, 48, 62;
    SPY 67 30
Frederick the Wise, **RENAISSANCE 91** 43, 58, 60
Frederick, Prince, **BOAT 36** 33
Freedom space station, **SPACE EXPLORATION 71** 59
freemen, **VIKING 50** 28
    freight, **TRAIN 39** 26-27, 48, 49
freighters, **BOAT 36** 51
Frémont, John, **EXPLORER 31** 44
French Trotter, **HORSE 33** 38
frequency, **ENERGY 76** 35, 40-43; **FORCE & MOTION 78** 46, 48-49, 50, 51;
    LIGHT 75 42, 63
    high, **ELECTRONICS 90** 20, 40-41, 43
frequency modulation, see FM
frescoes, **ARCHAEOLOGY 56** 20-21; **BUILDING 58** 53, 59;
    RENAISSANCE 91 8, 24
Fresnel, Augustin, **LIGHT 75** 17, 36
Freud, Sigmund, **HUMAN BODY 87** 59, 63;
    MEDICINE 88 47
Frey, **VIKING 50** 52, 53, 62
friction, **ENERGY 76** 14, 31;
    FORCE & MOTION 78 18, 26, 38-39, 40
    heat, **ENERGY 76** 20, 21, 24
Friedman, William F., **SPY 67** 27
Friesian horse, **HORSE 33** 41
Friesland, **FLAG 16** 30
frigate birds, **BIRD 1** 29
frilled shark, **FISH 20** 58;
    SHARK 40 6, 55
Frobisher, Martin, **EXPLORER 31** 40
frog shells, **SHELL 9** 12
frogs, **JUNGLE 54** 19; **LIFE 84** 30, 53; **POND & RIVER 6** 8, 9, 38, 39; **REPTILE 26** 7
    African bullfrog, **AMPHIBIAN 41** 30, 44,
    American bullfrog, **AMPHIBIAN 41** 22-23, 27
    Asian bullfrog, **AMPHIBIAN 41** 54-55
    Asian painted, **AMPHIBIAN 41** 21, 30, 45
    bones, **SKELETON 3** 21, 30, 56
    camouflage, **AMPHIBIAN 41** 14-15, 20-21
    diet, **AMPHIBIAN 41** 6, 18-19, 58
    European, **AMPHIBIAN 41** 6, 36, 42-43
    evolution of, **EVOLUTION 85** 35, 44, 61
    flying, **AMPHIBIAN 41** 50-51
    fossils, **FOSSIL 19** 20, 42, 43
    hibernation, **AMPHIBIAN 41** 38,

North American leopard, **AMPHIBIAN 41** 24-27
    poisonous, **AMPHIBIAN 41** 56, 57; **JUNGLE 54** 35
    rare, **AMPHIBIAN 41** 60-61
    Reinwardt's flying, **JUNGLE 54** 54
    reproduction, **AMPHIBIAN 41** 32, 36-37, 40
    senses, **AMPHIBIAN 41** 22-23
    tomato, **JUNGLE 54** 33
    tree, **JUNGLE 54** 12, 29, 57
    treefrogs, **AMPHIBIAN 41** 24, 50-53, 59
    vocal sacs, **AMPHIBIAN 41** 33, 37
    see also amphibians, tadpoles
Froissart, Jean, **KNIGHT 43** 44;
    WRITING 48 27
frost, **DESERT 51** 6;
    WEATHER 28 20, 21
fruits, **EARLY PEOPLE 10** 9, 26;
    JUNGLE 54 8, 26, 58-59;
    PLANT 14 26-27, 30, 31;
    PREHISTORIC LIFE 52 53;
    TREE 5 38-41
    farming of, **FARM 66** 6, 38, 39 62
Fry, Elizabeth, **MEDICINE 88** 56
fuel, **MATTER 80** 40, 61;
    ENERGY 76 37, 54; **FORCE & MOTION 78** 40, 41; **SPACE EXPLORATION 71** 14, 15;
    TECHNOLOGY 89 53
    in cars,
        fuselage, **CAR 21** 32, 48
        injection, **CAR 21** 27, 44, 48, 49
        system, **CAR 21** 17, 38
    see also petrol
Fulani peoples, **AFRICA 61** 44-45, 46, 47;
    DESERT 51 47, 48, 57
fulcrum, **FORCE & MOTION 78** 16, 17, 34
Fuller, Buckminster, **FORCE & MOTION 78** 43;
    MATTER 80 41
fulmars, **BIRD 1** 51
fumaroles, **VOLCANO 38** 36-37
funeral pyres, **VIKING 50** 54, 55
funerals, **AFRICA 61** 40;
    ANCIENT ROME 24 30, 56, 57; **PYRAMID 53** 24, 28;
    RELIGION 68 9, 16, 33
fungi, **ECOLOGY 86** 14, 15, 40, 44; **LIFE 84** 32, 50, 51, 57;
    PLANT 14 6;
    POND & RIVER 6 19, 54
    tree, **TREE 5** 19, 20, 48, 49
funnels, **BOAT 36** 52
"funny bone", **SKELETON 3** 48
fur, **ARCHAEOLOGY 56** 30-31, 45;
    ARCTIC & ANTARCTIC 57 16, 17, 32, 49; **LIFE 84** 26, 53;
    WHALE 46 7, 15, 16, 58

clothes, **COSTUME 35** 6, 15, 16, 39; **RUSSIA 74** 14, 23
grooming, **MAMMAL 11** 44-47
mammalian, **MAMMAL 11** 20-21
tails, **MAMMAL 11** 28-29
furnaces, **INVENTION 27** 14, 15, 25; **TECHNOLOGY 89** 13, 16, 62
furniture, **ANCIENT ROME 24** 24, 25, 46
fuselage, **FLYING MACHINE 22** 23, 27, 34, 59
fusion, **ENERGY 76** 46, 48, 49
future, **FUTURE 100**;
    SPACE EXPLORATION 71 54-55, 58-59
Futurism, in art, **PERSPECTIVE 98** 54-55
Fyodorov, Ivan, **RUSSIA 74** 43
Fyrkat, **VIKING 50** 14, 22, 23

Gabon, **AFRICA 61** 40, 41, 47, 53
Gabriel, Archangel, **RELIGION 68** 56, 57
Gachet, Paul, **IMPRESSIONISM 92** 42
gadgets, **SPY 67** 12-21
gagaku, **DANCE 99** 36
Gagarin, Yuri, **ASTRONOMY 82** 34;
    EXPLORER 31 58;
    FUTURE 100 10; **RUSSIA 74** 41; **SPACE EXPLORATION 71** 19, 26
Gage, Phineas, **HUMAN BODY 87** 60
Gagnan, Emile, **SHIPWRECK 72** 46
gahnite, **CRYSTAL & GEM 25** 46
Gaia, **ANCIENT GREECE 37** 20
Gainsborough, Thomas, **DOG 32** 59;
    WATERCOLOUR 97 40

gaiters, COSTUME 35 37
gaits, HORSE 33 61
galagos, *see* bushbabies
galah, DESERT 51 30
Galapagos rift, VOLCANO 38 25
galaxies, ASTRONOMY 82 26, 62-63; TIME & SPACE 81 7, 25, 48, 60
Galen, Claudius, HUMAN BODY 87 8, 9, 10; MEDICINE 88 17, 18, 21, 24
galena, CRYSTAL & GEM 25 12, 18, 21, 53, 62; ROCK & MINERAL 2 48, 49, 57
gales, WEATHER 28 42, 43, 44
Galilee, Sea of, BIBLE LANDS 30 7, 30; RELIGION 68 49, 51
Galileo Galilei, ELECTRONICS 90 15; ENERGY 76 15; MATTER 80 13; TECHNOLOGY 89 32
microscopes, HUMAN BODY 87 12
moons, ASTRONOMY 82 51, 53; LIGHT 75 61
pressure, WEATHER 28 10
projectiles, FORCE & MOTION 78 26, 27
science of motion, FORCE & MOTION 78 24, 25
telescope, ASTRONOMY 82 20; INVENTION 27 28; LIGHT 75 20, 21; SPACE EXPLORATION 71 8
Galileo space probes, ASTRONOMY 82 58; SPACE EXPLORATION 71 43
gall bladder, HUMAN BODY 87 35, 36-37
Gall, Dr. Franz, CRIME & DETECTION 73 52
Gall, Franz Joseph, MEDICINE 88 46
Galla peoples, AFRICA 61 36
Galle, Johann, ASTRONOMY 82 56
galleons, BOAT 36 15; PIRATE 59 6, 20, 23
galleys, BOAT 36 20, 21; PIRATE 59 8-9, 14-15
galliard, DANCE 99 8
Gallimimus, DINOSAUR 13 36
gallows, CRIME & DETECTION 73 14, 16; PIRATE 59 56
galls, INSECT 17 42, 43, 61; TREE 5 41, 50
Galton, Francis, CRIME & DETECTION 73 44
Galvani, Luigi, ELECTRICITY 77 16, 24, 50; HUMAN BODY 87 22, 58; INVENTION 27 38; LIFE 84 23; MEDICINE 88 36

galvanometers, ELECTRICITY 77 24, 31, 34, 35; ELECTRONICS 90 10, 24; ENERGY 76 53
Gama, Vasco da, EARTH 83 34; EXPLORER 31 20, 63; MEDIEVAL LIFE 65 63
gambling, CRIME & DETECTION 73 14, 18, 25-26; EARLY PEOPLE 10 57; MEDIEVAL LIFE 65 54
game parks, AFRICA 61 6
gamebirds, BIRD 1 27, 38
gamelans, MUSIC 12 55
games, ANCIENT ROME 24 38; AFRICA 61 22-23; CHINA 55 50-51; VIKING 50 50
gametes, LIFE 84 38, 42
gamma rays, FUTURE 100 50; LIGHT 75 43
Gandhi, Mahatma, RELIGION 68 8, 36; WRITING 48 53
Ganesha, RELIGION 68 21
Ganges, River, RELIGION 68 9, 19, 20, 24
gangplanks, BOAT 36 49
gangs, CRIME & DETECTION 73 26, 50
Ganku, Kishi, CAT 29 31
gannets, BIRD 1 29, 40; SEASHORE 15 52, 54; SKELETON 3 30
Gaozu, Emperor, CHINA 55 18
Gapon, Father, RUSSIA 74 30
Garbo, Greta, CINEMA 34 23, 56
Garcia, G. S., COWBOY 45 11
garden eels, FISH 20 51
Garden of Eden, BIBLE LANDS 30 28
gardens, KNIGHT 43 37
garfish, FISH 20 11, 14
gargoyles, BUILDING 58 59
Garibaldi, FLAG 16 34
garlic, ANCIENT EGYPT 23 26
garnets, CRYSTAL & GEM 25 8, 44, 56, 57; EARTH 83 29, 40; ROCK & MINERAL 2 24, 25, 46, 55
Garrett, Elizabeth, MEDICINE 88 29
Garrett, Pat, COWBOY 45 45
garrisons, CASTLE 49 30-31
garrotting, CRIME & DETECTION 73 10
gars, FISH 20 9, 11, 14, 20
garters, COSTUME 35 36, 37, 42
gas, ENERGY 76 34, 35, 56, 61
lights, LIGHT 75 9, 52
natural, ENERGY 76 54, 55
gases, MATTER 80 7, 12, 20-21
atoms, MATTER 80 34, 37, 38
compounds, MATTER 80 26
noble, CHEMISTRY 79 20, 26, 32-33; MATTER 80 33
pressure, MATTER 80 39
states of matter, MATTER 80 22

Gassner, Carl, INVENTION 27 39
gastroliths, DINOSAUR 13 26
gastropods, FOSSIL 19 13, 15, 26, 27; SHELL 9 10-11, 12-15
gatehouses, KNIGHT 43 22, 24
gauchos, COWBOY 45 6, 12, 29, 48-51; HORSE 33 35
gauges, TRAIN 39 24, 25, 52
Gauguin, Paul, MONET 95 25; VAN GOGH 96 38, 39, 44-45; WATERCOLOUR 97 51
Gaul, ANCIENT ROME 24 11, 12, 47, 60
Gaulle, Charles de, *see* de Gaulle, Charles
Gaumont, Leon, CINEMA 34 21
gauntlets, ARMS & ARMOUR 4 25, 27, 36; KNIGHT 43 12-13, 15, 43; SPORT 8 17, 18, 50
Gauss, Karl, TIME & SPACE 81 40-41
Gaza, BIBLE LANDS 30 12
gazelles, DESERT 51 34, 46; MAMMAL 11 10, 26, 58
gazettas, MONEY 18 41
gears, FORCE & MOTION 78 20-23, 46, 53; TECHNOLOGY 89 21, 32-33, 34
gears, cars, CAR 21 39, 52, 53
changing, CAR 21 7, 27, 38
gearbox, CAR 21 38, 53
pulleys, CAR 21 6, 7
Gebel Barkal, PYRAMID 53 48, 53
geckos, DESERT 51 36; JUNGLE 54 40, 54; REPTILE 26 16, 20, 50-51, 55
leopard, REPTILE 26 29
geese, ANCIENT EGYPT 23 32, 61; ARCTIC & ANTARCTIC 57 14-15, 20; BIRD 1 15, 20, 33, 38; FARM 66 40, 60
Geffroy, Gustave, MONET 95 36, 59, 61
Geiger counters, MATTER 80 47, 53; TIME & SPACE 81 50, 51
Geissler, Johann H. W., LIGHT 75 52
Gelderlander, Dutch, HORSE 33 35, 40
gelding, HORSE 33 12
Gemini spacecraft, SPACE EXPLORATION 71 18, 27
gems, CRYSTAL & GEM 25 48-49, 58-59
gemstones, ROCK & MINERAL 2 6, 50-55; VOLCANO 38 39
cutting, ROCK & MINERAL 2 60-61
generators, ELECTRICITY 77 6; ENERGY 76 32, 34, 61; FORCE & MOTION 78 40, 51; TECHNOLOGY 89 35, 36

genes, EVOLUTION 85 50, 51, 52, 57; GORILLA 64 9; HUMAN BODY 87 13, 45, 48; LIFE 84 32, 33, 38, 50
DNA, LIFE 84 36, 37
dominant, EVOLUTION 85 33, 51
evolution, LIFE 84 42, 43
genetic code, EVOLUTION 85 47, 52, 55, 56
heredity, LIFE 84 40
origin, LIFE 84 57
recessive, EVOLUTION 85 33, 51
see also genetic engineering, genetics
genet, CAT 29 45
genetic engineering, FARM 66 28, 62, 63; FUTURE 100 36-39, 58, 59; LIFE 84 60-61
genetics, EVOLUTION 85 41, 58; FUTURE 100 10, 11, 34-36; LIFE 84 11, 34-37, 40; TECHNOLOGY 89 44, 60-61
research, MEDICINE 88 62, 63
variation, LIFE 84 32, 38, 39
see also genes, genetic engineering
Genghis Khan, BATTLE 63 14; FLAG 16 17; HORSE 33 32; RUSSIA 74 8, 9; SPY 67 9; CHINA 55 58
Genoa, PIRATE 59 14
genotype, LIFE 84 40, 41
geocentric universe, ASTRONOMY 82 11, 17, 18, 19, 51
geodes, CRYSTAL & GEM 25 63
geographical zones, ECOLOGY 86 7, 34
geography cone shells, SHELL 9 12
geology, ECOLOGY 86 22
periods in, EVOLUTION 85 17, 46, 61-63
geometrid moths, BUTTERFLY & MOTH 7 15, 49
geometry, TIME & SPACE 81 10, 14, 26
Euclidian, TIME & SPACE 81 40, 41
spacetime, TIME & SPACE 81 34, 35
George II, King of England, BATTLE 63 49; BOAT 36 33
George III, King of England, PIRATE 59 18
George IV, King of England, WITCH & WIZARD 70 15
George, St., CASTLE 49 30; FLAG 16 46, 47; KNIGHT 43 40; MEDIEVAL LIFE 65 59; RUSSIA 74 9, 21, 46
Georgia, RUSSIA 74 9, 12, 22
Georgian ballet, DANCE 99 29
geostationary orbit, ASTRONOMY 82 34

geothermal energy, **ENERGY 76** 58, 59
geothite, **CRYSTAL & GEM 25** 22
Gerasimov, Mikhail, **CRIME & DETECTION 73** 48
gerbils, **DESERT 51** 32; **MAMMAL 11** 9, 54, 56
Géricault, Théodore, **SHIPWRECK 72** 38
German shepherds, **DOG 32** 18, 42, 45, 60
Germany, **ANCIENT ROME 24** 8, 13; **BATTLE 63** 29, 31, 50, 55; **SPACE EXPLORATION 71** 15
architecture, **BUILDING 58** 22, 28, 36, 51
castles, **CASTLE 49** 18-21
currency, **MONEY 18** 25, 32, 33, 44
flags of, **FLAG 16** 28-29
magic, **WITCH & WIZARD 70** 13, 16, 22, 23
germs, **MEDICINE 88** 32-33, 34-35
Geronimo, **NORTH AMERICAN INDIAN 60** 48
Gervex, Henri, **IMPRESSIONISM 92** 18
Gestapo, **SPY 67** 56
gestation, **SHARK 40** 23
geysers, **EARTH 83** 40; **VOLCANO 38** 7, 12, 36-37
Gezer, **BIBLE LANDS 30** 20
Ghana, **AFRICA 61** 48, 54, 56, 60
Asante kingdom, **AFRICA 61** 43, 46
rulers, **AFRICA 61** 30, 32
Ghiberti, Lorenzo, **RENAISSANCE 91** 12, 14, 61
Ghirlandaio, Domenico, **RENAISSANCE 91** 13, 54
ghost crabs, **SHELL 9** 3
ghost dance, **DANCE 99** 18
ghost moths, **BUTTERFLY & MOTH 7** 53
giant African river snails, **SHELL 9** 13
giant gars, **FISH 20** 13
Giant Hugo, **SKELETON 3** 58
giant panda, **ECOLOGY 86** 27
giant pen shells, **SHELL 9** 17
Giant's Causeway, **CRYSTAL & GEM 25** 22; **ROCK & MINERAL 2** 16, 17
gibbets, **PIRATE 59** 57
gibbons, **GORILLA 64** 30-31, 32, 51; **JUNGLE 54** 44-45; **SKELETON 3** 51, 56
Gibraltar, **EXPLORER 31** 6; **GORILLA 64** 58
Gibson Desert, **DESERT 51** 7
Giffard, Henri, **FLYING MACHINE 22** 9
Gifford, Gilbert, **SPY 67** 28
Gila monsters, **DESERT 51** 28
Gilbert, John, **CINEMA 34** 20, 23, 29

Gilbert, Dr. William, **ENERGY 76** 22, 23
Gill, Eric, **WRITING 48** 45
Gillette, King C., **TECHNOLOGY 89** 39
Gillray, James, **WATERCOLOUR 97** 30
gills, **FISH 20** 8-9; **SHARK 40** 11, 32, 34, 36
operculum, **SHARK 40** 7-8, 28
ginger, **JUNGLE 54** 58
ginger cat, **CAT 29** 54
ginkgos, **FOSSIL 19** 60
ginseng, **MEDICINE 88** 15
Giorgione, **RENAISSANCE 91** 35, 46
Giotto di Bondone, **PERSPECTIVE 98** 10; **RENAISSANCE 91** 8-9
Giotto space probes, **ASTRONOMY 82** 59; **SPACE EXPLORATION 71** 44
Giovanni da Udine, **RENAISSANCE 91** 51
Giovanni di Paolo, **RENAISSANCE 91** 23
Gir forest, **CAT 29** 28
giraffes, **DINOSAUR 13** 14; **MAMMAL 11** 10, 48; **SKELETON 3** 59
girdles, **COSTUME 35** 13, 15
Girtin, Thomas, **WATERCOLOUR 97** 32, 33
Gish, Lillian, **CINEMA 34** 20
Gita, see Bhagavad Gita
Giverny, **MONET 95** 34-35, 52-53
Giza, **ANCIENT EGYPT 23** 11, 20-21; **MUMMY 44** 7, 36; **PYRAMID 53** 6, 26-27, 50
The Great Pyramid, **PYRAMID 53** 20-21
Pharaohs, **PYRAMID 53** 18, 19
pyramids, **PYRAMID 53** 16-17
gizzards, **BIRD 1** 8, 38
glaciers, **ARCTIC & ANTARCTIC 57** 9; **EARTH 83** 12, 18, 58-59; **ROCK & MINERAL 2** 13
gladiators, **ANCIENT ROME 24** 17, 28, 30-31; **ARMS & ARMOUR 4** 13
Glashow, Sheldon, **FORCE & MOTION 78** 63
glasnost, **RUSSIA 74** 36, 58
glass catfish, **FISH 20** 10
glass, **ARCHAEOLOGY 56** 8-9, 59; **BUILDING 58** 48; **CHEMISTRY 79** 10; **CRYSTAL & GEM 25** 7, 30, 57; **EARTH 83** 24, 25
jewellery, **VIKING 50** 26, 46, 47
making of, **TECHNOLOGY 89** 8-9, 29, 57
manufacture, **CHEMISTRY 79** 11, 13, 45, 62; **INVENTION 27** 6; **MATTER 80** 24-25
stained glass, **BUILDING 58** 50-51

glassware, **ANCIENT ROME 24** 42, 46
glassworts, **DESERT 51** 11; **POND & RIVER 6** 58, 61
glauberite, **CRYSTAL & GEM 25** 41
glazes, **BUILDING 58** 42, 44
Gleyre, Charles, **IMPRESSIONISM 92** 10-11, 12, 16; **MONET 95** 10
gliders, **FLYING MACHINE 22** 10-11, 58-59, 60
gliding, **JUNGLE 54** 54-55
global warming, **ECOLOGY 86** 16, 19; **FUTURE 100** 15; **WEATHER 28** 60, 61
glomerulus, **HUMAN BODY 87** 12, 38
Glossopteris, **FOSSIL 19** 37
gloves, **COSTUME 35** 21, 27, 39, 57; **SPACE EXPLORATION 71** 30, 31; **SPORT 8** 22, 26, 37, 57
glucose, **LIFE 84** 8, 9, 16
photosynthesis, **LIFE 84** 17
respiration, **LIFE 84** 18-19
glue, **TECHNOLOGY 89** 9, 18, 25
glycerine, **WATERCOLOUR 97** 7
glyphs, **PYRAMID 53** 56-57, 58-59
gnats, **POND & RIVER 6** 16
gneiss, **EARTH 83** 29; **ROCK & MINERAL 2** 10, 11, 25
gnomons, **ASTRONOMY 82** 14, 38
goalkeepers, **SPORT 8** 7, 16
goatherd, **FARM 66** 54
goats, **DESERT 51** 42, 46, 59, 60; **FARM 66** 6, 45, 54, 55; **MAMMAL 11** 10; **SKELETON 3** 34
Gobi Desert, **DESERT 51** 7, 38, 49, 63
gobies, **FISH 20** 50, 51; **SEASHORE 15** 34, 35, 51
Godafoss, **VIKING 50** 53
Goddard, Robert, **ASTRONOMY 82** 34
Godiva, Lady, **HORSE 33** 46
gods, **ANCIENT EGYPT 23** 24-25; **VIKING 50** 7, 14, 52-53
see also under individual names
Godunov, Boris, **RUSSIA 74** 20, 44
Goes, Hugo van der, **RENAISSANCE 91** 20, 21
Goethe, Johann von, **EVOLUTION 85** 13; **WITCH & WIZARD 70** 16
goggles, **ARCTIC & ANTARCTIC 57** 53, 57
Gogh, Vincent van, *see* Van Gogh, Vincent
Gogol, Nikolai, **RUSSIA 74** 44
gold, **CHEMISTRY 79** 15, 18, 46, 47; **MATTER 80** 11, 16, 17; **MUMMY 44** 43, 45; **RUSSIA 74** 19, 24, 28; **TECHNOLOGY 89** 12, 30
archaeological finds, **ARCHAEOLOGY 56** 8, 21, 26, 50

arts and crafts, **AZTEC 47** 50; **CHINA 55** 56
Asante, **AFRICA 61** 56-57
gold rush, **ROCK & MINERAL 2** 6, 58, 59; **RUSSIA 74** 14
jewellery, **ANCIENT EGYPT 23** 56; **AZTEC 47** 51; **CHINA 55** 48; **VIKING 50** 6, 46, 47
masks, **AZTEC 47** 54; **MUMMY 44** 18
prospecting, **MATTER 80** 26
purity of, **CRYSTAL & GEM 25** 52
threads, **COSTUME 35** 11, 16, 17, 21
treasures, **PIRATE 59** 22, 36, 46
Gold Coast, **AFRICA 61** 10
gold dust, **MONEY 18** 29, 50
gold leaf, **WRITING 48** 29, 47
Goldberg, Whoopi, **CINEMA 34** 29
Golden Temple, **RELIGION 68** 38
goldfish, **FISH 20** 18
Goldwyn, Samuel, **CINEMA 34** 28
golf, **SPORT 8** 58-61
Goliath, **BIBLE LANDS 30** 44
gondolas, **BOAT 36** 21, 32, 34
Gondwana, **FOSSIL 19** 12, 37
gongs, **MUSIC 12** 6, 54
goniometers, **CRYSTAL & GEM 25** 12
Gonzaga family, **RENAISSANCE 91** 26
Goodnight, Charles, **COWBOY 45** 37, 39
Goodyear, Charles, **CHEMISTRY 79** 52
goose, *see* geese
Gorbachev, Mikhail, **RUSSIA 74** 36, 58, 59
Gordievsky, Oleg, **SPY 67** 35, 43
Gorgosaurus, **DINOSAUR 13** 25
gorillas, **GORILLA 64** 8, 36, 42-49; **JUNGLE 54** 41, 44
babies, **GORILLA 64** 48-49
communication, **GORILLA 64** 32, 33, 37
defences, **GORILLA 64** 34, 42, 43
family life, **GORILLA 64** 44-45, 46
food, **GORILLA 64** 42, 44, 45, 47
intelligence, **GORILLA 64** 36-37
mating, **GORILLA 64** 32
nests, **GORILLA 64** 44, 45, 47
poaching of, **GORILLA 64** 62-63
Gorm, King, **VIKING 50** 60, 61
gospel, **RELIGION 68** 50, 51
Gossaert, Jan, **RENAISSANCE 91** 58, 59
Gosse, Philips, **SEASHORE 15** 30, 32
Gothic, art, **RENAISSANCE 91** 6, 10, 16-17
script, **WRITING 48** 51
type, **WRITING 48** 43, 44

Goths, MEDIEVAL LIFE 65 6
Gotland, VIKING 50 18, 27, 29, 58
Gould, Stephen Jay,
    EVOLUTION 85 58
gourds, AFRICA 61 20, 60, 61;
    AZTEC 47 22, 23, 57;
    DESERT 51 47; PLANT 14 38
Gouzenko, Igor, SPY 67 35
governors,
    FORCE & MOTION 78 53
Gowers, William,
    MEDICINE 88 31
gowns, COSTUME 35 12, 16, 30, 38
Goya, Francisco de, GOYA 93;
    MANET 94 36, 42, 46
    "black" paintings, GOYA 93
    50-55
    cartoons, GOYA 93 12-13, 20-21
    The Circumcision, GOYA 93 9
    The Disasters of War,
    GOYA 93 28, 40-41
    Dona Isabel de Porcel,
    GOYA 93 37
    frescoes, GOYA 93 32-33
    The Great He-Goat,
    GOYA 93 50-51
    "House of the Deaf Man",
    GOYA 93 48-50, 54, 56
    The Majas, GOYA 93 36
    The Milkmaid of Bordeaux,
    GOYA 93 58, 59
    Self-portrait with Dr. Arrieta,
    GOYA 93 46-47
    self-portraits, GOYA 93 7, 26,
    43, 57
    Tío Paquete, GOYA 93 49
    The Witches Sabbath,
    GOYA 93 31, 51
Goya, Javier, GOYA 93 22, 26, 60
Gozan, BIBLE LANDS 30 29, 44
Gozzoli, CAT 29 32
Graafian follicle,
    HUMAN BODY 87 43
Grace, W.G., SPORT 8 28
gradients, TRAIN 39 20, 22, 23, 39
Grafton Galleries, London,
    MONET 95 48
Graham, Martha, DANCE 99
    10, 55, 56, 57
grain, EARLY PEOPLE 10 8, 31;
    FARM 66 6, 62
    cereals, FARM 66 28-29
    harvesting, FARM 66 20-21
    storage, FARM 66 42-43
    threshing, FARM 66 22-25
    see also granaries
Gramme, Z. T., ELECTRICITY 77 37
Granada, CASTLE 49 16, 17
granaries, AFRICA 61 17;
    BUILDING 58 22; FARM 66
    32, 40-43
Grand Canal, CHINA 55 7,
    38-39, 60
Grand Canyon, DESERT 51 11;
    EARTH 83 48; EXPLORER 31
    33; FOSSIL 19 8; ROCK &
    MINERAL 2 21

Grand Central Station,
    TRAIN 39 48
granite, BUILDING 58 16, 18;
    DESERT 51 9; EARTH 83 7, 25,
    48, 51; PYRAMID 53 32, 34;
    SEASHORE 15 9, 63
    rock, CRYSTAL & GEM 25 8,
    30, 39, 43;
    ROCK & MINERAL 2 8, 13,
    16, 42; VOLCANO 38 8
Grant, Cary, CINEMA 34 27
Grant, Professor Robert,
    EVOLUTION 85 20
granulated brittlestars,
    SKELETON 3 24
grapes, ANCIENT EGYPT 23 48
graphic equalizers,
    ELECTRONICS 90 17
graphite, CHEMISTRY 79 27, 48;
    CRYSTAL & GEM 25 14;
    MATTER 80 40, 41;
    ROCK & MINERAL 2 48
graptolites, FOSSIL 19 12
grass, ARCTIC & ANTARCTIC 57
    9, 19, 36; FARM 66 14, 28, 35,
    54; POND & RIVER 6 61;
    SEASHORE 15 8, 13, 17
    eel grass, POND & RIVER 6
    47, 58
    reed grass, POND & RIVER 6 6
grasshoppers, INSECT 17 8, 13,
    22, 26
grassland, ECOLOGY 86 7, 8,
    48-49; FARM 66 16
grassland butterflies,
    BUTTERFLY & MOTH 7 28
Grauballe Man, FOSSIL 19 21
grave goods, ARCHAEOLOGY 56
    23, 30-31; MUMMY 44 30-31
    status symbols,
    ARCHAEOLOGY 56 6, 26-27
gravestones, VIKING 50 57
Gravey, Marcus, FLAG 16 54
gravitation, ASTRONOMY 82 37,
    55, 63
gravity, ASTRONOMY 82 21, 35,
    45, 62; ENERGY 76 14, 15, 22,
    44; FORCE & MOTION 78 27,
    32-33, 47, 53; MATTER 80
    60-61, 63
    Big Bang, ENERGY 76 62-63
    black holes,
    TIME & SPACE 81 46, 47
    Einstein,
    FORCE & MOTION 78 60-63
    Jupiter, ASTRONOMY 82 58
    mass, ENERGY & MOTION 76 16
    Moon, ASTRONOMY 82 40, 42
    Neptune, ASTRONOMY 82 56;
    TIME & SPACE 81 28-29
    Newton,
    FORCE & MOTION 78
    28-29, 30
    Saturn, ASTRONOMY 82 53
    spacetime, SPACE
    EXPLORATION 71 30; TIME
    & SPACE 81 42-45

spinning top, FORCE &
    MOTION 78 56, 57
    Sun, ASTRONOMY 82 36
    weight, FORCE &
    MOTION 78 34-35
Gray, Asa, EVOLUTION 85 42
Gray, Elisha, ENERGY 76 39
Gray, Stephen,
    ELECTRICITY 77 10
Gray, Thomas, VOLCANO 38 54
grazing, ECOLOGY 86 35, 48
Great Barrier Reef,
    OCEAN 62 23, 25
Great Basin Desert,
    DESERT 51 6, 21, 27
Great Bear, ARCTIC &
    ANTARCTIC 57 37
great danes, DOG 32 14, 38,
    57, 60
Great Dividing Range,
    EXPLORER 31 38
great green turban shells,
    SHELL 9 13
Great Lakes, EARTH 83 12
great pond snails, SHELL 9 14
Great Pyramid,
    ANCIENT EGYPT 23 20-21,
    38; PYRAMID 53 16-17, 18,
    20-21
    construction, PYRAMID 53 30,
    32, 36
    layout, PYRAMID 53 23
    rooms, PYRAMID 53 22, 23, 24
Great Sandy Desert,
    DESERT 51 7, 9
Great Victoria Desert,
    DESERT 51 7
Great Wall of China, CHINA 55
    6, 16, 18, 60; ROCK &
    MINERAL 2 35
Great Western Railway,
    TRAIN 39 50, 55, 61
great white sharks, FISH 20
    59, 61
Great Zimbabwe, AFRICA 61 11;
    ARCHAEOLOGY 56 56
    see also Zimbabwe
Greater Swiss, DOG 32 44
Grebel, Stephen, CAR 21 21
grebes, BIRD 1 29, 51;
    POND & RIVER 6 30, 31
Greco, El, MANET 94 36
Greece, ANCIENT GREECE 37;
    ANCIENT ROME 24 6, 36,
    62-63; ARCHAEOLOGY 56 15;
    BIBLE LANDS 30 16, 54-55;
    PERSPECTIVE 98 8, 9;
    WHALE 46 6, 7, 32, 33
    art, ARCHAEOLOGY 56 17,
    48-49, 56
    astronomy, ASTRONOMY 82
    6-7, 14; SHIPWRECK 72 32
    astronomers,
    ASTRONOMY 82 10-11, 22
    battles, BATTLE 63 6, 44
    building, BUILDING 58 17, 18,
    32, 44

colonies, ANCIENT GREECE 37
    15, 26, 27, 42
    currency,
    MONEY 18 20, 23, 40, 41
    dances DANCE 99 9, 31, 44, 54
    dress, COSTUME 35 8, 9, 34, 60
    farming, FARM 66 6-8, 35, 52
    festivals, ANCIENT
    GREECE 37 24-25, 41, 50
    flags, FLAG 16 8, 38-39
    games, ANCIENT GREECE 37
    34-35, 44-45
    medicine, ANCIENT GREECE 37
    58-59; MEDICINE 88, 16-17, 50
    mummies,
    MUMMY 44 19, 42-43
    mythology, ANCIENT
    GREECE 37 8, 22, 39, 41
    philosophy, ANCIENT
    GREECE 37 36, 46-47, 58
    politics, ANCIENT GREECE 37
    6, 18-19, 30, 36
    religion, ANCIENT GREECE 37
    19, 20-23, 24; RELIGION 68
    12-13
    slaves, ANCIENT GREECE 37
    18, 32, 33, 34
    temples, ANCIENT GREECE 37
    17, 25, 26-27
    theatre, ANCIENT GREECE 37
    34, 38, 39
    trade, ANCIENT GREECE 37 10,
    14, 15, 52; ARCHAEOLOGY 56 21
    volcanoes,
    VOLCANO 38 19, 39
    witchcraft, WITCH &
    WIZARD 70 12, 17, 21, 37
Greek, language, WRITING 48
    10, 50
    alphabet, WRITING 48 15, 16
green silver-line moths,
    BUTTERFLY & MOTH 7 38
Green Table, The, DANCE 99 18
Greenaway, Kate,
    WATERCOLOUR 97 44
greenhouse effect,
    ASTRONOMY 82 42, 47;
    ECOLOGY 86 19
greenhouse gases,
    FUTURE 100 18;
    WEATHER 28 17, 61
greenhouses, FARM 66 36
Greenland, EXPLORER 31 12-13,
    57; MUMMY 44 7, 63;
    WEATHER 28 61;
    WHALE 46 37, 62
    Eric the Red, VIKING 50 21
    flags, FLAG 16 41
    Inuit peoples, ARCTIC &
    ANTARCTIC 57 8, 50
Greenpeace, FLAG 16 18
greenstone,
    CRYSTAL & GEM 25 51
Greenwich, England,
    ASTRONOMY 82 27
Greenwich Mean Time,
    WEATHER 28 13

grenades, ARMS & ARMOUR 4 52-53; BATTLE 63 36, 37; PIRATE 59 29
grenadiers, BATTLE 63 8, 37
Gresley, Sir Nigel, TRAIN 39 47
Grey, Zane, COWBOY 45 61
greyhounds, DOG 32 15, 34, 35, 46-49
Griffith, D. W., CINEMA 34 21, 39
griffons, EAGLE 69 35, 58
Grimaldi, Francesco, LIGHT 75 35, 36, 37
Grimaldi, Mary, WATERCOLOUR 97 23
Grimaldi, William, WATERCOLOUR 97 23
Grimes Graves, ARCHAEOLOGY 56 50
Grimm, Brothers, WITCH & WIZARD 70 18, 19
Grisi, Carlotta, DANCE 99 56
groats, MONEY 18 46
Gropius, Walter, PERSPECTIVE 98 57
gros, MONEY 18 34
grotesques, WRITING 48 28
ground loom, DESERT 51 59
grouper, FISH 20 47
grouse, BIRD 1 13, 19, 38, 52
Gruber, Dr. Samuel, SHARK 40 54
Grünewald, Matthias, RENAISSANCE 91 42, 43
Gryodus, DINOSAUR 13 58
Gryphaea, FOSSIL 19 16
guanaco, DESERT 51 43
guardrooms, KNIGHT 43 23
guards, TRAIN 39 29, 34, 50, 51
Guatemala, PYRAMID 53 56, 58; VOLCANO 38 13
gudgeons, POND & RIVER 6 25
guenons, GORILLA 64 22, 23, 25
guereza, GORILLA 64 24; JUNGLE 54 41
Guiana Plateau, OCEAN 62 8
guide dogs, DOG 32 45
guidon, FLAG 16 12, 42
guilds, MEDIEVAL LIFE 65 48, 50-52, 58
Guillemot, Maurice, MONET 95 60
guillemots, BIRD 1 18, 50; SKELETON 3 47
guimple, COSTUME 35 14
guinea pigs, SKELETON 3 17
guineas, MONEY 18 47
Guinevere, KNIGHT 43 41
guitarfish, SHARK 40 8-9
guitars, DANCE 99 17; MUSIC 12 26, 27
  acoustic MUSIC 12 42-43
  bass, MUSIC 12 60
  electric, MUSIC 12 58-59, 60-61
  Spanish, MUSIC 12 42
gulags, RUSSIA 74 35, 36, 39, 45
guldens, MONEY 18 32, 62

gullet, HUMAN BODY 87 24, 27, 34, 36
Gulliver's Travels, SPACE EXPLORATION 71 36
gulls, BIRD 1 16, 28, 33, 37; POND & RIVER 6 58; SEASHORE 15 34, 54-55, 60
  black-backed, SEASHORE 15 31
  herring, SEASHORE 15 52, 54
gulpers, FISH 20 48
gum arabic, WATERCOLOUR 97 6, 7, 10, 38
gun dogs, DOG 32 9, 16, 50, 51
gunbelts, ARMS & ARMOUR 4 60
gunboats, PIRATE 59 54
Gunnbjørn, VIKING 50 20
gunners, BATTLE 63 26-29, 34-35
gunpowder, ARMS & ARMOUR 4 38, 39, 46; BATTLE 63 28, 29, 46-47; CHEMISTRY 79 10, 38, 62; PIRATE 59 49
guns, BATTLE 63 46-49; COWBOY 45 22-23, 26-27, 44-46; CRIME & DETECTION 73 10, 11, 17, 58; SPY 67 24, 36, 54
  ancient, CASTLE 49 21, 36, 62-63; KNIGHT 43 30, 63
  ballistics, CRIME & DETECTION 73 42
  cannons, KNIGHT 43 60-61
  field, BATTLE 63 26-29; SPY 67 24
  Gatling, BATTLE 63 30-31
  gun ports, CASTLE 49 19, 29, 37
  gun-running, CRIME & DETECTION 73 26, 29
  lock-pick, SPY 67 59
  machine, BATTLE 63 30-31, 50; SPY 67 24, 54
  muskets, BATTLE 63 42-43
  piton, SPY 67 58, 59
  revolvers, BATTLE 63 43
  rifles, BATTLE 63 42, 43, 50-51
  Vickers, FLYING MACHINE 22 19, 23
  volley guns, BATTLE 63 46
gunwales, BOAT 36 10
gurnard, FISH 20 30, 32
Guru Granth Sahib, RELIGION 68 38, 39
Guru Nanak, RELIGION 68 38, 39
Gustavus Adolphus, King of Sweden, BATTLE 63 46
Gutenberg, Johannes, BIBLE LANDS 30 61; INVENTION 27 26, 27; TECHNOLOGY 89 48; WRITING 48 36, 39, 40
  bible, WRITING 48 43
  typeface, WRITING 48 44, 45
Guthrum, King, VIKING 50 17
gutters, BUILDING 58 28
Guys, Constantin, IMPRESSIONISM 92 8, 9

Guzman, Abimael, SPY 67 55
gwindel, CRYSTAL & GEM 25 31
gybing, BOAT 36 22
gymkhanas, HORSE 33 59
gymnastics, SPORT 8 42
gymnosperms, FOSSIL 19 38, 39
gypsies, HORSE 33 46-47
gypsum, CRYSTAL & GEM 25 18, 23; DESERT 51 9; EARTH 83 20, 21; ROCK & MINERAL 2 21, 45, 49
gyrfalcons, ARCTIC & ANTARCTIC 57 25
gyroscopes, FORCE & MOTION 78 56-57

H

Haber, Fritz, CHEMISTRY 79 39, 63
Habila peoples, AFRICA 61 16
habitat, ECOLOGY 86 7, 25, 26, 30; LIFE 84 33, 38, 53
Hades, ANCIENT GREECE 37 60; RELIGION 68 12, 13
Hadley, John, INVENTION 27 34
Hadrian, BIBLE LANDS 30 55
Hadrian's Wall, ANCIENT ROME 24 14, 40
Hadza peoples, AFRICA 61 18
haematology, MEDICINE 88 31
haemoglobin, CHEMISTRY 79 31, 51
haemophilia, MEDICINE 88 62
hagfish, FISH 20 8, 9, 12
Hague, The, VAN GOGH 96 6, 14-15, 16
Hahn, Otto, MATTER 80 54
hail, WEATHER 28 14
hailstones, WEATHER 28 36, 37
hair, HUMAN BODY 87 50, 51; MAMMAL 11 20-21, 27, 44-47
  hairstyles, COSTUME 35 18, 28-29, 59
  see also wigs
hairdriers, INVENTION 27 55

hairless dogs, DOG 32 36
hairy crabs, SHELL 9 27
halberds, CHINA 55 10, 15
Halder, Jacob, KNIGHT 43 15
Halema'uma'u, Hawaii, VOLCANO 38 22
halfbeaks, FISH 20 35
half-crowns, MONEY 18 51
halfpennies, MONEY 18 23, 28, 46, 48
halibut, FISH 20 25
halite, CRYSTAL & GEM 25 26
Hall, Asaph, ASTRONOMY 82 49
Hall, Chester Moor, INVENTION 27 28
Halley, Edmond, FORCE & MOTION 78 32; TIME & SPACE 81 29
Halley Station, ARCTIC & ANTARCTIC 57 61
Halley's comet, ASTRONOMY 82 58-59; ROCK & MINERAL 2 43; SPACE EXPLORATION 71 44
Halloween, WITCH & WIZARD 70 11
hallucinations, WITCH & WIZARD 70 33, 49
Hals, Frans, MANET 94 26, 50-51
Halsted, William, MEDICINE 88 50
halteres, INSECT 17 8, 13, 32
Halton Moor, VIKING 50 37, 46, 47
Hamilton, Richard, PERSPECTIVE 98 60
Hamilton, Sir William, ANCIENT GREECE 37 42, 48; WATERCOLOUR 97 28
Hamman, BIBLE LANDS 30 38
hammer and sickle, FLAG 16 14, 35, 57
hammerhead sharks, FISH 20 59; SHARK 40 6, 16, 19, 23
hammers, EARLY PEOPLE 10 12; SPORT 8 40; VIKING 50 43, 46, 53, 63
hammocks, BOAT 36 28
Hammurabi, King, BIBLE LANDS 30 50; MEDICINE 88 9
Hampson Air Liquifier, ENERGY 76 27
hamsters, DESERT 51 32, 37; MAMMAL 11 9, 44, 52-53; SKELETON 3 30
Han dynasty, CHINA 55 7, 21, 36
  warfare, CHINA 55 14, 49
hand-axes, ARMS & ARMOUR 4 6-7
handbags, COSTUME 35 31, 36, 39
handball, SPORT 8 36
handbells, MUSIC 12 54
handcuffs, ARMS & ARMOUR 4 55; CRIME & DETECTION 73 13, 32

handkerchieves, COSTUME 35
18, 39, 44
handwriting, WRITING 48 52-53
experts, CRIME &
DETECTION 73 43
hangers, ARMS & ARMOUR 4
16-17
hang-gliders,
FLYING MACHINE 22 10,
60-61, 62
hanging, CRIME &
DETECTION 73
12-13, 22, 58; PIRATE 59
56-57, 59
Hanna, Bill, CINEMA 34 50
Hannibal, ANCIENT ROME 24 7;
ELEPHANT 42 44, 46
Hanseatic League,
MEDIEVAL LIFE 65 7, 47
Hanuman, monkey god,
GORILLA 64 59;
RELIGION 68 21
Hapiru, BIBLE LANDS 30 12, 13
Haraden, Jonathan, PIRATE 59 53
Harald Bluetooth, King,
VIKING 50 22, 26, 60-61
Harare, AFRICA 61 7
Hardin, John Wesley,
COWBOY 45 45
hardness, CRYSTAL & GEM 25
18, 27, 32, 34, 51
Hardy, Oliver, CINEMA 34 54
hares, ARCTIC & ANTARCTIC 57
24, 36; MAMMAL 11 9;
SKELETON 3 17
harlequin frogfish, FISH 20 21
harmonicas, MUSIC 12 17
harmonics,
FORCE & MOTION 78 48
harness, BATTLE 63 10;
EARLY PEOPLE 10 44, 47, 48,
53; HORSE 33 30-31, 34
harpoons, ANCIENT EGYPT 23
45; BOAT 36 11, 30-31;
EARLY PEOPLE 10 20, 21, 26;
WHALE 46 37, 46, 49, 52
harps, ANCIENT EGYPT 23 50;
MEDIEVAL LIFE 65 26, 56;
MUSIC 12 26, 34, 35;
VIKING 50 50
Harran, BIBLE LANDS 30 10
harriers, EAGLE 69 11, 12, 26, 38
Harrington, Sir John,
INVENTION 27 54;
MEDICINE 88 35
Harrison, Rex, CINEMA 34 33
Hart, William S, COWBOY 45 60
Hartog, Dirk, EXPLORER 31 38
harvest, MEDIEVAL LIFE 65 12-14
festival, DANCE 99 19, 32
harvesting,
by hand, FARM 66 20-21
by machine, FARM 66 26-27
Harvey, William,
HUMAN BODY 87 12, 24, 28,
30; INVENTION 27 43; LIFE 84
27; MEDICINE 88 24-25, 30

Hasmonaean kingdom,
BIBLE LANDS 30 54, 56
Hasting, VIKING 50 16
Hastings, battle of,
KNIGHT 43 8-9
hatchetfish, FISH 20 21
Hathor, ANCIENT EGYPT 23 28,
31, 51, 58, 60
hats, COSTUME 35 46-47, 50;
COWBOY 45 20-21, 53, 57, 60
Hatshepsut, Queen,
ANCIENT EGYPT 23 10, 41;
EXPLORER 31 8-9;
PYRAMID 53 41
hat-trick, SPORT 8 27
Hauksbee, Francis,
ELECTRICITY 77 10;
ENERGY 76 18; FORCE &
MOTION 78 38
Hauptmann, Bruno, CRIME &
DETECTION 73 22
Hauran, BIBLE LANDS 30 25
Haussmann, Baron,
MONET 95 7
Hauy, the Abbé, CRYSTAL &
GEM 25 14, 15
Hawaii, EXPLORER 31 34;
VOLCANO 38 19, 23, 40, 44
Harris's hawk, DESERT 51 31
hawk's-eye,
CRYSTAL & GEM 25 33
hawkbill turtles,
SHELL 9 31, 52
Hawker Hart, FLYING
MACHINE 22 24, 39
hawkers, WRITING 48 60
Hawking, Stephen,
FORCE & MOTION 78 61;
MATTER 80 63
Hawkins, Benjamin W.,
DINOSAUR 13 9, 55
Hawkins, Jim,
PIRATE 59 60-61
Hawkins, John,
PIRATE 59 23, 38
hawkmoths, JUNGLE 54 50
hawks, BIRD 1 59; EAGLE 69
40-41
African harrier, EAGLE 69 11,
38, 39
broad-winged, EAGLE 69 58
Cooper's, EAGLE 69 29, 53
crane, EAGLE 69 39
goshawk, EAGLE 69 20, 26,
40, 57
Sparrowhawk, EAGLE 69 25,
40, 41
haworthia, DESERT 51 18
hawthorns, POND & RIVER 6
15; TREE 5 36, 38
hay, FARM 66 20, 34, 35, 45
Hayashi, Kenji, SPY 67 47
Haynes, CAR 21 63
hazels, TREE 5 23, 31, 61
Hazor, BIBLE LANDS 30 24
headboards,
TRAIN 39 54-55, 57

headgear, AFRICA 61 26
headlamps, TRAIN 39 13, 16, 19, 44
headphones, SPY 67 16, 18, 22
heart, HUMAN BODY 87 24, 28-33,
35; MEDICINE 88 54-55
ageing, HUMAN BODY 87 49
attacks, MEDICINE 88 7, 59
muscles, HUMAN BODY 87 20,
28, 29
respiration,
HUMAN BODY 87 26
heart-urchins, FOSSIL 19 33;
SHELL 9 21
heartwoods, TREE 5 16, 17
heat, ENERGY 76 14, 15, 22, 24,
26-27; MATTER 80 16, 20,
22, 30
capacity, ENERGY 76 21
energy, ENERGY 76 6, 20-21,
25, 57; FORCE &
MOTION 78 38, 40, 41;
MATTER 80 61
Big Bang, ENERGY 76 62
fire, ENERGY 76 10-11
fuel, ENERGY 76 37, 54
measurement,
ENERGY 76 36, 37
exchanger, ENERGY 76 47
fluid theory, ENERGY 76
18-19, 44
latent, MATTER 80 23
and liquids, MATTER 80 18
nuclear power,
ENERGY 76 46
Sun, ENERGY 76 48
and work, MATTER 80 38, 39
heating elements,
INVENTION 27 54
Heaviside, Oliver,
ELECTRONICS 90 11, 13
heavy metal, MUSIC 12 61
Hebrew alphabet,
WRITING 48 15, 16
Hebrews, BIBLE LANDS 30
12-13, 58, 60-61;
RELIGION 68 42, 47
Hebrides, VIKING 50 17, 38
Hebron, BIBLE LANDS 30 6
Hedeby,
VIKING 50 12, 26, 31, 44
hedgehogs, DESERT 51 34, 35;
MAMMAL 11 8, 24-25, 51;
SKELETON 3 30, 58
Hedin, Sven, EXPLORER 31 17
Hedley, William, TRAIN 39 11
heeling, BOAT 36 23
Hegelbord, battle of,
BATTLE 63 42
Heh, PYRAMID 53 48
Hektor, ANCIENT GREECE 37
12, 13, 55
Helen, ANCIENT GREECE 37 12, 14
Helgø, VIKING 50 19
helicopters, FUTURE 100 8, 27;
INVENTION 27 58;
SHIPWRECK 72 9, 35, 41, 43;
TECHNOLOGY 89 29

origin, FLYING MACHINE 22 52
Heliobatis, FISH 20 13
heliocentric universe,
ASTRONOMY 82 18,
heliodors, CRYSTAL & GEM 25
7, 38, 39, 59
heliographs, BATTLE 63 52
Heliopolis, PYRAMID 53 44, 45
helium, ASTRONOMY 82 31, 37,
38, 45; MATTER 80 46, 47, 57,
62; TIME & SPACE 81 39, 60
in sun, MATTER 80 60
Hellenistic Period, ANCIENT
GREECE 37 7, 42, 58, 62
Helluland, VIKING 50 21
helmets, ARMS & ARMOUR 4
28-29; BATTLE 63 11, 38, 44;
COSTUME 35 9, 12, 13;
EARLY PEOPLE 10 47, 53
Anglo-Saxon, ARMS &
ARMOUR 4 14
Bronze Age, ARMS &
ARMOUR 4 11
close, KNIGHT 43 14, 16, 46
Greek,
ARMS & ARMOUR 4 12
Indian,
ARMS & ARMOUR 4 33
iron, KNIGHT 43 12-13
Iron Age,
ARMS & ARMOUR 4 11
Japanese, ARMS &
ARMOUR 4 36, 37
mask-like, KNIGHT 43 42, 43
medieval,
ARMS & ARMOUR 4 26;
KNIGHT 43 14-15, 29
Roman, ANCIENT ROME 24
10, 31, 33, 50; ARMS &
ARMOUR 4 12, 13
in sports, SPORT 8 10, 16,
18, 22
Viking,
VIKING 50 6, 13, 14, 15
Helmholtz, Hermann,
HUMAN BODY 87 53
hematite, CRYSTAL &
GEM 25 17, 21, 37, 45; ROCK
& MINERAL 2 32, 33, 46, 56
Hemiptera, INSECT 17 8
Hemlingby, VIKING 50 27
Hendrix, Jimi, MUSIC 12 59
Heng, Zhang,
VOLCANO 38 52
Henle, Jakob, MEDICINE 88
30, 33
Henriques, Alphonso,
FLAG 16 37
Henry I, King of England,
KNIGHT 43 32
Henry II, King of England,
CASTLE 49 23; MEDIEVAL
LIFE 65 42; WITCH &
WIZARD 70 16
Henry III, King of England,
MEDIEVAL LIFE 65 24;
PIRATE 59 18

Henry IV, King of England, **Castle 49** 22; **Medieval Life 65** 26; **Witch & Wizard 70** 13
Henry VII, King of England, **Witch & Wizard 70** 14
Henry VIII, King of England, **Archaeology 56** 32, 34; **Horse 33** 45; **Medieval Life 65** 7; **Shipwreck 72** 18; **Spy 67** 40 royal arms, **Flag 16** 11, 16
Henry the Navigator, **Explorer 31** 20; **Flag 16** 37
Henry, Edward, **Crime & Detection 73** 45
Henry, Joseph, **Electricity 77** 28, 29, 34, 35; **Electronics 90** 19; **Weather 28** 13
Henson, William, **Flying Machine 22** 12-13; **Invention 27** 58, 59
Henson Organisation, **Cinema 34** 45
hepatitis, **Medicine 88** 42, 63
Hepburn, Audrey, **Cinema 34** 37
Hephaistos, **Ancient Greece 37** 20, 21, 22
hepialid moths, **Butterfly & Moth 7** 44
Heracles (Herakles), **Cat 29** 29; **Ancient Greece 37** 22, 48, 52
herald moths, **Butterfly & Moth 7** 51
heraldry, **Flag 16** 10-11, 32; **Knight 43** 48-49; **Medieval Life 65** 24
heralds, **Castle 49** 24
herbal therapies, **Medicine 88** 8, 12-13
  Arabic, **Medicine 88** 21
  drugs, **Medicine 88** 7, 40, 42
  eastern, **Medicine 88** 14-15
  Greek, **Medicine 88** 16
herbivores, **Ecology 86** 12, 48; **Mammal 11** 14, 50, 63; **Pond & River 6** 10, 12, 17; **Skeleton 3** 34, 36
herbs, **Ancient Rome 24** 45, 54; **Aztec 47** 38, 39; **Early People 10** 8, 9; **Medieval Life 65** 17, 19, 60, 61
  in magic, **Witch & Wizard 70** 8, 33-35
Herculaneum, Italy, **Archaeology 56** 9, 25, 28-29; **Cat 29** 46; **Volcano 38** 11, 26, 30-31, 33, 47, 60
Hercules, **Ancient Rome 24** 16, 31, 43, 61
heredity, **Evolution 85** 33, 50, 51, 52
Herero peoples, **Africa 61** 24

heretics, **Medieval Life 65** 31
hermaphrodites, **Pond & River 6** 8
Hermes, **Ancient Greece 37** 28
hermit butterflies, **Butterfly & Moth 7** 30
hermit crabs, **Skeleton 3** 25
Hero of Alexandria, **Invention 27** 32
Herod, King, **Bible Lands 30** 39, 56-57, 62; **Religion 68** 42, 55
Herodium, **Bible Lands 30** 57
Herodotos, **Ancient Greece 37** 35, 56; **Mummy 44** 14, 15, 46; **Pyramid 53** 36
heroin, **Plant 14** 58
herons, **Bird 1** 9, 21, 40, 44; **Pond & River 6** 12, 30, 31; **Skeleton 3** 18, 53
Herophilus, **Medicine 88** 17
herring, **Fish 20** 10, 52, 58; **Ocean 62** 26
Herring, John, **Horse 33** 39
Herschel, Caroline, **Astronomy 82** 29
Herschel, John, **Astronomy 82** 29
Herschel, Sir William, **Astronomy 82** 24-25, 54-55; **Crime & Detection 73** 44; **Light 75** 20, 40, 42; **Technology 89** 58, 59
Hertz, Heinrich, **Electricity 77** 57, 60; **Electronics 90** 12, 13, 24; **Energy 76** 40, 42, 51; **Invention 27** 52; **Time & Space 81** 33
hessonite, **Crystal & Gem 25** 44
hetairai, **Ancient Greece 37** 31, 36, 39
Hetepheres, **Pyramid 53** 9, 47
Heterodontosaurus, **Dinosaur 13** 36
Hetpheres, **Ancient Egypt 23** 12
Hevelius, Johannes, **Astronomy 82** 40
Hewitt, William Grailly, **Writing 48** 7
Heyerdahl, Thor, **Ancient Egypt 23** 38; **Boat 36** 9
Hezekiah, **Bible Lands 30** 46
hibernation, **Butterfly & Moth 7** 51; **Ecology 86** 53; **Life 84** 7, 58
hibiscus, **Jungle 54** 40; **Plant 14** 25
Hickok, Wild Bill, **Cowboy 45** 42-43, 47, 59
hickories, **Tree 5** 28, 33, 47, 59
hieratic script, **Writing 48** 12-13
hieroglyphs, **Ancient Egypt 23** 34, 35; **Mummy 44** 10, 16, 28, 33; **Pyramid 53** 18, 38, 46; **Writing 48** 12-13

Hieron, King, **Force & Motion 78** 14, 15, 18
hi-fi, **Electronics 90** 43, 60
high jump, **Sport 8** 40
High Priest's breastplate, **Crystal & Gem 25** 60
high-heels, **Costume 35** 27, 36, 51
high-tension battery, **Electricity 77** 19
highwaymen, **Arms & Armour 4** 48-49; **Crime & Detection 73** 14, 52, 56
hi-hat drum, **Fish 20** 19
Hillary, Edmund, **Future 100** 10
hillforts, **Archaeology 56** 12, 25
Hills, Robert, **Watercolour 97** 38
Himalayas, **Earth 83** 49
himation, **Ancient Greece 37** 40, 43
Hinckley, John, **Crime & Detection 73** 58
Hindemith, Paul, **Dance 99** 17
Hinduism, **Religion 68** 18-19, 22-23
  gods, **Religion 68** 20-21
Hipparchus, **Astronomy 82** 10
Hipparion, **Horse 33** 8
Hippidion, **Horse 33** 8
hippies, **Costume 35** 6, 58-59
hippocamp, **Ancient Greece 37** 7
Hippocrates, **Ancient Greece 37** 58, 59; **Human Body 87** 8, 9, 58, 60; **Medicine 88** 16-17, 24, 26
hippopotamuses, **Ancient Egypt 23** 22, 44, 60, 61; **Mammal 11** 10, 26
hipposandal, **Horse 33** 29
hips, **Human Body 87** 7, 15-19, 46
Hiram, King, **Bible Lands 30** 40
Hiroshige, Ando, **Cat 29** 21; **Impressionism 92** 54; **Monet 95** 22, 43, 54, 55; **Perspective 98** 48, 49; **Van Gogh 96** 37
  Tsukuda Beneath a Full Moon, **Monet 95** 22
Hispaniola, **Pirate 59** 20, 26-27, 38
Hispano-Suiza, **Car 21** 12
histology, **Life 84** 14-15, 25
Hitachi, **Spy 67** 47
Hitchcock, Alfred, **Cinema 34** 23, 61
Hitler, Adolf, **Crime & Detection 73** 21; **Flag 16** 28
Hittites, **Bible Lands 30** 13, 50; **Early People 10** 50
HIV, **Medicine 88** 42, 63
hives, **Insect 17** 58-59

hoards, **Viking 50** 49
hobble skirts, **Costume 35** 50
hockey, **Sport 8** 16-17
Hockney, David, **Cat 29** 54; **Pyramid 53** 62
Hodgkin, Dorothy, **Chemistry 79** 20
hoes, **Africa 61** 53
Hogan, Paul, **Cinema 34** 59
Hogarth, William, **Goya 93** 23; **Perspective 98** 7
Hokusai, Katsushika, **Volcano 38** 6, 57
Holbein, Hans the Younger, **Perspective 98** 32-33; **Renaissance 91** 43, 58, 59; **Watercolour 97** 22, 24
holey dollars, **Money 18** 50
Holland, **Ancient Rome 24** 13; **Whale 46** 57
holly, **Plant 14** 37; **Tree 5** 11, 26
Hollywood, **Cinema 34** 18, 20-21, 24, 33, 36; **Dance 99** 8, 47, 51, 54
Holman Island, **Arctic & Antarctic 57** 21
holocephaleans, **Fish 20** 9, 20
holograms, **Electronics 90** 15
holography, **Light 75** 58-59
holosteans, **Fish 20** 9, 11, 13, 41
holsters, **Arms & Armour 4** 60; **Cowboy 45** 8, 22-23, 27
Holy Land, **Castle 49** 34-35; **Medieval Life 65** 7, 28
Holy Roman Empire, **Medieval Life 65** 6
Holy Spirit, **Religion 68** 48, 52
Homarus, **Fossil 19** 31
homburg hat, **Costume 35** 50
home runs, **Sport 8** 22
home shopping, **Future 100** 30, 59
homeopathy, **Medicine 88** 44
homeostasis, **Life 84** 26
Homer, **Ancient Greece 37** 7, 11, 12; **Archaeology 56** 14; **Horse 33** 22, 58; **Shipwreck 72** 59; **Witch & Wizard 70** 16
hominoids, **Gorilla 64** 8-9
Homo, **Fossil 19** 13, 58-59
Homo erectus, **Early People 10** 14-15, 18; **Evolution 85** 63; **Skeleton 3** 28
Homo habilis, **Archaeology 56** 55
Homo sapiens, **Prehistoric Life 52** 56
Homo sapiens sapiens, **Early People 10** 22-23; **Skeleton 3** 28
Honduras, **Pyramid 53** 56
honey, **Insect 17** 43, 58-59
honeybees, **Insect 17** 43, 52, 58-59

honeysuckle, PLANT 14 20
Hong Kong, CHINA 55 63
Hooch, Pieter de,
    PERSPECTIVE 98 60
Hoogstraten, Samuel van,
    PERSPECTIVE 98 36-37
Hook, Captain, PIRATE 59 61,62
Hooke, Robert, ASTRONOMY 82
    50; HUMAN BODY 87 12, 24;
    LIFE 84 10; LIGHT 75 22, 23
Hooker, Joseph, EXPLORER 31 50
hooped skirts, COSTUME 35 42
hoopoes, BIRD 1 39
Hoover, John Edgar, CRIME &
    DETECTION 73 24; SPY 67
    40, 41
Hoover, William,
    INVENTION 27 55
hooves, SKELETON 3 57
Hopis, DESERT 51 61
Hopkinson, Francis,
    FLAG 16 24
Hoplophoneus, CAT 29 9;
    FOSSIL 19 55
Hoplopteryx, SKELETON 3 12
hoppers, CRYSTAL & GEM 25 21
Horemakhet, PYRAMID 53 27
hormones, HUMAN BODY 87 36,
    40-41, 42; LIFE 84 26, 27;
    MEDICINE 88 42
Hormuz, EXPLORER 31 17
Horn, Cape, EXPLORER 31 24
horn book, WRITING 48 51
hornbeam, TREE 5 32
hornblende,
    CRYSTAL & GEM 25 23
Hornelund, VIKING 50 42
hornets, INSECT 17 38, 46, 50
horns, armour, KNIGHT 43
    8-9, 52-53; VIKING 50 37, 39
horns, car, CAR 21 10, 11
horns, cups, ARCHAEOLOGY 56
    26, 30-31, 34, 44
horns, musical, MUSIC 12 15,
    20, 22
    French, MUSIC 12 9, 24
horse equipment,
    ARCHAEOLOGY 56 30-31
horseflies, INSECT 17 33
horsepower, ENERGY 76 30,
    INVENTION 27 24
horses, DESERT 51 35, 42, 43, 49;
    HORSE 33; MAMMAL 11 10,
    28, 50, 58; NORTH
    AMERICAN INDIAN 60 28,
    39, 48;
    ancient, AFRICA 61 44, 47;
    ANCIENT ROME 24 13, 22,
    34, 35
    Arab, HORSE 33 38-39, 42
    in battle, BATTLE 63 7, 10, 20,
    26; HORSE 33 22-23, 42-45;
    KNIGHT 43 20-21
    birth, HORSE 33 14-15
    bones, SKELETON 3 14, 36, 59
    cowboys, COWBOY 45 6-8,
    12-13, 19, 32-35

evolution, EVOLUTION 85 23,
    41, 48, 62; MAMMAL 11 13, 14
    extinct, DINOSAUR 13 22, 27,
    61; PREHISTORIC LIFE 52 8,
    45, 49
    farm, FARM 66 9, 13, 40
    grooming, MAMMAL 11 46
    harness, EARLY PEOPLE 10 44,
    47, 48, 53
    mares, HORSE 33 12-14, 26
    mythical, HORSE 33 7, 22-23
    racehorses, HORSE 33 10-11,
    58-60
    riding, EARLY PEOPLE 10
    46, 60
    Shire, HORSE 33 28-29, 50-51
    thoroughbreds, HORSE 33 38,
    54, 59, 62
    Viking, VIKING 50 36, 40,
    41, 56
    wild, HORSE 33 20-21, 36-37
    see also ponies
horseshoe crabs, FOSSIL 19 60
horseshoes, CASTLE 49 61;
    EARLY PEOPLE 10 49;
    HORSE 33 28-29, 48;
    INVENTION 27 15;
    WITCH & WIZARD 70 30
horsetails, FOSSIL 19 36, 37
Horus, BIBLE LANDS 30 24;
    MUMMY 44 20, 34, 43, 44;
    WITCH & WIZARD 70 29
    Egyptian god,
    ANCIENT EGYPT 23 19, 25,
    27, 56; PYRAMID 53 18, 27,
    28, 38, 52
Hory, Elmyr de, CRIME &
    DETECTION 73 21
Hoschedé, Alice, MONET 95
    28-29, 38, 49, 53
Hoschedé, Ernest,
    IMPRESSIONISM 92 42
hose, COSTUME 35 16, 17, 22
Hospitallers,
    KNIGHT 43 56-57
hot springs, VOLCANO 38 24,
    25, 36, 37
hotpants, COSTUME 35 59
hounds, DOG 32 34, 35, 48, 49
Hounsfield, Godfrey,
    FUTURE 100 11
houppelande, COSTUME 35
    16, 23
hourglass, TIME & SPACE 81 16
house martins, BIRD 1 44, 47
houseflies,
    INSECT 17 18, 21, 32
houses,
    African, AFRICA 61 8-9,
    12-13, 14, 16
    desert, DESERT 51 44, 45
    medieval, MEDIEVAL LIFE 65
    14, 16-17, 19
    polar, ARCTIC &
    ANTARCTIC 57 60-61
    Roman, ANCIENT ROME 24
    23, 24, 25

tribal, JUNGLE 54 38-39
    Viking, VIKING 50 22-23,
    32-35
    see also architecture, building
hovercrafts,
    FORCE & MOTION 78 39;
    FUTURE 100 10
Howard, Luke, WEATHER 28 28
Howard, Trevor,
    CINEMA 34 56
howdahs, ELEPHANT 42 53
howitzers, BATTLE 63 32, 33
Hoyle, Sir Fred,
    ASTRONOMY 82 47;
    LIFE 84 54; MATTER 80 63;
    TIME & SPACE 81 26, 38, 39
Huang Ti, mythical Emperor,
    MEDICINE 88 14-15
Hubble, Edwin,
    ASTRONOMY 82 62;
    TIME & SPACE 81 46, 49
Hubble Space Telescope,
    ASTRONOMY 82 7, 34-35, 57;
    FUTURE 100 43, 50;
    SPACE EXPLORATION 71 53;
    TIME & SPACE 81 45, 49
Hudson, Henry, EXPLORER 31
    40-42
Hudson's Bay Company,
    BOAT 36 12
Huggins, Williams,
    ASTRONOMY 82 61
Hughes, David,
    ELECTRONICS 90 42
Hui Zong, Emperor,
    CHINA 55 30-31, 32, 54
huias, BIRD 1 36
hulcs, BOAT 36 16, 17, 24
hulls, BOAT 36 14, 27, 47, 54
human beings,
    EVOLUTION 85 15, 39;
    FOSSIL 19 20, 21, 58-59;
    LIFE 84 11, 14, 18, 23;
    MAMMAL 11 8, 21, 23, 58
    body structure,
    HUMAN BODY 87;
    SKELETON 3 6-9
    arms, SKELETON 3 7,
    48-49, 63
    bones, SKELETON 3 62-63
    brain, SKELETON 3 6, 26
    hands, SKELETON 3 7, 9,
    48, 49
    legs, SKELETON 3 10,
    54-57, 62
    mammary glands,
    MAMMAL 11 36-37
    muscles,
    SKELETON 3 48, 54
    nose, SKELETON 3 28, 62
    pelvis, SKELETON 3 39,
    44-47, 62
    ribs,
    SKELETON 3 8, 42-43, 62
    skull, SKELETON 3 10, 11,
    26-29
    spine, SKELETON 3 40-41

early, EARLY PEOPLE 10 6-7,
    10; MAMMAL 11 14;
    PREHISTORIC LIFE 52 9,
    55-57
    Homo erectus, EARLY
    PEOPLE 10 14-15, 18;
    EVOLUTION 85 63
    Homo sapiens sapiens,
    EARLY PEOPLE 10 22-23
human population,
    ECOLOGY 86 58-61
human sacrifice, EARLY
    PEOPLE 10 38, 52, 55, 58
Humber, CAR 21 55
Humboldt, Alexander von,
    EXPLORER 31 50;
    JUNGLE 54 60
humerus, SKELETON 3 48-49, 62
humidity, ECOLOGY 86 41;
    WEATHER 28 10, 22, 23, 63
hummingbirds, BIRD 1 8, 16,
    20, 29;
    JUNGLE 54 25; PLANT 14 25
humours, bodily,
    MEDICINE 88 17, 22, 26
humus, EARTH 83 52, 53;
    ECOLOGY 86 22, 23
Hundred Years War,
    BATTLE 63 36, 63;
    KNIGHT 43 30;
    MEDIEVAL LIFE 65 7, 28
Hunefer, PYRAMID 53 29, 44
Hungary, BATTLE 63 18;
    FLAG 16 32; MONEY 18
    19, 63
Hunter, John and William,
    MEDICINE 88 27
hunter-gatherers, AFRICA 61 15,
    18, 19; ARCHAEOLOGY 56
    44-45, 47; EARLY PEOPLE 10
    9, 60; ECOLOGY 86 58
    Bushmen, EARLY PEOPLE 10
    28-29
    Ice Age, EARLY PEOPLE 10
    20-21, 26-27
hunting, ARCTIC &
    ANTARCTIC 57 50-51;
    JUNGLE 54 46-47, 52-53;
    NORTH AMERICAN
    INDIAN 60 12-13, 28-30,
    38-40; RUSSIA 74 11, 13, 25
    ancient times,
    ANCIENT EGYPT 23 44, 45;
    ANCIENT ROME 24 58;
    AZTEC 47 14, 15
    in deserts, DESERT 51 46
    horses, HORSE 33 22-23,
    46, 61
    Ice Age, NORTH AMERICAN
    INDIAN 60 6
    Inuit, NORTH AMERICAN
    INDIAN 60 60-61
    medieval, KNIGHT 43 50-51;
    MEDIEVAL LIFE 65 15, 19
    as sport, SPORT 8 52, 54
    sub-arctic, NORTH AMERICAN
    INDIAN 60 58-59

Viking, **VIKING 50** 35, 36
see also hunters-gatherers
Hupmobile, **CAR 21** 63
hurdy-gurdys, **CASTLE 49** 45
hurricanes, **FUTURE 100** 14;
   OCEAN 62 12; **SHIPWRECK 72**
   11; **WEATHER 28** 7, 13, 42, 43
  eye, **WEATHER 28** 44, 45
Hurt, John, **CINEMA 34** 44
huskies, **DOG 32** 47, 56, 57
hussars, **BATTLE 63** 18, 25
huts, **DESERT 51** 44, 45;
   EARLY PEOPLE 10 10, 11, 18
Hutton, James, **EARTH 83** 8,
  22, 60
Huxley, Aldous, **FUTURE 100** 9
Huygens, Christiaan,
  ASTRONOMY 82 48, 53;
  CINEMA 34 7; **ENERGY 76** 14;
  FORCE & MOTION 78 47;
  INVENTION 27 23;
  LIGHT 75 34, 62
  Pendulum clocks,
   TIME & SPACE 81 17, 18
Huygens, space probes,
  SPACE EXPLORATION 71
  44-45
hyaenas, **MAMMAL 11** 9
hyalite, **CRYSTAL & GEM 25** 40
hybrids, **EVOLUTION 85** 41,
  50, 51
hydra, **LIFE 84** 32, 53
hydraulics, **FORCE &**
  MOTION 78 44;
  TECHNOLOGY 89 33, 39
hydrocarbons, **CHEMISTRY 79**
  36, 37, 49, 53
hydrochloric acid,
  CHEMISTRY 79 28, 38, 39, 42
hydroelectric energy,
  ENERGY 76 57, 58
  power, **ELECTRICITY 77** 44, 45;
   RUSSIA 74 14, 15
hydrogen, **ASTRONOMY 82** 43;
  CHEMISTRY 79 18, 40, 46;
  EARTH 83 16, 17;
  LIFE 84 8, 9, 55;
  MATTER 80 6, 18, 30, 34;
  TECHNOLOGY 89 63
  atoms, **MATTER 80** 48, 53, 62
  atomic weight,
   CHEMISTRY 79 16
  in balloons, **MATTER 80** 21
  Big Bang, **TIME &**
   SPACE 81 60
  fuels, **MATTER 80** 40, 41
  gas, **CHEMISTRY 79** 25, 27,
   33, 36, 39
  hydrocarbons,
   CHEMISTRY 79 30, 48,
   49, 60
  isotopes, **ENERGY 76** 46;
   MATTER 80 52, 57
  ions, **CHEMISTRY 79** 42, 43, 44;
   ENERGY 76 35;
   MATTER 80 49
  nuclei, **MATTER 80** 57

on other planets,
  ASTRONOMY 82 50, 52, 53, 55
respiration, **LIFE 84** 18-19
solar system,
  ASTRONOMY 82 37, 38, 43
in water, **CHEMISTRY 79** 20,
  29, 46; **MATTER 80** 36, 51
hydrogen bomb, **ENERGY 76** 47;
  MATTER 80 57; **RUSSIA 74**
  40, 41
hydroids, **OCEAN 62** 11, 21;
  SEASHORE 15 39
hydrometers, **CHEMISTRY 79** 61;
  FORCE & MOTION 78 15
hydrophones, **SPY 67** 52, 54
hydroponics, **FARM 66** 36
hyenas, **DESERT 51** 35;
  DOG 32 7-9, 19
Hygeia, **ANCIENT ROME 24** 54
hygrometers, **WEATHER 28** 11,
  22, 23, 63
Hyksos, **BIBLE LANDS 30** 12
Hylestad, **VIKING 50** 43, 51
Hymenoptera, **INSECT 17** 8
hyperspace, **TIME & SPACE 81** 63
hyphae, **LIFE 84** 20, 51
Hypsilophodon, **FOSSIL 19** 49
Hyracotherium, **DINOSAUR 13** 61
hyrax, **MAMMAL 11** 11, 58
Hyrcanus, **BIBLE LANDS 30** 56

Iban Dyak peoples,
  DANCE 99 32
Ibibio peoples, **AFRICA 61** 35
Ibis, **ANCIENT EGYPT 23** 28;
  JUNGLE 54 9; **MUMMY 44** 45
Ibn Fadhlan, **VIKING 50** 19, 55
Ibo peoples, **AFRICA 61** 40, 62
Icarus, **BIRD 1** 10; **FLYING**
  MACHINE 22 6
ice, **CRYSTAL & GEM 25** 6, 62;
  EARTH 83 7, 14, 18-19;
  FOSSIL 19 6, 20, 54;
  ROCK & MINERAL 2 13

Arctic, **ARCTIC &**
  ANTARCTIC 57 6, 8, 57, 62
density, **EARTH 83** 16
erosion, **EARTH 83** 54
pack ice, **ARCTIC &**
  ANTARCTIC 57 9
sheets, **EARTH 83** 7, 35
Ice Age, **EARTH 83** 7, 12, 13, 14;
  EVOLUTION 85 9, 17, 62, 63;
  FOSSIL 19 15, 20, 54, 59;
  PREHISTORIC LIFE 52 6, 18,
  58-59
  art, **EARLY PEOPLE 10** 24-25
  clothes, **EARLY PEOPLE 10**
   22, 32
  fire-making, **EARLY**
   PEOPLE 10 16
  hunters, **EARLY PEOPLE 10**
   20-21, 26-27
  people, **EARLY PEOPLE 10** 18-19
  Pleistocene period,
   EARTH 83 18, 41, 58, 63;
   MAMMAL 11 13-15
  weather, **WEATHER 28** 60
ice fish, **ARCTIC &**
  ANTARCTIC 57 16
ice hockey, **SPORT 8** 18-19
Ice Man, **ARCHAEOLOGY 56** 42-43
ice skates, **VIKING 50** 40
icebergs, **ARCTIC &**
  ANTARCTIC 57 6-7, 9, 10-11;
  OCEAN 62 11, 54;
  SHIPWRECK 72 28;
  WEATHER 28 20
icebreakers, **ARCTIC &**
  ANTARCTIC 57, 11;
  BOAT 36 49
Iceland, **EXPLORER 31** 10, 12;
  VIKING 50 6, 20, 25, 53;
  VOLCANO 38 11, 12, 24, 34;
  WEATHER 28 61
  flag, **FLAG 16** 42-43
Icelandic pony, **HORSE 33** 12
Iceman, **MUMMY 44** 56-57
ichthyosaurs, **FOSSIL 19** 13, 44,
  46, 47; **SKELETON 3** 13
ichthyostega, **FOSSIL 19** 42
icons, **RUSSIA 74** 18, 46, 47, 50
identity parade,
  CRIME & DETECTION 73 50
ideograms, **WRITING 48** 8
idocrase, **CRYSTAL & GEM 25** 12
igloos, **ARCTIC & ANTARCTIC 57**
  60, 61; **NORTH AMERICAN**
  INDIAN 60 60
igneous rocks, **EARTH 83**
  24-25, 28, 48
iguanas, **DINOSAUR 13** 6, 7, 8,
  26; **REPTILE 26** 18, 28, 56
Iguanodon, **DINOSAUR 13** 8-9,
  40, 59; **FOSSIL 19** 50;
  PREHISTORIC LIFE 52 33;
  SKELETON 3 12, 58
Iliad, The, **ANCIENT GREECE 37**
  12; **ARMS & ARMOUR 4** 12
ilimba, **MUSIC 12** 55
ilium, **SKELETON 3** 44-45, 46-47

Illinois, **FLAG 16** 24
Imhotep, **ANCIENT EGYPT 23**
  20, 34; **MEDICINE 88** 8;
  PYRAMID 53 10, 11, 13
immune system, **LIFE 84** 28-29
immunization, **MEDICINE 88**
  32, 35, 63
immunology, **MEDICINE 88** 42
implants, **FUTURE 100** 41;
  MEDICINE 88 54-55
Impressionism,
  IMPRESSIONISM 92;
  MANET 94 20, 47, 52-55;
  MONET 95 18, 24-25;
  VAN GOGH 96 32-33, 36, 40;
  WATERCOLOUR 97 19,
  50-52, 58
  "London Impressionists,"
   IMPRESSIONISM 92 61
  Neo-Impressionism,
   IMPRESSIONISM 92 58, 59
Inca peoples, **EXPLORER 31**
  30-33; **JUNGLE 54** 60;
  MUMMY 44 52, 53, 55;
  PIRATE 59 20-21
  Empire, **AZTEC 47** 6, 7, 10-11
  Spanish conquest,
   AZTEC 47 62, 63
incandescent lamps,
  ELECTRICITY 77 42, 43, 47
incantations, **WITCH &**
  WIZARD 70 32, 33, 42, 46
incarnations, **RELIGION 68** 23,
  34, 48
incense, **WITCH & WIZARD 70**
  27, 58, 59
inchworms, **BUTTERFLY &**
  MOTH 7 15, 43
India, **ANCIENT GREECE 37** 7,
  62, 63; **BATTLE 63** 20, 52;
  BIBLE LANDS 30 28, 31, 54;
  EARTH 83 32, 36;
  VOLCANO 38 11, 50
  buildings, **BUILDING 58** 13,
   48, 57, 60
  currency, **MONEY 18** 19, 22,
   38, 55
  dances, **DANCE 99** 46, 47
   bharata natyam,
    DANCE 99 20, 25, 34, 35
   kathak, **DANCE 99** 16
   kathakali, **DANCE 99** 21,
    26, 27, 29
   orissi, **DANCE 99** 39
  early trade, **EXPLORER 31** 10,
   17-20
  East Indian Railways,
   TRAIN 39 16
  forests, **JUNGLE 54** 48, 63
  scripts, **WRITING 48** 8, 32
  space, **SPACE**
   EXPLORATION 71 13
  tigers, **CAT 29** 30-31
  weapons, **ARMS &**
   ARMOUR 4 32-35, 50, 51;
   BATTLE 63 38, 39, 40
  weather, **WEATHER 28** 31, 38

I

witchcraft, WITCH & WIZARD 70 50, 51
Indian Ocean, AFRICA 61 48; EXPLORER 31 8, 18, 20, 25; PIRATE 59 36, 46, 51; VOLCANO 38 11, 23, 35
Indian snakeheads, FISH 20 9
indicators, CHEMISTRY 79 42, 61
indigenous peoples, DESERT 51 36
Indonesia, EXPLORER 31 17-18, 20, 49; JUNGLE 54 48, 59; VOLCANO 38 11, 20, 35, 37; WHALE 46 62; WITCH & WIZARD 70 52, 53
Indra, RELIGION 68 20
Indri, GORILLA 64 11
induction, ELECTRICITY 77 29, 34, 46, 58
coils, ELECTRICITY 77 35, 60
motors, ELECTRICITY 77 35, 40, 41
inductors, ELECTRONICS 90 18-19, 23, 40
power supply, ELECTRONICS 90 31
filter, ELECTRONICS 90 34
Indus Civilization, ARCHAEOLOGY 56 8, 14; EARLY PEOPLE 10 40
Indus, River, BIBLE LANDS 30 52; EXPLORER 31 10
Industrial Revolution, FARM 66 14; TECHNOLOGY 89 34
inertia, FORCE & MOTION 78 30-31, 52
infantry, BATTLE 63 8-9, 15, 42
armour, BATTLE 63 46-47
close combat, BATTLE 63 44-45
infections, LIFE 84 26, 27, 51
informers, SPY 67 46, 47
infrared light, ASTRONOMY 82 30, 32, 62; ENERGY 76 48; LIGHT 75 40-41, 42-43; TECHNOLOGY 89 7, 58-59
beams, TIME & SPACE 81 55
signals, FUTURE 100 47, 50, 51
Ingenhousz, Jan, ENERGY 76 50; LIFE 84 16; LIGHT 75 50
Inglefield clips, FLAG 16 7
Ingolf, VIKING 50 20
ingots, MONEY 18 7, 11, 50
ink, ANCIENT ROME 24 40, 41; INVENTION 27 18, 19
ancient, WRITING 48 11, 12, 16
invisible, SPY 67 22
medieval, WRITING 48 26-27, 29
modern, WRITING 48 51, 56
printing, WRITING 48 39
Inkerman, battle of, BATTLE 63 61, 62

inkwells, WRITING 48 50-51
inlays, BUILDING 58 17, 45, 60
Innes, George, HORSE 33 48
Inquisition, GOYA 93 28-30, 42-45, 48; MEDIEVAL LIFE 65 7
insectivores, MAMMAL 11 8, 56
insects, EVOLUTION 85 11, 22, 25, 55; INSECT 17 6-9, 10-11; LIFE 84 47, 48-49, 53; PLANT 14 36, 37, 40, 43
antennae, INSECT 17 7, 12, 16-17
camouflage, INSECT 17 44-45; JUNGLE 54 50-51, 53
eggs, INSECT 17 22, 23, 24, 26
evolution, EVOLUTION 85 49, 61
eyes, INSECT 17 7, 14-15, 27
feeding, INSECT 17 20-21
fossils, FOSSIL 19 30, 52, 54, 60
leaf insects, INSECT 17 19, 44-45
legs, INSECT 17 16, 17, 18-19
metamorphosis, INSECT 17 24-25, 26-29
nests, INSECT 17 50-51, 52-53
polar, ARCTIC & ANTARCTIC 57 16, 18, 19
predators, JUNGLE 54 52-53
primitive, DINOSAUR 13 13, 24, 51, 61; PREHISTORIC LIFE 52 22-23, 42
senses, INSECT 17 7, 16-17, 20; LIFE 84 24
skeletons, SKELETON 3 22-23
sting, INSECT 17 8, 14, 38, 39
water insects, INSECT 17 18, 48-49
insulation, ELECTRICITY 77 17, 28, 35, 48; ENERGY 76 61
insulators, ELECTRICITY 77 20-21, 23
insulin, FUTURE 100 9; MEDICINE 88 42-43; TECHNOLOGY 89 60
insurance, CRIME & DETECTION 73 18, 31, 59
integrated circuits, ELECTRICITY 77 63; ELECTRONICS 90 52-53, 54, 58, 62
amplifier, ELECTRONICS 90 31
radio, ELECTRONICS 90 7, 39
interbreeding, EVOLUTION 85 22, 40
internal combustion, TECHNOLOGY 89 36, 42
International Code of Signals, FLAG 16 18-19
Internet, FUTURE 100 12, 31, 59
Interpol, CRIME & DETECTION 73 36
intestines, ELEPHANT 42 24; HUMAN BODY 87 7, 32-37, 41
Inti, AZTEC 47 33, 37

Inuit peoples, ARCTIC & ANTARCTIC 57 50-51; NORTH AMERICAN INDIAN 60 9, 60-61, 63; VIKING 50 21; WHALE 46 37, 49, 52, 56
art, ARCTIC & ANTARCTIC 57 21, 43, 46, 50-51
early, EARLY PEOPLE 10 20-21
houses, ARCTIC & ANTARCTIC 57 60-61
hunting, ARCTIC & ANTARCTIC 57 21, 43, 51
mummies, MUMMY 44 7, 63
inventions, INVENTION 27; CHINA 55 22-23
inverse square law, ELECTRICITY 77 11
invertebrates, EVOLUTION 85 46, 60; LIFE 84 49, 53; PREHISTORIC LIFE 52 12-17, 19; SHELL 9 7, 8; SKELETON 3 22-25
invisible ink, SPY 67 22
in-vitro fertilization, MEDICINE 88 7
Ionia, ANCIENT GREECE 37 6, 7, 27, 42
Ionides, Basil, CAT 29 51
ions, CHEMISTRY 79 39, 42, 43, 44; MATTER 80 33, 46, 51, 58
bonds, CHEMISTRY 79 20, 21, 44
electrolysis, CHEMISTRY 79 46, 47
Ipi, PYRAMID 53 32, 35
Iran, BIBLE LANDS 30 48, 52; CAT 29 38, 46
see also Persia
Iraq, BIBLE LANDS 30 10, 28, 48, 50; EXPLORER 31 6-7
Ireland, DANCE 99 39; EXPLORER 31 13; FLAG 16 47; VIKING 50 17, 46
iridescence, CRYSTAL & GEM 25 17
Iridium, PREHISTORIC LIFE 52 60
iris, PLANT 14 20, 33; POND & RIVER 6 7, 11, 15, 21
Irish Draught horse, HORSE 33 47, 58
"Irish Mail" train, TRAIN 39 37
Irish Thoroughbred, HORSE 33 58
iroko, TREE 5 59
iron, ARCHAEOLOGY 56 38, 48, 58; CHEMISTRY 79 18, 20, 22, 45; CHINA 55 22, 56; CRYSTAL & GEM 25 39, 44, 46, 50; MATTER 80 12, 16, 27
casting TECHNOLOGY 89 16-17
in Earth EARTH 83 7, 20, 29, 40; VOLCANO 38 9, 33
invention of, INVENTION 27 14, 15, 16, 55

Iron-Age, EARLY PEOPLE 10 48, 50, 52
iron-working, AFRICA 61 53; EARLY PEOPLE 10 50-51, 52, 53
magnetism, ENERGY 76 22, 23
oxide, EARTH 83 11, 50
production, CHEMISTRY 79 40, 41
tools, ARCHAEOLOGY 56 8, 34
wrought, BUILDING 58 38, 56; TECHNOLOGY 89 13
Iron Age, ARCHAEOLOGY 56 40, 58-59; EARLY PEOPLE 10 30, 32, 48-49
ARCHAEOLOGY 56 52, 58; BUILDING 58 13
objects, ARCHAEOLOGY 56 36-37
weapons, ARMS & ARMOUR 4 10-11
Iron Cross, FLAG 16 28
Iron Curtain, SPY 67 38, 39
Ironbridge Gorge, ARCHAEOLOGY 56 60-61
Iroquois peoples, NORTH AMERICAN INDIAN 60 12, 15-18, 21
Iroquois League, NORTH AMERICAN INDIAN 60 14
irrigation, DESERT 51 14, 15; FARM 66 29, 30
ancient, ARCHAEOLOGY 56, 28, 46
Irwin, James, ASTRONOMY 82 34
Isaac, BIBLE LANDS 30 10
Isabella, Queen, EXPLORER 31 22-23
ischium, SKELETON 3 44-45, 46-47
Ischnacanthus, FISH 20 12
Ischyromys, FOSSIL 19 54
Ishtar, BIBLE LANDS 30 48-51
Isis, ANCIENT ROME 24 20, 48, 50, 52; MUMMY 44 20, 21, 34
Islam, ANCIENT EGYPT 23 63; MEDIEVAL LIFE 65 44, 45; RELIGION 68 54-55, 58-59
flags, FLAG 16 14
medicine, MEDICINE 88 20-21
Qur'an, RELIGION 68 56-57
whirling dervishes, DANCE 99 34
see also Muslims, Muhammad
Isle of Man, CAT 29 13, 59; VIKING 50 17, 37
Isleworth, VAN GOGH 96 8-10
isobars, WEATHER 28 15
isopods, SHELL 9 26
isotopes, ENERGY 76 46; MATTER 80 49, 52; SKELETON 3 60

Israel, **Bible Lands 30** 10, 12,
20, 48; **Explorer 31** 6
Israelites, **Bible Lands 30**
20-21, 24, 34, 36;
Religion 68 42, 44, 45, 47
Issigonis, Alec, **Car 21** 30
Istanbul, **Ancient Rome 24** 62
Italian heavy draught horses,
Horse 33 41
italics, **Writing 48** 42, 44, 51
Italy, **Battle 63** 25, 38, 44;
Building 58 33, 36, 39, 44;
Explorer 31 11
ancient, **Ancient Greece 37**
7, 14, 24, 63; **Ancient
Rome 24** 6, 7, 36, 58
currency, **Money 18** 13, 23,
32, 63
fashions, **Costume 35** 14 19,
20, 23
flags, **Flag 16** 34-35
magic, **Witch & Wizard 70**
15, 30, 31
railways, **Train 39** 63
Renaissance,
Renaissance 91
clothes, **Costume 35** 16-17
volcanoes, **Volcano 38** 35,
40, 48, 53
weather, **Weather 28** 10,
11, 51
Ivan the Terrible, **Russia 74** 9,
20, 23, 26; **Spy 67** 40
Ivar the Boneless, **Viking 50** 7
ivies, **Tree 5** 48
ivory, **Ancient Egypt 23** 6, 41;
China 55 20, 26, 46;
**North American
Indian 60** 10, 52, 60-61;
Pirate 59 42;
Shipwreck 72 55
in archaeology,
Archaeology 56 16-17
elephants, **Elephant 42** 18,
20, 32
mammoth,
Elephant 42 10, 11
miniatures,
Watercolour 97 22-23
products, **Elephant 42** 52,
54-55
trade, **Elephant 42** 56-57,
62-63
ivy, **Plant 14** 39
Iwo Jima, **Flag 16** 25

J

jacanas, **Bird 1** 33
jackals, **Desert 51** 35;
Dog 32 19, 24-26, 34;
Mammal 11 43, 51
jackaroos, **Cowboy 45** 56
jack-asses, **Horse 33** 27
jackdaws, **Bird 1** 52
jackets, **Costume 35** 23, 29,
50, 57
Jackson, Glenda,
Cinema 34 36
Jackson, Samuel,
Watercolour 97 41
Jacob, **Bible Lands 30** 10
Jacobson's organ,
Horse 33 13
jade, **Aztec 47** 37, 52, 53, 54;
China 55 10, 16, 32, 51;
Crystal & Gem 25 50, 51;
Rock & Mineral 2 52, 53
jadeite, **Crystal & Gem 25** 51
Jaguar, **Car 21** 2, 59
jaguars, **Cat 29** 14, 33, 34-35
Jai Singh, Maharajah,
Light 75 7
Jainism, **Religion 68** 36-37
James I, King of Scotland,
Pirate 59 26;
Witch & Wizard 70 15
James, Frank,
Cowboy 45 44; **Crime &
Detection 73** 11
James, Jesse, **Cowboy 45** 44;
Crime & Detection 73
11-13
James, St., **Medieval Life 65** 42
Jansky, Karl, **Astronomy 82** 32
Janssen, Zacharias, **Light 75**
20, 22
Japan, **Battle 63** 16, 36, 38, 40;
Cat 29 7, 24, 44, 48;
Explorer 31 56;
Whale 46 49, 50, 56, 57
art, **Impressionism 92**
54-55, 56, 57; **Manet 94**
36-37, 40, 56; **Monet 95** 22,
36, 37, 43, 61;
Perspective 98 48-49;
Van Gogh 96 31, 36-37, 47
building, **Building 58** 11, 58
castles, **Castle 49** 36-37
currency, **Money 18** 12, 52,
53, 63
dances, **Dance 99** 11, 40
bugaku, **Dance 99** 30, 36, 43

buloh, **Dance 99** 43
kabuki, **Dance 99** 25, 41,
43, 50
noh, **Dance 99** 16, 28, 29
flags, **Flag 16** 11, 15, 52-53
knights, **Knight 43** 58-59
Kuroda, Seiki,
Impressionism 92 61
masks, **Witch &
Wizard 70** 55
pirates, **Pirate 59** 55
railways, **Train 39** 16, 47
space, **Space
Exploration 71** 15
volcanoes, **Volcano 38** 54,
57, 60, 63
weapons, **Arms &
Armour 4** 36-37
weather, **Weather 28** 45
Japanese language,
Writing 48 31
Jarre, Jean-Michel,
Music 12 62
Jason, **Ancient Greece 37** 23
jasper, **Crystal & Gem 25** 32, 33
Java, **Volcano 38** 20, 37, 57
court dancers, **Dance 99**
22, 23
Java man, **Skeleton 3** 29
javelins, **Ancient Rome 24** 11,
13; **Battle 63** 36, 44;
Knight 43 46; **Sport 8** 40
jawless fishes, **Fish 20** 8, 9, 12
jaws, **Human Body 87** 15, 48,
56, 57
development,
Human Body 87 49
jays, **Bird 1** 21, 24, 25, 41
jazz, **Music 12** 14, 15, 22, 23
dance, **Dance 99** 9
jeans, **Costume 35** 59, 60
Jefferson, Thomas,
Evolution 85 14, 15;
Explorer 31 42
Jeffreys, Alec, **Crime &
Detection 73** 45
Jehoiakim, King,
Bible Lands 30 50
Jehu, King, **Bible Lands 30** 49
Jelling Stone, **Viking 50** 9, 23,
60-61
jellyfish, **Arctic &
Antarctic 57** 12;
Ocean 62 28, 41, 43;
Seashore 15 38
Jenkins, Ab, **Car 21** 23
Jenner, Edward, **Medicine 88** 32
jennet, **Horse 33** 27
jenny donkey, **Horse 33** 24, 27
jerboa, **Desert 51** 32, 37
jerkin, **Costume 35** 20, 26
Jericho, **Bible Lands 30** 8, 29,
42-43
Jerusalem, **Religion 68** 42-44,
50-52; **Viking 50** 6, 26
archaeology, **Bible Lands 30**
62, 63

battle, **Bible Lands 30** 46,
50, 55
biblical, **Bible Lands 30** 20,
38, 56, 59
Crusades, **Castle 49** 34, 35;
Knight 43 54;
Medieval Life 65 28, 42,
44, 45
Temple, **Bible Lands 30**
20-21, 54-55
wailing wall,
Bible Lands 30 57
jesters, **Castle 49** 45;
Medieval Life 65 58
Jesus Christ, **Ancient
Rome 24** 62;
Bible Lands 30 32, 40, 58,
60; **Religion 68** 48-49, 52-53
the cross,
Religion 68 50-51
jet, **Crystal & Gem 25** 54;
Fossil 19 36
jet fins, **Shipwreck 72** 47
jet power, **Future 100** 8, 9, 10
jet propulsion, **Force &
Motion 78** 31
jets,
aircrafts, **Flying
Machine 22** 36, 39, 44-45
engines, **Technology 89** 15,
36-37, 53
jewellery, **Costume 35** 16, 18,
36, 58; **Dance 99** 22, 34, 37;
Desert 51 54, 55, 56-57;
Knight 43 38-39, 49;
Shark 40 40-41, 46, 60
African, **Africa 61** 28, 57
ancient, **Archaeology 56** 26,
36, 49; **Early People 10** 34,
35, 57
bronze age,
Early People 10 44-45
Egyptian, **Pyramid 53** 40,
42, 43, 52-53
iron age, **Early People 10**
48-49
on mummies, **Mummy 44**
16, 18, 21, 25
Roman, **Ancient Rome 24**
19, 43, 63
Russian, **Russia 74** 8, 15, 20
Viking, **Viking 50** 18, 31,
46-49
jewels, **Pirate 59** 31, 36-37
Jews, **Bible Lands 30** 54, 55,
57-58, 60
Bible, **Religion 68** 43, 44,
46-48
trade, **Bible Lands 30** 38-40
Jewstones, **Fossil 19** 17
Jezebel, **Bible Lands 30** 24
Jezebel butterfly, **Butterfly &
Moth 7** 33
jiggers, **Boat 36** 40
jird, Shaw's, **Desert 51** 32
Joan of Arc, St., **Castle 49** 33;
Medieval Life 65 22

Joan of Navarre,
WITCH & WIZARD 70 13
Jodrell Bank Observatory,
ASTRONOMY 82 33
John Dory, **FISH 20** 20, 34
John, King of England,
MEDIEVAL LIFE 65 19, 25
John, St., **KNIGHT 43** 56-57;
RELIGION 68 48, 49, 51
John the Baptist,
BIBLE LANDS 30 57
Johnson, Amy, **EXPLORER 31** 56
Johnson, Celia, **CINEMA 34** 56
Johnson, Charles, **PIRATE 59** 41,
42, 47, 61
Johnston, David,
VOLCANO 38 14
joints, architectural,
BUILDING 58 9
joints, bone, **HUMAN BODY 87**
18-19, 46, 49
joists, **BUILDING 58** 44, 45
jojoba, **PLANT 14** 58
Jolly Roger, **BOAT 36** 29;
PIRATE 59 34-35
Jolson, Al, **CINEMA 34** 22
Jonah and the whale,
SHIPWRECK 72 58;
WHALE 46 12, 55
Jones, John Paul, **PIRATE 59**
52-53
Jongkind, Johan-Barthold,
MONET 95 7, 10, 24, 25
Jooss, Kurt, **DANCE 99** 18
Jordan, **BIBLE LANDS 30** 33, 35,
57, 59
Jordan, River, **BIBLE LANDS 30**
30, 40, 56
Jordanian desert, **DESERT 51** 8,
11, 19, 60
Jorvik, *see* Vikings
Joseph, **BIBLE LANDS 30** 10, 11,
28; **RELIGION 68** 49
Joseph, Chief, **NORTH**
AMERICAN INDIAN 60 39
Joseph I, King of Spain,
GOYA 93 38, 41, 42
Joshua, **SPY 67** 8
Joule, James Prescott,
ELECTRICITY 77 24;
ENERGY 76 20, 24, 25, 36;
FORCE & MOTION 78 40;
MATTER 80 38, 39
joules, **ELECTRICITY 77** 24, 25
jousts, **CASTLE 49** 48; **HORSE 33**
44-45; **KNIGHT 43** 44-45;
MEDIEVAL LIFE 65 26
Juarez, Benito, **MANET 94** 42
Judaea, **BIBLE LANDS 30** 54,
55, 56
Judah, **BIBLE LANDS 30** 20-21,
48, 50, 54; **RELIGION 68** 44
Judaism, **RELIGION 68** 42-47
Judas, **ANCIENT ROME 24** 62
Judean Hills, **BIBLE LANDS 30**
12, 13, 34
judo, **SPORT 8** 49

Judson, Whitcomb,
INVENTION 27 7
jugglers, **MEDIEVAL LIFE 65** 54
juke boxes, **ELECTRONICS 90** 56
Julia, **ANCIENT ROME 24** 9, 18
Julius II, Pope,
RENAISSANCE 91 53
Julius Tomb,
RENAISSANCE 91 55
Rome, **RENAISSANCE 91** 50,
51, 58
Sistine Chapel,
RENAISSANCE 91 56
Julius Caesar, *see* Caesar
jumbo jets, *see* Boeing 747
jumpers, **COSTUME 35** 53
jumping bean moths,
BUTTERFLY & MOTH 7 56
junctions, **TRAIN 39** 32, 35, 50
Jung, Carl, **MEDICINE 88** 47
junglefowl, **BIRD 1** 27
jungles, **JUNGLE 54**
see also forests
junipers, **ANCIENT EGYPT 23** 26;
TREE 5 31
junks, **BOAT 36** 24, 34, 35;
CHINA 55 23, 38, 60-61;
PIRATE 59 54;
SHIPWRECK 72 16, 17
Jupiter, planet,
ASTRONOMY 82 8, 50-51, 58;
SPACE EXPLORATION 71 42,
43; **TIME & SPACE 81** 14, 15
orbit, **ASTRONOMY 82** 36, 37
satellites, **ASTRONOMY 82** 20
storms, **ASTRONOMY 82** 56
Jupiter, Roman god,
ANCIENT ROME 24 50
Jurassic Period, **DINOSAUR 13**
56, 58, 59;
EVOLUTION 85 61
Justinian I, Byzantine Emperor,
MEDIEVAL LIFE 65 6;
SPY 67 46

Ka, **MUMMY 44** 12
Ka'bah, **RELIGION 68** 54, 55, 59
kabuki, **DANCE 99** 25, 30, 41, 50
kachinas, **DESERT 51** 61; **NORTH**
AMERICAN INDIAN 60 46-47
Kaifeng, **CHINA 55** 22, 54
Kalahari Desert,
AFRICA 61 6, 8, 14, 19;
DESERT 51 34, 35, 44, 46;
EARLY PEOPLE 10 28
Kaleidoscope Moth,
BUTTERFLY & MOTH 7 53
kalengo, **MUSIC 12** 50
Kali, **RELIGION 68** 18, 20
Kalmyk, **RUSSIA 74** 12
Kandinsky, Wassili,
VIKING 50 19;
WATERCOLOUR 97 58, 60
Kane, Paul, **NORTH AMERICAN**
INDIAN 60 59
kangaroos, **DESERT 51** 32, 57;
JUNGLE 54 56; **MAMMAL 11**
8, 9, 58; **SKELETON 3** 52
fossils, **FOSSIL 19** 55, 56, 57
reproduction,
MAMMAL 11 30-31
Kangxi, Emperor, **CHINA 55** 62
Kansas, River,
EXPLORER 31 33
Kanzi, **GORILLA 64** 36
Kapoor, Anish,
WATERCOLOUR 97 61
Kara Kum, **DESERT 51** 7, 34
Karamojong peoples,
AFRICA 61 25, 26
karate, **SPORT 8** 49
Karloff, Boris,
ANCIENT EGYPT 23 16;
CINEMA 34 61;
MUMMY 44 40
karma, **RELIGION 68** 22, 25, 27
Karnak, **PYRAMID 53** 26, 41
Kasparov, Gary, **FUTURE 100** 44
Katep, **PYRAMID 53** 9
katsura, **TREE 5** 26
Kaupang, **VIKING 50** 26
Kawah Idjen, Java,
VOLCANO 38 20, 21
kayaks, **ARCTIC &**
ANTARCTIC 57 51;
BOAT 36 10, 11, 21; **EARLY**
PEOPLE 10 20, 21; **NORTH**
AMERICAN INDIAN 60 60-61
Kazakhstan, **RUSSIA 74** 12, 23
Kazan, **RUSSIA 74** 20, 23

keels, **BOAT 36** 17, 19, 23, 34
keeps, **CASTLE 49** 10;
KNIGHT 43 22, 23
keepsakes, **MONEY 18** 23, 25
Kelly, "Machine Gun", **CRIME**
& DETECTION 73 13
Kelly, Gene, **CINEMA 34** 42;
DANCE 99 8
Kelly, Ned, **COWBOY 45** 57;
CRIME & DETECTION 73 16
Kelly, Orry, **CINEMA 34** 37
kelpies, **DOG 32** 56
Kenilworth castle, **CASTLE 49** 13
Kennedy, John F.,
CRIME & DETECTION 73 58;
RUSSIA 74 37
Kennel Clubs, **DOG 32** 39, 52
Kent, William, **BOAT 36** 33
Kenya, **AFRICA 61** 7, 28, 29;
DANCE 99 39; **EXPLORER 31**
16; **FLAG 16** 54
Maasai peoples,
AFRICA 61 42
Turkana peoples,
AFRICA 61 18-19
Kepler, Johannes,
ASTRONOMY 82 18-19;
FORCE &
MOTION 78 32, 33;
LIGHT 75 11;
TIME & SPACE 81 14
Kerameikos, **ANCIENT**
GREECE 37 48
keratin, **CAT 29** 15;
ELEPHANT 42 17; **HORSE 33**
28; **REPTILE 26** 24; **SHELL 9** 8;
WHALE 46 25
Kerner, Annette, **CRIME &**
DETECTION 73 37
keros, **AZTEC 47** 7, 50, 63
kestrels, **BIRD 1** 16, 27, 34, 37
American, **EAGLE 69** 11, 47, 58
European, **EAGLE 69** 19, 46, 58
Mauritian, **EAGLE 69** 47
ketches, **PIRATE 59** 30
Ketchum, Black Jack,
CRIME & DETECTION 73 13
Kettering, C. F., **FUTURE 100** 11
kettles, **INVENTION 27** 54
keyboards, musical,
ELECTRONICS 90 7, 56, 57;
MUSIC 12 44
electronic, **MUSIC 12** 62
keyboards, typing,
WRITING 48 58-59
keys, **CASTLE 49** 61;
VIKING 50 28, 33
keys, musical, **MUSIC 12** 11, 12, 13
Keyser, Jacob de,
PERSPECTIVE 98 27
keystones, **BUILDING 58** 32
KGB, **RUSSIA 74** 20, 34, 36;
SPY 67 35, 43, 57-58
Khafra, **PYRAMID 53** 6, 16-19,
26-27
Khmelnitsky, Bogdan,
RUSSIA 74 22

Khnum, **ANCIENT EGYPT 23** 25
Khonsu, **ANCIENT EGYPT 23** 31
Khorana, Har Gobind,
  LIFE 84 37
Khrushchev, Nikita,
  RUSSIA 74 36, 37
Khufu, **ANCIENT EGYPT 23** 20,
  38; **MUMMY 44** 7;
  PYRAMID 53 18, 19
  funeral boat,
    PYRAMID 53 28-29
  Great Pyramid, **PYRAMID 53**
    16-17, 20, 23
  portraits, **PYRAMID 53** 18, 21
khur, **DESERT 51** 34;
  HORSE 33 17
kiang, **HORSE 33** 16-17
Kidd, William, **PIRATE 59** 46, 57
kidnapping, **CRIME &**
  DETECTION 73 22, 23;
  SPY 67 43
kidneys, **HUMAN BODY 87** 12,
  38-39, 40
  dialysis, **MEDICINE 88** 54-55
  kidney machines,
    FUTURE 100 10
Kiev, **RUSSIA 74** 8;
  VIKING 50 26, 29
Kikuyu peoples, **AFRICA 61** 28,
  42, 62
  dance, **DANCE 99** 39
Kilauea volcano, Hawaii,
  VOLCANO 38 22, 23, 40, 43
Kilby, Jack, **ELECTRONICS 90**
  52, 53
Kilimanjaro, Mt., **AFRICA 61** 7;
  ROCK & MINERAL 2 7
  Kilimanjaro tusks,
    ELEPHANT 42 20
kilns, **TECHNOLOGY 89** 8, 34
kilowatts,
  ELECTRICITY 77 25, 46
Kimberley, South Africa,
  VOLCANO 38 39
kimberlite,
  CRYSTAL & GEM 25 34
kimono, **DANCE 99** 28, 29, 30,
  36, 41
Kimura, Motoo,
  EVOLUTION 85 54
kinetic energy, **ENERGY 76** 12,
  15, 16-17; **FORCE &**
  MOTION 78 40, 41;
  MATTER 80 61
Kinetoscope, **CINEMA 34** 12,
  16, 62
King Kong, **GORILLA 64** 42
King William Island,
  ARCTIC & ANTARCTIC 57 53
kingfishers, **BIRD 1** 14, 40;
  POND & RIVER 6 30
Kingsford Smith, Charles,
  FLYING MACHINE 22 32
Kingsley, Charles, **POND &**
  RIVER 6 49
Kingsley, Mary, **EXPLORER 31** 49
Kinski, Klaus, **CINEMA 34** 61

Kipling, Rudyard,
  CAT 29 7, 33; **ELEPHANT 42**
  26; **REPTILE 26** 58
Kircher, Athanasius,
  VOLCANO 38 8
Kirchhoff, Gustav,
  ASTRONOMY 82 30, 31;
  ELECTRONICS 90 22
Kirov Ballet, **DANCE 99** 12
Kissi pennies, **MONEY 18** 54, 55
Kissi peoples, **AFRICA 61** 36
kitchens, **CASTLE 49** 40-41, 47
kites, birds, **EAGLE 69** 29, 31,
  38-39
kites, paper, **CHINA 55** 22, 50,
  51; **FLYING MACHINE 22** 10,
  11; **WEATHER 28** 43
  "kite planes", **FLYING**
    MACHINE 22 60
kithara, **ANCIENT GREECE 37**
  23, 34
kitharistes, **ANCIENT**
  GREECE 37 33
kits, **MUSIC 12** 29
kiwis, **BIRD 1** 55
Kiyonaga, Torii,
  IMPRESSIONISM 92 55
Klee, Paul, **PERSPECTIVE 98** 56,
  57; **WATERCOLOUR 97** 58, 61
Klein, Oscar, **TIME &**
  SPACE 81 59
Klimt, Gustav,
  WATERCOLOUR 97 55
klippes, **MONEY 18** 42
klystron, **ELECTRONICS 90** 26, 41
knees, **HUMAN BODY 87** 18, 19,
  21, 30
  kneecaps,
    HUMAN BODY 87 15
knickerbockers, **COSTUME 35**
  22, 23, 52
knickers, **COSTUME 35** 36, 50
knifefish, **FISH 20** 21, 48
knights, **BATTLE 63** 7, 10, 12, 45;
  KNIGHT 43;
  MEDIEVAL LIFE 65 8, 14, 27,
  63; **PIRATE 59** 16-17
  arms and armour,
    ARMS & ARMOUR 4 24-25,
    26-27
  education, **KNIGHT 43**
    10-11, 39
  family, **KNIGHT 43** 37, 38
  jousting, **ARMS &**
    ARMOUR 4 28-29, 30-31
  knighthood, **BATTLE 63** 58
  peace time, **KNIGHT 43** 34-35
  religious orders,
    KNIGHT 43 53, 56-57
  royal champions,
    KNIGHT 43 42
  tourneys, **MEDIEVAL LIFE 65**
    26-27
  at war, **MEDIEVAL LIFE 65** 24,
    25, 28-29
Knights Hospitaller,
  CASTLE 49 35

Knights Templar, **CASTLE 49** 34
knives, **AFRICA 61** 47, 49;
  ARMS & ARMOUR 4 22-23,
  50, 62; **COWBOY 45** 38, 49;
  SPY 67 12, 32, 36, 37
  ancient, **EARLY PEOPLE 10** 21,
    32, 46, 51
  Aztec peoples, **AZTEC 47** 23,
    28, 36, 38
knobkerries, **AFRICA 61** 46
Knossos, **ANCIENT GREECE 37** 6,
  7; **WRITING 48** 10
Koberg, Anthony,
  RENAISSANCE 91 40
Koch, Robert, **LIFE 84** 12, 28;
  MEDICINE 88 32-33
Koestler, Arthur, **FUTURE 100** 10
Kofi-Karikari, King,
  AFRICA 61 10, 56
Koh-i-noor diamond,
  ROCK & MINERAL 2 50
kohl, **DESERT 51** 53;
  EARLY PEOPLE 10 34
kokerboom tree, **DESERT 51** 20
Kokoshnik, **RUSSIA 74** 12, 51
Kolff, Wilhelm, **FUTURE 100** 10
Komarov, Vladimir,
  SPACE EXPLORATION 71 34
Komsomol, **RUSSIA 74** 39, 53
Konik ponies, **HORSE 33** 20
kopeks, **MONEY 18** 44, 45, 62
Koran, *see* Qur'an
Korea, **FLAG 16** 52;
  WITCH & WIZARD 70 55
Koryusai, Isoda,
  IMPRESSIONISM 92 55
Kos, **ANCIENT GREECE 37** 42, 59
Kota peoples, **AFRICA 61** 40
koto, **MUSIC 12** 38
Kouri, **ANCIENT GREECE 37** 6
Krak des Chevaliers,
  CASTLE 49 35; **KNIGHT 43** 55
Kraken, **OCEAN 62** 34
Krebs, Hans, **LIFE 84** 19, 23
Kremlin, **RUSSIA 74** 25-27,
  30, 45
Krishna, **RELIGION 68** 18, 20,
  1, 23
krona, **MONEY 18** 44
krones, **MONEY 18** 42, 43, 62
kronors, **MONEY 18** 45
krugerrands, **MONEY 18** 55
Kuanyama peoples,
  AFRICA 61 16-17, 24
Kuanyin, **CHINA 55** 26, 27
Kuba peoples, **AFRICA 61** 21,
  31, 46, 58
Kublai Khan, **CHINA 55** 8, 58,
  59; **DESERT 51** 63;
  EXPLORER 31 17
Knights Templar,
  CASTLE 49 34
Kubrick, Stanley, **CINEMA 34** 35
Kuiper, Gerard P.,
  ASTRONOMY 82 55
kulan, **DESERT 51** 34; **HORSE 33**
  7, 12, 17

kung fu, **SPORT 8** 48
Kunz, George,
  CRYSTAL & GEM 25 49
kunzite,
  CRYSTAL & GEM 25 42, 49
Kuo Min Tang party,
  FLAG 16 58
Kuroda, Seiki,
  IMPRESSIONISM 92 61
Kurosawa, Akira, **CINEMA 34**
  49, 58
Kurru, **PYRAMID 53** 48
kurus, **MONEY 18** 40, 41
Kutuzov, Mikhail, **RUSSIA 74** 22
Kuyu peoples, **AFRICA 61** 41
Kwakiutl, **DANCE 99** 33
kyanite, **CRYSTAL & GEM 25** 20
kylix, **ANCIENT GREECE 37** 49
Kyoto, **VOLCANO 38** 11
Kyzyl Kum, **DESERT 51** 7, 34

La Brea, **FOSSIL 19** 21
labels, **INSECT 17** 63
labradorite, **CRYSTAL &**
  GEM 25 17
labradors, **DOG 32** 21
laburnums, **TREE 5** 28, 41
labyrinth, **ANCIENT**
  GREECE 37 9
Lacewing, **BUTTERFLY &**
  MOTH 7 7, 22, 34
Lachish, **BIBLE LANDS 30** 35,
  46-47
  Fosse Temple,
    BIBLE LANDS 30 31, 37
  solar shrine,
    BIBLE LANDS 30 53
Lackey Moth, **BUTTERFLY &**
  MOTH 7 10-11
Lacroix, Alfred, **VOLCANO 38** 32
lacrosse, **NORTH AMERICAN**
  INDIAN 60 24-25; **SPORT 8** 17
lactic acid, **CHEMISTRY 79** 41,
  48, 49

ladders, CASTLE 49 24, 26
lading, SHIPWRECK 72 54
Laennec, René, INVENTION 27 43; MEDICINE 88 28-29
Lafayette, FLAG 16 26
Lafitte, Jean, PIRATE 59 53
Lagash, WRITING 48 9
Lagonda, CAR 21 59
Lagunillas Canyon, VOLCANO 38 56
Lahmu, BIBLE LANDS 30 48
Laing, Gordon, DESERT 51 62
Lake, Stuart, COWBOY 45 43
lakes, ECOLOGY 86 54
Lakshmi, RELIGION 68 18
Lalique, René, CAR 21 62
Lamarck, Jean Baptiste de, EVOLUTION 85 12-13, 32, 33
lamas, RELIGION 68 28, 29
lamb and flag, FLAG 16 18
Lammas, feast, KNIGHT 43 36
lamp shells, see brachiopods
lampreys, FISH 20 9, 12, 34
lamps, ANCIENT ROME 24 25; CASTLE 49 38; CHINA 55 43; ELECTRICITY 77 42, 43, 47
lance pennons, FLAG 16 12
Lancelot, KNIGHT 43 41
lances, ARMS & ARMOUR 4 8, 15, 31; BATTLE 63 45; KNIGHT 43 18, 33
lance rests, KNIGHT 43 15, 44-45
Landelle, Gabriel de la, FLYING MACHINE 22 52
Landru, Henri-Désiré, CRIME & DETECTION 73 23
landscapes, PERSPECTIVE 98 28
Landseer, Sir Edwin, CAT 29 8
Landsknechts, KNIGHT 43 60-61
Landsteiner, Karl, LIFE 84 29; MEDICINE 88 50
Lang, Fritz, CINEMA 34 19, 46, 61
Langerhans, Paul, HUMAN BODY 87 41
Langley, Samuel Pierpoint, FLYING MACHINE 22 13
Lango peoples, AFRICA 61 46
langurs, GORILLA 64 23, 24
L'Anse aux Meadows, VIKING 50 21
Lao Zi, CHINA 55 26
Laocoön, RENAISSANCE 91 47, 50
Lao-tzu, RELIGION 68 30, 32
laparoscopes, TECHNOLOGY 89 57
lapilli, VOLCANO 38 16, 26, 29
lapis lazuli, ANCIENT EGYPT 23 41, 56; ARCHAEOLOGY 56 50; WATERCOLOUR 97 6, 7, 13; WRITING 48 29
gemstone, CRYSTAL & GEM 25 50, 56, 58, 60; ROCK & MINERAL 2 33, 52
Laplace, Pierre Simon, ASTRONOMY 82 37

lappet moths, BUTTERFLY & MOTH 7 4, 55
Lapps, ARCTIC & ANTARCTIC 57 38, 39, 48, 59
Lapstrakes, BOAT 36 16, 17, 18, 31
larches, TREE 5 31, 32, 44, 58
larvae, ARCTIC & ANTARCTIC 57 16; SHELL 9 10, 24, 32
larval fish, FISH 20 24, 25
laryngoscope, MEDICINE 88 60
larynx, HUMAN BODY 87 19, 23, 25
Las Vegas, PYRAMID 53 63
Lascaux, ARCHAEOLOGY 56 62-63
lasers, CRYSTAL & GEM 25 28, 58; ELECTRONICS 90 47, 49, 63; FUTURE 100 10, 51
beams, MEDICINE 88 52-53; TIME & SPACE 81 54, 57
light, LIGHT 75 56-57, 58, 59; TECHNOLOGY 89 58-59, 63
cutting, TECHNOLOGY 89 26, 35
measuring, TECHNOLOGY 89 30
surgery, TECHNOLOGY 89 57, 58, 59
surveying, TECHNOLOGY 89 23
printers, ELECTRONICS 90 62
Lasseter, John, CINEMA 34 52
lateral line, FISH 20 8, 15, 28, 52
latex, JUNGLE 54 59
lathes, TECHNOLOGY 89 10-11
Latin, ANCIENT ROME 24 40
inscriptions, WRITING 48 16
Latin America, WITCH & WIZARD 70 14, 48, 49
latitude, ASTRONOMY 82 14, 15, 27, 28; INVENTION 27 34, 35; SHIPWRECK 72 32; TIME & SPACE 81 18, 40
Latvia, FLAG 16 57
Lauda, Niki, CAR 21 33
Laue, Max von, CRYSTAL & GEM 25 14, 15
Lauer, Jean-Philippe, PYRAMID 53 12
launching, BOAT 36 26, 46
laurel wreaths, ANCIENT ROME 24 7, 9
Laurel, Stan, CINEMA 34 54
laurels, TREE 5 7
lava, EARTH 83 35, 44-45, 61; ROCK & MINERAL 2 10, 17, 18-19; SEASHORE 15 9; VOLCANO 38 18, 19, 23, 40
Lavoisier, Antoine Laurent, CHEMISTRY 79 16, 18, 30, 31; ENERGY 76 21; LIFE 84 18; MATTER 80 28, 30; WEATHER 28 6
Lavoisier, Marie-Anne, MATTER 80 28

Law of Conservation of Energy, FORCE & MOTION 78 40
Law of Conservation of Momentum, FORCE & MOTION 78 36
Law of Gravity, FORCE & MOTION 78 28, 32, 35
lawmen, COWBOY 45 42-45, 47
lawn tennis, SPORT 8 30
Lawrence, Ernest, MATTER 80 59
laws, CRIME & DETECTION 73 8, 9, 10, 12
Laws of Motion, FORCE & MOTION 78 28, 29, 40
Lawson, William, EXPLORER 31 38
Le Carré, John, SPY 67 58
Le Corbusier, CAR 21 34
Le Verrier, Urbain, ASTRONOMY 82 56
lead, CHEMISTRY 79 12, 23; CRYSTAL & GEM 25 10, 53; MATTER 80 6, 11, 22, 24; ROCK & MINERAL 2 48, 57
metallic properties, TECHNOLOGY 89 14
lead-acid accumulators, INVENTION 27 39
lead-acid battery, ELECTRICITY 77 19
Leadenhall Street, CAT 29 31
leaf butterflies, BUTTERFLY & MOTH 7 54
leaf mines, INSECT 17 42
leaf moths, BUTTERFLY & MOTH 7 55
leafhoppers, INSECT 17 36
Leakey, Louis, FOSSIL 19 59
Leakey, Mary, FOSSIL 19 58
Leakey, Richard, EARLY PEOPLE 10 7, 10; FOSSIL 19 59
Lean, David, CINEMA 34 59
leap years, TIME & SPACE 81 27
Lear, Edward, BIBLE LANDS 30 38; CAT 29 58; FISH 20 32
leather, ARCHAEOLOGY 56 30, 31; EARLY PEOPLE 10 32; ELEPHANT 42 56
leatherworking, CASTLE 49 50
leather carp, FISH 20 15
leather jacket, FISH 20 35
leaves, ECOLOGY 86 8-9, 44; JUNGLE 54 11, 13; PLANT 14 10, 34-35, 53; TREE 5 28-31, 46-47
Leavitt, Henrietta, ASTRONOMY 82 60
Lebanon, BIBLE LANDS 30 22, 41; EXPLORER 31 6, 9
Leclanché, Georges, ELECTRICITY 77 18
leclanché cell, ENERGY 76 23

Lee, Bruce, SPORT 8 48
Lee, Christopher, CINEMA 34 60
Lee, Sir Henry, KNIGHT 43 15
Lee, Robert E., BATTLE 63 51
Lee, Spike, CINEMA 34 28
Lee Enfield rifles, BATTLE 63 51
leeboards, BOAT 36 34, 35
leeches, MEDICINE 88 22, 26; POND & RIVER 6 9, 13
Leeuwenhoek Antoni Van, INVENTION 27 29; HUMAN BODY 87 12, 13, 33
left-hand rule, ELECTRICITY 77 27
Léger, Fernand, WATERCOLOUR 97 60
legionaries, ANCIENT ROME 24 10-11, 13, 14
Leibniz, Gottfried Wilhelm, ELECTRONICS 90 46; ENERGY 76 16, 17; TIME & SPACE 81 29
Leif the Lucky, VIKING 50 6, 21, 24
Leigh, Vivien, CINEMA 34 37
lemmings, ARCTIC & ANTARCTIC 57 16, 24, 36; ECOLOGY 86 28, 33; MAMMAL 11 38
lemons, TREE 5 39
lemurs, GORILLA 64 6, 10-11, 33; JUNGLE 54 26; MAMMAL 11 8, 9, 19, 29
ring-tailed, SKELETON 3 40
Lenin, Vladimir, FLAG 16 18; MUMMY 44 6; RUSSIA 74 29, 30, 31, 34
Leningrad, FLAG 16 57
Lenoir, Étienne, CAR 21 6, 48; INVENTION 27 48
lenses, INVENTION 27 28, 29, 40, 41; LIGHT 75 44, 55, 58
achromatic, LIGHT 75 17, 21, 23
camera, LIGHT 75 24-25, 37
concave, LIGHT 75 16, 17, 20
convex, LIGHT 75 16-17, 20
eye, LIGHT 75 18, 19
focal length, LIGHT 75 16, 19, 20, 22
microscope, LIGHT 75 22-23, 37
telescope, LIGHT 75 20-21
Leonardo da Vinci, EVOLUTION 85 10; LIGHT 75 10; MEDICINE 88 24; TECHNOLOGY 89 6; WRITING 48 52
anatomy drawings, HUMAN BODY 87 15, 20, 42; INVENTION 27 42; SKELETON 3 7, 48
drawing techniques, RENAISSANCE 91 37
experiments, scientific, RENAISSANCE 91 38-39
flying machines, FLYING MACHINE 22 6-7; INVENTION 27 58

landscapes, RENAISSANCE **91** 35
Mona Lisa, RENAISSANCE **91** 36
on perspective, PERSPECTIVE **98** 24, 28
"Vitruvian Man", RENAISSANCE **91** 30
Leonov, Aleksei, SPACE EXPLORATION **71** 13, 19, 26
leopard butterflies, BUTTERFLY & MOTH **7** 19, 23
leopard cats, CAT **29** 40
leopard tortoises, SHELL **9** 30
leopards, CAT **29** 10-11, 32-33; GORILLA **64** 35, 42; JUNGLE **54** 46; MAMMAL **11** 53
Lepidodendron, FOSSIL **19** 36
Lepidoptera, INSECT **17** 8
Lepidostrobus, FOSSIL **19** 36
Lepidotes, FOSSIL **19** 16, 35
leptons, MONEY **18** 41
Lermontov, Mikhail, RUSSIA **74** 44
Leroy, Louis, MONET **19**, 29, 57
Lesbos, ANCIENT GREECE **37** 31
Lesotho, AFRICA **61** 14
lesser spotted dogfish, FISH **20** 29, 60
lesser weaver, FISH **20** 55
letterpress, INVENTION **27** 26
leukaemia, MEDICINE **88** 30, 42
Levant, BIBLE LANDS **30** 11, 30
levers, FORCE & MOTION **78** 10, 16-17; TECHNOLOGY **89** 32
  balance, FORCE & MOTION **78** 34
  clock, FORCE & MOTION **78** 46, 47
  machines, FORCE & MOTION **78** 22-23, 30, 31
Lewis, David, WATERCOLOUR **97** 31
Lewis, John Frederick, WATERCOLOUR **97** 39
Lewis, Meriwether, EXPLORER **31** 42, 45, 63
Leyden jar, ELECTRICITY **77** 8, 9, 10, 12, 13; ELECTRONICS **90** 20
Li Shizhen, CHINA **55** 29
libraries, WRITING **48** 43, 62-63
Libya, BIBLE LANDS **30** 52; MONEY **18** 23
lice, INSECT **17** 40, 41
lichen, ARCTIC & ANTARCTIC **57** 18, 38; JUNGLE **54** 10; POND & RIVER **6** 54; TREE **5** 8, 21
  composition, PLANT **14** 6
  indicator species, ECOLOGY **86** 52
Lichstenstein, Roy, CASTLE **49** 21; PERSPECTIVE **98** 60, 61

Liebig, Justus von, MATTER **80** 27
life, LIFE **84**; TIME & SPACE **81** 22, 31, 39
  cycle, LIFE **84** 31, 52
  origin of, EVOLUTION **85** 56-57, 60
lifeboats, BOAT **36** 56, 58, 59; SHIPWRECK **72** 29, 38, 39
  equipment, SHIPWRECK **72** 42, 43
  German, SHIPWRECK **72** 41
  rescue, SHIPWRECK **72** 8, 40
lifebuoys, SHIPWRECK **72** 43
lifejackets, BOAT **36** 58, 59, 62
lift, FORCE & MOTION **78** 42, 45
ligaments, HUMAN BODY **87** 19, 23
liger, CAT **29** 59
light, LIGHT **75** 42, 60-61; MATTER **80** 20, 30, 51, 63; TIME & SPACE **81** 17, 41, 48, 61
  in art, PERSPECTIVE **98** 28-29
  black holes, FORCE & MOTION **78** 61; TIME & SPACE **81** 46, 47
  colours, MATTER **80** 32, 56
  electric, LIGHT **75** 52-53
  energy, ENERGY **76** 15, 22, 25; FORCE & MOTION **78** 29, 40, 51
  gravity, TIME & SPACE **81** 42, 43
  infra-red, ENERGY **76** 48; LIGHT **75** 40-41, 42-43; TECHNOLOGY **89** 7, 58-59
  laser, LIGHT **75** 56-57, 58, 59
  measurement, TIME & SPACE **81** 54, 56
  optical inventions, INVENTION **27** 28-29
  polarized, LIGHT **75** 48-49
  rays, ELECTRICITY **77** 60
  relativity, TIME & SPACE **81** 34, 36
  spectrum, ENERGY **76** 43
  speed, ENERGY **76** 44, 45; FORCE & MOTION **78** 58-59, 62; TIME & SPACE **81** 14, 32-33, 35
  Sun, ENERGY **76** 6, 48
  ultraviolet, ENERGY **76** 42; LIGHT **75** 41, 43, 45
  waves, ENERGY **76** 40
  white, LIGHT **75** 28-29, 32-33, 39
light bulbs, ELECTRICITY **77** 19, 43, 46, 47, 54; LIGHT **75** 52-53
light years, ASTRONOMY **82** 60, 62, 63; TIME & SPACE **81** 7, 48
lighthouses, BOAT **36** 58; BUILDING **58** 63; ELECTRICITY **77** 36, 37; INVENTION **27** 35; LIGHT **75** 8, 17

saving shipwrecks, SHIPWRECK **72** 34, 35
lighting, ENERGY **76** 58; FUTURE **100** 19; LIGHT **75** 52-53
lightning, ELECTRICITY **77** 6, 7, 12, 41; ENERGY **76** 6, 19; LIGHT **75** 6; WEATHER **28** 36, 37, 51
  conductors, ELECTRICITY **77** 8, 10
lights, car, CAR **21** 20-21, 41, 50
lignin, TREE **5** 26
lignite, ROCK & MINERAL **2** 37
lilies, JUNGLE **54** 49; PLANT **14** 16, 17, 25, 34
  water, PLANT **14** 48, 49; POND & RIVER **6** 34, 42-43, 44
limbo dancing, DANCE **99** 11
Limbourg brothers, RENAISSANCE **91** 16; WATERCOLOUR **97** 12-13
limes, TREE **5** 41
limestone, CHEMISTRY **79** 28, 40, 48, 49; EARTH **83** 17, 27, 63; PYRAMID **53** 32; ROCK & MINERAL **2** 20, 24, 34-35
  caves, ROCK & MINERAL **2** 22-23
  in deserts, DESERT **51** 11
  near sea, SEASHORE **15** 10-11, 42, 43
  Solvay process, CHEMISTRY **79** 62, 63
  weathering, EARTH **83** 50, 51, 55
Limousines, CAR **21** 13
limpets, POND & RIVER **6** 53, 59; SEASHORE **15** 28-29, 33, 59
Lincoln, Abraham, BOAT **36** 32; CRIME & DETECTION **73** 11; SPY **67** 30, 31
Lindbergh, Charles, CRIME & DETECTION **73** 22; EXPLORER **31** 57; FLYING MACHINE **22** 26, 32
Lindholm Høje, VIKING **50** 57
Lindisfarne, VIKING **50** 16
Lindisfarne Gospels, CAT **29** 6
Lindow Man, ARCHAEOLOGY **56** 36; CRIME & DETECTION **73** 9; MUMMY **44** 59
Lindow Woman, CRIME & DETECTION **73** 58; MUMMY **44** 58
Linear B, WRITING **48** 10
linen, ARCHAEOLOGY **56** 34, 40-41; COSTUME **35** 8, 9, 10, 12, 14, 28, 51; VIKING **50** 30, 44
liners, BOAT **36** 36, 38, 54-57; SHIPWRECK **72** 28, 29

Linnaeus, CAT **29** 10, 44
Lion gate, ANCIENT GREECE **37** 11
lion-dogs, DOG **32** 35, 58
lionfishes, FISH **20** 31, 54, 55
lions, ANCIENT EGYPT **23** 44, 60; CAT **29** 7, 13, 15, 21; DESERT **51** 34, 35, 43; ECOLOGY **86** 11, 48; MAMMAL **11** 16, 28, 42, 48
  Africa, CAT **29** 28-29
  ancient, DINOSAUR **13** 25
  bones, SKELETON **3** 17, 35, 36, 53
  cubs, CAT **29** 25
  evolution, CAT **29** 8-9
  "ligers" and "tigons", CAT **29** 59
  mating, CAT **29** 24
Lippershey, Hans, ASTRONOMY **82** 20, 22
Lippi, Filippino, RENAISSANCE **91** 18
Lippi, Fra Filippo, RENAISSANCE **91** 23
liquefaction, EARTH **83** 42
liquid crystal display, CRYSTAL & GEM **25** 62; ELECTRONICS **90** 44-45, 59
  fax machine, ELECTRONICS **90** 61
  laser printer, ELECTRONICS **90** 62
  mobile phone, ELECTRONICS **90** 63
  remote control, ELECTRONICS **90** 60
liquids, FORCE & MOTION **78** 14, 15, 44; MATTER **80** 11, 13, 18-19
  and atoms, MATTER **80** 34, 38
  crystals, MATTER **80** 15
  measurement, MATTER **80** 10
  state of matter, MATTER **80** 6, 12, 22
lira, MONEY **18** 40, 41
lire, MONEY **18** 23, 36, 37
liroconite, CRYSTAL & GEM **25** 24
Lister, Joseph, INVENTION **27** 43; MEDICINE **88** 48-49
lithification, EARTH **83** 26
lithosphere, EARTH **83** 20, 40, 43, 49; VOLCANO **38** 9, 13
Lithostrotion, FOSSIL **19** 22
Little Big Horn, battle of, BATTLE **63** 53
Little Mermaid, The, SHIPWRECK **72** 59
liver, HUMAN BODY **87** 32, 34-37, 44; LIFE **84** 14, 15
Liverpool and Manchester Railway, TRAIN **39** 6, 12, 13
liverworts, JUNGLE **54** 8; PLANT **14** 6, 7; POND & RIVER **6** 54; TREE **5** 53
Livia, ANCIENT ROME **24** 9, 50, 59

living stone, DESERT 51 19
Livingstone, David,
        EXPLORER 31 19, 46-47, 63;
        JUNGLE 54 61
lizards, DESERT 51 26, 28;
        JUNGLE 54 16, 32, 55;
        LIFE 84 26, 33, 53;
        REPTILE 26 10, 20, 28-29, 46
    basilisks, REPTILE 26 57
    bones, SKELETON 3 20
    extinct, DINOSAUR 13 6, 58,
        60, 61
    fossils, FOSSIL 19 20, 44, 45, 46
    garden, REPTILE 26 55
    Mexican beaded,
        REPTILE 26 42
    monitor, REPTILE 26 19-20,
        45, 58
    plated, REPTILE 26 24, 28
    sand, REPTILE 26 10, 14
    tegu, AMPHIBIAN 41 7;
        REPTILE 26 7, 52-53
    see also iguana
llamas, AZTEC 47 12, 24, 42, 51;
        DESERT 51 7, 43;
        FARM 66 13; MAMMAL 11 10
Lloyd, Harold, CINEMA 34 20
loaches, FISH 20 16
load, FORCE & MOTION 78 8,
        9, 43
    friction, FORCE &
        MOTION 78 39
    inertia, FORCE & MOTION 78
        30-31
    levers, FORCE & MOTION 78
        16, 17
    pulley, FORCE & MOTION 78
        78 18
lobe-finned fishes, FISH 20 9, 13
lobster moth caterpillars,
        BUTTERFLY & MOTH 7 53
lobsters, DINOSAUR 13 60;
        SEASHORE 15 44, 46-47;
        SHELL 9 22-23, 27, 47;
        SKELETON 3 24
    crustaceans, FOSSIL 19 30, 31
    spiny, OCEAN 62 18
    squat, OCEAN 62 19
Loches, CASTLE 49 22, 23, 33, 39
lock-picks, CRIME &
        DETECTION 73 37; SPY 67 59
locks, INVENTION 27 7
Lockyer, Norman,
        ASTRONOMY 82 31
locomotives, INVENTION 27 32,
        33; TRAIN 39 36, 44, 60
    diesel, TRAIN 39 7, 38
    diesel-electric, TRAIN 39 7,
        12, 26, 40
    electric, TRAIN 39 38, 39, 56
    "Gladstone", TRAIN 39 44
    "John Bull", TRAIN 39 19
    "Mallard", TRAIN 39 41,
        46, 47
    "Puffing Billy", TRAIN 39 11
    "Rocket", TRAIN 39 13
    steam, TRAIN 39 12-15, 52-53

"Tom Thumb", TRAIN 39 18
locust-bean moths, BUTTERFLY
        & MOTH 7 42
locusts, DESERT 51 24, 25;
        ECOLOGY 86 31; INSECT 17
        18, 19, 22, 61
lodestones, INVENTION 27 34
Loeb, Richard, CRIME &
        DETECTION 73 23
Loewe, Siegmund,
        ELECTRONICS 90 52
log cabins, BUILDING 58 10, 11, 41
logarithms, INVENTION 27 30
logboats, BOAT 36 6, 14, 15
logging, JUNGLE 54 62-63
logic, in computers,
        ELECTRONICS 90 8, 9, 45, 57
    circuit, ELECTRONICS 90 50, 51
logo, WRITING 48 61
Loire, River, CASTLE 49 14-15
Loki, VIKING 50 53
L'Ollonais, PIRATE 59 26, 27
Lomonosov, Mikhail,
        ASTRONOMY 82 28, 49
London, ANCIENT ROME 24 38;
        CAT 29 16, 31, 50-51;
        MONET 95 48, 50-51;
        VAN GOGH 96 8, 10;
        VIKING 50 16
    archaeological finds,
        ARCHAEOLOGY 56 10-11,
        48-49, 52-53
    Chatham and Dover
        Railway, TRAIN 39 49
    North Eastern Railway,
        TRAIN 39 46
    Metropolitan Police,
        CRIME & DETECTION 73 10,
        11, 35, 50
    Tower of, CASTLE 49 10, 32
London, Jack, ARCTIC &
        ANTARCTIC 57 40, 41
Long John Silver,
        ARMS & ARMOUR 4 40;
        PIRATE 59 60
long jump, SPORT 8 41
longbows, ARMS & ARMOUR 4
        18-21; BATTLE 63 36;
        KNIGHT 43 30-31
Longfellow, Henry,
        VAN GOGH 96 8
longhorn cattle, VIKING 50 38
longitudes, ASTRONOMY 82 14,
        15, 27, 28; INVENTION 27 34,
        35; SHIPWRECK 72 32, 33;
        TIME & SPACE 81 18, 19, 40
long-nosed gars, FISH 20 20
longships, VIKING 50 8-11
long-tailed tits, BIRD 1 49
Lonsdale, Kathleen,
        CHEMISTRY 79 27
looms, AZTEC 47 42;
        INVENTION 27 35, 37;
        TECHNOLOGY 89 34;
        VIKING 50 44, 45
loons, ARCTIC &
        ANTARCTIC 57 21

loosejaws, FISH 20 18
Lord's, cricket ground,
        SPORT 8 27
lords, CASTLE 49 48-49
Lorenzetti, Ambrogio,
        PERSPECTIVE 98 10, 62
lorgnettes, COSTUME 35 36
lorises, GORILLA 64 10, 12-13
    lowland, GORILLA 64 44-45
lotus, ANCIENT EGYPT 23 13, 26;
        CHINA 55 27, 54, 57;
        MUMMY 44 19, 24, 30;
        PLANT 14 28; RELIGION 68
        20, 23, 29
lotus position, RELIGION 68 24,
        26, 27
Lotus Sutra, CHINA 55 25;
        WRITING 48 31
Lotz, Wolfgang, SPY 67 58
Loud, John H., INVENTION 27 19
loudspeakers, ELECTRICITY 77
        53, 61, 62; INVENTION 27 52;
        MUSIC 12 58;
        TECHNOLOGY 89 59
Louis IX, King of France,
        MEDIEVAL LIFE 65 26
Louis XII, King of France,
        KNIGHT 43 15;
        RENAISSANCE 91 37
Louis XIII, King of France,
        CRYSTAL & GEM 25 48
Louis XIV, King of France,
        BATTLE 63 62; DANCE 99 37;
        PIRATE 59 19; RUSSIA 74 24
Louisiana, EXPLORER 31 42-43
Louk, Mordecai, SPY 67 29
Louvre, MANET 94 8-9, 46, 61
Louvre pyramid, PYRAMID 53 63
Love, Nat, COWBOY 45 18
Lovell, Bernard,
        ASTRONOMY 82 33
Lovell, Stanley, SPY 67 12
Lovelock, James, ECOLOGY 86
        62; ENERGY 76 57
Low, Edward, PIRATE 59 30, 59
Lowell, Percival,
        ASTRONOMY 82 48, 57
Lower, Richard,
        MEDICINE 88 25
Lozano, David, COWBOY 45 8
Lucan, "Lucky", CRIME &
        DETECTION 73 23
Lucas, George, CINEMA 34 61
Lucius, ANCIENT ROME 24 40
Lucky Luke, COWBOY 45 21
"Lucy", earliest skeleton,
        ARCHAEOLOGY 56 6, 42;
        EARLY PEOPLE 10 6, 7
Lucy of Syracuse, St.,
        MEDICINE 88 23
lugsails, BOAT 36 24, 25, 42
Luke, St., BIBLE LANDS 30 59;
        RELIGION 68 51
Lumière brothers, Auguste and
        Louis, CINEMA 34 16, 17, 24;
        FUTURE 100 8; INVENTION 27
        50; LIGHT 75 26

luminescence, LIGHT 75 45
luminous organs, FISH 20 18, 39
Luna space probes, SPACE
        EXPLORATION 71 18, 46
Lunar Rover, SPACE
        EXPLORATION 71 23
lung ti, MUSIC 12 11
lungfish, DINOSAUR 13 56;
        FISH 20 8, 9, 32, 45;
        FOSSIL 19 35, 42;
        PREHISTORIC LIFE 52 24
lungs, HUMAN BODY 87 20,
        24-27, 35; LIFE 84 15, 27
    blood, HUMAN BODY 87 29,
        31, 32
lungworms,
        POND & RIVER 6 59
Lunokhod explorer, SPACE
        EXPLORATION 71 46
Lusaka, Zambia,
        VOLCANO 38 50
Lusi-tano, COWBOY 45 13
lutes, MEDIEVAL LIFE 65 26, 56,
        57; MUSIC 12 36-37, 40, 41
Luther, Martin, MEDIEVAL
        LIFE 65 62; RELIGION 68 53;
        RENAISSANCE 91 42-43
Luxor, PYRAMID 53 26
lychees, CHINA 55 55
Lycopodium, FOSSIL 19 36
lycopods, FOSSIL 19 36, 40
lycra, TECHNOLOGY 89 7
Lydia, ANCIENT GREECE 37 6,
        35, 52
Lyell, Charles, EVOLUTION 85
        17, 20, 28, 29
lyme-hounds, DOG 32 40
lymph, HUMAN BODY 87 37,
        40-41
    lymphatic system,
        LIFE 84 29
lynching, CRIME & DETECTION
        73 12
lynxes, ARCTIC & ANTARCTIC
        57 36; CAT 29 10, 36-37, 38;
        MAMMAL 11 21
Lyot, Bernard,
        ASTRONOMY 82 38
lyre, ANCIENT EGYPT 23 51;
        MUSIC 12 34
lyrebirds, BIRD 1 28

Maasai peoples, **AFRICA 61** 6, 30

clothes, **AFRICA 61** 24, 26, 29

games, **AFRICA 61** 23

raids, **AFRICA 61** 42

Maat, **PYRAMID 53** 45

macaques, **GORILLA 64** 24, 34, 53, 61

barbary, **GORILLA 64** 58

bonnet, **GORILLA 64** 28

Japanese, **GORILLA 64** 29, 58

lion-tailed, **GORILLA 64** 22, 28

long-tailed, **GORILLA 64** 33

pig-tailed, **GORILLA 64** 29

Sulawesi crested, **GORILLA 64** 29, 32

Macarius, Joannes, **INVENTION 27** 35

macaws, **BIRD 1** 21, 24, 26; **JUNGLE 54** 23, 55

Macedonia, **ANCIENT GREECE 37** 6, 7, 46, 62; **EXPLORER 31** 10

maces, **ARMS & ARMOUR 4** 31, 50; **BATTLE 63** 38, 45; **KNIGHT 43** 9, 18-19; **TREE 5** 42

Macewen, Sir William, **MEDICINE 88** 49

Machaerus, **BIBLE LANDS 30** 57

Machiavelli, Niccolò, **RENAISSANCE 91** 13

machine guns, **BATTLE 63** 30-31, 50; **SPY 67** 24, 54

machine tools, **TECHNOLOGY 89** 10, 38

machines, **FORCE & MOTION 78** 6, 7, 10, 16; **TECHNOLOGY 89** 6, 32-33, 35

accelerators, **FORCE & MOTION 78** 62

complex, **FORCE & MOTION 78** 22-23

energy, **FORCE & MOTION 78** 41

gears, **FORCE & MOTION 78** 20

lubricants, **FORCE & MOTION 78** 39

pulley, **FORCE & MOTION 78** 18

wedge, **FORCE & MOTION 78** 8-9, 12

wheel, **FORCE & MOTION 78** 10-11

Machu Picchu, **AZTEC 47** 13, 18, 19, 30

Mackenzie, Alexander, **EXPLORER 31** 44, 63

MacKenzie, Compton, **SHIPWRECK 72** 58

mackerels, **FISH 20** 8, 10, 19, 58; **FOSSIL 19** 18, 19, 35; **OCEAN 62** 10, 27

Maclean, Donald, **SPY 67** 35, 57

MacMahon, Marshall, **MANET 94** 44, 50

macuta, **MONEY 18** 54

Madaba, **BIBLE LANDS 30** 59

Madagascar, **AFRICA 61** 21, 40; **GORILLA 64** 10, 11; **PIRATE 59** 46-47, 49; **VOLCANO 38** 35

madeira, **WHALE 46** 38, 49

Madi peoples, **AFRICA 61** 61

Mafia, **CRIME & DETECTION 73** 25-27; **SPY 67** 43, 55

Magellan, Ferdinand, **ASTRONOMY 82** 15, 46; **EARTH 83** 30, 34; **EXPLORER 31** 24-25, 63

maggots, **INSECT 17** 16, 24, 32, 33

Maghara, **PYRAMID 53** 14

magic, **ANCIENT EGYPT 23** 26-27; **EARLY PEOPLE 10** 36, 37; **RELIGION 68** 11, 14, 32, 33

circle, **WITCH & WIZARD 70** 9, 58, 59

cookery, **WITCH & WIZARD 70** 34-35

modern, **WITCH & WIZARD 70** 58, 59

powers, **WITCH & WIZARD 70** 12, 28

sites, **WITCH & WIZARD 70** 26-27

spells, **MUMMY 44** 12, 16, 20, 40

tools, **WITCH & WIZARD 70** 42, 51

magic lantern, **CINEMA 34** 6, 7-8, 16

magicians, **WITCH & WIZARD 70** 12-14, 28, 46

magma, **EARTH 83** 7, 25, 29, 38; **ROCK & MINERAL 2** 7, 10, 16, 18; **VOLCANO 38** 8, 14, 47, 57

channels, **VOLCANO 38** 22

mantle, **VOLCANO 38** 8, 12, 13, 22

reservoir, **VOLCANO 38** 13, 14, 25, 39

Magna Carta, **MEDIEVAL LIFE 65** 25

magnesium, **CHEMISTRY 79** 18, 22, 25, 40; **EARTH 83** 7, 15, 20

magnetic field, **ASTRONOMY 82** 39, 43, 44, 51; **EARTH 83** 6, 35, 60, 61; **MATTER 80** 52, 57, 58, 59

ocean floor, **EARTH 83** 36, 38, 39

Magnetic resonance imaging, *see* MRI

magnetism, **ENERGY 76** 32, 36, 45; **FORCE & MOTION 78** 51, 55, 62; **MATTER 80** 12, 60

and electricity, **ELECTRICITY 77** 26-27, 34-35; **ENERGY 76** 23, 23, 24

electromagnetic waves, **LIGHT 75** 42

fluid theory, **ENERGY 76** 18-19

see also electromagnetism

magnetite, **CRYSTAL & GEM 25** 37, 60; **ROCK & MINERAL 2** 15, 49

magneto, **FLYING MACHINE 22** 42

magnetrons, **ELECTRONICS 90** 18, 26, 40

magnets, **INVENTION 27** 44

magnetic tapes, **ELECTRONICS 90** 10, 11; **INVENTION 27** 46, 47

Magnier, Constantin, **DOG 32** 61

magnification, **LIGHT 75** 17, 23

magnolias, **PREHISTORIC LIFE 52** 60; **TREE 5** 25, 26, 52

magpies, **BIRD 1** 19, 26, 41, 44

Magritte, René, **FUTURE 100** 32; **PERSPECTIVE 98** 58

Mahabharata, **RELIGION 68** 20

mahari, temple dance, **DANCE 99** 39

Mahavira, **RELIGION 68** 36, 37

Mahdi, **AFRICA 61** 42

mahogany, **BUILDING 58** 8; **JUNGLE 54** 10, 62; **TREE 5** 59

mahouts, **ELEPHANT 42** 41, 45

Maiasaura, **DINOSAUR 13** 44, 46

Maiden Castle, **CASTLE 49** 6

maidenhair, **FOSSIL 19** 60

mail armour, **ARMS & ARMOUR 4** 15, 24; **KNIGHT 43** 12-13, 28

Maine coon, **CAT 29** 57

maize, **AZTEC 47** 13, 23, 24, 25; **FARM 66** 6, 32; **NORTH AMERICAN INDIAN 60** 16-17, 32-33; **PLANT 14** 54

husk bag, **NORTH AMERICAN INDIAN 60** 39

"Major Martin", **SPY 67** 27

Major, Gen. Scipio, **SPY 67** 40

make-up, **CINEMA 34** 34-35, 42; **MUMMY 44** 30

mako shark, **FISH 20** 61

malachite, **CRYSTAL & GEM 25** 24, 50, 51; **ROCK & MINERAL 2** 33; **RUSSIA 74** 15

Malaise trap, **INSECT 17** 63

malaria, **MEDICINE 88** 26, 44, 63

Malaya, **EXPLORER 31** 21

Malaysia, **JUNGLE 54** 8, 48; **WITCH & WIZARD 70** 53

Maldive Islands, **WHALE 46** 38

Mali, **AFRICA 61** 9, 15, 34, 61, 63

Empire, **AFRICA 61** 6, 30, 48

mallards, **BIRD 1** 11, 25, 27; **SKELETON 3** 30

Mallarmé, Stéphane, **MANET 94** 37, 48, 49, 60; **MONET 95** 36, 51

Malle, Louis, **CINEMA 34** 62

mallets, **SPORT 8** 61

Malpighi, Marcello, **MEDICINE 88** 25, 30

Malpus, **ANCIENT ROME 24** 15

Malta, **EXPLORER 31** 6; **PIRATE 59** 16-17

Malta cats, **CAT 29** 51

Malraux, **DANCE 99** 28

Maltese dogs, **DOG 32** 10, 58

Malthus, Rev. Thomas, **EVOLUTION 85** 34; **TIME & SPACE 81** 22

Mamluks, **KNIGHT 43** 54

mammals, **ELEPHANT 42** 12, 13, 37, 38; **EVOLUTION 85** 25, 27, 41, 46; **FISH 20** 6, 7, 42, 45; **LIFE 84** 22, 24, 26, 31; **MAMMAL 11** 8-11

birth, **MAMMAL 11** 34-35

bones, **SKELETON 3** 14-17

defence, **MAMMAL 11** 21, 24-27, 28

egg-laying, **EVOLUTION 85** 42, 43

extinct, **DINOSAUR 13** 24, 60; **PREHISTORIC LIFE 52** 44-47, 50-51

communication, **MAMMAL 11** 28-29, 40-41

evolution, **EVOLUTION 85** 26, 47, 62-63; **MAMMAL 11** 13-14

of humans, **EVOLUTION 85** 39

feeding, **MAMMAL 11** 16, 17, 48-49

fossilized, **FOSSIL 19** 45, 54-57, 61

genetic code, **EVOLUTION 85** 55

group behaviour, **MAMMAL 11** 43, 44

mammary glands, **HUMAN BODY 87** 6, 47, 49; **MAMMAL 11** 6, 36-37

reproduction, **MAMMAL 11** 30-35

senses, **MAMMAL 11** 16-17, 24

mammen, **VIKING 50** 41, 44, 60

mammen axes, **VIKING 50** 7, 44

mammoths, **ELEPHANT 42** 9, 10-11, 21; **EVOLUTION 85** 17, 44, 54, 62; **FOSSIL 19** 17, 20, 21, 54; **PREHISTORIC LIFE 52** 9, 58

ivory, **ELEPHANT 42** 54

skeletons, **SKELETON 3** 13, 14

Ma'mun, Caliph, **PYRAMID 53** 22
man of war, ship, **PIRATE 59** 59
manades, **COWBOY 45** 52-53
manakins, **JUNGLE 54** 62
manatees, **MAMMAL 11** 11, 37;
  WHALE 46 7, 44-45
Manchu Dynasty,
  CHINA 55 18, 46, 62;
  FLAG 16 58
mandarin fish, **FISH 20** 17
Mandela, Nelson,
  FUTURE 100 11
mandolin, **MUSIC 12** 37
mandrake, **MEDICINE 88** 16, 23;
  PLANT 14 58
mandrills, **GORILLA 64** 32;
  JUNGLE 54 45
Mandrin, Louis, **CRIME &**
  DETECTION 73 56
Manet, Edouard, **GOYA 93** 37,
  43, 57; **IMPRESSIONISM 92**
  8-9, 17; **MANET 94**;
  MONET 95 12, 20, 22, 25;
  VAN GOGH 96 31, 36;
  WATERCOLOUR 97 50
  biography,
    IMPRESSIONISM 92 62
  family, **MANET 94** 6, 22, 24,
    26, 46
  influence of,
    IMPRESSIONISM 92 11, 16,
  wife, Suzanne, **MANET 94**
    26-27, 44-45, 61
  paintings,
    The Absinthe Drinker,
      MANET 94 12-13, 38, 39
    The Balcony,
      MANET 94 46-47
    A Bar at the Folies-Bergère,
      MANET 94 58-59
    "Beggar-philosopher"
      series, **MANET 94** 9, 13,
      38-39
    The Bullfight,
      MANET 94 19, 36
    Café paintings,
      MANET 94 48, 57
    Déjeuner sur l'Herbe,
      MANET 94 21, 24-25, 32
    Eva Gonzalès,
      MANET 94 34-35
    The Execution of Emperor
      Maximilian,
      MANET 94 42-43, 45
    The Fifer,
      MANET 94 33, 39, 40-41
    Music in the Tuileries,
      MANET 94 14, 15, 16-17
    Nana, **MANET 94** 56
    Olympia,
      IMPRESSIONISM 92 18;
      MANET 94 8, 28-29, 32, 37
    The Plum, **MANET 94** 57, 58
    The Races at Longchamp,
      IMPRESSIONISM 92 48-49
    The Street Singer,
      MANET 94 21

Manet, Eugène,
  IMPRESSIONISM 92 58, 60
Manet, Julie,
  IMPRESSIONISM 92 45
mangabeys, **GORILLA 64** 22, 24
manganese, **CRYSTAL & GEM 25**
  17, 39, 44, 51; **EARTH 83** 38;
  TECHNOLOGY 89 14
Mangbetu peoples, **AFRICA 61** 52
mangoes, **TREE 5** 43
mangosteens, **GORILLA 64** 40
mangrove swamps, **FISH 20**
  32, 36
mangroves, **JUNGLE 54** 8, 9, 16,
  48; **TREE 5** 18
manillas, **MONEY 18** 9, 54;
  PIRATE 59 38
manna, **INSECT 17** 60
Mannerism, **RENAISSANCE 91**
  56, 60, 61
manors, **KNIGHT 43** 36;
  MEDIEVAL LIFE 65 10, 12,
  14-15
manta rays, **FISH 20** 57
Mantegna, Andrea,
  IMPRESSIONISM 92 11;
  PERSPECTIVE 98 20-21, 22,
  61; **RENAISSANCE 91** 26,
  27, 35
Mantell, Dr. Gideon,
  DINOSAUR 13 8, 9;
  EVOLUTION 85 18, 19;
  FOSSIL 19 50
Mantell, Mary Ann,
  DINOSAUR 13 8
mantellas, **AMPHIBIAN 41**
  56-57, 61
mantids, **INSECT 17** 15, 19,
  40, 44
mantle, molluscs, **SHELL 9** 10,
  32, 36
mantras, **RELIGION 68** 28, 29
mantua gown, **COSTUME 35** 30
Mantz, Paul, **MANET 94** 41, 49
manure, **FARM 66** 8, 14, 34, 41
manuscripts, **WRITING 48**
  26-29
  illuminated,
    WATERCOLOUR 97 8, 10-13
  Indian, **WATERCOLOUR 97**
    20-21
  Limbourg brothers,
    WATERCOLOUR 97 12-13
  Persian, **WATERCOLOUR 97**
    7, 18
Manutius, Aldus, **WRITING 48** 42
Manx Loghtan sheep,
  VIKING 50 37, 38
Many-plume Moth,
  BUTTERFLY & MOTH 7 47
Maori peoples, **DANCE 99** 18;
  FLAG 16 48, 49
maple leaf, **FLAG 16** 14, 48, 49
maples, **FOSSIL 19** 39; **TREE 5**
  28, 36, 40, 57
  field, **TREE 5** 8
  Japanese, **TREE 5** 26, 27

leaf, **FLAG 16** 14, 48, 49
  Norway, **TREE 5** 20-21
  sugar, **NORTH AMERICAN**
    INDIAN 60 16, 22; **TREE 5** 46
  syrup, **TREE 5** 23
maps, **ARCHAEOLOGY 56** 14, 26;
  ARCTIC & ANTARCTIC 57 7;
  FOSSIL 19 15, 62;
  TECHNOLOGY 89 31
mappa mundi, map of the
  world, **EARTH 83** 8, 34;
  WATERCOLOUR 97 8, 26
  mythical, **PIRATE 59** 60
  navigation, **PIRATE 59** 24;
    SHIPWRECK 72 32
  of oceans, **EARTH 83** 39
  spy, **SPY 67** 13, 20, 21, 32
map-wing butterflies,
  BUTTERFLY & MOTH 7 35
Marathi language,
  WRITING 48 36-37
marathon, **ANCIENT**
  GREECE 37 19
maravedis, **MONEY 18** 39
marble, **BUILDING 58** 17, 44, 60;
  EARTH 83 28; **ROCK &**
  MINERAL 2 8, 24, 26-27, 39
marbles, game, **SPORT 8** 57
Marc, Franz, **HORSE 33** 41;
  WATERCOLOUR 97 58
Marco Polo, **HORSE 33** 32;
  EXPLORER 31 16, 17, 63
Marconi, Guglielmo,
  ELECTRICITY 77 55, 57, 60,
  61; **ELECTRONICS 90** 13, 25;
  ENERGY 76 41;
  INVENTION 27 52
Marcus, Siegfried, **ENERGY 76** 30
Marcus Aurelius,
  ANCIENT ROME 24 9
Maremmana, **COWBOY 45** 6
Marengo, **HORSE 33** 42
mares, **HORSE 33** 12-14, 26
Marey, Etienne Jules,
  CINEMA 34 10, 11
margays, **CAT 29** 40
margin shells, **SHELL 9** 42
María Luisa, Queen of Spain,
  GOYA 93 11, 14, 34-35
Mariana Trench,
  OCEAN 62 8-9, 47, 53
Marie Antoinette, Queen of
  France, **WRITING 48** 52
marigolds, **POND & RIVER 6** 7
Mariner, space probes,
  ASTRONOMY 82 45, 48;
  SPACE EXPLORATION 71 46
Mark, St., **FLAG 16** 34;
  RELIGION 68 51, 53
marker flags, **FLAG 16** 23
markers, **SPORT 8** 60
markets, **AFRICA 61** 18, 48;
  MEDIEVAL LIFE 65 55
  market halls,
    BUILDING 58 22, 24
  market towns, **VIKING 50** 26
markkas, **MONEY 18** 44, 62

Markland, **VIKING 50** 21
Markov, Georgi, **SPY 67** 36, 43
marks, **MONEY 18** 32, 33, 42, 62
marlinspike shells, **SHELL 9** 43
Marlowe, Christopher, **WITCH**
  & WIZARD 70 16
marmosets, **MAMMAL 11** 8
marooning, **PIRATE 59** 48-49
marque, letters of, **PIRATE 59** 18
marriages,
  African, **AFRICA 61** 24, 25
  Roman, **ANCIENT ROME 24** 22
marrow, **HUMAN BODY 87**
  16-17, 33
Mars, god, **ANCIENT ROME 24**
  16, 51, 52
Mars, planet, **ASTRONOMY 82** 7,
  48-49, 57; **FUTURE 100** 11, 56,
  57, 59; **ROCK &**
  MINERAL 2 41
  asteroid belt,
    ASTRONOMY 82 58
  orbit, **ASTRONOMY 82** 18, 19,
    36, 37
Mars space probes, **SPACE**
  EXPLORATION 71 35, 44, 47
Marsh, Othniel Charles,
  FOSSIL 19 50
marshlands,
  BUILDING 58 62, 63
marsupials, **FOSSIL 19** 55,
  56-57, 61; **MAMMAL 11** 8, 9,
  13, 14; **PREHISTORIC**
  LIFE 52 50
  reproduction,
    MAMMAL 11 30-31
martial arts, **SPORT 8** 48
Martin, John, **PERSPECTIVE 98**
  46, 47
Martini, Simone,
  RENAISSANCE 91 10, 11
Marx, Karl, **RUSSIA 74** 32;
  TECHNOLOGY 89 34
Mary, *see* Virgin Mary
Mary, Queen of Scots, **SPY 67**
  25, 28, 41; **TRAIN 39** 45
Mary Celeste, **SHIPWRECK 72** 9
Mary Rose, **ARCHAEOLOGY 56** 9,
  32-35, 38; **SHIPWRECK 72** 14,
  18, 19, 57
Masaccio, **PERSPECTIVE 98** 14-15;
  RENAISSANCE 91 7, 18-19, 54
Masada, **BIBLE LANDS 30** 35,
  55, 57
Maserati, **CAR 21** 26
masked crabs, **SHELL 9** 43
masks, **ARMS & ARMOUR 4** 30,
  37, 62; **NORTH AMERICAN**
  INDIAN 60 9-10, 54-55;
  PYRAMID 53 54, 61;
  WITCH & WIZARD 70 10, 22,
  44-46
  African, **AFRICA 61** 58-59
  dance, **DANCE 99** 16, 32-33
  Inuit, **ARCTIC &**
  ANTARCTIC 57 51; **NORTH**
  AMERICAN INDIAN 60 61

H AMERICAN
, 17
, MUMMY 44
39
ELIGION 68 16-17
sacrificial, AZTEC 47 36
South American, AZTEC 47
53, 54-55
Masolino di Panicale,
RENAISSANCE 91 18-19
masons, CASTLE 49 7, 10,
56-57; PYRAMID 53 30, 34
Maspero, Gaston,
MUMMY 44 36
masquerades, AFRICA 61 35, 58,
62-63; DANCE 99 29
mass, physical, FORCE &
MOTION 78 31, 32, 34-35;
MATTER 80 6, 55, 58; TIME
& SPACE 81 37, 41, 44
and momentum,
FORCE & MOTION 78 36, 37,
54, 58
Sun, FORCE & MOTION 78 61
in universe, MATTER 80
61, 62
mass, religious,
MEDIEVAL LIFE 65 30, 38;
RELIGION 68 50
massage, MEDICINE 88 37, 44-45
masseter muscles,
SKELETON 3 27, 34, 35
Massetognathus,
DINOSAUR 13 57
Massine, Leonide, CINEMA 34
57; DANCE 99 17
Massopondylus, DINOSAUR 13
23, 42
mastabas, PYRAMID 53 7, 10, 41
Mästermyr, VIKING 50 43
Masterson, Bat, COWBOY 45 43
mastiffs, DOG 32 44, 45, 56, 57
masts, BOAT 36 25, 40, 57
Mata Hari, SPY 67 56
matches, INVENTION 27 7, 21
Materia Medica, MEDICINE 88
19, 21
maticaes, MONEY 18 55
Matisse, Henri,
WATERCOLOUR 97 55
Matmata, Tunisia,
DESERT 51 45
matrices, WRITING 48 37
matter, ENERGY 76 20, 46;
MATTER 80; TIME &
SPACE 81 42, 46, 60
conduction, ENERGY 76 36
living, MATTER 80 6, 10, 42-43
particle theory, ENERGY 76
18-19
states of matter, MATTER 80
22-23, 38
Universe, ENERGY 76 62-63
Matthew, St., RELIGION 68 51
Mau Mau campaign, FLAG 16 34
Maui volcano, Hawaii,
VOLCANO 38 16, 22

Mauna Loa volcano, Hawaii,
VOLCANO 38 22
Maupassant, Guy de,
MONET 95 40
Mauve, Anton, VAN GOGH 96
14, 44
maxillae, SKELETON 3 28, 62
Maximilian, Emperor,
KNIGHT 43 15;
MANET 94 42-43
Maxwell, James Clerk,
ELECTRICITY 77 60;
ENERGY 76 40, 42, 43, 45;
LIGHT 75 42
electric signals,
ELECTRONICS 90 11, 12, 24
electromagnetic waves,
TIME & SPACE 81 32-33
May Day, MEDIEVAL LIFE 65 54;
RUSSIA 74 34, 56, 57
Maya peoples,
ARCHAEOLOGY 56 11, 15;
EXPLORER 31 31;
JUNGLE 54 22
blood rituals, PYRAMID 53 58
hieroglyphs,
EARLY PEOPLE 10 40, 41, 59;
WRITING 48 11
Mayan Civilization,
AZTEC 47 6, 8, 62
pyramids, PYRAMID 53
56-57, 59
Mayer, Luigi, PYRAMID 53 17
mayflies, POND & RIVER 6 13,
17, 50-51
maypoles, TREE 5 58
Mbuti peoples, AFRICA 61 19, 62
McCormick, Cyrus,
FARM 66 26
McCosker, Dr. John,
SHARK 40 29, 54
McLaren, Norman,
CINEMA 34 52
McSween, Susan,
COWBOY 45 58
Meager, Michael,
COWBOY 45 42
measurement, INVENTION 27
16-17, 34
Mecca, RELIGION 68 54-57, 59
medallions, CASTLE 49 31
medals, BATTLE 63 58-59, 62;
PIRATE 59 59
Medea, WITCH & WIZARD 70 16
Medes, BIBLE LANDS 30 52
medical instruments,
INVENTION 27 42-43
Medici family,
RENAISSANCE 91 12, 32, 55
Medici, Lorenzo de',
MEDIEVAL LIFE 65 62;
RENAISSANCE 91 32-33
Medici, Piero de', CAT 29 32
medicine, ARCTIC &
ANTARCTIC 57 55;
MEDICINE 88;
SEASHORE 15 17, 20-21, 23

advances, FUTURE 100
40-41, 48-49
African, AFRICA 61 35, 38-39
American Indian, NORTH
AMERICAN INDIAN 60
10-11, 15, 30-31
Arabic, MEDICINE 88 20-21
Ayurvedic, MEDICINE 88
10, 14
Aztec, AZTEC 47 38-39
books on, WRITING 48 26
Chinese, MEDICINE 88 12,
14-15
complementary,
MEDICINE 88 44-45
Egyptian, ANCIENT
EGYPT 23 26-27;
MUMMY 44 11, 40, 62
general practice,
MEDICINE 88 60-61
Greek, ANCIENT GREECE 37
58-59; MEDICINE 88 1
6-17, 50
herbal, CHINA 55 28-29
Islamic, MEDICINE 88 20-21
medieval, MEDIEVAL LIFE 65
44, 45, 60-61
prehistoric,
EARLY PEOPLE 10 8
Roman, ANCIENT ROME 24
54, 55; MEDICINE 88
18-19, 50
and technology,
TECHNOLOGY 89 56-57
traditional, MEDICINE 88
12-15, 40-41
tribal, JUNGLE 54 42-43
wounded soldiers,
BATTLE 63 60-61
medicine bags,
WITCH & WIZARD 70 42, 47
medicine men, MEDICINE 88
10-11, 12-13; WITCH &
WIZARD 70 44, 46, 53
Medina, RELIGION 68 54-56
meditation, RELIGION 68 24,
26-28, 39
Mediterranean lands, ANCIENT
GREECE 37 8, 12, 14, 52;
ANCIENT ROME 24 6, 7, 45;
BIBLE LANDS 30 38, 41-42;
EXPLORER 31 6-7, 9, 11-14
Mediterranean Sea,
OCEAN 62 8, 55;
SHIPWRECK 72 12, 13, 58;
VIKING 50 6, 26
medlars, TREE 5 39
Medusa,
ANCIENT GREECE 37 23
meerkat, DESERT 51 35
megaliths, ARCHAEOLOGY 56 26;
EARLY PEOPLE 10 38
Megalosaurus, DINOSAUR 13 8,
25; FOSSIL 19 50
Megazostrodon,
DINOSAUR 13 57
megrim, FISH 20 25

Meickle, Andrew,
INVENTION 27 25
meiosis, LIFE 84 30, 38, 42
melanite, CRYSTAL & GEM 25 44
melting point, MATTER 80 22
Melville, Herman,
SHIPWRECK 72 38;
WHALE 46 11, 38
memorials, BATTLE 63 62, 63
memory, electronic,
ELECTRONICS 90 8, 9, 56-57
microprocessors,
ELECTRONICS 90 58, 59
printers, ELECTRONICS 90 62
robots, ELECTRONICS 90 60
telephones, ELECTRONICS 90
6, 7
Memphis, PYRAMID 53 8, 13, 18,
41, 50
Mende peoples, AFRICA 61 28,
36, 37
Mendel, Gregor, EVOLUTION 85
33, 50-51, 58; LIFE 84 40-41
Mendeleyev, Dmitri,
CHEMISTRY 79 22, 23, 25, 33;
ELECTRONICS 90 37;
MATTER 80 32, 33;
RUSSIA 74 41
Mengs, Anton, GOYA 93 11, 16,
19, 57
Menkaura, PYRAMID 53
16-19, 33
Mensheviks, RUSSIA 74 31
menstruation,
HUMAN BODY 87 43, 49
mental illnesses,
MEDICINE 88 8, 46-47
Mentuhotep, PYRAMID 53 41
Mercalli, Guiseppe,
VOLCANO 38 48
Mercalli scale, EARTH 83 42;
VOLCANO 38 48-49
Mercedes, CAR 21 10, 26, 27
merchants, CHINA 55 46, 50, 58;
MEDIEVAL LIFE 65 17,
46-47, 51
mercury, CHEMISTRY 79 23, 24,
28, 30, 31; MATTER 80 16, 20;
ROCK & MINERAL 2 57;
TECHNOLOGY 89 41
cell, CHEMISTRY 79 47
lamps, LIGHT 75 53
Mercury, god,
ANCIENT ROME 24 51, 53
Mercury, planet,
ASTRONOMY 82 33, 37,
44-45; SPACE EXPLORATION 71
46; TIME & SPACE 81 42
Mereret, PYRAMID 53 42, 43
Mereruka, PYRAMID 53 10
mergansers, BIRD 1 37;
SKELETON 3 30
Merib, PYRAMID 53 25
meridians, ASTRONOMY 82 11,
13, 14, 27
merkhet, INVENTION 27 22
Merlin, WITCH & WIZARD 70 17

merlons, **Castle 49** 26;
Knight 43 23, 24
mermaid, **Whale 46** 7, 44
mermaid's purse, **Fish 20** 43
Merneptah, Pharaoh,
Bible Lands 30 20
Meroe, **Pyramid 53** 44, 48, 52-53
merry-go-round, **Horse 33** 63
Merychippus, **Horse 33** 8
Mesa Verde,
Archaeology 56 29
Mesoamerica, **Aztec 47** 8-9, 16-17
Mesohippus, **Horse 33** 8-9
Mesolimulus, **Fossil 19** 60
mesolite, **Crystal & Gem 25** 22
mesons, **Time & Space 81** 37
Mesopotamia,
Ancient Greece 37 63;
Bible Lands 30 14, 27, 38, 50; **Building 58** 12, 13
cuneiform script,
Early People 10 40;
Writing 48 8-9
mesosaurs,
Prehistoric Life 52 29
Mesozoic era,
Evolution 85 46, 61
mess, **Boat 36** 28
Messel, Oliver,
Watercolour 97 56
Messiah, **Religion 68** 44, 48, 52
Messier, Charles,
Astronomy 82 60
metabolism, **Human Body 87** 40-41; **Life 84** 7, 18, 21, 56
metals, **Aztec 47** 7, 50-51;
Energy 76 19, 20, 43, 45;
Matter 80 6, 16-17, 50;
Technology 89 6, 11, 12-13
alloys, **Chemistry 79** 24;
Matter 80 12
analysis, **Chemistry 79** 58-59
atoms, **Chemistry 79** 38;
Matter 80 51
burning, **Matter 80** 30
casting, **Early People 10** 42, 43, 48
conservation of,
Archaeology 56 34-35
crystal structure,
Matter 80 14
electrons, **Energy 76** 43
as elements, **Chemistry 79** 16, 18, 24-25
ores, **Chemistry 79** 34;
Energy 76 10;
Rock & Mineral 2 56-57
oxides, **Chemistry 79** 12, 30
periodic table, **Matter 80** 32
precious, **Aztec 47** 7, 50-51;
Rock & Mineral 2 6, 58-59
reactivity, **Chemistry 79** 36
recycling, **Technology 89** 62
smelting, **Chemistry 79** 10, 11
symbols, **Chemistry 79** 13

uses, **Technology 89** 14-17
see also under individual metals
metalwork, **Africa 61** 52, 53, 54-55; **Ancient Rome 24** 42, 43; **Castle 49** 60-61
metamorphosis, **Fish 20** 24, 25, 26; **Life 84** 31, 53; **Pond & River 6** 12, 48
meteorites, **Astronomy 82** 40, 44, 58-59; **Rock & Mineral 2** 40-41
collisions, **Prehistoric Life 52** 11, 13, 60-61;
Volcano 38 44, 55
iron, **Crystal & Gem 25** 8
meteorology, **Weather 28** 10
meteors, **Astronomy 82** 40, 43, 58-59
meters, **Energy 76** 24, 36, 42, 43
Metesky, George, the "Mad Bomber",
Crime & Detection 73 52
Methodius, St., **Russia 74** 19, 42
methylated spirits,
Energy 76 34, 37
metric system,
Time & Space 81 11, 54
Metro, **Train 39** 56, 57
Metro Goldwyn Mayer Studios, **Cinema 34** 21, 27
metronome, **Force & Motion 78** 46
Mexico, **Cat 29** 35, 40;
Mummy 44 55;
Weather 28 18;
Whale 46 19, 40
currency, **Money 18** 38, 62
flag, **Flag 16** 54
"The Maximilian Affair",
Manet 94 42-43
pyramids, **Pyramid 53** 6, 54-55, 56, 58
Quetzal dance,
Dance 99 32, 39
trade, **Explorer 31** 30-32
volcanoes, **Volcano 38** 35, 59
MG, **Car 21** 63
MI5, **Spy 67** 42, 50, 57, 58
MI6, **Spy 67** 11, 35, 42, 58
Miami, **North American Indian 60** 21
mica, **Crystal & Gem 25** 8, 15, 30, 38; **Earth 83** 20, 23, 28; **Rock & Mineral 2** 8, 42, 46, 49
mice, **Mammal 11** 16, 22, 49, 58
nest, **Mammal 11** 32, 54
reproduction,
Mammal 11 32-33
tracks, **Mammal 11** 61, 62
Michelangelo,
Medieval Life 65 7, 62;
Renaissance 91 54-55;
Technology 89 23;
Writing 48 52
David, **Renaissance 91** 54

Pieta, **Renaissance 91** 7
Sistine Chapel,
Renaissance 91 56-57
Michelet, Jules, **Van Gogh 96** 8, 14
Michelin, **Car 21** 60
Michelson, Albert, **Force & Motion 78** 58
microchips, **Electronics 90** 36, 54-55, 59; **Future 100** 33, 43, 58; **Invention 27** 62-63;
Technology 89 49, 54
computers,
Electronics 90 51
memory, **Electronics 90** 57
microelectronics, **Invention 27** 46, 62-63
microfilm, **Spy 67** 21
micromoths, **Tree 5** 8, 51
micromounts, **Crystal & Gem 25** 63
microphones, **Electronics 90** 6, 7, 42, 43, 63; **Energy 76** 41; **Music 12** 58; **Spy 67** 17-18, 45, 48
hidden, **Spy 67** 16, 19
use in telephones,
Electricity 77 58, 59
microprocessors,
Electronics 90 51, 56, 58-59; **Future 100** 45, 52
computer, **Electronics 90** 57
fax, **Electronics 90** 61
filters, **Electronics 90** 34
microscopes, **Chemistry 79** 17;
Light 75 60-61, 62;
Matter 80 10, 35, 38, 51;
compound, **Light 75** 22-23
electron, **Crime & Detection 73** 46
invention of, **Invention 27** 28, 29, 63
lens, **Light 75** 22-23, 37
in medicine, **Medicine 88** 25, 30-31, 51
microsurgery, **Medicine 88** 51
microwaves, **Electronics 90** 40-41, 60; **Light 75** 42, 43
microwave ovens,
Energy 76 34, 35
Midas, King, **Crime & Detection 73** 49
Mid-Atlantic Ridge,
Earth 83 37, 38, 39;
Ocean 62 9, 46-47
Middle Ages,
Archaeology 56 12, 18, 52-53; **Farm 66** 14, 37, 60;
Medieval Life 65;
Watercolour 97 10-13, 49, 54
castles, **Castle 49**
fashions, **Costume 35** 14-15
midgets, **Skeleton 3** 58
midilid moths, **Butterfly & Moth 7** 46
Miescher, Friedrich, **Life 84** 34

migration, **Arctic & Antarctic 57** 14-15, 16;
Early People 10 14-15;
Shark 40 19, 56
milk, **Farm 66** 44-48, 54, 55
Milky Way, **Astronomy 82** 32, 62, 63; **Time & Space 81** 7, 48, 60
Miller, Arthur, **Witch & Wizard 70** 25
Miller, Hugh, **Evolution 85** 17
Miller, Stanley, **Evolution 85** 57; **Life 84** 54, 55
miller's thumb, **Fish 20** 42
millet, **Early People 10** 54;
Farm 66 6, 42
Millet, Jean François,
Impressionism 92 40;
Monet 95 6; **Van Gogh 96** 12-13, 22, 36
Millikan, Robert,
Electronics 90 26
millipedes, **Fossil 19** 30;
Insect 17 9; **Prehistoric Life 52** 13, 28
millstones, **Farm 66** 28; **Force & Motion 78** 10, 53
Milne, A.A., **Watercolour 97** 45
Milne, John, **Volcano 38** 54
Milton, John,
Perspective 98 46
mime, **Ancient Rome 24** 36, 37
mimicry, **Jungle 54** 50, 51
minarets, **Building 58** 36;
Religion 68 58, 59
minerals, **Africa 61** 7;
Chemistry 79 18, 31, 32, 42;
Matter 80 13, 15; **Rock & Mineral 2** 8-9, 48-49
deposits, **Chemistry 79** 24;
Earth 83 8, 20-23
deserts, **Desert 51** 8, 9
erosion, **Earth 83** 54
geophagy, **Elephant 42** 42, 43
oil, **Chemistry 79** 58
plants, **Plant 14** 8, 9
soil, **Earth 83** 52, 53
volcanic, **Volcano 38** 19, 25, 37, 38
weathering, **Earth 83** 50
Minerva, **Ancient Rome 24** 38, 50
Ming dynasty, **China 55** 9, 40, 59, 60
civil service, **China 55** 21
porcelain, **China 55** 56, 58
mini dress, **Costume 35** 58
miniatures, **Watercolour 97** 22-25
mining, **Arctic & Antarctic 57** 6, 62;
Chemistry 79 12, 18, 24;
Russia 74 14, 39
coal, **Archaeology 56** 60
flint, **Archaeology 56** 50
Minkowski, Hermann, **Time & Space 81** 34, 35, 38

...ER 6 12, 36
...ANCIENT
... 9, 10, 40;
...OGY 56 10, 51
...NCIENT
GREECE 37 8, 9
minstrels, MEDIEVAL LIFE 65 26
Miocene period, MAMMAL 11 13, 14
Mir space station, SPACE EXPLORATION 71 29, 30, 36-37
mirages, LIGHT 75 15
Mirbeau, Octave, IMPRESSIONISM 92 38
mirror carps, FISH 20 15
mirror writing, WRITING 48 53
mirrors, INVENTION 27 28, 35; MUMMY 44 30; PERSPECTIVE 98 11, 34, 44; SPY 67 15, 49
concave, LIGHT 75 12-13
in magic, WITCH & WIZARD 70 14, 53, 54
mirs, RUSSIA 74 17
missals, KNIGHT 43 56-57
missiles, ARMS & ARMOUR 4 8-9; SPY 67 38, 53, 54, 57
missionaries, AFRICA 61 33
Mississippi, FLAG 16 24
Mississippi, River, ROCK & MINERAL 2 11
Missouri, River, EXPLORER 31 43, 45
mist, WEATHER 28 23, 30, 48, 56
mistletoe, PLANT 14 44; TREE 5 21, 49
Mistral, Frederic, COWBOY 45 52
Mitchell, Bill, CAR 21 26
mites, DESERT 51 17
Mithras, ANCIENT ROME 24 50, 51
mitochondria, LIFE 84 10, 11, 18, 57
mitosis, LIFE 84 30
mitre shells, SHELL 9 50
mitres, CASTLE 49 23
mitten crabs, SHELL 9 56
mittens, COSTUME 35 12, 19, 41, 44
Mix, Tom, COWBOY 45 21, 24, 60
Mixtec Civilization, AZTEC 47 8, 9
mixtures, CHEMISTRY 79 14-15, 24, 28; MATTER 80 6, 26-27
moas, FOSSIL 19 21
moats, CASTLE 49 26, 28, 36; KNIGHT 43 22, 24
mob caps, COSTUME 35 35
mobile phones, ELECTRONICS 90 60, 63; FUTURE 100 11, 12, 28, 53
Moby Dick, SHIPWRECK 72 38; WHALE 46 11, 38

moccasins, EARLY PEOPLE 10 60
Moche peoples, AZTEC 47 10, 28; MUMMY 44 52, 54; PYRAMID 53 54
models, CINEMA 34 44, 45, 52
Mohammed, see Muhammed
Mohawk peoples, NORTH AMERICAN INDIAN 60 14, 16, 62
Mohenjo Daro, ARCHAEOLOGY 56 8
Mohs, Friedrich, CRYSTAL & GEM 25 18, 19; MATTER 80 13
Mohs scale, EARTH 83 21; ROCK & MINERAL 2 49
Moissan, Henri, CHEMISTRY 79 26
Mojave Desert, DESERT 51 6, 28, 30, 33
Moldavia, RUSSIA 74 23, 59
molecules, CHEMISTRY 79 8, 14, 38; ENERGY 76 13, 14, 15, 20, 28; MATTER 80 7, 35, 36-37; TIME & SPACE 81 58
artificial, MATTER 80 44-45
changing states, CHEMISTRY 79 7
compounds, CHEMISTRY 79 20
food, ENERGY 76 52
and heat, MATTER 80 38-39
kinetic energy, ENERGY 76 16, 37
mass, CHEMISTRY 79 16, 17
motion, ENERGY 76 36, 44, 45, 48; MATTER 80 20, 38-39
polymers, CHEMISTRY 79 54, 56, 57
waves, ENERGY 76 40
moles, animal, DESERT 51 36; MAMMAL 11 8, 16, 56-57; SKELETON 3 16
moles, espionage, SPY 67 11, 50
molluscs, FISH 20 7, 35; LIFE 84 30, 49, 53; SHELL 9 8, 36, 40, 44; SKELETON 3 24, 25
bivalves, SHELL 9 16-17
deep-sea, OCEAN 62 10, 34, 58; SEASHORE 15 26-29, 42-43; SHELL 9 54
edible, SHELL 9 34, 35
evolution, EVOLUTION 85 26, 32, 55
fossils, FOSSIL 19 26-29, 31, 46; PREHISTORIC LIFE 52 6, 18, 38-39; SEASHORE 15 10, 11
fresh water, SHELL 9 56-57
land, SHELL 9 58-59
making, SHELL 9 10-11, 32-33
moloch, DESERT 51 29
Mombasa, AFRICA 61 48
momentum, FORCE & MOTION 78 36-37, 53

angular, FORCE & MOTION 78 54-55, 56
linear, FORCE & MOTION 78 30, 54
Mona Lisa, RENAISSANCE 91 36
monarch butterflies, BUTTERFLY & MOTH 7 11, 17, 18, 23
monasteries, KNIGHT 43 52; RUSSIA 74 18; VIKING 50 16, 46; WRITING 48 24
rules, MEDIEVAL LIFE 65 38-39
Tibetan Buddhist, RELIGION 68 28, 29
Monet, Camille, IMPRESSIONISM 92 14-15, 38, 54; MONET 95 14, 16, 25, 30
Monet, Claude, IMPRESSIONISM 92 7, 10, 38, 43; MANET 94 52-53, 54-55, 61; MONET 95; VAN GOGH 96 33; WATERCOLOUR 97 51
biography, IMPRESSIONISM 92 62; MONET 95 62
Japanese influence, IMPRESSIONISM 92 54; PERSPECTIVE 98 49
photography, influence of, IMPRESSIONISM 92 29
paintings
The Artist's Garden at Giverny, MONET 95 52
The Boat, MONET 95 36-37
Boats: Regatta at Argenteuil, MONET 95 21
Camille on her Deathbed, MONET 95 30-31
Cathedrals series, MONET 95 44-47
Clouds, MONET 95 60
Le Déjeuner sur l'Herbe, MONET 95 10-11, 12-13
floating studio, MONET 95 20-23
Gare Saint-Lazare, MONET 95 26-27, 50
Grainstacks series, MONET 95 42
Impression, Sunrise, IMPRESSIONISM 92 19; MONET 95 24
London, Houses of Parliament, MONET 95 50-51
The Manneporte, Etretat, MONET 95 40-41
Morning, with Weeping Willows, MONET 95 60
On the Beach at Trouville, MONET 95 16-17
Poplars series, MONET 95 42, 43
The Promenade, MONET 95 30, 32, 33
Red Boats, MONET 95 9, 22-23
The Road from Chailly, MONET 95 10, 11

train paintings, IMPRESSIONISM 92 32, 33
Waterlilies series, MONET 95 53, 54, 56-59
Waterlily decorations, MONET 95 60-61
Woman in the Green Dress, MONET 95 25
Woman with a Parasol, MONET 95 32-33, 42
Women in the Garden, MONET 95 14, 15
money, EARLY PEOPLE 10 56-57; MONEY 18
see also under individual countries
money-laundering, CRIME & DETECTION 73 26
money orders, MONEY 18 12, 58
Mongolia, EXPLORER 31 19
herdsmen, COWBOY 45 29, 35
Mongols, BATTLE 63 14, 44; CHINA 55 23, 58-59, 60; RUSSIA 74 8, 9, 12, 13
mongoose, MAMMAL 11 9; REPTILE 26 58-59
mongrels, DOG 32 38, 53, 60, 61
"Monkey", Chinese hero, GORILLA 64 58
monkey cup, JUNGLE 54 52
monkey puzzle, FOSSIL 19 36, 37
monkeys, GORILLA 64 6; JUNGLE 54 31, 44; MAMMAL 11 8, 21, 29; SKELETON 3 15, 31
communication, GORILLA 64 32-33, 36, 50
defences, GORILLA 64 34-35
myths, GORILLA 64 58-59
as pets, GORILLA 64 60
types of,
capuchin, GORILLA 64 16, 17, 20-21
colobus, GORILLA 64 22, 24, 53; JUNGLE 54 10, 41
douroucoulis, JUNGLE 54 29
guenon, GORILLA 64 22, 23, 25
guereza, JUNGLE 54 11
howler, GORILLA 64 16, 18
leaf, GORILLA 64 22, 25
mangabeys, GORILLA 64 22, 24
mona, GORILLA 64 23, 24, 25
patas, GORILLA 64 26
proboscis, GORILLA 64 23
sakis, GORILLA 64 16
spider, GORILLA 64 16, 18-19; JUNGLE 54 20
squirrel, GORILLA 64 16, 17
titis, GORILLA 64 16, 17
vervet, GORILLA 64 25, 26, 35
woolly, GORILLA 64 16, 18, 19; JUNGLE 54 45, 60
see also baboons, macaques

monks, MEDIEVAL LIFE 65 6, 25, 38-39; RELIGION 68 25-28, 35, 37
Capuchin, MUMMY 44 60-61
monocoque, FLYING MACHINE 22 23, 24
monoplanes, FLYING MACHINE 22 15, 18, 22, 25
monorails, TRAIN 39 58-59
Monroe, Marilyn, CINEMA 34 37, 63
monsoon, WEATHER 28 31, 38, 39
monsters, WRITING 48 29
Montenegro, FLAG 16 38
Montergon, MONET 95 28
Montgolfier brothers, INVENTION 27 58
Montmartre, VAN GOGH 96 30-31
Montreal, EXPLORER 31 42
Monument Valley, ROCK & MINERAL 2 12
monuments, ARCHAEOLOGY 56 26-27, 53
Moody, Christopher, PIRATE 59 35
moon moths, BUTTERFLY & MOTH 7 36-37, 44, 58
Moon, ASTRONOMY 82 8, 20, 40-41; FORCE & MOTION 78 6, 20, 32; SPACE EXPLORATION 71 8, 11; TIME & SPACE 81 9, 12, 26, 54; WEATHER 28 10, 58
atmosphere, EARTH 83 10, 11
eclipse, ASTRONOMY 82 39
exploration, ASTRONOMY 82 34; SPACE EXPLORATION 71 46
gravity, FORCE & MOTION 78 34, 57
landings, FLAG 16 25; SPACE EXPLORATION 71 18, 23
lunar modules, SPACE EXPLORATION 71 22, 23
lunar year, ASTRONOMY 82 8, 10
men on, EXPLORER 31 58-59; FUTURE 100 10; SPACE EXPLORATION 71 19, 22-24, 27
motion, ASTRONOMY 82 21, 37; FORCE & MOTION 78 28
natural resources, FUTURE 100 56; ROCK & MINERAL 2 41
orbit, EARTH 83 12; TIME & SPACE 81 28, 29, 42
Solar System, TIME & SPACE 81 14, 15
tides, FORCE & MOTION 78 33
moons, ASTRONOMY 82 49, 50-51, 52, 55
moonstones, CRYSTAL & GEM 25 16, 45

Moore, George, MANET 94 37, 60
moorhens, BIRD 1 33, 50
moose, ARCTIC & ANTARCTIC 57 34-35, 40
moraine, EARTH 83 58
Moratín, Leandro Fernandéz, GOYA 93 29, 44, 58, 59
morays, FISH 20 48, 50
More, Sir Thomas, WATERCOLOUR 97 22
Moreau, Gustave, WATERCOLOUR 97 43
Morgan, Captain Henry, BOAT 36 29; CRIME & DETECTION 73 58; PIRATE 59 26-27, 42
Morgan, Thomas Hunt, EVOLUTION 85 41, 51
morganite, CRYSTAL & GEM 25 38, 39
Morisot, Berthe, IMPRESSIONISM 92 11, 44, 46-47; MANET 94 32, 41, 46-47; MONET 95 14, 24, 48; WATERCOLOUR 97 50
biography, IMPRESSIONISM 92 62
The Cradle, IMPRESSIONISM 92 19
Getting out of Bed, IMPRESSIONISM 92 45
In the Dining Room, IMPRESSIONISM 92 58
Lady at her Toilette, IMPRESSIONISM 92 46-47
Summer's Day, IMPRESSIONISM 92 35
Morley, Edward, FORCE & MOTION 78 58
Mormon butterfly, BUTTERFLY & MOTH 7 11, 17, 18, 23
morning suit, COSTUME 35 50
Morocco, AFRICA 61 27; DANCE 99 15; FLAG 16 14; MONEY 18 19, 54, 63
Morosaurus, DINOSAUR 13 19
Morozov, Pavlik, RUSSIA 74 53
morphine, MEDICINE 88 16, 50
Morpho butterfly, BUTTERFLY & MOTH 7 6, 24-25, 35
Morris, William, DOG 32 29; WATERCOLOUR 97 47, 48-49, 56
"Morris", COWBOY 45 21
Morse, Samuel, ELECTRICITY 77 57; ELECTRONICS 90 24; ENERGY 76 38; WEATHER 28 13
Morse Code, BOAT 36 58; SHIPWRECK 72 36, 37; SPY 67 24, 32
flag signalling, FLAG 16 18
"Morse tape", ELECTRONICS 90 48
telegraphic receiver, ELECTRICITY 77 31, 57
mortars, BATTLE 63 32-33, 34-35

Morton, Samuel, "Nails", CRIME & DETECTION 73 58
mosaic, ANCIENT ROME 24 24, 36, 37, 48, 58; ARCHAEOLOGY 56 53; AZTEC 47 48, 52, 53, 55; BUILDING 58 44
mosasaurs, DINOSAUR 13 48, 60; PREHISTORIC LIFE 52 39
mosasaurus, DINOSAUR 13 52
Moscow, RUSSIA 74 39, 43, 48, 51
architecture, RUSSIA 74 26, 34
metro, RUSSIA 74 37
University, RUSSIA 74 36, 40
Moses, BIBLE LANDS 30 12, 26; RELIGION 68 42, 43, 47
mosques, AFRICA 61 8; BUILDING 58 36, 58, 61; RELIGION 68 54, 56, 58; WRITING 48 34
mosquitoes, ECOLOGY 86 63; INSECT 17 12, 32, 49, 61; POND & RIVER 6 16
Mossad, SPY 67 43
moss, ARCTIC & ANTARCTIC 57 10, 18, 36; PLANT 14 6, 7, 46; POND & RIVER 6 54, 55; TREE 5 21, 48, 53
mother-of-pearl, OCEAN 62 58-59; SHELL 9 13, 36, 37; WRITING 48 33
Mother of Pearl butterfly, BUTTERFLY & MOTH 7 32
moths, BUTTERFLY & MOTH 7 36-37, 52-53; ECOLOGY 86 53; EVOLUTION 85 36, 41, 49, 58; INSECT 17 10, 16, 34-35
Arctic, ARCTIC & ANTARCTIC 57 19
camouflage, BUTTERFLY & MOTH 7 54-55; JUNGLE 54 50, 51; TREE 5 55
cocoons, BUTTERFLY & MOTH 7 38-39
day-flying, BUTTERFLY & MOTH 7 48-49
definition, BUTTERFLY & MOTH 7 6-7
desert, DESERT 51 24
endangered, BUTTERFLY & MOTH 7 58-59
Hawk-moths, BUTTERFLY & MOTH 7 14-15, 42-45
largest, JUNGLE 54 55
mimicry, BUTTERFLY & MOTH 7 56-57
silk, BUTTERFLY & MOTH 7 40-41
temperate, BUTTERFLY & MOTH 7 42-43
tropical, BUTTERFLY & MOTH 7 44-47
motion, ENERGY 76 14, 15, 16-17; FORCE & MOTION 78
particles, ENERGY 76 20-21

motmots, BIRD
motor nerves, HUMAN BODY 87
motorcycle, FORCE & MOTION 78 23, 53
motors, ENERGY 76 8, 30, 31
motte and bailey, CASTLE 49 8-9; KNIGHT 43 22
moulds, FOSSIL 19 6, 26
body, ARCHAEOLOGY 56 28
papermaking, WRITING 48 22-23
stone, ARCHAEOLOGY 56 50
type, WRITING 48 37
moulting, DOG 32 12, 30
mounds, burial, ARCHAEOLOGY 56 12-14, 26-27
Mount Washington Railway, TRAIN 39 23
mountain dogs, DOG 32 12, 44, 56
mountain gorilla, GORILLA 64 46-47, 60
mountain railways, TRAIN 39 22, 23
mountain rescue dogs, DOG 32 56
mountains, ECOLOGY 86 7, 52-53; PREHISTORIC LIFE 52 6-7, 10; ROCK & MINERAL 2 6, 24
Africa, AFRICA 61 7
Alps, EARTH 83 46, 48, 58
Andes, EARTH 83 47
Antarctic, ARCTIC & ANTARCTIC 57 11
Himalayas, EARTH 83 49
Rockies, EARTH 83 46
volcanic, EARTH 83 45
weather, WEATHER 28 52, 53
mourners, MUMMY 44 13, 29, 47
clothes, COSTUME 35 28, 40
mouse, spiny, DESERT 51 33
mouth organs, MUSIC 12 17
mouthbrooders, FISH 20 44
mouthpieces, MUSIC 12 8-9, 10, 12
Mozambique, AFRICA 61 33, 34
MRI, MEDICINE 88 39
mucus, FISH 20 6, 14, 47
mud, BUILDING 58 12-13, 29
mudskippers, FISH 20 32, 33; FOSSIL 19 42, 43; JUNGLE 54 17
mudstone, EARTH 83 27, 28, 29
mugging, CRIME & DETECTION 73 16
"mug-shots", CRIME & DETECTION 73 50, 53
Muhammad, Prophet, MEDIEVAL LIFE 65 44; RELIGION 68 54-57; WRITING 48 34

sharks' sense of, SHARK 40 18-19

shipwrecks, SHIPWRECK 72 22, 32, 33

surveying, INVENTION 27 34-35; TECHNOLOGY 89 30-31

"navvies", TRAIN 39 6, 20

Nawidamak, Queen, PYRAMID 53 52

Nazareth, BIBLE LANDS 30 40, 57; RELIGION 68 49

Nazca Civilization, AZTEC 47 10

Nazis, FLAG 16 3, 29

Ndebele peoples, AFRICA 61 8

Ndembu peoples, AFRICA 61 38

Neanderthals, ARCHAEOLOGY 56 43; EVOLUTION 85 63; FOSSIL 19 59; SKELETON 3 28

early humans, PREHISTORIC LIFE 52 56-57

Ice Age life, EARLY PEOPLE 10 18-19

Neave, Richard, CRIME & DETECTION 73 48, 49

Nebamun, CAT 29 47

Nebuchadnezzar, BIBLE LANDS 30 50; CAT 29 29

nebulae, ASTRONOMY 82 26, 60, 61, 62

necklace shells, SHELL 9 42

necklaces, COSTUME 35 6, 18, 48, 58; EARLY PEOPLE 10 35, 45, 56, 57; MUMMY 44 8, 54, 55

neck-rings, EARLY PEOPLE 10 45, 48; VIKING 50 37, 47

neckties, COSTUME 35 37

necropolis, ARCHAEOLOGY 56 43

nectar, JUNGLE 54 24, 25, 52; PLANT 14 22, 23, 25, 42

needles, sewing, INVENTION 27 15, 42, 46, 47

needles, trees, TREE 5 11, 30, 31, 53

Neferirkara, PYRAMID 53 38

Nefer-Maat, PYRAMID 53 15

Nefertiabet, PYRAMID 53 25

Nefertiti, ANCIENT EGYPT 23 10, 55

Negev Desert, DESERT 51 7, 16

Negri, Pola, CINEMA 34 20

Neith, PYRAMID 53 39

Nelson, Admiral, FLAG 16 19; WRITING 48 53

Nelson's column, CAT 29 8

Neo-Impressionism, IMPRESSIONISM 92 58, 59; VAN GOGH 96 32, 34

Neolithic age, ARCHAEOLOGY 56 43, 45, 50

buildings, ARCHAEOLOGY 56 53

neon lights, CINEMA 34 24

Nepal, MONEY 18 17

nephrite, CRYSTAL & GEM 25 51

nephrons, HUMAN BODY 87 38, 39

Neptune, planet, ASTRONOMY 82 36, 56-57

Neptune, Roman god, ANCIENT ROME 24 31; OCEAN 62 9; WHALE 46 54

Neptunea, FOSSIL 19 27

Nero, ANCIENT ROME 24 8

nerve cells, HUMAN BODY 87 59, 60, 62, 63; LIFE 84 11, 25

nerves, HUMAN BODY 87 6, 30, 58-61; LIFE 84 23, 24, 25, 26

intercostal, HUMAN BODY 87 25

muscles, HUMAN BODY 87 21, 23

peripheral, HUMAN BODY 87 35

sensory, HUMAN BODY 87 52, 54-55, 56

skin, HUMAN BODY 87 50

nervous system, LIFE 84 15, 25, 31

Ness, Eliot, CRIME & DETECTION 73 24

nests, BIRD 1 44-47; JUNGLE 54 36-37; TREE 5 51

unusual, BIRD 1 48-49

netball, SPORT 8 21

Netherlands, BATTLE 63 58; FLAG 16 30-31; MONEY 18 19, 34, 35, 62

Dutch art, PERSPECTIVE 98 38-39

nets, BOAT 36 44-45; WHALE 46 41, 58, 59, 61

nettles, PLANT 14 36

neurology, MEDICINE 88 60

neurons, HUMAN BODY 87 59, 60, 62, 63; LIFE 84 11, 25

neutron star, TIME & SPACE 81 45, 56

neutrons, ELECTRONICS 90 26; ENERGY 76 46, 47; MATTER 80 52, 53, 58, 62; TIME & SPACE 81 37, 58, 60

New Forest ponies, HORSE 33 37

New Guinea, JUNGLE 54 38, 39, 44, 57

mummies, MUMMY 44 63

New Ireland, WITCH & WIZARD 70 57

New Orleans, PIRATE 59 53

New Providence, PIRATE 59 31, 35

New World, EXPLORER 31 22-23, 33

New York, EXPLORER 31 40, 57; MONET 95 34, 35

New Zealand, CAT 29 55; DANCE 99 18; EXPLORER 31 14, 34; VOLCANO 38 36, 37; WEATHER 28 60

currency, MONEY 18 50, 51, 63

"the southern cross", FLAG 16 48-49

Newcomen, Thomas, ENERGY 76 28, 29; INVENTION 27 32, 33; TECHNOLOGY 89 36; TRAIN 39 10

Newfoundland, EXPLORER 31 12-13, 40; VIKING 50 6, 21; WEATHER 28 48; WHALE 46 59

Newfoundland dog, DOG 32 56

Newgate Prison, PIRATE 59 57

newspapers, WRITING 48 49

newsreel, CINEMA 34 16

Newton, Isaac, CRYSTAL & GEM 25 16; ENERGY 76 18, 40; PERSPECTIVE 98 46; TECHNOLOGY 89 58

atomic theory, TIME & SPACE 81 58

clockwork universe, FORCE & MOTION 78 28; TIME & SPACE 81 6, 9, 28-29

on friction, FORCE & MOTION 78 38

gravity, TIME & SPACE 81 32, 37, 42, 44

laws, FORCE & MOTION 78 30-31, 37, 40, 57, 60

optics, LIGHT 75 28-29, 34-35

Principia, FORCE & MOTION 78 29

telescope, ASTRONOMY 82 7, 20-21, 23

Newton, Thomas, COWBOY 45 9

newts, AMPHIBIAN 41 16, 40, 48, 49; POND & RIVER 6 9, 19, 38-39

California, AMPHIBIAN 41 13

fire-bellied, AMPHIBIAN 41 28, 40, 48

marbled, AMPHIBIAN 41 22, 48

palmate, AMPHIBIAN 41 31, 34-35, 48

great crested, AMPHIBIAN 41 7, 12, 48, 61

nibs, WRITING 48 51, 53

Nicaragua, VOLCANO 38 62

Nicholas I, Tsar of Russia, CAT 29 51; RUSSIA 74 20, 25

Nicholas II, Tsar of Russia, RUSSIA 74 20, 21, 24, 25, 30-32

Nicholas, St., RUSSIA 74 27

Nicholson, William, ELECTRICITY 77 32

nickel, ROCK & MINERAL 2 57

nickelodeons, CINEMA 34 12

niello work, DESERT 51 50, 54

niello, VIKING 50 6, 46, 49

Niepce, Joseph, LIGHT 75 24, 25; INVENTION 27 40

Niépce, Nicéphore, CINEMA 34 10

Niger, River, EXPLORER 31 19

Nigeria, AFRICA 61 22, 35, 37, 62; CAT 29 33; DANCE 99 35; WEATHER 28 36

legend, AFRICA 61 40

masks, AFRICA 61 58-59

witchcraft, WITCH & WIZARD 70 41

see also Yoruba peoples

Nightingale, Florence, BATTLE 63 60; MEDICINE 88 56

nightingales, BIRD 1 47, 52

nightjars, BIRD 1 31, 35, 53

Nijinsky, Vaslav, DANCE 99 44, 54, 55; RUSSIA 74 48, 49

Nile, River, AFRICA 61 10; ANCIENT EGYPT 23 6, 8; ANCIENT ROME 24 59; CAT 29 47; ROCK & MINERAL 2 7

gods, ANCIENT EGYPT 23 24

mummies, MUMMY 44 10, 34, 44

pyramid sites, PYRAMID 53 7, 8, 16, 30

source of, EXPLORER 31 46-47

Nilgiri Hills, JUNGLE 54 63

Nîmes, ANCIENT ROME 24 26

Nimrud, BIBLE LANDS 30 23, 33, 42, 43, 49

Nineveh, ARCHAEOLOGY 56 20; BIBLE LANDS 30 28, 46

Ninga peoples, DANCE 99 15

ninja, SPY 67 40

Ninurta, BIBLE LANDS 30 49

Nipa, FOSSIL 19 38

Nipkow, Paul, INVENTION 27 56

Nirvana, RELIGION 68 25, 26, 28

nitric acid, CHEMISTRY 79 6, 12, 39, 42, 54

salt, CHEMISTRY 79 44

TNT, CHEMISTRY 79 53

nitrogen, ASTRONOMY 82 37, 42, 43, 57; CHEMISTRY 79 18, 23, 26, 37; LIFE 84 8, 17, 18, 20; MATTER 80 7, 30-31; WEATHER 28 6

air, CHEMISTRY 79 28, 29, 32; MATTER 80 34

ammonia, CHEMISTRY 79 39

in coal, MATTER 80 40

cycle, ECOLOGY 86 20, 21

fertilizers, CHEMISTRY 79 63

nuclei, MATTER 80 52

TNT, CHEMISTRY 79 53

nitrogen cycle, ECOLOGY 86 20-21

nitrogen dioxide, CHEMISTRY 79 6

nitroglycerine, CHEMISTRY 79 62

nitrous oxide, MEDICINE 88 48

Nix, Evett, **Cowboy 45** 43
Nixie tubes,
Electronics 90 45
Nkimba society, **Africa 61** 32
Noah, **Bible Lands 30** 32, 50
Noah's Ark, **Boat 36** 16;
Shipwreck 72 58
Nobel, Alfred,
Chemistry 79 62
Nobel Prize, **Russia 74** 40, 41, 45
Nobile, Umberto,
Arctic & Antarctic 57 20
Nobili, Leopold,
Electricity 77 24
noble gases,
Chemistry 79 20, 26, 32-33
periodic table,
Chemistry 79 23
nobles, **Money 18** 46
Nofret, **Pyramid 53** 14
Nola, **Ancient Rome 24** 14
nomads, **Africa 61** 8, 12, 14,
18; **Arctic & Antarctic 57**
48-49; **Desert 51** 44-45, 49,
56, 58; **Russia 74** 13, 23
Nonius horse, **Cowboy 45** 13;
Horse 33 38
Nonnebakken, **Viking 50** 22, 48
Nordenskjöld, Nils, **Arctic &
Antarctic 57** 52
Nore lightship,
Shipwreck 72 34
Norgay, Tenzing,
Future 100 10
Normandy, **Monet 95** 16-17,
40-41; **Viking 50** 10, 16
Normans, **Castle 49** 10;
Knight 43 8-9;
Medieval Life 65 7;
Viking 50 10, 35, 38
weaponry, **Arms &
Armour 4** 14-15
Norris, William, **Train 39** 17
North America,
Building 58 31, 36, 41, 62;
Cat 29 9, 10, 36;
Explorer 31 42-45;
Witch & Wizard 70
44-47, 58
animals, **Arctic &
Antarctic 57** 34, 36,
38-39
North American Indians,
Early People 10 34, 60-61;
Horse 33 34, 46, 56-57;
**North American
Indian 60**
games, **North American
Indian 60** 24-25, 27, 29
graves, **North American
Indian 60** 18, 36, 52-53
hunting, **North American
Indian 60** 12-13, 28-30, 38-40
language, **North American
Indian 60** 9, 46, 63
modern, **North American
Indian 60** 62-63

music, **North American
Indian 60** 14, 26-27, 37
potlatch, **North American
Indian 60** 56-57
shamans, **North American
Indian 60** 9-11, 22-23, 54
totem poles, **North
American Indian 60** 52-53
see also under individual tribes
North Pole, **Arctic &
Antarctic 57** 6, 20, 55;
Explorer 31 52-53, 55;
Flag 16 42; **Weather 28**
17, 40
Northern Ireland, **Money 18** 46
northern lights, **Arctic &
Antarctic 57** 7
northern marblewing
butterflies, **Butterfly &
Moth 7** 31
Northwest Passage,
Explorer 31 40-42
Norton, Elizabeth, **Cat 29** 57
Norway, **Explorer 31** 12-13;
Flag 16 42-43; **Money 18**
13, 42, 43, 62; **Monet 95** 39;
Whale 46 49, 51, 57, 58
Norwich School,
Watercolour 97 34
nose, **Human Body 87** 56-57
Nostradamus, **Future 100** 8,
11; **Witch & Wizard 70** 15
notes, **Money 18** 12, 13
printing, **Money 18** 16, 17
notes, musical, **Music 12** 6,
8, 26
notodontid moths,
Butterfly & Moth 7 55
Notre Dame, **Rock &
Mineral 2** 35
nova, **Astronomy 82** 18, 61
Noverre, Jean-George,
Dance 99 44
Novgorod, **Viking 50** 22
Nuba peoples, **Africa 61** 22
Nubia, **Africa 61** 10;
Archaeology 56 41, 51;
Pyramid 53 48-49
pharaohs,
Pyramid 53 50-51
queens, **Pyramid 53** 52-53
nuclear bombs, **Matter 80**
28, 54, 55
nuclear force, **Force &
Motion 78** 62, 63
nuclear power, .
Electricity 77 45; **Force &
Motion 78** 41; **Time &
Space 81** 37
accidents, **Future 100** 11
reactions, **Chemistry 79** 18,
35; **Energy 76** 44, 45, 46-47
fission, **Energy 76** 56
fusion, **Astronomy 82**
38-39, 60
reactors, **Matter 80** 52, 54,
55, 57

nucleic acids, **Life 84** 9, 14,
34, 54
viruses, **Life 84** 58, 59
nucleus, **Chemistry 79** 16, 22,
35; **Life 84** 10, 11, 14;
Matter 80 48, 50, 56, 63;
Time & Space 81 58
components, **Matter 80**
52-53, 58-59
DNA, **Life 84** 34
fission, **Matter 80** 54
fusion, **Matter 80** 57, 60
nuée ardente,
Volcano 38 16, 32
nummulites, **Shell 9** 44
nunataks, **Arctic &
Antarctic 57** 11
nungu, **Music 12** 51
nuns, **Medieval Life 65** 22, 38
Nupe peoples, **Africa 61** 8
Nureyev, Rudolf,
Russia 74 48
Nuri, **Pyramid 53** 48, 50, 51
nurses, **Battle 63** 60
nursing, **Medicine 88** 49, 56-57
Nut, **Mummy 44** 21, 25
Nutcracker, The,
Dance 99 52, 53
nuthatches, **Bird 1** 32, 33, 60;
Tree 5 21
Nuthetes, **Dinosaur 13** 25
nutmegs, **Tree 5** 42
nutrition, **Life 84** 20-21
nuts, **Tree 5** 40-43, 51
nylon, **Chemistry 79** 56;
Costume 35 55, 56;
Technology 89 7, 28
nymphalid butterflies,
Butterfly & Moth 7 6, 9,
26, 34, 56
Nyos, Lake, **Volcano 38** 20, 55
Nyuserra, **Pyramid 53** 38

Oahu volcano, Hawaii,
Volcano 38 22
oak, **Building 58** 8, 22, 26, 38
Oakes, Roger,
Watercolour 97 57
Oakley, Annie,
Cowboy 45 59; **Sport 8** 55
oaks, **Pond & River 6** 19, 55;
Tree 5 50, 51, 52, 59
English, **Tree 5** 8, 25, 33
Turkey, **Tree 5** 25, 41
oarfish, **Fish 20** 48
oars, **Boat 36** 8, 10, 17, 20-21
oases, **Desert 51** 7, 13, 14, 18
Oates, Captain, **Arctic &
Antarctic 57** 54, 58
oats, **Farm 66** 6, 28
oban, **Money 18** 52
obelisks, **Ancient Egypt 23** 29
oboes, **Music 12** 9, 12, 13
obol, **Money 18** 41
observatories,
Astronomy 82 10, 18,
26-27; **Light 75** 7, 21;
Time & Space 81 9, 26, 32
Berlin, **Astronomy 82** 56
Paris, **Astronomy 82**
28, 50, 52
Royal Greenwich,
Astronomy 82 25, 27, 28
space, **Space
Exploration 71** 42, 52-53
obsidian, **Archaeology 56** 50;
Aztec 47 15, 28, 52, 54;
Rock & Mineral 2 16, 19, 29
occipital bones,
Skeleton 3 29, 63
occultists, **Witch &
Wizard 70** 12, 13, 15, 26
oceans, **Earth 83** 7, 14, 18, 22;
Ecology 86 8, 24, 38-39;
Ocean 62
Arctic, **Earth 83** 18;
Ocean 62 8
Atlantic, **Earth 83** 30, 34, 36,
48; **Ocean 62** 7-9, 13-14, 26
floor, **Earth 83** 32, 30-33
food web, **Ecology 86**
12-13
formation, **Earth 83** 6, 25,
36, 38-39
Indian, **Earth 83** 32, 36;
Ocean 62 7-8, 24
Pacific, **Earth 83** 30, 32, 36,
38; **Ocean 62** 11-12, 24, 46

Southern, OCEAN 62 8
trenches, EARTH 83 36, 37
zones, OCEAN 62 10, 40-41, 42-43
see also sea
ocelots, CAT 29 14, 40
Ockels, Wubbo, SPACE EXPLORATION 71 17, 33
ocotillo, DESERT 51 18
octant, INVENTION 27 34, 35
Octavian, PIRATE 59 11
Octavian, *see* Augustus
October Revolution, RUSSIA 74 30-31, 35
octopus, FISH 20 49; OCEAN 62 10, 32, 34-35; SEASHORE 15 26; SHELL 9 8, 18
Odin, VIKING 50 37, 53, 58, 62
Odonata, INSECT 17 8
Odysseus, ANCIENT GREECE 37 12, 13, 14, 21
Odyssey, The, ANCIENT GREECE 37 12; SHIPWRECK 72 59
Oedipus, King, ANCIENT GREECE 37 39
Oersted, Hans Christian, ELECTRICITY 77 26, 27, 38; ELECTRONICS 90 10, 11, 24; ENERGY 76 23, 24
oesophagus, HUMAN BODY 87 24, 27, 34, 36
offerings, PYRAMID 53 24-25
officers, BATTLE 63 16
Ogoni peoples, AFRICA 61 58
Ohm, Georg Simon, ELECTRICITY 77 22-23; ELECTRONICS 90 16
Ohm's law, ELECTRONICS 90 22, 23
ohms, ELECTRICITY 77 23, 25
oil, EARTH 83 27, 57; ENERGY 76 52, 54, 55, 56; FOSSIL 19 15, 40, 41; OCEAN 62 60-62
  biochemistry, CHEMISTRY 79 50
  as blubber, WHALE 46 16, 46, 50, 58
  chemical analysis, CHEMISTRY 79 58
  crude, CHEMISTRY 79 6, 15
  deposits, DESERT 51 9
  in plants, PLANT 14 13, 15, 58
  see also essential oils
oil lamps, INVENTION 27 20, 21
oil paints, PERSPECTIVE 98 29
oil tankers, SHIPWRECK 72 30-31
ointments, WITCH & WIZARD 70 33-35, 37, 40
Ojibwa peoples, NORTH AMERICAN INDIAN 60 16, 22, 58-59
Olaf Haraldsson, King, VIKING 50 62
Olbers, Heinrich, TIME & SPACE 81 25

Old Bear, NORTH AMERICAN INDIAN 60 10
Old Calabar, River, PIRATE 59 45
Old Faithful, geyser, VOLCANO 38 7, 37
Oldenburg, HORSE 33 40
Oldsmobile CAR 21 8, 62
Olduvai Gorge, FOSSIL 19 59
olive branch, FLAG 16 15
olive oil, ANCIENT GREECE 37 40, 41, 44, 51
olives, TREE 5 39
olivine, CRYSTAL & GEM 25 45; ROCK & MINERAL 2 15, 17, 43, 54
Olmec peoples, ARCHAEOLOGY 56 7, 13; AZTEC 47 8, 9; EARLY PEOPLE 10 59; PYRAMID 53 54
Olympia, ANCIENT GREECE 37 6, 26, 33, 44
Olympic games, ANCIENT GREECE 37 7, 44-45; DANCE 99 49; FLAG 16 22, 23; SPORT 8 38
Olympus, Mt., ANCIENT GREECE 37 20
Omaha, NORTH AMERICAN INDIAN 60 29, 35
Omega Workshop, FLAG 16 19
omnivores, PREHISTORIC LIFE 52 8; SKELETON 3 35
onager, HORSE 33 7, 12, 16-17
onions, PLANT 14 15, 33
Onohippidium, HORSE 33 8
Ontario, badge of, FLAG 16 44
Ontario, Lake, SHIPWRECK 72 24, 25
ootheca, INSECT 17 23
opals, CRYSTAL & GEM 25 19, 25, 40-41; ROCK & MINERAL 2 51
opaque objects, LIGHT 75 46, 47
Oparin, Alexandr, LIFE 84 55, 56, 57
Opel Kadett, CAR 21 24
Opel Vectra, SPY 67 46
operating theatre, MEDICINE 88 49, 50
operculum, FISH 20 7, 8, 59
ophiuroids, FOSSIL 19 32
opium, CHINA 55 62, 63; PLANT 14 58
Opium Wars, FLAG 16 59
opossums, FOSSIL 19 61; MAMMAL 11 8, 20, 27, 31
Oppenheimer, Robert, MATTER 80 55
opthalmologists, MEDICINE 88 18
  optic nerves, HUMAN BODY 87 52-53, 60, 63; LIGHT 75 18
optical printers, CINEMA 34 43, 44-45
optics, INVENTION 27 28-29, 40; PERSPECTIVE 98 6
  fibre optics, LIGHT 75 54, 55

optometers, LIGHT 75 19
oracles, ANCIENT GREECE 37 24, 25
oral rehydration therapy, ORT, MEDICINE 88 63
orang pendeks, GORILLA 64 59
Orangerie, Paris, MONET 95 60-61
orangutans, GORILLA 64 38-41; JUNGLE 54 63; PREHISTORIC LIFE 52 54
  and humans, GORILLA 64 8
  intelligence, GORILLA 64 36, 37
  poaching, GORILLA 64 63
  worship of, GORILLA 64 58
orbits, ASTRONOMY 82 11, 18, 37; FORCE & MOTION 78 29, 32-33, 53; TIME & SPACE 81 28, 29, 42
  atoms, TIME & SPACE 81 58
  comets, ASTRONOMY 82 58
  gravity, TIME & SPACE 81 46
  planets, ASTRONOMY 82 37, 38, 56, 57; TIME & SPACE 81 14-15
  satellites, ASTRONOMY 82 34, 40, 44-45
orchestras, MUSIC 12 12, 30
orchids, JUNGLE 54 63; PLANT 14 23, 24, 46, 47; TREE 5 21
  mantis, JUNGLE 54 53
  one-day, JUNGLE 54 13
  otter, JUNGLE 54 33
  slipper, JUNGLE 54 24, 49
orders, BATTLE 63 58-59
Ordovician period, EVOLUTION 85 60
φre, MONEY 18 42, 43
öre, MONEY 18 44, 45
Oregon Trail, EXPLORER 31 44; HORSE 33 35
Orellana, Francisco de, EXPLORER 31 63
ores, CHEMISTRY 79 10, 12, 18, 25; INVENTION 27 14; MATTER 80 6, 15, 16; TECHNOLOGY 89 12, 14
  types of, ROCK & MINERAL 2 6, 56-57
organic compounds, CHEMISTRY 79 8, 9, 48-49
  analysis, CHEMISTRY 79 60
  chemistry, CHEMISTRY 79 63
  synthesis, CHEMISTRY 79 52-53
organs, bodily, LIFE 84 14-15, 22, 30
  organ transplants, FUTURE 100 10, 11, 40
organs, pipe, MUSIC 12 18-19
Orient Express, TRAIN 39 31, 43, 49
oriflamme, FLAG 16 26
Orion, ASTRONOMY 82 6, 60, 61, 63; PYRAMID 53 47

Orion lunar module, SPACE EXPLORATION 71 22, 23
Orleans, Duke of, CASTLE 49 10
Orlov, Count Grigory, RUSSIA 74 25
Orlov Trotter, HORSE 33 38
Ornithomimus, DINOSAUR 13 42
ornithopters, FLYING MACHINE 22 6-7
Ornithosuchus, DINOSAUR 13 7
Orpheus, ANCIENT GREECE 37 23; DANCE 99 31; MUSIC 12 34
orreries, TIME & SPACE 81 14
orthoceratoids, FOSSIL 19 29
orthoclase, CRYSTAL & GEM 25 8, 12, 16, 18, 19
Orthodox Church, RUSSIA 74 9, 18-19, 56
orthogonals, PERSPECTIVE 98 12, 62
Orthoptera, INSECT 17 8
Orwell, George, FUTURE 100 14
Orycteropus, FOSSIL 19 54
oryx, DESERT 51 37, 51
Oscan alphabet, WRITING 48 6
Oscars, CINEMA 34 37, 39, 53, 62
oscillation, ENERGY 76 41, 40; FORCE & MOTION 78 46-47
oscillators, ELECTRONICS 90 30, 32-33, 48
oscilloscopes, ELECTRONICS 90 15, 19, 20, 33
Osiris, ANCIENT EGYPT 23 10, 19, 25, 60; MUMMY 44 13, 34-35, 49; PYRAMID 53 29, 32; WRITING 48 13
osmosis, LIFE 84 20, 23
ospreys, BIRD 1 53; EAGLE 69 10, 13, 27, 36
osteichthians, FISH 20 9
osteopathy, MEDICINE 88 44-45
osteostracans, FISH 20 12
ostraca, PYRAMID 53 32; WRITING 48 6, 13
ostracods, SHELL 9 24, 54
ostrakon, ANCIENT GREECE 37 19
ostrich feathers, COSTUME 35 47, 51
ostriches, BIRD 1 17, 32, 41, 54; DESERT 51 30, 42, 57, 60; FOSSIL 19 21, 53; SKELETON 3 57
  similarity with dinosaurs, DINOSAUR 13 36, 37
Oswald, Lee Harvey, CRIME & DETECTION 73 58
otoscope, MEDICINE 88 28, 60
otterhounds, DOG 32 53
otters, MAMMAL 11 9, 49, 62; POND & RIVER 6 37, 57
Otto I, King of Germany, MEDIEVAL LIFE 65 6

Otto, Nikolaus, ENERGY 76 30; INVENTION 27 48
Ottoman Empire, MEDIEVAL LIFE 65 63; PIRATE 59 14, 16-17
ouabain, JUNGLE 54 43
outlaws, CRIME & DETECTION 73 11-13, 52, 56
outriggers, BOAT 36 14-15, 21, 45
ovaries, HUMAN BODY 87 40, 42-43
ovens, CASTLE 49 40
overgrazing, DESERT 51 42
overshoes, COSTUME 35 38
Ovid, ANCIENT ROME 24 34; RENAISSANCE 91 32, 33, 47
oviduct, HUMAN BODY 87 43
Ovimbundu peoples, AFRICA 61 31
ovum, HUMAN BODY 87 42, 43, 44, 48
Owen, Samuel, SHIPWRECK 72 8
Owen, Sir Richard, DINOSAUR 13 8; EVOLUTION 85 18, 19; FOSSIL 19 50
owl coins, MONEY 18 20, 22
owls, ARCTIC & ANTARCTIC 57 24; BIRD 1 12, 35, 42-43; EAGLE 69 48-50; ECOLOGY 86 10, 28, 44
chicks, EAGLE 69 13, 14
desert, DESERT 51 30, 31
senses, EAGLE 69 51
skeleton, SKELETON 3 19, 30, 33, 56
oxen, FARM 66 8, 12-15, 48; SKELETON 3 57
Oxford bags, COSTUME 35 53
oxygen, CHEMISTRY 79 18, 23, 24, 26; ENERGY 76 51, 54, 50; EVOLUTION 85 56, 57, 61; LIFE 84 8, 9, 27, 57; MATTER 80 6, 7, 16, 18
air, CHEMISTRY 79 28, 29; MATTER 80 34, 39
atmospheric, EARTH 83 10, 11, 50, 62
burning, CHEMISTRY 79 30, 35; ENERGY 76 52, 53; MATTER 80 30-31
carbohydrates, CHEMISTRY 79 49, 60
in coal, MATTER 80 40
in crystals, CRYSTAL & GEM 25 6, 8, 14, 15
discovery, WEATHER 28 6
gas, MATTER 80 20, 21
living processes, CHEMISTRY 79 31, 34, 51
oxidation, CHEMISTRY 79 40-41
photosynthesis, LIFE 84 17
respiration, LIFE 84 15, 18-19

water, CHEMISTRY 79 18, 20, 29, 46; EARTH 83 16, 17; MATTER 80 36, 51
oystercatchers, BIRD 1 39; SEASHORE 15 54
oysters, FOSSIL 19 16, 26; POND & RIVER 6 59; SEASHORE 15 26-27, 43, 53; SHELL 9 8, 32, 34, 36
pearls, OCEAN 62 58-59
ozone, CHEMISTRY 79 33, 34; WEATHER 28 61
ozone layer, ARCTIC & ANTARCTIC 57 62, 63; EARTH 83 11; LIGHT 75 41; VOLCANO 38 35
creation of, ECOLOGY 86 36
damage to, FUTURE 100 11, 15, 18

pacas, MAMMAL 11 9, 52-53
pacemakers, FUTURE 100 40, 41; MEDICINE 88 54-55
Pachycephalosaurus, DINOSAUR 13 28, 29
Pacific, ARCTIC & ANTARCTIC 57 8; EARTH 83 30, 32, 36, 38; VOLCANO 38 10, 11, 24; WEATHER 28 7, 45, 52
crossing, FLYING MACHINE 22 32
"the Great South Sea" EXPLORER 31 34
James Cook, EXPLORER 31 34, 37
tribes, WITCH & WIZARD 70 10, 30, 52, 56
pack ice, SHIPWRECK 72 11, 38
Packard, CAR 21 22
pacu, FISH 20 34
paddleball, SPORT 8 36
paddlefish, FISH 20 9
paddles, BOAT 36 20, 21, 30, 42

Paganini, Niccolo, MUSIC 12 30
Page, Jimmy, MUSIC 12 61
pages, CASTLE 49 43, 46; KNIGHT 43 10
pagoda stones, FOSSIL 19 29
pagodas, CHINA 55 26
paidogogus, ANCIENT GREECE 37 33
paidotribes, ANCIENT GREECE 37 33
Paige, CAR 21 62
painite, CRYSTAL & GEM 25 56
paint, BUILDING 58 52, 53; TECHNOLOGY 89 9, 51; WATERCOLOUR 97 15, 28, 29, 37, 39
oil, PERSPECTIVE 98 29
paintings, ARCHAEOLOGY 56 8, 16; EARLY PEOPLE 10 22, 24, 34; SHIPWRECK 72 8, 38
Ancient Egypt, PYRAMID 53 7, 25, 41
Buddhist, ARCHAEOLOGY 56 29, 51
cave, ARCHAEOLOGY 56 9, 16, 57, 62
Chinese, CHINA 55 30, 32-33, 54
frescoes, ARCHAEOLOGY 56 20-21
Impressionist, IMPRESSIONISM 92
tomb, PYRAMID 53 15, 24, 33
wall, ARCHAEOLOGY 56 51
water colours, WATERCOLOUR 97
see also under individual artists
Paiute peoples, NORTH AMERICAN INDIAN 60 40-41
Pakistan, EXPLORER 31 10
Palaeocene period, MAMMAL 11 12, 14
palaeogeography, EARTH 83 26
Palaeolithic age, ARCHAEOLOGY 56 44, 57, 62
weapons, ARMS & ARMOUR 4 6-7
Palaeoniscus, FISH 20 12
palaeontologists, DINOSAUR 13 52, 53; ELEPHANT 42 8
Palaeophis, FOSSIL 19 44
Palaeotherium, FOSSIL 19 14
Palaeozoic era, EVOLUTION 85 46, 60, 61
palatine bones, SKELETON 3 28, 63
Palermo, MUMMY 44 60
Palestine, Ancient, BIBLE LANDS 30 22, 33, 52-54; MONEY 18 20, 24; RELIGION 68 42, 48
archaeology, BIBLE LANDS 30 62-63
Bronze Age, BIBLE LANDS 30 14, 16
culture, BIBLE LANDS 30 42

food, BIBLE LANDS 30 30-31
trade, BIBLE LANDS 30 38
palettes, VAN GOGH 96 22, 45, 57
palfreys, KNIGHT 43 20
palisades, CASTLE 49 6, 26
Pallas, Peter Simon, CAT 29 57
palm fruit, ANCIENT EGYPT 23 47, 49
Palmer, David Daniel, MEDICINE 88 45
Palmer, Harry, SPY 67 58
Palmer, Samuel, WATERCOLOUR 97 28, 42, 43
Palmieri, Luigi, VOLCANO 38 52, 53
palmistry, WITCH & WIZARD 70 36
palms, DESERT 51 15, 18; FOSSIL 19 38; JUNGLE 54 8; TREE 5 12, 13, 32, 42
fruit, JUNGLE 54 27
oil, JUNGLE 54 40
products, JUNGLE 54 30-31, 48
rattan, JUNGLE 54 26, 49
wax, JUNGLE 54 30
palps, INSECT 17 7, 17, 20
Pan, ANCIENT GREECE 37 20, 22, 41; ANCIENT ROME 24 48, 51
Panama, EXPLORER 31 23
Panathenaea, ANCIENT GREECE 37 7, 16, 25, 44
pancreas, HUMAN BODY 87 34, 36, 40, 41
pandas, MAMMAL 11 9, 50
Pandavas, RELIGION 68 20
panelling, BUILDING 58 54, 55
Pangaea, FOSSIL 19 12, 13
Panhard Levassor, CAR 21 8, 12, 23
paniers, COSTUME 35 30, 42
panning, CRYSTAL & GEM 25 25, 52
panpipes, AZTEC 47 57; MUSIC 12 10
pansies, PLANT 14 7
pantaloons, COSTUME 35 41
panther groupers, FISH 20 19
panthers, CAT 29 14, 22-23, 33
pantograph, TRAIN 39 38, 39
pantomime, DANCE 99 40
Papago peoples, NORTH AMERICAN INDIAN 60 7, 44, 50-51
paper, CHINA 55 25, 32; TECHNOLOGY 89 24, 62; WRITING 48 22-23
invention, CHINA 55 23, 24; INVENTION 27 7, 19; WATERCOLOUR 97 6, 18
paper knives, WRITING 48 56
Papin, Denis, INVENTION 27 55
Papua New Guinea, DANCE 99 32; EXPLORER 31 14; JUNGLE 54 38, 56, 63; WITCH & WIZARD 70 10, 30, 56

papyrus, **ANCIENT EGYPT 23** 32, 38; **EARLY PEOPLE 10** 41; **MUMMY 44** 12, 13; **PYRAMID 53** 30, 31, 32, 39

Egyptian, **INVENTION 27** 18; **WRITING 48** 12-13

plant, **WRITING 48** 20; **PLANT 14** 49

scroll, **ANCIENT GREECE 37** 30, 33, 48

para, **MONEY 18** 41

parables, **RELIGION 68** 53

parachutes, **FLYING MACHINE 22** 10, 60; **SPY 67** 20, 21 32

paracils, **BOAT 36** 10, 11

Parade, **DANCE 99** 30

parades, **KNIGHT 43** 15, 44; **MEDIEVAL LIFE 65** 58-59

Paradoxides, **FOSSIL 19** 30

paraffin, **TECHNOLOGY 89** 41

Paragon propeller, **FLYING MACHINE 22** 30

Paraguay, **FLAG 16** 55

Parahippus, **HORSE 33** 8

parallax, **TIME & SPACE 81** 49

parallel bars, **SPORT 8** 42

paramedics, **MEDICINE 88** 58

Paramount Studios, **CINEMA 34** 21

Parasaurolophus, **DINOSAUR 13** 10, 28, 29

parasites, **ARCHAEOLOGY 56** 6, 42, 46, 63; **FISH 20** 6, 46, 47; **LIFE 84** 21, 47; **SEASHORE 15** 48; **TREE 5** 21

parasitism, **ECOLOGY 86** 30, 46, 47

parasols, **COSTUME 35** 19

parchment, **WATERCOLOUR 97** 10, 11; **WRITING 48** 20-21

making, **WRITING 48** 21

pardons, **CRIME & DETECTION 73** 14, 16

Paré, Ambroise, **MEDICINE 88** 26, 54

parietal bones, **SKELETON 3** 29, 63

Paris, **CAT 29** 61; **MANET 94** 14-15, 44-45, 56; **MONET 95** 7, 60-61; **VAN GOGH 96** 28-38, 44, 56

Gare de Lyons, **TRAIN 39** 17

Metro, **TRAIN 39** 57

Observatory, **ASTRONOMY 82** 28, 50, 52

Salons, **IMPRESSIONISM 92** 6, 18-19, 45

Paris Commune, **MANET 94** 44-45, 51

Paris, Matthew, **KNIGHT 43** 13; **WATERCOLOUR 97** 8

Park, Nick, **CINEMA 34** 53

parkas, **ARCTIC & ANTARCTIC 57** 49

Parker, George, **CRIME & DETECTION 73** 40, 47, 49

Parkes, Alexander, **INVENTION 27** 60; **MATTER 80** 44; **TECHNOLOGY 89** 26

Parkfield, California, **VOLCANO 38** 61

parliament, medieval, **MEDIEVAL LIFE 65** 24

Parnassus, Mt., **ANCIENT GREECE 37** 25

parrotfishes, **FISH 20** 31, 35

parrots, **BIRD 1** 27, 34, 36, 37; **JUNGLE 54** 41; **SKELETON 3** 18, 30

Parry, Sir William, **ARCTIC & ANTARCTIC 57** 53; **EXPLORER 31** 51, 53

Parsa, **BIBLE LANDS 30** 52

Parsons, Sir Charles, **ELECTRICITY 77** 42; **ENERGY 76** 28, 32, 33

parthenogenesis, **INSECT 17** 36, 43

Parthenon, **ANCIENT GREECE 37** 7, 16, 17; **ARCHAEOLOGY 56** 63; **ROCK & MINERAL 2** 13

particle accelerators, **ENERGY 76** 45; **TIME & SPACE 81** 37, 59

particle theory, **LIGHT 75** 34-35, 36, 44

particles, **TIME & SPACE 81** 51, 52

quantum theory, **TIME & SPACE 81** 53

partridges, **BIRD 1** 26

Parvati, **RELIGION 68** 20, 21

pas de deux, **DANCE 99** 21, 56

Pascal, Blaise, **FORCE & MOTION 78** 44; **INVENTION 27** 31; **WEATHER 28** 52

passenger service, **TRAIN 39** 7, 52, 62

passion flowers, **PLANT 14** 18

passion fruits, **GORILLA 64** 19

Passover, **RELIGION 68** 42, 46, 47

Pasternak, Boris, **RUSSIA 74** 44, 45

Pasteur, Louis, **EVOLUTION 85** 13; **LIFE 84** 28, 54; **MATTER 80** 42; **MEDICINE 88** 32, 35, 48, 57

Patagonian Desert, **DESERT 51** 6, 43

patchboxes, **COSTUME 35** 18

patella, *see* kneecap

Pathé, **CINEMA 34** 13, 16, 19

path-finding, **DESERT 51** 9, 13, 62

pathogens, **LIFE 84** 28, 58

Patrick, St., **FLAG 16** 47; **REPTILE 26** 27

Paul, St., **MEDIEVAL LIFE 65** 42; **VIKING 50** 59, 60

Pavarotti, Luciano, **WHALE 46** 27

Pavlov, Ivan, **HUMAN BODY 87** 58; **RUSSIA 74** 40

Pavlova, Anna, **DANCE 99** 29, 53, 54; **RUSSIA 74** 48

Pazyryk, **ARCHAEOLOGY 56** 30-31

pea urchins, **SHELL 9** 21

Peacock throne, **CRYSTAL & GEM 25** 37

peacocks, **BIRD 1** 19, 26, 27, 28; **FARM 66** 60; **SKELETON 3** 47

pearl crabs, **SHELL 9** 53

pearls, **COSTUME 35** 11, 45, 48; **CRYSTAL & GEM 25** 32, 54, 55, 56; **FOSSIL 19** 26; **SHELL 9** 8, 12, 36-37

from oysters, **OCEAN 62** 59

pears, **TREE 5** 25

Peary, Robert, **ARCTIC & ANTARCTIC 57** 58; **EXPLORER 31** 52, 63; **FLAG 16** 24

peasants, **CASTLE 49** 53, 54; **KNIGHT 43** 36, 37; **MEDIEVAL LIFE 65** 8, 10-13, 28

food, **MEDIEVAL LIFE 65** 18, 19

revolt, **MEDIEVAL LIFE 65** 7, 10

peasecod belly, **COSTUME 35** 20, 21

peat, **ARCTIC & ANTARCTIC 57** 10; **FOSSIL 19** 6, 21, 40; **ROCK & MINERAL 2** 37

peatbogs, **ARCHAEOLOGY 56** 9, 36-37

pebbles, **ROCK & MINERAL 2** 6, 14-15; **SEASHORE 15** 8-11

pedlars, **MEDIEVAL LIFE 65** 14, 46, 55

Peel, Sir Robert, **CRIME & DETECTION 73** 10

peepshows, **CINEMA 34** 7; **PERSPECTIVE 98** 12, 36-37, 39

Pegasus, **ANCIENT GREECE 37** 23; **FLAG 16** 14; **HORSE 33** 22

pegmatites, **CRYSTAL & GEM 25** 25, 38, 43, 45

Pei, I. M., **PYRAMID 53** 63

Peking Man, **FOSSIL 19** 59

Pekingeses, **DOG 32** 20, 34, 58, 60

Pelée, Mt., **ROCK & MINERAL 2** 9; **VOLCANO 38** 15, 32

pelican's foot shells, **SHELL 9** 43

pelobates, **FOSSIL 19** 42

Peloponnese, **ANCIENT GREECE 37** 7, 22

pelota, **SPORT 8** 37

Pemberton, Dr. John, **CINEMA 34** 25

pen shells, **SHELL 9** 17

pence, **MONEY 18** 14, 18, 28, 50

pencils, **INVENTION 27** 7, 18; **SPY 67** 36

pendants, **EARLY PEOPLE 10** 35, 44, 49; **VIKING 50** 7, 31, 46

pendulum, **FORCE & MOTION 78** 46, 47, 48; **INVENTION 27** 22, 23

clock, **FORCE & MOTION 78** 25, 47

earthquake detector, **FORCE & MOTION 78** 30

penguins, **ARCTIC & ANTARCTIC 57** 10, 28-29; **BIRD 1** 17; **SEASHORE 15** 56

Emperor, **ARCTIC & ANTARCTIC 57** 30-31

penicillin, **FUTURE 100** 9; **MEDICINE 88** 42

Peninsular War, **BATTLE 63** 21, 48, 57

penis, **HUMAN BODY 87** 39, 42, 44

Penkowsky, Oleg, **SPY 67** 57

penniä, **MONEY 18** 44, 45, 62

pennies, **MONEY 18** 44, 46, 48, 51

penny arcade, **CINEMA 34** 12

pens, **INVENTION 27** 18, 19; **SPY 67** 12, 13, 19; **TECHNOLOGY 89** 39, 48; **WRITING 48**

modern, **WRITING 48** 53

quill, **WRITING 48** 53, 57

Pentacrinites, **FOSSIL 19** 33

peplos, **ANCIENT GREECE 37** 16, 42; **COSTUME 35** 9

Pepy I, **PYRAMID 53** 39

Pepy II, **ANCIENT EGYPT 23** 10; **PYRAMID 53** 39

Pepys, Samuel, **PERSPECTIVE 98** 37

perch, **FISH 20** 8, 9

Percheron, **HORSE 33** 50-51

percussion, **MEDICINE 88** 28-29; **MUSIC 12** 48-49, 54-55

drums, **MUSIC 12** 50-51, 52-53

see also under individual instruments

peregrine falcons, **BIRD 1** 14, 42

Peress, Joseph, **SHIPWRECK 72** 48

perfume, **EARLY PEOPLE 10** 34

Pergamum, **ANCIENT GREECE 37** 6, 62, 63; **WRITING 48** 21

peridot, **CRYSTAL & GEM 25** 42, 45, 49, 61

Perikles, **ANCIENT GREECE 37** 16, 17, 18, 27

periodic table, **CHEMISTRY 79** 22-23, 33; **ELECTRONICS 90** 37 **MATTER 80** 32-33

metals, **CHEMISTRY 79** 25

non-metals, **CHEMISTRY 79** 26

peripatus, **INSECT 17** 10

periscopes, **BATTLE 63** 54

Perissodactyla, **HORSE 33** 6

periwigs, **COSTUME 35** 28, 29

periwinkles, POND & RIVER 6 59; SEASHORE 15 26, 28, 30, 33; SHELL 9 47
Perkin, William, LIGHT 75 33
permafrost, ARCTIC & ANTARCTIC 57 9; RUSSIA 74 11, 15, 39
Permian period, EVOLUTION 85 61
Perlution 85 MUMMY 44 62
Perrin, Jean, MATTER 80 38
Perrot, Jules, DANCE 99 13, 56
Persephone, ANCIENT GREECE 37 20, 21, 60
Persepolis, BIBLE LANDS 30 52-53
Perseus, ANCIENT GREECE 37 23
Persia, ANCIENT GREECE 37 6, 16, 18, 54; BUILDING 58 43; EXPLORER 31 10, 17-18
Ancient, RELIGION 68 40, 41, 46; WITCH & WIZARD 70 20, 21, 37
Persian peoples, ANCIENT ROME 24 62; BIBLE LANDS 30 52-53
weapons, ARMS & ARMOUR 4 32
see also Iran
Persian cats, CAT 29 46, 49, 50, 56
Persian Gulf, OCEAN 62 60
Persian language, old, WRITING 48 9
perspective, fourth dimension, TIME & SPACE 81 34
perspective, in art, PERSPECTIVE 98 6-7; RENAISSANCE 91 28-29, 52, 61
aerial, PERSPECTIVE 98 28-29
foreshortening, PERSPECTIVE 98 7, 22, 38, 62
linear, PERSPECTIVE 98 6, 12, 24, 52
natural, PERSPECTIVE 98 24
in paintings, PERSPECTIVE 98 16, 20-21, 50
vanishing points, PERSPECTIVE 98 6, 13, 25, 62
perturbation, ASTRONOMY 82 56
Peru, CAT 29 34, 35, 37; EXPLORER 31 30-32, 50; MONEY 18 17, 38, 62; VOLCANO 38 57
desert, DESERT 51 6
mummies, MUMMY 44 52-54
paso, COWBOY 45 8, 50
pyramids, PYRAMID 53 54
Perugino, Pietro, BIBLE LANDS 30 61
Peruzzi, Baldassare, RENAISSANCE 91 50
Pesetas, MONEY 18 38, 63

pesos, MONEY 18 23, 62
pesticides, ECOLOGY 86 60, 61, 62, 63; FARM 66 62, 63
pests, ECOLOGY 86 30, 61; FARM 66 13, 18, 19, 50
control, ECOLOGY 86 37; FUTURE 100 16, 26, 28, 59
Peter, St., RELIGION 68 52
Peter Pan, PIRATE 59 61, 62
Peter the Great, Tsar of Russia, FLAG 16 56; RUSSIA 74 16, 18, 20-22
Peter the Hermit, KNIGHT 43 54
Peters, Arno, TIME & SPACE 81 41
Petit, Alfred le, WATERCOLOUR 97 31
Petit, Georges, MONET 95 35, 43
Petrarch, RENAISSANCE 91 6, 13
petrels, ARCTIC & ANTARCTIC 57 22
Petrie, W. M. F., BIBLE LANDS 30 62
petrochemicals, CHEMISTRY 79 6, 15
petrol, CAR 21 6, 26, 45, 49; ENERGY 76 30, 31, 37, 54
petroleum, CHEMISTRY 79 36, 52, 58, 63; TECHNOLOGY 89 18, 41, 51
Petrushka, DANCE 99 52
pets, MUMMY 44 44, 46
monkeys, GORILLA 64 60
Pettit Smith, Francis, BOAT 36 38
Peugeot, CAR 21 22, 62
pewter, ARCHAEOLOGY 56 35, 40, 48; VIKING 50 46
pH scale, CHEMISTRY 79 42, 43; ECOLOGY 86 17, 23
phalanges, HUMAN BODY 87 14-15, 18, 51
phalaropes, BIRD 1 28
phantasmagoria show, CINEMA 34 7
phantoms, WITCH & WIZARD 70 24
pharaohs, ANCIENT EGYPT 23 10-11; MUMMY 44 7, 18, 36-37; PYRAMID 53 8-9, 18-19, 50-51; RELIGION 68 42, 47
see also individual names
Pharisees, BIBLE LANDS 30 55
pharmaceutical industry, MEDICINE 88 42
pharmacists, MEDICINE 88 40-41
pharmacy, SHIPWRECK 72 52
Pharos of Alexandria, BIBLE LANDS 30 41; SHIPWRECK 72 34
pheasants, BIRD 1 19, 38, 56-57; CASTLE 49 42
Phenakistoscope, CINEMA 34 8
Philadelphia, PIRATE 59 52
Philby, Kim, SPY 67 35, 57

Philip II, SHIPWRECK 72 22
Philip of Macedon, ARCHAEOLOGY 56 42
Philippines, EXPLORER 31 20; VOLCANO 38 17, 35, 56
Philistines, BIBLE LANDS 30 13, 20, 22, 44
Phillips, Horatio, FLYING MACHINE 22 30
Phillips, John, PIRATE 59 48
Phoenicia, BIBLE LANDS 30 20, 48, 55
Phoenicians, BIBLE LANDS 30 22-23, 34, 36; EARLY PEOPLE 10 40; PIRATE 59 8
art, BIBLE LANDS 30 21-22, 41-43, 49
alphabet, WRITING 48 14, 16
the first traders, EXPLORER 31 6-7, 14
phoenix, FLAG 16 52
phonographs, INVENTION 27 46
phosphorus, CHEMISTRY 79 23, 26, 37, 40
photochronographs, CINEMA 34 10
photocopiers, ELECTRICITY 77 14-15; ELECTRONICS 90 54
photoelectric effect, ELECTRICITY 77 52, 62
photography, BATTLE 63 62; PERSPECTIVE 98 44, 45, 55, 61; SPY 67 12-15, 28, 53
aerial, ARCHAEOLOGY 56 12-13
in Cinema, CINEMA 34 10-11, 46
holograms, LIGHT 75 58-59
infra-red, ARCHAEOLOGY 56 14
invention of, INVENTION 27 40-41, 50; LIGHT 75 24-25
micro, SPY 67 23
site, ARCHAEOLOGY 56 22
underwater, ARCHAEOLOGY 56 32-33
photonics, ELECTRONICS 90 62
photons, ENERGY 76 42, 43, 44, 45; LIGHT 75 44, 51; MATTER 80 51, 59, 60; TIME & SPACE 81 52, 53
and laser, TECHNOLOGY 89 58-59
photosynthesis, CHEMISTRY 79 34, 36, 50; ENERGY 76 50-51, 52, 54; LIFE 84 8, 10, 16-17; POND & RIVER 6 10, 20, 46
carbon, ECOLOGY 86 18-19
light in, ECOLOGY 86 8-9; LIGHT 75 50, 51
oxygen, EARTH 83 10
plants, LIFE 84 6, 20, 52
respiration, LIFE 84 18, 19
photovoltaic effect, ELECTRICITY 77 52, 53
phrenology, MEDICINE 88 46

physiology, MEDICINE 88 17, 30
physiotherapy, MEDICINE 88 44
piano, ELEPHANT 42 55; MUSIC 12 44, 45, 46-47
Piazzi, Guiseppe, ASTRONOMY 82 58
Piazzi Smyth, Charles, PYRAMID 53 47
Picasso, Pablo, ANCIENT GREECE 37 9; DANCE 99 30; GOYA 93 43; PERSPECTIVE 98 52, 53
Invention in perspective, WATERCOLOUR 97 60
Piccard, Jacques, EXPLORER 31 60; OCEAN 62 53
piccolos, MUSIC 12 11
pichard, FISH 20 58
Pickford, Mary, CINEMA 34 18, 21
pickpockets, CRIME & DETECTION 73 8
pictograms, WRITING 48 8
picture palaces, CINEMA 34 24-25
picture-writing, EARLY PEOPLE 10 40, 41, 58
piddock shells, SHELL 9 49
pieces of eight, PIRATE 59 22, 36, 44
pied wagtails, BIRD 1 45
piedmont ringlets, BUTTERFLY & MOTH 7 31
pierid butterflies, BUTTERFLY & MOTH 7 11, 56
Piero della Francesca, PERSPECTIVE 98 18-19; RENAISSANCE 91 30, 31
piezoelectricity, CRYSTAL & GEM 25 30, 31, 62; ELECTRICITY 77 52, 53
pigeons, BIRD 1 6, 9, 38, 44
carrier, BATTLE 63 52; SPY 67 20, 21
"piggin' string", COWBOY 45 34
pigments, CHEMISTRY 79 10, 44, 60; EARLY PEOPLE 10 25, 34; ROCK & MINERAL 2 32-33; VAN GOGH 96 19, 46
colour, TECHNOLOGY 89 50-51
pigs, CASTLE 49 54, 55; FARM 66 40, 56-57, 62, 63; MAMMAL 11 10 16; SKELETON 3 52
pike eels, FISH 20 48
Pike, Zebulon, EXPLORER 31 44
pikes, FISH 20 11, 48; KNIGHT 43 30
pile lighthouses, SHIPWRECK 72 35
piles, BUILDING 58 62
pilgrimages, KNIGHT 43 52-53; MEDIEVAL LIFE 65 32, 42-43, 54; RELIGION 68 20, 38, 54, 58

pill bug, **Insect 17** 9
pilot fish, **Fish 20** 46
pilots, **Flying Machine 22** 16-17
Piltdown butterfly fraud, **Butterfly & Moth 7** 58
pilum, **Ancient Rome 24** 11
Pima peoples, **North American Indian 60** 7, 44, 50-51
Pinatubo, Mt., Philippines, **Volcano 38** 17, 35, 36
pince-nez, **Costume 35** 36
pincer grip, **Skeleton 3** 49
pine processionary moths, **Butterfly & Moth 7** 15
pine white butterflies, **Butterfly & Moth 7** 29
pineal gland, **Human Body 87** 40, 52, 57, 62
pineapples, **Plant 14** 46
pines, **Tree 5** 30, 31, 33, 51
  bristlecone, **Tree 5** 16
  London, **Tree 5** 54
  Scots, **Tree 5** 10, 11, 45
Pinewood Studios, **Cinema 34** 31
ping-pong, **Sport 8** 34
Pinkerton, Allan, **Crime & Detection 73** 11, 37; **Spy 67** 30, 31
Pinkertons, **Cowboy 45** 42
pinnacles, **Desert 51** 11
pinnas, **Shell 9** 17
Pinter, Harold, **Cinema 34** 28
Pinto, **Cowboy 45** 19
Pioneer space probes, **Astronomy 82** 46, 50, 53; **Space Exploration 71** 42
Piotrovsky, Comrade, **Spy 67** 29
pipefish, **Fish 20** 16, 22, 23, 44; **Pond & River 6** 59; **Seashore 15** 35, 50
pipes, musical, **Medieval Life 65** 10, 56, 57, 61; **Music 12** 18-19
pipes, smoking, **Africa 61** 15; **North American Indian 60** 10-11, 20, 34, 53
  medicine pipes, **North American Indian 60** 10-11
  peace pipes, **North American Indian 60** 23
Piranesi, G.B., **Perspective 98** 59
piranha, **Fish 20** 35; **Jungle 54** 16
pirarucus, **Fish 20** 9
pirates, **Crime & Detection 73** 28, 29, 58; **Pirate 59**; **Skeleton 3** 9; **Spy 67** 47
  anti-piracy measures, **Pirate 59** 58-59
  punishment, **Pirate 59** 56-57
  ships, **Boat 36** 21, 28, 29; **Shipwreck 72** 17, 22

women, **Pirate 59** 23, 33, 44
Pirckheimer, Willibald, **Renaissance 91** 27, 40
Pisan, Christine de, **Medieval Life 65** 23
Pisano, Giovanni, **Renaissance 91** 10, 19
Pisano, Nicola, **Renaissance 91** 19
Pissarro, Camille, **Impressionism 92** 39, 40, 43, 58; **Monet 95** 7, 24, 48; **Van Gogh 96** 33, 58; **Watercolour 97** 50
  biography, **Impressionism 92** 62
  The Climbing Path, l'Hermitage, **Impressionism 92** 35
  colours, **Impressionism 92** 21
  etchings, **Impressionism 92** 19
  Lordship Lane Station, Dulwich, **Impressionism 92** 33
  Peasant Women Planting Pea Sticks, **Impressionism 92** 40-41
  Self-Portrait, **Impressionism 92** 11
  Woman and Child at the Well, **Impressionism 92** 40
  Woman in a Field, **Impressionism 92** 59
Pissarro, Lucien, **Van Gogh 96** 29
pistols, **Arms & Armour 4** 46-47, 58-59; **Battle 63** 43, 46, 48; **Pirate 59** 28, 37, 48, 50; **Sport 8** 54; **Spy 67** 36, 37, 43
  Apache, **Arms & Armour 4** 51
  Derringer, **Arms & Armour 4** 57, 61
  holster, **Arms & Armour 4** 41, 48-49
  pocket, **Arms & Armour 4** 57, 59
  wheel-lock, **Arms & Armour 4** 38, 39
pistons, **Train 39** 10, 14, 15, 40
pit viper, *see* rattlesnake
pitches, musical, **Music 12** 6, 8, 9, 26
pitches, **Sport 8** 6, 10, 16, 26
pitchforks, **Castle 49** 53
pitching, **Sport 8** 23
pitchstone, **Rock & Mineral 2** 16
pits, **Archaeology 56** 10, 22-23, 25, 59
  rubbish, **Archaeology 56** 7, 29
pittas, banded, **Jungle 54** 15
pituitary glands, **Human Body 87** 40, 43, 57

Pizarro, Francisco, **Explorer 31** 30, 32; **Pirate 59** 21
placenta, **Human Body 87** 40, 44-47
placentals, **Fossil 19** 54, 56, 57; **Prehistoric Life 52** 50-51
placoderms, **Fossil 19** 34; **Prehistoric Life 52** 18, 20-21
plagues, **Medieval Life 65** 7, 60, 61
plaice, **Fish 20** 25, 26, 27
Planck, Max, **Energy 76** 43; **Light 75** 44; **Time & Space 81** 54
  Planck time, **Time & Space 81** 56, 60, 61
planes, **Tree 5** 27, 33, 41, 55
planetaria, **Astronomy 82** 19, 36, 52, 54
planets, **Astronomy 82** 11, 36-37, 61; **Space Exploration 71** 8, 42, 46-47; **Time & Space 81** 8, 14-15, 28, 48
  motion, **Astronomy 82** 18-19, 21, 58
  zodiac, **Astronomy 82** 7, 17
  see also under individual planets
planks, **Boat 36** 16-17, 46
plankton, **Arctic & Antarctic 57** 12, 46, 47, 63; **Earth 83** 32; **Fish 20** 35, 49, 52, 57; **Seashore 15** 15, 44; **Shark 40** 8, 24, 32, 35
  marine food chain, **Shell 9** 24
  types, **Ocean 62** 22-23, 26-28
  zooplankton, **Ecology 86** 38
Planorbis, **Fossil 19** 27
plant remains, **Archaeology 56** 36, 44, 46-47
plantations, **Pirate 59** 39
Planté, Gaston, **Electricity 77** 18; **Invention 27** 39
plants, **Early People 10** 8, 10, 26, 30; **Earth 83** 50, 52-53; **Evolution 85** 24, 30, 31; **Insect 17** 42-43
  carnivorous, **Plant 14** 40-41; **Jungle 54** 52
  climbers, **Plant 14** 38-39; **Jungle 54** 7, 12, 20-21
  deep-sea, **Ocean 62** 10, 16, 26
  defence, **Plant 14** 36-37
  desert, **Desert 51** 18-21, 36
  extinct, **Dinosaur 13** 10, 11, 23, 26; **Prehistoric Life 52** 7-8, 10-12, 22
  evolution, **Evolution 85** 61, 62
  fertilization, **Plant 14** 11, 22, 26
  fossils, **Fossil 19** 21, 36-39, 40

  in food chain, **Ecology 86** 12
  medicinal, **Jungle 54** 42-43
  mountain, **Plant 14** 50-51
  parasitic, **Plant 14** 44-45
  photosynthesis, **Ecology 86** 8-9; **Life 84** 50, 52-53; **Plant 14** 10, 14-15, 42
  poisonous, **Jungle 54** 34-35, 42
  polar, **Arctic & Antarctic 57** 9, 10, 18-19
  pollination, **Plant 14** 22-23, 24-25
  reproduction, **Plant 14** 26-27, 32-33
  shoots, **Plant 14** 8, 9, 14
  shore, **Seashore 15** 12, 16-17
  in space, **Space Exploration 71** 38, 58
  varieties, **Evolution 85** 30-31, 50, 51
  water plants, **Plant 14** 34, 48-49
  see also flowers, roots
plaques, **China 55** 19, 49
plasma, blood, **Human Body 87** 32-33
plasma, gas, **Matter 80** 56, 57, 63
plaster, **Building 58** 52-53, 55
plastic, **Boat 36** 13, 21, 43, 62, 63; **Costume 35** 36, 56, 58; **Future 100** 54, 55; **Technology 89** 26-27, 28-29
  Bakelite, **Matter 80** 44-45
  initial synthetics, **Chemistry 79** 53, 54-55
  invention of, **Invention 27** 60-61, 62
  new, **Chemistry 79** 56, 57
plastic money, **Money 18** 6, 58, 59
Plataea, **Ancient Greece 37** 6
Plateau, Joseph, **Cinema 34** 8
plateaux, **Earth 83** 48-49
platelets, **Human Body 87** 32-33
Plateosaurus, **Dinosaur 13** 39
plates, Earth,
  Australian, **Volcano 38** 11
  movements, **Fossil 19** 12-13, 56
  oceanic, **Ocean 62** 9, 46
  Pacific, **Volcano 38** 10, 22
  tectonic, **Volcano 38** 10, 11, 12, 24
platform shoes, **Costume 35** 24, 25, 59
platinum, **Chemistry 79** 23, 27, 36, 37; **Crystal & Gem 25** 52, 53; **Rock & Mineral 2** 6, 58
Plato, **Dance 99** 9; **Force & Motion 78** 6; **Human Body 87** 24, 58, 60; **Renaissance 91** 7, 53

dialogues, ANCIENT GREECE 37 47
on "elements", MATTER 80 8, 9
Platte, River, EXPLORER 31 44
platypus, FOSSIL 19 56, 57; MAMMAL 11 8, 16, 40, 52
burrow, MAMMAL 11 56
reproduction, MAMMAL 11 31
Plautus, ANCIENT ROME 24 36
plays, MEDIEVAL LIFE 65 58-59
plectrums, MUSIC 12 37, 43, 44
Pleistocene period, EARTH 83 18, 41, 58, 63; MAMMAL 11 13-15
pleochroism, CRYSTAL & GEM 25 36, 43, 49
Plesiosaurs, DINOSAUR 13 48, 58, 62; FOSSIL 19 6, 44, 46, 47; PREHISTORIC LIFE 52 38-39; SKELETON 3 13
Pleurotomaria, FOSSIL 19 61
Plimsoll line, BOAT 36 49
Pliny the Elder, ANCIENT ROME 24 54; EVOLUTION 85 8, 9; MEDICINE 88 18; RENAISSANCE 91 18, 50
Pliny the Younger, VOLCANO 38 26, 27
Pliocene period, MAMMAL 11 13, 14
ploughs, ENERGY 76 8, 9; FARM 66 8-10, 17, 33; INVENTION 27 7; TECHNOLOGY 89 44
ploughing, FARM 66 11-14; HORSE 33 50-51
plovers, BIRD 1 30, 33, 36, 51
plumb lines, CASTLE 49 57; INVENTION 27 29
plums, TREE 5 39
plus-fours, COSTUME 35 52
plus-twos, COSTUME 35 52
Pluto, god, ANCIENT GREECE 37 60
Pluto, planet, ASTRONOMY 82 36, 37, 56-57
poachers, ELEPHANT 42 55, 56, 62, 63; GORILLA 64 62-63
pochette, MUSIC 12 29
po-chung, MUSIC 12 54
Pocohontas, NORTH AMERICAN INDIAN 60 19
Poe, Edgar Allan, MANET 94 37, 49
poetry, ANCIENT GREECE 37 7, 12, 23, 33; CHINA 55 30, 32, 55
point sizes, WRITING 48 38, 44
Pointe-à-Pitre, Guadeloupe, VOLCANO 38 51
pointers, DOG 32 16, 19, 50, 51
pointillism, VAN GOGH 96 32, 34, 40-41
poison, CRIME & DETECTION 73 22, 47; ECOLOGY 86 41, 49, 57; PLANT 14 58-59; SPY 67 36, 43

arsenic, CRIME & DETECTION 73 20, 46
cyanide, CRIME & DETECTION 73 23
Poissy, MONET 95 29, 34
Poitiers, battle of, BATTLE 63 7, 36, 63; KNIGHT 43 32
Polacanthus, DINOSAUR 13 32
Poland, BATTLE 63 45; MONEY 18 32, 63
polar bears, MAMMAL 11 56; WHALE 46 7, 42
polarization, TIME & SPACE 81 53
Pole Star, ASTRONOMY 82 12, 13, 25, 60
pole vault, SPORT 8 41
Poles, ASTRONOMY 82 12, 14, 27; EARTH 83 35, 36
exploration, FUTURE 100 9
polar ice, EARTH 83 18-19
police, CRIME & DETECTION 73 8, 15, 29, 38
agencies, CRIME & DETECTION 73 34-35
mounted, CRIME & DETECTION 73 10, 33, 35, 55; HORSE 33 54, 56
riot, CRIME & DETECTION 73 26, 34
uniforms, CRIME & DETECTION 73 10, 11, 32-33
weapons, ARMS & ARMOUR 4 54-55
WPCs, CRIME & DETECTION 73 33
Politian, RENAISSANCE 91 33, 50
Pollaiuolo, Antonio del, ANCIENT GREECE 37 21
pollen, ARCHAEOLOGY 56 6, 47; ARCTIC & ANTARCTIC 57 18; FOSSIL 19 39 LIFE 84 38, 44
in natural history, ECOLOGY 86 34
pollen grain, PLANT 14 22, 23, 26
pollination, ECOLOGY 86 7; EVOLUTION 85 21, 22, 50; JUNGLE 54 24-25, 27; LIFE 84 41, 52
by animals, TREE 5 36-37
by insects, LIFE 84 19, 39, 46; TREE 5 34-35
by wind, TREE 5 32-33
polling, COWBOY 45 31
pollution, ARCHAEOLOGY 56 63; CHEMISTRY 79 29, 32, 36, 63; EAGLE 69 9, 13, 36, 39; ENERGY 76 31, 54, 56, 61
control, FUTURE 100 16-19, 22, 24; TRAIN 39 7, 18, 58, 62
and fishing, WHALE 46 58, 59, 61
human impact, ECOLOGY 86 60
nuclear, ARCTIC & ANTARCTIC 57 38

ozone layer, CHEMISTRY 79 34
pollutants, WEATHER 28 19
water, ECOLOGY 86 16, 54, 62; OCEAN 62 24, 62; SEASHORE 15 20, 58, 62-63
polo, SPORT 8 61
Polo, Marco, CHINA 55 8, 59; DESERT 51 63; EXPLORER 31 16-17, 63; SHIPWRECK 72 16
polonaise dress, COSTUME 35 30
polyester, COSTUME 35 55
polyethylene, CHEMISTRY 79 56, 57
polyethylene glycol, SHIPWRECK 72 57
Polykleitos, ANCIENT GREECE 37 41
polymers, CHEMISTRY 79 49, 54-55, 57; TECHNOLOGY 89 26-27
Polynesia, EXPLORER 31 14-15, 35, 51
polyps, SHELL 9 51, 52
polytheism, RELIGION 68 57
polyvinyl chloride, PVC, CHEMISTRY 79 55, 56, 57
Pomeranians, DOG 32 59
pommel horse, SPORT 8 43
Pomo peoples, NORTH AMERICAN INDIAN 60 42-43
Pompeii, ARCHAEOLOGY 56 9, 25, 28-29; BUILDING 58 12; FOSSIL 19 20; ROCK & MINERAL 2 19
eruption of Vesuvius, ANCIENT ROME 24 57; VOLCANO 38 26-29
mummies, MUMMY 44 9
Pompey, General, BIBLE LANDS 30 54, 56
ponchos, AZTEC 47 44
pond skaters, INSECT 17 46
ponds, POND & RIVER 6
ponies, ARCTIC & ANTARCTIC 57 58; COWBOY 45 12, 17
Exmoor, HORSE 33 20
Fell, HORSE 33 36, 62
Haflinger, HORSE 33 38, 51-52
Icelandic, HORSE 33 12
polo, HORSE 33 40, 59
Shetland, HORSE 33 6, 41, 62-63; MAMMAL 11 58
Pontius Pilate, BIBLE LANDS 30 55
Pontormo, Jacopo, RENAISSANCE 91 56, 61
Pony Express, HORSE 33 62
pony-trekking, HORSE 33 60
poodles, DOG 32 38, 55, 62, 63
pooping, BOAT 36 27
Pope, Alexander, FORCE & MOTION 78 28
Popes, ANCIENT ROME 24 63; MEDIEVAL LIFE 65 6, 28, 31, 62; RELIGION 68 52, 53

Adrian IV, RENAISSANCE 91 59
Julius II, RENAISSANCE 91 50, 51, 53, 58
Leo X, RENAISSANCE 91 50, 52
Nicholas V, RENAISSANCE 91 50
Paul III, RENAISSANCE 91 51
Popham, Sir Home, FLAG 16 18, 19
poplars, FOSSIL 19 39; POND & RIVER 6 7; TREE 5 25, 26
Popocatépetl, Mexico, VOLCANO 38 62
Popov, Alexander, RUSSIA 74 40
Popov, Dusko, SPY 67 27, 56
Popov, Leonid, SPACE EXPLORATION 71 13
Popova, Lyubov, PERSPECTIVE 98 53
poppies, PLANT 14 13, 29, 58
population, ECOLOGY 86 6, 7, 12
distribution, ECOLOGY 86 25
dynamics, ECOLOGY 86 28-29
explosion, ECOLOGY 86 31, 59; FUTURE 100 16, 17, 38, 58
growth, ARCHAEOLOGY 56 46; ECOLOGY 86 11, 30-31, 33
Porana, FOSSIL 19 39
Porcel, Dona Isabel de, GOYA 93 36, 37
porcelain, BUILDING 58 42, 60; CHINA 55 22, 56, 58; PIRATE 59 47; SHIPWRECK 72 16, 17, 56, 57
insulator, ELECTRICITY 77 2, 21
porches, BUILDING 58 57
porcupine fish, FISH 20 15, 34, 39, 62
porcupines, MAMMAL 11 9, 27
Porosphaera, FOSSIL 19 17
porpoises, MAMMAL 11 10; SKELETON 3 51; WHALE 46 10, 12, 48, 60
porpoising, WHALE 46 19, 32
port, ship side, BOAT 36 7, 21, 39, 52
port light, BOAT 36 52
Port Jackson sharks, FISH 20 43, 60
Port Royal, Jamaica, PIRATE 59 45
portcullis, CASTLE 49 12, 18, 28; KNIGHT 43 24
Porter, Cole, CINEMA 34 27
porters, TRAIN 39 48, 50
portholes, BOAT 36 56
Portinari, Tommaso, RENAISSANCE 91 21
Portugal, AFRICA 61 6, 31, 33, 48; BATTLE 63 59; FLAG 16 36-37; MONEY 18 19, 38, 39, 55

early navigation, **EXPLORER 31** 20-21

Portugues, Bartholomew, **PIRATE 59** 27

Portuguese man-o'-war, **FISH 20** 46

Poseidon statue, **SHIPWRECK 72** 15

Poseidonia, **ANCIENT GREECE 37** 24, 26, 60

positron, **ENERGY 76** 45

possums, **MAMMAL 11** 8, 9, 20, 29

posters, **WRITING 48** 45

postholes, **ARCHAEOLOGY 56** 8, 25, 52, 58

Postman Butterfly, **BUTTERFLY & MOTH 7** 16, 17, 22, 57

postmortems, **CRIME & DETECTION 73** 40, 47

Potamotherium, **FOSSIL 19** 55

potassium, **CHEMISTRY 79** 22, 25, 34, 46; **EARTH 83** 20

potassium permanganate, **MATTER 80** 20, 29

potato stones, **CRYSTAL & GEM 25** 7, 23

potatoes, **FARM 66** 8, 19, 32-34; **JUNGLE 54** 59; **PLANT 14** 14-15, 33, 54

potential, **ELECTRICITY 77** 22, 23, 25, 52

potential energy, **ECOLOGY 86** 10

potentiometer, **ELECTRONICS 90** 17

potions, **WITCH & WIZARD 70** 17, 27, 32, 34

pottery, **JUNGLE 54** 38; **NORTH AMERICAN INDIAN 60** 7, 44, 50; **TECHNOLOGY 89** 6, 8, 34, 62; **WRITING 48** 6, 13

African, **AFRICA 61** 15, 52

ancient, **ARCHAEOLOGY 56** 8, 50-51

Aztec, **AZTEC 47** 22, 23, 46-47

Chinese, **CHINA 55** 56

conservation of, **ARCHAEOLOGY 56** 38-39

desert peoples, **DESERT 51** 47, 60, 61

fake, **ARCHAEOLOGY 56** 55-56

in graves, **MUMMY 44** 8, 52, 54

Greek, **ANCIENT GREECE 37** 10, 11, 48-49; **ARCHAEOLOGY 56** 17

in Iron Age, **EARLY PEOPLE 10** 50, 58

making, **ARCHAEOLOGY 56** 60

Peublo, **NORTH AMERICAN INDIAN 60** 46-47

Roman **ANCIENT ROME 24** 42, 47; **ARCHAEOLOGY 56** 48-49

Russian, **RUSSIA 74** 44, 50, 51, 55

tomb figures, **CHINA 55** 13, 16, 52

pottos, **GORILLA 64** 10, 12, 34; **SKELETON 3** 51

Poulsen, Valdemar, **INVENTION 27** 47

poultices, **MEDICINE 88** 12-13

poultry, **FARM 66** 40, 58-61, 63

pounds, **MONEY 18** 19, 28, 47, 51

Pourville, **MONET 95** 38

powder horns, **PIRATE 59** 49

powdered wigs, **COSTUME 35** 32

Powell, John Wesley, **EARTH 83** 48

power, **ENERGY 76** 56, 58; **FORCE & MOTION 78** 6, 22, 41

power cables, **ELECTRICITY 77** 21, 23, 40, 45

power stations, **ELECTRICITY 77** 41, 44-45, 46; **FUTURE 100** 17, 18

Powers, Gary, **SPY 67** 39

Powhatan peoples, **NORTH AMERICAN INDIAN 60** 18-19

Pozzo, Andrea, **PERSPECTIVE 98** 40-41

Pozzuoli, Italy, **VOLCANO 38** 57

Praeneste, **ANCIENT ROME 24** 49

Pratt, William, **INVENTION 27** 31

Pravaz, Charles Gabriel, **INVENTION 27** 42

Pravda, **RUSSIA 74** 43

prawns, **INSECT 17** 9; **OCEAN 62** 27, 58; **SEASHORE 15** 22, 30, 33; **SHELL 9** 24, 40, 44; **SKELETON 3** 24

Praxinoscope, **CINEMA 34** 9, 10

precession, **FORCE & MOTION 78** 56, 57

precipitates, **CHEMISTRY 79** 35, 44, 58

precipitation, **WEATHER 28** 40

predators, **ECOLOGY 86** 7, 11, 12, 15; **LIFE 84** 21, 24, 46, 47

predation, **ECOLOGY 86** 30-31

prehensile tails, **SKELETON 3** 20, 25, 40

Prémaray, Jules de, **MONET 95** 6

Pre-Raphaelites, **WATERCOLOUR 97** 46-47, 48-49

Presley, Elvis, **DANCE 99** 9

presses, binding, **WRITING 48** 46-47

papermaking, **WRITING 48** 22-23

printing, **WRITING 48** 40-41

pressure, **FORCE & MOTION 78** 38, 44, 54

Price, Karen, **CRIME & DETECTION 73** 48, 49

prickly pears, **DESERT 51** 21

Prienne, **WRITING 48** 15

priestesses, **ANCIENT EGYPT 23** 19, 30, 51

Priestley, Joseph, **ELECTRICITY 77** 10; **EVOLUTION 85** 21; **LIGHT 75** 50; **MATTER 80** 21

oxygen discovery, **CHEMISTRY 79** 28, 29, 30; **ENERGY 76** 50, 51; **WEATHER 28** 6

plant respiration, **LIFE 84** 16, 17

priests, **ANCIENT EGYPT 23** 28-31; **MEDIEVAL LIFE 65** 13, 30, 56, 60; **RELIGION 68** 13, 33, 40, 48; **WITCH & WIZARD 70** 20, 21, 50, 54

African, **AFRICA 61** 32, 34-35, 41

primates, **FOSSIL 19** 55; **MAMMAL 11** 8, 14, 36, 58; **PREHISTORIC LIFE 52** 9, 45, 54

communication, **GORILLA 64** 32-33

defences, **GORILLA 64** 34-35

definition of, **GORILLA 64** 6

endangered, **GORILLA 64** 62-63

intelligence, **GORILLA 64** 6, 36-37, 50, 56

nocturnal, **GORILLA 64** 12-13, 16

primitive, **GORILLA 64** 6, 10-11

primroses, **TREE 5** 53

Prinsep, James, **WATERCOLOUR 97** 33

printer, laser, **ELECTRONICS 90** 62

printing, **MEDIEVAL LIFE 65** 40, 62; **TECHNOLOGY 89** 48, 51; **WATERCOLOUR 97** 44-45; **WRITING 48** 40-41

hand press, **WRITING 48** 41

invention of, **INVENTION 27** 18, 26-27

moveable type, **WRITING 48** 37

typesetting, **WRITING 48** 38-39

woodblock, **WRITING 48** 36, 42

prints, **CRIME & DETECTION 73** 40, 42, 46

prisms, **ASTRONOMY 82** 21, 30, 31, 38; **INVENTION 27** 29, 51; **LIGHT 75** 40, 44, 54, 55

prison, **CASTLE 49** 10, 14, 32-33; **CRIME & DETECTION 73** 9, 13, 31, 52; **PIRATE 59** 56-57

prisoners, **BATTLE 63** 57

private investigators, **CRIME & DETECTION 73** 36, 37

privateers, **PIRATE 59** 6, 18-19, 52-53

New World, **PIRATE 59** 22-23, 26

proa, **BOAT 36** 21

probability, **TIME & SPACE 81** 50, 51

proboscis, **INSECT 17** 21, 34

Procarcharadon, **FISH 20** 61

Procolophon, **DINOSAUR 13** 56

Proconsul, **FOSSIL 19** 55

Procoptodon, **FOSSIL 19** 57

Proctor, John, **WITCH & WIZARD 70** 24

production, films, **CINEMA 34** 28, 31

post-production, **CINEMA 34** 29, 48-49

prohibition, **CRIME & DETECTION 73** 24, 26

projectors, **CINEMA 34** 7, 11, 16, 19; **LIGHT 75** 10, 26-27

Prokofiev, Sergei, **RUSSIA 74** 48

propellers, **BOAT 36** 7, 36, 37, 38-39; **FLYING MACHINE 22** 24, 25, 30-33

Prophaethon, **FOSSIL 19** 53

prophecies, **WITCH & WIZARD 70** 13, 15

Prophet Muhammed, *see* Muhammed

prophets, **RELIGION 68** 41, 48, 54, 55

props, **CINEMA 34** 38-39

prosimians, **GORILLA 64** 10, 32

prosthesis, **MEDICINE 88** 54-55

proteins, **CHEMISTRY 79** 8, 34, 50, 51; **ECOLOGY 86** 20; **LIFE 84** 9, 11, 18, 57; **TECHNOLOGY 89** 9

antibodies, **LIFE 84** 28, 29

DNA, **LIFE 84** 36, 37, 61

enzymes, **LIFE 84** 7, 20

Proterosuchus, **DINOSAUR 13** 7

Protestants, **MEDIEVAL LIFE 65** 62; **RELIGION 68** 53

protoceretops, **FOSSIL 19** 49

protons, **CHEMISTRY 79** 16, 22; **ELECTRONICS 90** 26; **ENERGY 76** 46; **MATTER 80** 52, 53, 58-59; **TIME & SPACE 81** 58, 60

Protoreaster, **FOSSIL 19** 32

Proust, Antonin, **MANET 94** 16, 21, 24, 49

proustite, **CRYSTAL & GEM 25** 10

Prud'hon, Pierre Paul, **VAN GOGH 96** 26

Prussia, **BATTLE 63** 20, 42, 48, 58; **MONEY 18** 32, 33

Przewalski, **COWBOY 45** 12

Przhevalsky, Nicolay, **EXPLORER 31** 17

Psalms, **WRITING 48** 24, 28-29
psalters, **MEDIEVAL LIFE 65** 40;
    WATERCOLOUR 97 11;
    WRITING 48 24-25
psaltery, **MUSIC 12** 39
Psaronius, **FOSSIL 19** 37
Psion, **FUTURE 100** 52
Psittacosaurus,
    DINOSAUR 13 29
Psyche, **ANCIENT GREECE 37** 22
psychiatry, **MEDICINE 88** 46-47
psychoanalysis, **FUTURE 100** 32;
    MEDICINE 88 46
psychology, **CRIME &**
    DETECTION 73 52
Ptah, **PYRAMID 53** 11, 32
ptarmigans, **ARCTIC &**
    ANTARCTIC 57 17, 20, 25;
    BIRD 1 31
Pteraclis, **FISH 20** 31
pteranodon, **FOSSIL 19** 52;
    SKELETON 3 51
Pterodactylus,
    DINOSAUR 13 58;
    FOSSIL 19 52
pterosaurs, **BIRD 1** 6;
    FOSSIL 19 13, 44, 52;
    PREHISTORIC LIFE 52 40-41, 61
pterothysanid moths,
    BUTTERFLY & MOTH 7 44
Ptolemy, **ASTRONOMY 82** 10,
    11, 18, 19; **LIGHT 75** 14;
    TIME & SPACE 81 12
Ptolemy II, King,
    BIBLE LANDS 30 54
Ptychodus, **FOSSIL 19** 34
pubis, **SKELETON 3** 44-45, 46-47
publishers, **WRITING 48** 60-61
pueblos, **ARCHAEOLOGY 56** 9,
    29; **DESERT 51** 45
Puerto Rico, **FLAG 16** 55
pufferfishes, **FISH 20** 38, 39, 54
puffins, **BIRD 1** 18, 29;
    SEASHORE 15 52, 55;
    SKELETON 3 18
Pugin, A.W.N., **BUILDING 58** 42
pulleys, **ENERGY 76** 12, 13,
    25, 30; **FORCE &**
    MOTION 78 10, 11, 18-19;
    TECHNOLOGY 89 32-33
  lever,
    FORCE & MOTION 78 16, 17
  machines,
    FORCE & MOTION 78 22
Pullman, George,
    TRAIN 39 30
Pullman Company,
    TRAIN 39 30, 31
pulsar, **ASTRONOMY 82** 60, 61;
    TIME & SPACE 81 44, 45, 56
pulse rate, **MEDICINE 88**
    28-29, 57
pumas, **CAT 29** 10, 25, 36-37
pumice, **ROCK & MINERAL 2** 19;
    VOLCANO 38 16, 21, 28, 35
pumps, **COSTUME 35** 25;
    ENERGY 76 8, 13, 28, 29

punctures, **CAR 21** 13, 58, 60
punk rockers,
    COSTUME 35 6, 58, 59
punting, **BOAT 36** 6, 20, 34
pupa, **BUTTERFLY & MOTH 7**
    20-21, 22-23; **INSECT 17** 6,
    21, 35
puppets, **CINEMA 34** 6, 44, 45;
    PIRATE 59 62
Puritan dresses,
    COSTUME 35 27
Push Comes to Shove,
    DANCE 99 45
Pushkin, Aleksandr,
    ARMS & ARMOUR 4 46;
    RUSSIA 74 18, 44
push-ups, **SPORT 8** 43
Puttin' on the Ritz,
    DANCE 99 51
putting, **SPORT 8** 60
Puyi, Last Emperor,
    CHINA 55 9, 62, 63;
    FUTURE 100 8
PVC, **CHEMISTRY 79** 55, 56, 57
pygmies, **AFRICA 61** 18, 19
pygmy devil, **FISH 20** 57
pyjamas, **COSTUME 35** 52
Pyle, Howard, **PIRATE 59** 7, 49
Pyramid of the Giant Jaguar,
    PYRAMID 53 58, 59
Pyramid of the Magician,
    PYRAMID 53 58
Pyramid of the Niches,
    PYRAMID 53 55
Pyramid of the Sun,
    PYRAMID 53 54
Pyramid Texts,
    PYRAMID 53 7, 22, 47
pyramidions,
    PYRAMID 53 44-45
pyramids, **BUILDING 58** 16;
    EARLY PEOPLE 10 38, 59;
    FORCE & MOTION 78 8;
    PYRAMID 53
  building, **ARCHAEOLOGY 56**
    13, 53; **PYRAMID 53** 32-37
  Egyptian, **ANCIENT EGYPT 23**
    20-21; **MUMMY 44** 7, 10,
    12, 36
  foundations, **PYRAMID 53**
    30, 31, 50
  Mesoamerican, **AZTEC 47** 17
  planning, **PYRAMID 53** 30-31
  of queens, **PYRAMID 53** 17,
    19, 51
  steps, **PYRAMID 53** 7, 14, 47
  ventilation,
    PYRAMID 53 23, 46, 47
pyrite, **CRYSTAL & GEM 25** 13,
    21, 50; **ROCK & MINERAL 2**
    15, 45, 47, 59
pyrotechnicists,
    CINEMA 34 43
pyroxenes,
    CRYSTAL & GEM 25 8, 14, 53;
    ROCK & MINERAL 2 8, 9,
    17, 43

Pythagoras,
    ANCIENT GREECE 37 46, 58;
    EVOLUTION 85 10; **TIME &**
    SPACE 81 8, 10; **WITCH &**
    WIZARD 70 12
  theorem, **TIME & SPACE 81** 6,
    11, 26, 34
  theory of musical harmony,
    RENAISSANCE 91 31
pythons, **REPTILE 26** 12-13, 20,
    26; **SKELETON 3** 36-37, 40
pyxis, **ANCIENT GREECE 37** 15,
    40, 49

Qadesh, Battle of,
    BIBLE LANDS 30 13
qanum, **MUSIC 12** 39
Qianlong, Emperor, **CHINA 55**
    32, 62-63
Qin dynasty, **CHINA 55** 6, 18, 34
qin zither, **MUSIC 12** 38
Qing dynasty, **CHINA 55** 9
  civil service, **CHINA 55**
    20, 21
  fall, **CHINA 55** 62-63
  jewellery, **CHINA 55** 48, 49
  kite festivals, **CHINA 55** 50
Qingming festival,
    CHINA 55 13, 50
quadrants, **ASTRONOMY 82** 12,
    25, 26, 29; **INVENTION 27** 29
quadrille, **DANCE 99** 46
quagga, **HORSE 33** 18-19
quantum physics, **ENERGY 76**
    42; **FORCE & MOTION 78**
    61-63
quantum theory, **LIGHT 75** 44,
    63; **TIME & SPACE 81** 36,
    50-53, 59
  length, **TIME & SPACE 81** 54
  time, **TIME & SPACE 81** 8,
    9, 56
quarks, **MATTER 80** 58, 60, 62;
    TIME & SPACE 81 58-59

quarries, **PYRAMID 53** 32
quarter horses, **COWBOY 45** 13,
    17, 19, 32
quartz, **CRYSTAL & GEM 25** 15,
    21, 30-33; **EARTH 83** 20, 21,
    55; **ROCK & MINERAL 2** 8,
    16, 42, 59
  crystals, **ELECTRONICS 90** 7,
    15, 32; **ROCK & MINERAL 2**,
    6, 44, 45, 47
  in clocks,
    ELECTRONICS 90 15, 60
  in detectors,
    ELECTRONICS 90 36
  in radars,
    ELECTRONICS 90 40, 61
  in resonators,
    ELECTRONICS 90 34
  formation, **ROCK &**
    MINERAL 2 11
  polishing, **ROCK &**
    MINERAL 2 61
  properties, **ROCK &**
    MINERAL 2 48, 49
quartzite, **CRYSTAL & GEM 25** 8,
    9, 30
Quaternary period,
    EVOLUTION 85 62
queen butterflies, **BUTTERFLY &**
    MOTH 7 22
Queensland blue heelers,
    DOG 32 42
querns, **EARLY PEOPLE 10** 31
Quetzal dance, **DANCE 99** 39
Quetzalcoat, **PYRAMID 53** 56,
    57, 60
quffas, **BOAT 36** 11
quills, **BIRD 1** 20, 27;
    WRITING 48 53, 57
quinine, **MEDICINE 88** 26, 44;
    PLANT 14 59; **TREE 5** 22
quirts, **COWBOY 45** 11-12, 51,
    53, 57
quivers, **ARMS & ARMOUR 4** 19,
    62; **CASTLE 49** 27;
    SPORT 8 53
Qumran, **BIBLE LANDS 30** 58
quoits, **ARMS & ARMOUR 4**
    34-35
Qur'an, **RELIGION 68** 54-57;
    WRITING 48 34-35

R

Ra, ANCIENT EGYPT **23** 38;
WITCH & WIZARD **70** 30
"Way of the Sun God",
ANCIENT EGYPT **23** 22
rabbitfish, FISH **20** 9, 20, 54
rabbits, CASTLE **49** 54;
MAMMAL **11** 9, 60, 62, 63;
SKELETON **3** 30, 46, 58
rabies, DOG **32** 35, 62;
MEDICINE **88** 32
raccoon dogs, DOG **32** 26, 27
racehorses, HORSE **33** 10-11,
58-60
races, CAR **21** 32
rachis, BIRD **1** 20
racketball, SPORT **8** 37
rackets, SPORT **8** 32-33, 35, 36
Rackham, Jack, PIRATE **59**
32-33
racoons, MAMMAL **11** 9
radar, BOAT **36** 53, 58; SPY **67**
16, 52; WEATHER **28** 13, 14
navigation, SHIPWRECK **72**
33, 34
X-ray vision,
FUTURE **100** 50, 51
radiation, ENERGY **76** 62;
MATTER **80** 56, 62, 63;
TECHNOLOGY **89** 59;
WEATHER **28** 61
electromagnetic,
ENERGY **76** 39, 40-43;
MATTER **80** 6, 59
heat, ENERGY **76** 26, 43
light, ENERGY **76** 42
neutrons, MATTER **80** 53
photons, MATTER **80** 51
radiation fog, WEATHER **28**
48, 49
radio, ELECTRONICS **90** 6, 36,
38, 48; SHIPWRECK **72** 29,
37, 42; SPY **67** 22, 23, 32;
TECHNOLOGY **89** 49
car, ELECTRONICS **90** 60
communication,
ELECTRICITY **77** 55-57
developments in,
FUTURE **100** 50, 52
invention, ELECTRICITY **77** 55;
FUTURE **100** 8, 9;
INVENTION **27** 52-53, 62
operators, SPY **67** 32, 33
pocket, ELECTRONICS **90** 53
portable, FUTURE **100** 53
receivers, SPY **67** 13, 16, 22, 49

signals, FORCE & MOTION **78**
49; ELECTRONICS **90** 18;
SPY **67** 18, 42, 48-50;
TIME & SPACE **81** 18,
35, 61
radio waves,
ELECTRONICS **90** 12, 13, 36,
49; ENERGY **76** 38, 39, 40, 41;
LIGHT **75** 42;
TIME & SPACE **81** 32, 33,
45, 49
communications,
ELECTRICITY **77** 62-63
detection, ELECTRONICS **90** 28
invention,
ELECTRICITY **77** 60-61
pulsars, TIME & SPACE **81** 56
radar, ELECTRONICS **90** 40;
TIME & SPACE **81** 55
Sun, ENERGY **76** 6
telephone,
ELECTRONICS **90** 25
telescopes, ASTRONOMY **82**
27, 32-33, 46, 62;
LIGHT **75** 42
television, ENERGY **76** 35
radioactivity,
CHEMISTRY **79** 19, 53;
ELECTRICITY **77** 47; LIGHT **75**
43; MATTER **80** 46-47, 48, 60;
TIME & SPACE **81** 37
radioactive decay,
MATTER **80** 54, 58, 59, 62
radioactive waste,
ENERGY **76** 46, 47, 56
radiocarbon dating,
ARCHAEOLOGY **56** 54;
MUMMY **44** 56, 58-59
radiometers, LIGHT **75** 35
radiotherapy, MEDICINE **88** 38,
53; TECHNOLOGY **89** 57
radium, CHEMISTRY **79** 19, 22,
33, 35
radius, SKELETON **3** 48-49,
50-51, 62
Radjedef, PYRAMID **53** 9, 29
Raedwald, King,
ARCHAEOLOGY **56** 7, 27
raffia, AFRICA **61** 21
rafters, BUILDING **58** 9,
20-21, 24
rafts, BOAT **36** 6, 8-9
Ragnarök, VIKING **50** 37, 51
Rahotep, PYRAMID **53** 14
raids, VIKING **50** 16-17
railways, BATTLE **63** 20;
RUSSIA **74** 34, 38-39;
TECHNOLOGY **89** 12, 36, 37,
42; TRAIN **39** 13, 19, 23, 29
companies, TRAIN **39** 54
construction, TRAIN **39**
20-21
earliest, TRAIN **39** 6, 8-9
lines, TECHNOLOGY **89** 17, 23;
TRAIN **39** 24-25
overhead, TRAIN **39** 58-59
railroads, COWBOY **45** 38-39

rails, TRAIN **39** 11, 20, 24-25
flanged, TRAIN **39** 10, 25
monorail, FUTURE **100** 25,
27, TRAIN **39** 59
overhead, TRAIN **39** 58
underground, TRAIN **39**
56-57, 58
see also trains
Raimondi, Marcantonio,
RENAISSANCE **91** 53
rain, WEATHER **28** 6, 7, 15, 30
downpour, WEATHER **28**
24, 36
measurement, WEATHER **28**
30, 62, 63
torrential, WEATHER **28** 31,
38, 44, 51
rainbow trout, FISH **20** 18
rainbows, LIGHT **75** 29;
WEATHER **28** 51, 58, 59
rainfall, DESERT **51** 6, 10;
JUNGLE **54** 6, 8, 62
rainforests, AFRICA **61** 7;
ECOLOGY **86** 56-57;
TREE **5** 12, 13
see also tropical rainforests
rainshadow, WEATHER **28** 54, 55
rakes, FARM **66** 21, 23, 34, 35
Raleigh, Walter, EXPLORER **31**
22; PIRATE **59** 18
ram-headed god, ANCIENT
EGYPT **23** 18
ram's horn snails, SHELL **9** 14
Rama, RELIGION **68** 21
Ramadan, RELIGION **68** 54
Ramayana, RELIGION **68** 20
Rambert, Marie, DANCE **99** 56
Ramesses II, the great,
AFRICA **61** 10; MUMMY **44**
28, 36, 41, 50;
PYRAMID **53** 32
in the Bible, BIBLE LANDS **30**
12-13
builder, ANCIENT EGYPT **23**
11, 29
Ramesses III, Pharaoh,
ANCIENT EGYPT **23** 16;
MUMMY **44** 40
Ramesses VI, Pharaoh,
ANCIENT EGYPT **23** 22
Ramesses IX, Pharaoh,
ANCIENT EGYPT **23** 22
ramps, PYRAMID **53** 36-37
ramrods, ARMS & ARMOUR **4**
38-39, 46
Ramsey, William,
CHEMISTRY **79** 32
Ramsgate, VAN GOGH **96** 8
ranches, COWBOY **45** 28-29;
FARM **66** 48; JUNGLE **54** 62
Rancho la Brea, CAT **29** 8
Randall, John,
ELECTRONICS **90** 40
Raneferef, PYRAMID **53** 38
Rank, J. Arthur, CINEMA **34** 21
Rankine, William, FORCE &
MOTION **78** 40

ranks, BATTLE **63** 16-17
ransom, CRIME &
DETECTION **73** 22, 23, 50
Ranvaik, VIKING **50** 17
Raphael, ANCIENT GREECE **37**
47; MANET **94** 24;
RENAISSANCE **91** 48, 49
Vatican frescoes,
RENAISSANCE **91** 52-53
rapid transport system
TRAIN **39** 38, 56, 62, 63
rapiers, ARMS & ARMOUR **4**
42-45; BATTLE **63** 40, 41
Ras Shamra, BIBLE LANDS **30** 24
Rasputin, Grigori, RUSSIA **74** 30
Rastrelli, Bartolomeo,
RUSSIA **74** 28, 29
ratfish, FISH **20** 9, 20
rats, MAMMAL **11** 44-45, 54, 56
kangaroo rats,
DESERT **51** 32, 33
tracks, MAMMAL **11** 61, 62
tree, MAMMAL **11** 29
rattans, BOAT **36** 16
rattles, MUSIC **12** 48, 51, 56
ravens, ARCTIC &
ANTARCTIC **57** 20; BIRD **1** 34
Ravning Enge, VIKING **50** 23
Ray, Charles, CINEMA **34** 33
ray-finned fishes, FISH **20** 9,12
rayon, CHEMISTRY **79** 53;
COSTUME **35** 52, 53
rays, fish, FISH **20** 13, 29, 56, 57;
FOSSIL **19** 18, 34;
OCEAN **62** 16-17, 27, 33
electric, OCEAN **62** 36-37
razor shells, SEASHORE **15** 26,
42; SHELL **9** 43
razorbills, SEASHORE **15** 52
razors, EARLY PEOPLE **10** 44, 49;
TECHNOLOGY **89** 39
Re, MUMMY **44** 25;
PYRAMID **53** 28, 39, 44
paintings, PYRAMID **53** 7, 45
reactions, chemical,
CHEMISTRY **79** 38-39, 40-41;
MATTER **80** 11, 20, 28, 30
reactivity, CHEMISTRY **79** 25, 33,
34, 36
Read, Mary,
PIRATE **59** 32, 35, 61
Reagan, Ronald, CRIME &
DETECTION **73** 58
reales, MONEY **18** 39
Realism, in art,
MONET **95** 8, 40
Rebek, Julian, LIFE **84** 54
Reber, Grote,
ASTRONOMY **82** 32
reconnaissance, BATTLE **63**
24-25
records, INVENTION **27** 46, 47;
TECHNOLOGY **89** 26
recording systems,
ELECTRONICS **90** 47
rectifiers, ELECTRONICS **90**
31, 37

rectum, HUMAN BODY 87 35, 37, 43
recycling, FUTURE 100 19, 20, 30; TECHNOLOGY 89 14, 62
forest, ECOLOGY 86 44, 45
nutrients, ECOLOGY 86 11, 14-17
waste, ECOLOGY 86 62
red admiral butterflies, BUTTERFLY & MOTH 7 6
Red Army, RUSSIA 74 31, 32, 33, 36
red blood cells, HUMAN BODY 87 17, 27, 32-33, 48; LIFE 84 11, 14, 27, 29
Red Cross, BATTLE 63 60; FLAG 16 21
red giants, ASTRONOMY 82 60
red lories, BIRD 1 26
red mullets, FISH 20 19
Red Sea, BIBLE LANDS 30 8, 13, 40; OCEAN 62 8, 25, 50; RELIGION 68 42; VOLCANO 38 24, 39
navigation, EXPLORER 31 8
red shift, ASTRONOMY 82 23, 61, 62
Red Square, RUSSIA 74 26, 27, 34, 57, 58
red-billed queleas, BIRD 1 38
Redi, Francesco, LIFE 84 54
redstarts, BIRD 1 46
redwoods, TREE 5 16, 22, 30, 31
reed buntings, BIRD 1 47
reed instruments, MUSIC 12 12-13, 16, 17
Reed Olsen, Oluf, SPY 67 22, 23
reed warblers, BIRD 1 44, 49
reeds, POND & RIVER 6 10, 32-35
giant, SEASHORE 15 59
Reeves, Alec, ELECTRONICS 90 47
Reeves, William, CINEMA 34 52
referee, SPORT 8 6, 13
refining, ELECTRICITY 77 32
reflecting telescopes, ASTRONOMY 82 21, 23, 26, 54
Reformation, MEDIEVAL LIFE 65 7, 62
art, RENAISSANCE 91 42-43
refracting telescopes, ASTRONOMY 82 23, 24, 25
refraction, CRYSTAL & GEM 25 18, 19, 47; INVENTION 27 28; LIGHT 75 14-15, 28-29, 34-35
double, LIGHT 75 48
refractive index, LIGHT 75 14, 54, 61
refractometers, CHEMISTRY 79 60
refrigeration, TECHNOLOGY 89 44, 46; INVENTION 27 54
regal tang, FISH 20 17

regiments, BATTLE 63 8, 18-19, 56
Regin, VIKING 50 43, 51
Re-Harakhty, ANCIENT EGYPT 23 30, 57
Rehoboam, BIBLE LANDS 30 20
Reid, Bill, WHALE 46 54
reincarnation, RELIGION 68 18, 25, 27
reindeer, ARCTIC & ANTARCTIC 57 38-39, 48-49; VIKING 50 20, 36, 38
reins, COWBOY 45 16-17, 26, 32-33; HORSE 33 30-31, 34
Reiter, Thomas, SPACE EXPLORATION 71 31
Rekhmire, Pharaoh, ENERGY 76 8; PYRAMID 53 30, 33, 34, 36
Relativity, Theory of, FUTURE 100 8; MATTER 80 55; TIME & SPACE 81 8, 10, 41
general theory, TIME & SPACE 81 42-45, 46, 62, 63
gravity, FORCE & MOTION 78 60
special theory, ENERGY 76 44-45; TIME & SPACE 81 34-37, 39, 42
speed of light, FORCE & MOTION 78 58-59; LIGHT 75 62, 63
relics, holy, MEDIEVAL LIFE 65 42, 54
religion, AZTEC 47 30-31, 32-33; EARLY PEOPLE 10 18, 22, 25, 36; RELIGION 68; VIKING 50 52-53
in Africa, AFRICA 61 32-33, 34-35, 42
medieval Europe, KNIGHT 43 52-53
symbols, MUMMY 44 11, 21, 30
Rembrandt, GOYA 93 18; MANET 94 26; PERSPECTIVE 98 39; VAN GOGH 96 23, 24
Remington, Frederic, COWBOY 45 12, 19, 42, 44; HORSE 33 57
remora, FISH 20 30
remote controls, ELECTRONICS 90 60; FUTURE 100 11, 20
Remus, ANCIENT ROME 24 6
Renaissance, MEDICINE 88 24-25, 26; MEDIEVAL LIFE 65 6, 7, 62-63; RENAISSANCE 91; WATERCOLOUR 97 26, 40
art, PERSPECTIVE 98 30-31
clothes, COSTUME 35 16-17
chronology, RENAISSANCE 91 62
Early, RENAISSANCE 91 14-15, 18, 61

High, RENAISSANCE 91 48-51, 60
Northern, RENAISSANCE 91 58-59
renal vessels, HUMAN BODY 87 38-39, 40
Renault, CAR 21 36-37, 38-41
Renoir, Auguste, IMPRESSIONISM 92 22, 26-27, 39; MANET 94 53, 61; MONET 95 6, 10, 15, 20; VAN GOGH 96 36
biography, IMPRESSIONISM 92 62
The Dance at the Moulin de la Galette, IMPRESSIONISM 92 27
Fruits from the Midi, IMPRESSIONISM 92 45
La Grenouillère, MONET 95 15
La Loge, IMPRESSIONISM 92 50
Madame Charpentier and her Children, IMPRESSIONISM 92 42
and painting, IMPRESSIONISM 92 10, 58
The Rower's Lunch, IMPRESSIONISM 92 34
Two Sisters, IMPRESSIONISM 92 22-23
Repin, Ilya, RUSSIA 74 46, 47
reproduction, HUMAN BODY 87 42-43, 44, 49; LIFE 84 6, 7, 40, 50
asexual, LIFE 84 32-33
human birth, HUMAN BODY 87 46-47
plants, LIFE 84 52
sexual, LIFE 84 30, 38-39, 43
reptiles, ECOLOGY 86 37, 41, 49; FISH 20 6, 8, 12; INSECT 17 8, 9; JUNGLE 54 15; LIFE 84 22, 31, 49, 53; REPTILE 26
babies, REPTILE 26 20-23, 34-35
body temperature, REPTILE 26 6, 14-15
camouflage, REPTILE 26 48-49
conservation, REPTILE 26 62-63
defence, REPTILE 26 46-47
evolution, EVOLUTION 85 26, 43, 61
extinct, PREHISTORIC LIFE 52 7-8, 28-32
flying, PREHISTORIC LIFE 52 40-41, 61
food, REPTILE 26 38-41
fossils, FOSSIL 19 12, 44-45, 46, 60
mammal-like, EVOLUTION 85 26, 61, 62; PREHISTORIC LIFE 52 30-31

marine, PREHISTORIC LIFE 52 20, 38-39, 61
reproduction, REPTILE 26 18-21
senses, REPTILE 26 16-17
shells, SHELL 9 9, 28, 58, 59
skeletons, SKELETON 3 13, 20, 40, 53
skin, REPTILE 26 24-25
teeth, REPTILE 26 8-9, 40-41
resin, TECHNOLOGY 89 26, 29, 51; TREE 5 10, 23
Resin-gall Moth, BUTTERFLY & MOTH 7 43
resinous electricity, ELECTRICITY 77 8
resistance, electrical, ELECTRICITY 77 22-23, 47, 48
coil, ELECTRICITY 77 25
wires, ELECTRICITY 77 24, 46
resistance, physical, FORCE & MOTION 78 24, 34, 39, 42
resistors, ELECTRONICS 90 16-17, 22, 40
radio, ELECTRONICS 90 52
telephone, ELECTRONICS 90 6
television, ELECTRONICS 90 39
variable, ELECTRONICS 90 31
resonance, FORCE & MOTION 78 48, 49
respiration, ECOLOGY 86 15, 19; ENERGY 76 50, 52; HUMAN BODY 87 7, 24-27, 33; LIFE 84 8, 9, 18-19
cells, LIFE 84 27
mitochondria, LIFE 84 10, 11, 16
photosynthesis, LIFE 84 16, 17
respiratory system, LIFE 84 15
restaurant cars, TRAIN 39 28, 30, 38, 42
resurrection, RELIGION 68 48, 50, 51
retiarius, ANCIENT ROME 24 31, 33
reticules, COSTUME 35 39
retina, LIGHT 75 18, 19, 56
retrievers, DOG 32 40, 41, 50, 51
senses, DOG 32 14-18, 27, 31
shows, DOG 32 38, 56, 63
skeleton, DOG 32 10, 11, 34, 35
tail, DOG 32 12
teeth, DOG 32 6-10, 12, 13
retzius shells, SHELL 9 49
Réunion island, VOLCANO 38 11, 23, 43, 47
Revere, Paul, HORSE 33 57
revolutions, FUTURE 100 9
revolvers, BATTLE 63 43
Colt, ARMS & ARMOUR 4 61
percussion, ARMS & ARMOUR 4 56

Pinfire, ARMS & ARMOUR 4 58-59

Remington, ARMS & ARMOUR 4 57

Smith & Wesson, ARMS & ARMOUR 4 61

Rewald, John, MONET 95 48

Rey, Dr. Felix, VAN GOGH 96 48

Reynaud, Emile, CINEMA 34 9, 51

Reynolds, Joshua, PERSPECTIVE 98 43

Rhamphorhyncus, FOSSIL 19 52

rheas, BIRD 1 17

rheostats, ELECTRICITY 77 22

Rhine, River, ANCIENT ROME 24 8, 62; CASTLE 49 18

Rhineland, VIKING 50 26, 39

rhinoceroses, DINOSAUR 13 30; MAMMAL 11 10, 14, 27, 45

Rhodes, ANCIENT GREECE 37 10, 14, 41, 51

rhodochrosite, CRYSTAL & GEM 25 17

rhododendrons, PLANT 14 35, 60

rhodonite, CRYSTAL & GEM 25 51

rhythm, MUSIC 12 50-51, 56

ribbon eels, FISH 20 48

ribbonfish, FISH 20 25

ribonucleic acid, *see* RNA

ribosomes, LIFE 84 11, 37

ribs, HUMAN BODY 87 7, 15, 17, 31
   muscles, HUMAN BODY 87 21, 23

rice, CHINA 55 34, 38, 44, 45; EARLY PEOPLE 10 54; PLANT 14 55

Rich, Buddy, MUSIC 12 52

Richard I, Lion Heart, King of England, HORSE 33 44-45; MEDIEVAL LIFE 65 29

Richard II, King of England, CASTLE 49 7, 22; MEDIEVAL LIFE 65 10, 26; RENAISSANCE 91 16

Richard III, King of England, CASTLE 49 32

Richardson, Lewis, WEATHER 28 15

Richelieu, Cardinal, SPY 67 41, 58

Richmann, Georg, ELECTRICITY 77 8

Richter, Charles F., VOLCANO 38 49

Richter scale, EARTH 83 42; VOLCANO 38 47, 48-49, 50

rickets, MEDICINE 88 35

ridges, VOLCANO 38 11, 12, 24-25

riding hat, COSTUME 35 47

Riemann, Bernhard, TIME & SPACE 81 41

rifles, ARMS & ARMOUR 4 41, 60-61; BATTLE 63 42, 43, 50-51; SPORT 8 54

Rigadin, CINEMA 34 23

rigging, BOAT 36 22, 25, 41

Rimington, Stella, SPY 67 42

Ring of Fire, VOLCANO 38 10, 11

ringed plovers, BIRD 1 30, 51

Ringrose, Basil, PIRATE 59 26, 42

rings, jewellery ANCIENT ROME 24 16, 19, 54

rings, planetary,
   Jupiter, ASTRONOMY 82 50
   Neptune, ASTRONOMY 82 56
   Saturn, ASTRONOMY 82 52-53
   Uranus, ASTRONOMY 82 55

Rio de Janeiro, MANET 94 6-7

Riojasuchus, DINOSAUR 13 57

Rite of Spring, The, DANCE 99 44, 56

rites, AFRICA 61 34-35, 40-41

Ritter, Wilhelm, LIGHT 75 41

river snails, SHELL 9 57

Rivera, Diego, AZTEC 47 24, 26; PYRAMID 53 55

rivers, EARTH 83 14, 54, 56, 57; ECOLOGY 86 54-55; JUNGLE 54 16-17, 32-33; POND & RIVER 6; ROCK & MINERAL 2 11
   estuary, ECOLOGY 86 50, 51
   flooding, ECOLOGY 86 23
   ocean floor, EARTH 83 39
   wetlands, ECOLOGY 86 16

rivets, KNIGHT 43 16; TECHNOLOGY 89 14, 18, 19

Rivière, Georges, IMPRESSIONISM 92 27

RNA, EVOLUTION 85 56, 57; LIFE 84 34, 36, 37, 59

roadrunners, DESERT 51 30

roads, FUTURE 100 9, 25
   automated highways, FUTURE 100 24, 59

robber crabs, SHELL 9 58

robbers, CRIME & DETECTION 73 23, 31, 56-57
   bank, CRIME & DETECTION 73 11, 16, 38, 56
   train, CRIME & DETECTION 73 11, 13, 17

Robert, Etienne, CINEMA 34 7

Roberta, DANCE 99 54

Roberts, Bartholomew, BOAT 36 29; PIRATE 59 31, 35, 39, 47

Roberts, David, ANCIENT EGYPT 23 22, 29

Roberts, Estelle, CRIME & DETECTION 73 37

Robin Hood, ARMS & ARMOUR 4 19; CRIME & DETECTION 73 26, 56

Robin Moth, BUTTERFLY & MOTH 7 37

robins, BIRD 1 9, 47, 53, 60

Robinson Crusoe, SHIPWRECK 72 58

robotic limbs, FUTURE 100 45, 48, 49

robots, CINEMA 34 44, 61; FUTURE 100 28, 29, 31, 58; SPACE EXPLORATION 71 54; TECHNOLOGY 89 43
   bomb disposal, FUTURE 100 43
   in industry, ELECTRONICS 90 60; FUTURE 100 42
   pets, FUTURE 100 59
   security, FUTURE 100 44, 59
   "smart", FUTURE 100 46-47
   sports, FUTURE 100 43
   surgery, FUTURE 100 49

rock 'n' roll, DANCE 99 59

rock art, ARCHAEOLOGY 56 16; DESERT 51 60

rock crystals, CRYSTAL & GEM 25 6, 16, 31, 32

rock music, MUSIC 12 60-61

rock pebblers, BIRD 1 24, 25

rock pools, SEASHORE 15 26, 30-33

rockets, FORCE & MOTION 78 27, 31; SPACE EXPLORATION 71 14-15, 19
   Ariane rocket, ASTRONOMY 82 35; SPACE EXPLORATION 71 12, 14-15, 35
   speed, FORCE & MOTION 78 58, 59
   V2, FORCE & MOTION 78 57

Rockies, EARTH 83 46

rocks, DESERT 51 8, 9, 10-11, 14; ECOLOGY 86 6, 19, 22, 23; ROCK & MINERAL 2 7, 8-9, 10-11
   crystals, ROCK & MINERAL 2 44, 61
   deep-sea, OCEAN 62 18-20, 46, 60
   igneous, EARTH 83 24-25, 28, 48; ROCK & MINERAL 2 16-17, 42
   metamorphic, EARTH 83 24, 28-29, 48; ROCK & MINERAL 2 24-25
   prehistoric, PREHISTORIC LIFE 52 10-11, 62-63
   sea-side, SEASHORE 15 6, 9, 10, 11
   sedimentary, EARTH 83 26-27, 28, 56; ROCK & MINERAL 2 20-21, 38
   in space, SPACE EXPLORATION 71 11, 23
   volcanic, ROCK & MINERAL 2 17, 18-19

rodents, FOSSIL 19 54, 56; MAMMAL 11 22, 54, 58, 63; SKELETON 3 34
   burrows, MAMMAL 11 55-57
   parental care, MAMMAL 11 32-33

teeth, MAMMAL 11 50, 62

rodeos, COWBOY 45 34-35, 58-59, 62-63; HORSE 33 56-57

Rodin, Auguste, MONET 95 35, 60; WATERCOLOUR 97 55

Roemer, Ole, LIGHT 75 60, 61

Roentgen, Wilhelm, FUTURE 100 34; HUMAN BODY 87 13; TECHNOLOGY 89 57

Roerich, Nikolai, RUSSIA 74 49

Rogers, Ginger, CINEMA 34 57; DANCE 99 54

Rogers, Roy, COWBOY 45 20, 60

Rogers, Will, COWBOY 45 34

Roget, P. M., INVENTION 27 50

Roi des Belges, CAR 21 12

roll, FLYING MACHINE 22 14, 40-41

rollers, birds, BIRD 1 12

rollers, mechanical, FORCE & MOTION 78 11, 18, 19, 20; INVENTION 27 12, 13

Rollo, VIKING 50 16

Rolls-Royce, CAR 21 12, 13, 63

ROM, ELECTRONICS 90 56, 58, 59

Roma, ANCIENT ROME 24 9

romals, COWBOY 45 17

Roman Britain, *see* Britain

Roman Catholics, RELIGION 68 52, 53

Roman numerals, ANCIENT ROME 24 40

Romanov, Mikhail, RUSSIA 74 20

Romanovs, RUSSIA 74 20, 21, 25

Romans, Ancient, ANCIENT ROME 24; PERSPECTIVE 98 10; PIRATE 59 10-11; PYRAMID 53 62; RENAISSANCE 91 50-53
   alphabet, WRITING 48 16-17
   archaeological discoveries, ARCHAEOLOGY 56 7-12, 57
      objects, ARCHAEOLOGY 56 48-49
      buildings, ARCHAEOLOGY 56 18-19, 52-53
   architecture, ANCIENT ROME 24 26; BUILDING 58 32, 34, 42, 58
   army, ANCIENT ROME 24 10, 12-13, 14; BATTLE 63 22, 44
   art, ANCIENT ROME 24 6, 25, 36, 42; RENAISSANCE 91 26, 30, 51, 58
   Biblical, BIBLE LANDS 30 39, 46-47, 54-55
   coins, MONEY 18 10, 36, 38, 40
   costume, COSTUME 35 10, 12, 18, 34, 60
   education, ANCIENT ROME 24 18, 20, 40

emperors, ANCIENT ROME 24 8-9, 22, 28, 62
Empire, ANCIENT ROME 24 7, 12, 62
farming, FARM 66 6, 12, 17, 20
law, CRIME & DETECTION 73 8, 9
magic, WITCH & WIZARD 70 12, 21, 22
medicine, MEDICINE 88 18-19, 50
mummies, MUMMY 44 17, 18, 42-43
religion, ANCIENT ROME 24 23, 50-53
Republic, ANCIENT ROME 24 6, 16
society, ANCIENT ROME 24 16 weapons, ARMS & ARMOUR 4 12-13
Romulus, ANCIENT ROME 24 6
Ronnesbaeksholm, VIKING 50 14
Röntgen, Wilhelm, ELECTRONICS 90 27; INVENTION 27 56
roofs, BUILDING 58 24-25
construction, BUILDING 58 20-21
covering, BUILDING 58 26-27
decoration, BUILDING 58 28-29, 53, 60
round, BUILDING 58 31
thatch, BUILDING 58 30-31
vaults, BUILDING 58 34-35
rooks, BIRD 1 25, 46
Roosevelt, Franklin D., ENERGY 76 47; MATTER 80 55
Roosevelt, Theodore, COWBOY 45 19
roots, PLANT 14 13, 15, 52, 65
adventitious, PLANT 14 14, 39
aerial, JUNGLE 54 18, 20; PLANT 14 46, 47
buttress, JUNGLE 54 15
main, PLANT 14 8, 10
stilt, JUNGLE 54 9
rope climbing, SPORT 8 43
roping, COWBOY 45 24, 32, 34-35, 50
Rosenquist, Gary, VOLCANO 38 14, 15
roses, PLANT 14 26-27, 37
Rosetta Stone, ANCIENT EGYPT 23 35; PYRAMID 53 32; WRITING 48 12
Rosinante, HORSE 33 42
Roskilde ships, VIKING 50 10-11, 15, 24-25
Ross, John, ARCTIC & ANTARCTIC 57 52
Ross, Sir James, ARCTIC & ANTARCTIC 57 53; EXPLORER 31 50

Rosse, Lord, ASTRONOMY 82 26, 62
Rosseli, Francesco, TIME & SPACE 81 12, 13
rostrum, INSECT 17 16, 30
rostrum camera, CINEMA 34 53
rosy periwinkles, JUNGLE 54 43
rotation, FORCE & MOTION 78 20, 21, 54, 57
Rothafel, Samuel, CINEMA 34 25
rouble, MONEY 18 44, 45, 62; RUSSIA 74 58
Rouen, MONET 95 38, 48
Rouen Cathedral, MONET 95 44-47
Round Table, KNIGHT 43 41
round-up, COWBOY 45 32, 48
modern, COWBOY 45 19
Rousseau, Henri, CAT 29 30
Rousseau, Théodore, IMPRESSIONISM 92 12
Roux, Emil, MEDICINE 88 32
Rover, CAR 21 62
rowans, TREE 5 28, 36, 38
rowing, BOAT 36 20, 31, 43, 58
Rowlandson, Thomas, WATERCOLOUR 97 28, 30, 54
Rowley, John, FORCE & MOTION 78 28
Roxy Cinema, New York, CINEMA 34 25
Royal Academy, Madrid, GOYA 93 7, 18, 25, 48
Royal Albert Bridge, TRAIN 39 21
royal assyrian butterflies, BUTTERFLY & MOTH 7 33
Royal Ballet, DANCE 99 45, 50
Royal Ballet School, DANCE 99 12
Royal Fusiliers, BATTLE 63 17
Royal Gold Cup, CASTLE 49 22
royal grammas, FISH 20 16
Royal Mail, TRAIN 39 37
Royal Opera House, DANCE 99 50
Royce, Henry, CAR 21 13
Rozier, François de, FLYING MACHINE 22 8
rubber, CHEMISTRY 79 52, 54; JUNGLE 54 59; MATTER 80 44, 45; SPORT 8 30, 34; TREE 5 22
latex, TECHNOLOGY 89 27
synthetic, CHEMISTRY 79 63
Rozier, Pilatre de, INVENTION 27 58
Rubens, Peter Paul, GOYA 93 51; MANET 94 10, 26; VAN GOGH 96 25; WATERCOLOUR 97 38

rubies, CRYSTAL & GEM 25 19, 36-37, 56; ROCK & MINERAL 2 51; RUSSIA 74 24
Rublev, Andrei, RUSSIA 74 46, 47
rudd, FISH 20 18
rudders, aeroplane, FLYING MACHINE 22 15, 21, 27, 41
mounting, BOAT 36 35
stern-post, BOAT 36 17, 25, 39, 52; SHIPWRECK 72 16, 17
ruddy daggerwing butterflies, BUTTERFLY & MOTH 7 35
Rufus, ANCIENT ROME 24 23
rugby, SPORT 8 14
rugs, DESERT 51 59
saddle, DESERT 51 45, 54, 58, 60
Ruiz, Colombia, VOLCANO 38 56
rulers, INVENTION 27 11, 16, 17; TIME & SPACE 81 10, 11, 34, 54
rum, BOAT 36 28
Rumford, Count, ENERGY 76 21
Runes, VIKING 50 58-59; WRITING 48 18
runner beans, PLANT 14 10, 38, 39
Runnin' Wild, DANCE 99 58
rushes, POND & RIVER 6 18, 32-35, 47
Ruskin, John, CRYSTAL & GEM 25 36, 43; WATERCOLOUR 97 15, 36, 40
Russell, Charles, COWBOY 45 26
Russia, ARCTIC & ANTARCTIC 57 48; BATTLE 63 20, 48, 59, 61; RUSSIA 74; SPACE EXPLORATION 71 8; WHALE 46 56, 58
architecture, BUILDING 58 11, 36
climate, RUSSIA 74 10, 11, 13, 52
currency, MONEY 18 41, 45
dances, DANCE 99 12, 23, 54, 55
festivals, RUSSIA 74 56-57
literature, RUSSIA 74 42-45, 53
money, MONEY 18 10, 11, 62
music, MUSIC 12 37
peoples, RUSSIA 74 12-13
religion, RUSSIA 74 18-19
science, RUSSIA 74 40-43
tsars, RUSSIA 74 20-21
expansion, RUSSIA 74 22, 23
Vikings in, VIKING 50 18-19, 22, 26
weather, WEATHER 28 54
see also Bolshevik Revolution

Russian blue, CAT 29 51, 55
Russian Federation, RUSSIA 74 58, 59
Russian language, WRITING 48 19, 53
Russo-Japanese War, BATTLE 63 20, 63
rust, CHEMISTRY 79 40, 41, 47; SHIPWRECK 72 29, 56
rustlers, COWBOY 45 31
Ruth, "Babe", SPORT 8 22
Rutherford, Ernest, CHEMISTRY 79 35; ELECTRICITY 77 54; MATTER 80 46, 48, 49, 53
rutile, CRYSTAL & GEM 25 27, 37, 57
rye, FARM 66 16, 28

S

Sabal, FOSSIL 19 38
sabbath, RELIGION 68 45, 46; WITCH & WIZARD 70 38
sabotage, SPY 67 32, 37
sabots, COWBOY 45 52
sabres, ARMS & ARMOUR 4 32-33, 44, 52-53; BATTLE 63 48
sabretooths, FOSSIL 19 21, 55, 56
Sachs, Julius, ENERGY 76 50
sacrifice, ANCIENT EGYPT 23 27; RELIGION 68 14, 23, 31; WITCH & WIZARD 70 48, 54
human, EARLY PEOPLE 10 38, 52, 55, 58; PYRAMID 53 6, 54, 58, 60
saddle-back caterpillars, BUTTERFLY & MOTH 7 57
saddles, ANCIENT ROME 24 13; COWBOY 45 14-15, 50-51, 56-57; HORSE 33 30-32, 56-57; KNIGHT 43 39

bags, COWBOY **45** 8, 13, 17, 53
blanket, COWBOY **45** 9, 17, 23
making, COWBOY **45** 8-9, 16
saddling, COWBOY **45** 16-17
sidesaddles, COWBOY **45** 8
sadhus, WITCH & WIZARD **70** 50
safe deposits,
    CRIME & DETECTION **73** 17
saguaro, DESERT **51** 21
Sahara Desert, AFRICA **61** 6, 23,
    44, 48; DESERT **51** 15, 44, 48,
    62; EXPLORER **31** 10-11,
    18-19, 22
Sahel, DESERT **51** 57
Sahura, PYRAMID **53** 38, 39
sailfish, FISH **20** 11, 30
sailing, ANCIENT ROME **24** 60;
    BOAT **36** 22, 28, 62-63;
    FORCE & MOTION **78**
    7, 42, 43
sailors, BOAT **36** 28-29, 30, 58
sails, BOAT **36** 24-25, 43;
    INVENTION **27** 25, 33;
    PIRATE **59** 40
    jib, BOAT **36** 23, 24, 27, 61
    lateen, BOAT **36** 20, 21, 25, 57
    main, BOAT **36** 23, 24, 41, 57
    making, BOAT **36** 26
    spinnaker, BOAT **36** 23, 60, 61
    yard, BOAT **36** 22, 25, 26, 41
St. Basil's Cathedral,
    RUSSIA **74** 26-28
St. Bernards, DOG **32** 44
St. Denis, Ruth, DANCE **99** 35
St. Elmo's Fire,
    WEATHER **28** 59
Saint-Exupéry, Antoine de,
    VOLCANO **38** 44
St. Helens, Mt., FUTURE **100** 11;
    ROCK & MINERAL **2** 18, 19;
    VOLCANO **38** 14, 35, 39
St. Hilaire, Geoffroy,
    CAT **29** 41
St. John, Order of,
    PIRATE **59** 16-17
St. Lawrence, River,
    EXPLORER **31** 42
St. Malo, PIRATE **59** 50-51
St. Petersburg,
    RUSSIA **74** 28-29, 48
St. Pierre, Martinique,
    VOLCANO **38** 16, 32-33
Sakara festival, DANCE **99** 11
Sakharov, Andrei,
    RUSSIA **74** 40
sakis, GORILLA **64** 16
Saladin, CASTLE **49** 34;
    MEDIEVAL LIFE **65** 45
Salam, Abdus, FORCE &
    MOTION **78** 63
salamandars, AMPHIBIAN **41**
    16, 17, 34, 61;
    REPTILE **26** 7
    European fire,
    AMPHIBIAN **41** 7, 46, 48
    giant, AMPHIBIAN **41** 10-11,
    41, 49

lungless, AMPHIBIAN **41**
    36, 46
    mandarin, AMPHIBIAN **41**
    7, 19, 31, 49
    tiger, AMPHIBIAN **41**
    28, 31, 46-47
Salamis,
    ANCIENT GREECE **37** 19, 54
salinity, EARTH **83** 30, 32;
    ECOLOGY **86** 25, 38, 42, 50
saliva, HUMAN BODY **87** 31, 34, 59
salmon, FISH **20** 7, 42;
    OCEAN **62** 38, 56-57;
    POND & RIVER **6** 23
Salome, BIBLE LANDS **30** 57
Salon Cinematographe,
    Sydney, CINEMA **34** 24
Salon des Refusés,
    MANET **94**
    22-23, 24, 28;
    MONET **95** 12, 25
Salone delle Prospettive,
    PERSPECTIVE **98** 30-31
Salons, Paris,
    IMPRESSIONISM **92** 6, 18-19,
    45; MANET **94** 12, 50, 51, 58;
    MONET **95** 12, 14, 24-25
salt, CHEMISTRY **79** 20, 21, 45;
    CRYSTAL & GEM **25** 17, 62;
    EARLY PEOPLE **10** 9;
    ROCK & MINERAL **2** 21, 47
    sea water, OCEAN **62** 8-9, 11
salt bush, DESERT **51** 19
Salter, Professor Stephen,
    FORCE & MOTION **78** 51
saltire cross, FLAG **16** 47
salt-marsh caterpillars,
    BUTTERFLY & MOTH **7** 42
salts, CHEMISTRY **79** 44-45, 49
    acids and bases,
    CHEMISTRY **79** 42
    analysis, CHEMISTRY **79** 31
    crystalline, 20, 21, 55
    insoluble, CHEMISTRY **79** 58
    metal, CHEMISTRY **79** 19,
    20, 24, 25
saluki, DESERT **51** 43
Salyut space station,
    SPACE EXPLORATION **71**
    13, 34, 36-37
Sam'al, BIBLE LANDS **30** 40
Samaria, BIBLE LANDS **30** 20,
    46, 48
samba, DANCE **99** 10
Samburu peoples, AFRICA **61** 29
samovars, RUSSIA **74** 55
sampans, BOAT **36** 34, 35
Samson, BIBLE LANDS **30** 33
samurai, BATTLE **63** 12, 16, 36,
    44; CASTLE **49** 36; FLAG **16**
    52; KNIGHT **43** 58-59
    Japanese, ARMS &
    ARMOUR **4** 36-37
San Andreas, VOLCANO **38**
    13, 61
San Francisco, VOLCANO **38**
    46, 57, 60, 61

San peoples, AFRICA **61** 7, 8,
    18, 19; DESERT **51** 20, 44, 46
Sanctorius, Santorio,
    HUMAN BODY **87** 34;
    MEDICINE **88** 28
sanctuaries, GORILLA **64** 61
sand, ARCHAEOLOGY **56** 10, 26,
    29, 43; DESERT **51** 8,
    12-13; ROCK & MINERAL **2**
    11, 14-15, 47
    storms, DESERT **51** 7
sand cats, CAT **29** 39
sand eels, FISH **20** 56
sand vipers, REPTILE **26** 15
sandals, ANCIENT ROME **24** 11;
    COSTUME **35** 8, 10, 59
sandbank, SHIPWRECK **72** 10
Sandby, Paul,
    WATERCOLOUR **97** 7
sand-dollars, FOSSIL **19** 33
sandglass, INVENTION **27** 23
sandgrouse, DESERT **51** 30, 31
sandpipers, BIRD **1** 36
sandstone, BUILDING **58** 17, 18,
    26, 47; PYRAMID **53** 32, 51;
    ROCK & MINERAL **2** 12, 14,
    21, 35; SEASHORE **15** 8-9, 63
    desert, DESERT **51** 9, 10
    layers, EARTH **83** 26, 27, 63
Sandviken, MONET **95** 39
sansa, MUSIC **12** 55
Santa Cruz, MONEY **18** 9
Santa Domingo, PIRATE **59** 23
Santo Domingo dogs,
    DOG **32** 36
Santorini, ANCIENT GREECE **37**
    50; VOLCANO **38** 19, 39
sapphires, CRYSTAL & GEM **25**
    36-37, 46, 56;
    ROCK & MINERAL **2** 51
sapwoods, TREE **5** 16, 17, 48
Saqqara, PYRAMID **53** 10-13,
    28, 32, 39
Sara peoples, AFRICA **61** 50
Saracens, KNIGHT **43** 55
Saragossa,
    GOYA **93** 8-9, 10, 24
sarangi, MUSIC **12** 41
Sarasvati, RELIGION **68** 18, 37
sarcophagi, MUMMY **44**
    28-29, 38; PYRAMID **53** 22
sarcopterygians, FISH **20** 9
Sardinia, EXPLORER **31** 6-7;
    MONEY **18** 37
Sargasso Sea, OCEAN **62** 8, 30, 38
sargassum, SEASHORE **15** 18, 33
Sargent, John Singer,
    IMPRESSIONISM **92** 60;
    MONET **95** 11, 36
    *Monet painting at the Edge
    of a Wood*, MONET **95** 11
Sargrove, John,
    ELECTRONICS **90** 22
satellite imaging,
    FUTURE **100** 14, 15
satellite tracking, WHALE **46**
    14, 61

satellites, ENERGY **76** 38, 39, 48,
    62; FUTURE **100** 56, 59;
    INVENTION **27** 63; SPY **67** 42
    artificial, ASTRONOMY **82**
    34-35, 43
    communications,
    ELECTRONICS **90** 13, 41, 60,
    63; SPACE EXPLORATION **71**
    48-49
    ecological information,
    FUTURE **100** 14, 15
    environmental,
    FUTURE **100** 11, 51
    European, SPACE
    EXPLORATION **71** 48, 50
    farming, TECHNOLOGY **89** 45
    geostationary,
    FUTURE **100** 12, 13
    KFA, SPY **67** 52
    launch, SPACE
    EXPLORATION **71** 48, 49;
    SPY **67** 38
    lost, SPACE
    EXPLORATION **71** 35
    Moon, ASTRONOMY **82** 40
    navigation systems,
    FUTURE **100** 24, 25;
    TECHNOLOGY **89** 30, 31
    observation, SPACE
    EXPLORATION **71** 50-51
    in space, SPACE
    EXPLORATION **71** 12, 15,
    18, 58
    Sputnik I, FUTURE **100**
    10, 12
    spy, SPY **67** 38, 52-54
    Telstar I, FUTURE **100** 10
    Uranus, ASTRONOMY **82** 55
    weather, FUTURE **100** 14;
    WEATHER **28** 12, 13, 14, 15
Sat-Hathor III, PYRAMID **53** 40
satin, COSTUME **35** 24, 25, 45
Saturn, planet,
    ASTRONOMY **82** 13, 18,
    52-53; SPACE
    EXPLORATION **71** 44, 45, 53
    density, ASTRONOMY **82** 45
    orbit, ASTRONOMY **82** 36, 37
Saturn rocket, SPACE
    EXPLORATION **71** 19
Saul, BIBLE LANDS **30** 20
saung-gauk, MUSIC **12** 35
savannahs, AFRICA **61** 6;
    ECOLOGY **86** 7, 48;
    GORILLA **64** 26-27
Savery, Roelandt Jacobsz,
    ANCIENT GREECE **37** 23;
    BIBLE LANDS **30** 28
Savery, Thomas,
    ENERGY **76** 28;
    INVENTION **27** 32
sawfish, FISH **20** 35, 56;
    SHARK **40** 8-9
sawflies, INSECT **17** 38-39
saws, BUILDING **58** 8-9;
    EARLY PEOPLE **10** 51;
    INVENTION **27** 11, 42

Sax, Adolphe, **Music 12** 14, 15, 24
saxhorns, **Music 12** 15, 24
Saxons, **Early People 10** 49, 50; **Farm 66** 13; **Medieval Life 65** 6; **Pirate 59** 12
saxophones, **Music 12** 9, 12, 14-15
scabbards, **Arms & Armour 4** 12, 33, 36, 41
scaffolding, **Pyramid 53** 34
scaled dragon fish, **Fish 20** 38
scales, **Invention 27** 16
scallops, **Fossil 19** 18, 19, 26; **Ocean 62** 34-35; **Seashore 15** 26, 37, 59; **Shell 9** 16, 34, 35, 42
Scandinavia, **Arctic & Antarctic 57** 38, 39, 48; **Explorer 31** 12; **Monet 95** 39; **Witch & Wizard 70** 10, 29, 36
houses, **Building 58** 7, 11, 22
Scania, **Flag 16** 44
scanners, **Medicine 88** 38-39, 52; **Space Exploration 71** 56, 57; **Technology 89** 57
scapolite, **Crystal & Gem 25** 7, 49
scarabs, **Ancient Egypt 23** 14, 24, 35, 57; **Mummy 44** 16, 21, 25, 44
scarves, **Costume 35** 9, 53, 59
scavengers, **Ecology 86** 48
Scelidosaurus, **Dinosaur 13** 20, 38
Scheckter, Jody, **Car 21** 33
Scheele, Carl Wilhelm, **Light 75** 41
Scheuchzer, Johann, **Evolution 85** 10; **Fossil 19** 14, 36
Schiaparelli, Giovanni, **Astronomy 82** 48; **Life 84** 62, 63
Schleicher K 23, **Flying Machine 22** 58-59
Schliemann, Heinrich, **Ancient Greece 37** 11, 12; **Archaeology 56** 14; **Early People 10** 63
Schmidt, Johannes, **Fish 20** 49
schools, **Writing 48** 50-51
schooners, **Boat 36** 43; **Pirate 59** 53
Schrödinger, Erwin, **Time & Space 81** 50-51
Schulze, Johann Heinrich, **Invention 27** 40
Schwann, Theodor, **Life 84** 14; **Medicine 88** 30
Schwarzschild, Karl, **Time & Space 81** 46, 62
schwenkel, **Flag 16** 6

science fiction, **Future 100** 27, 40, 44
writers, **Future 100** 8, 9, 10
scientists, **Arctic & Antarctic 57** 61, 63
scimitars, **Arms & Armour 4** 17, 32
scissors, **Force & Motion 78** 8, 17; **Invention 27** 6; **Shipwreck 72** 53; **Technology 89** 10-11
Scleropages, **Fish 20** 44
Scorel, Jan van, **Renaissance 91** 58, 59
scorpionfish, **Fish 20** 46, 54, 55
scorpions, **Desert 51** 24; **Ecology 86** 41; **Jungle 54** 56; **Pond & River 6** 51; **Shell 9** 7, 27
fossil, **Prehistoric Life 52** 23, 28
invertebrates, **Insect 17** 9;
scoters, **Bird 1** 37; **Skeleton 3** 23
Scotland, **Battle 63** 39, 41; **Cat 29** 44, 59; **Money 18** 13, 19, 23, 46; **Weather 28** 12
culture, **Dance 99** 23
flag, **Flag 16** 47
navigation, **Viking 50** 17
Scotland Yard, **Crime & Detection 73** 10, 22
Scott, Captain Robert, **Arctic & Antarctic 57** 54-55, 56, 58; **Explorer 31** 54-55; **Flag 16** 42
scramblers, **Spy 67** 48
scraper solecurtus, **Shell 9** 42
screenplay, **Cinema 34** 28
screw shells, **Shell 9** 43
screws, **Boat 36** 38, 39; **Force & Motion 78** 9, 12-13
scribes, **Early People 10** 41; **Medieval Life 65** 40, 41, 47; **Pyramid 53** 31; **Writing 48** 7, 12, 35
Ancient Egypt, **Ancient Egypt 23** 32-35
scrimshaw, **Whale 46** 51
scripts, **Writing 48**
Chancery, **Writing 48** 51
Demotic, **Ancient Egypt 23** 34
Gothic, **Writing 48** 28
Hieratic, **Ancient Egypt 23** 34, 35
Indian, **Writing 48** 8, 32
Kufic, **Writing 48** 34
Naski, **Writing 48** 34
Nasta'liq, **Writing 48** 35
scriptures, **Religion 68** 18, 25, 43, 55
scrolls, **Writing 48** 21, 32, 42
scrubland, **Ecology 86** 7, 8

scuba diving, **Ocean 62** 48, 50, 52-55; **Shipwreck 72** 9, 46, 47
sculling, **Boat 36** 21
sculpture, **Renaissance 91** 14-15, 54-55
ancient, **Archaeology 56** 8 16-17; **Early People 10** 22, 24, 58
Scupi, Yugoslavia, **Volcano 38** 46
scurvy, **Pirate 59** 43
scythes, **Farm 66** 20, 35
Scythians, **Archaeology 56** 30
sea anemones, **Arctic & Antarctic 57** 12, 13; **Fish 20** 46, 47
sea catfish, **Fish 20** 31, 44
sea cow, **Whale 46** 44; **Mammal 11** 11
sea lion, **Arctic & Antarctic 57** 44; **Fish 20** 60; **Mammal 11** 9; **Skeleton 3** 51; **Whale 46** 15, 26
Steller's, **Whale 46** 23, 30, 31, 63
sea monsters, **Ocean 62** 19, 33-34, 42
sea otter, **Whale 46** 7, 58
sea spiders, **Arctic & Antarctic 57** 12-13
sea stickleback, **Fish 20** 40
sea urchins, **Arctic & Antarctic 57** 12; **Ocean 62** 11, 18-19, 29, 58; **Shell 9** 20-21, 34, 49; **Skeleton 3** 24
sea, **Ocean 62** 8-9; **Prehistoric Life 52** 6-10, 16-21
bed, **Archaeology 56** 32-33; **Ocean 62** 16-17, 44-45
wrecks, **Ocean 62** 54-55
see also oceans
seadragons, **Fish 20** 23
seahorses, **Fish 20** 22, 23, 44; **Ocean 62** 17; **Skeleton 3** 25
sea-lavender, **Pond & River 6** 61
sea-lilies, **Fossil 19** 12, 32, 33
seals, on manuscripts, **China 55** 17, 21, 24, 51; **Early People 10** 20, 21, 26; **Writing 48** 8, 57
Ancient Egypt, **Ancient Egypt 23** 34, 35
medieval, **Castle 49** 23, 34; **Medieval Life 65** 2 2, 25, 46
seals, marine, **Arctic & Antarctic 57** 33, 44-45, 51; **Mammal 11** 20, 58, 59, 63; **Ocean 62** 36, 38; **Seashore 15** 54, 56, 57
Baikal, **Whale 46** 14, 58, 63

common, **Whale 46** 14
crabeater, **Whale 46** 14, 22, 25
elephant, **Whale 46** 14, 28, 40-41
leopard, **Whale 46** 14, 22
skeleton, **Skeleton 3** 58
skin, **Whale 46** 19, 20
sea-scorpions, **Fossil 19** 31; **Seashore 15** 35
sea-shells, **Evolution 85** 10, 11, 32
seashore, **Ecology 86** 25, 42-43; **Rock & Mineral 2** 14-15; **Seashore 15**
sea-slugs, **Seashore 15** 26, 30
sea-snails, **Seashore 15** 28
seasons, **Tree 5** 12, 30, 46, 47
sea-urchins, **Fossil 19** 13, 17, 19, 33; **Seashore 15** 24, 28, 50, 60
seaweeds, **Ecology 86** 13, 42, 43; **Fossil 19** 17, 18, 19, 24; **Ocean 62** 20-21, 30, 58; **Seashore 15** 18-21, 58-59
giant, **Seashore 15** 24
"holdfast" roots, **Seashore 15** 22-23
Secret Services, American, **Spy 67** 42, 54
Austrian, **Spy 67** 41
German, **Spy 67** 56
Polish, **Spy 67** 25
Soviet, **Spy 67** 35, 43, 57-58
secret societies, **Africa 61** 36, 59, 62, 63
Ekpo, **Africa 61** 35
secretary bird, **Eagle 69** 10, 26, 44, 45
security officers, **Crime & Detection 73** 29
sed festival, **Pyramid 53** 12, 41
sedges, **Pond & River 6** 6, 19, 32-35
sediment, **Earth 83** 30, 31, 32, 48; **Rock & Mineral 2** 12, 13, 20, 38
sedimentation, **Earth 83** 26, 56-57, 62
Seebeck, Thomas, **Electricity 77** 52
Seebeck effect, **Electricity 77** 52, 53
seeds, **Ecology 86** 9; **Jungle 54** 26-27, 58; **Life 84** 6, 23, 31, 52; **Plant 14** 8, 11, 13; **Tree 5** 14-15, 40-43
dispersal, **Ecology 86** 44; **Plant 14** 26, 27, 30-31
fossilized, **Fossil 19** 38, 39
seedlings, **Plant 14** 10, 28
sowing of, **Farm 66** 16-17, 30
Segovia, **Castle 49** 16
Seine, River, **Monet 95** 20-23, 34, 38
seine net, **Boat 36** 44

seismic waves, EARTH 83 40, 41, 42-43
seismographs, SPY 67 52, 53; VOLCANO 38 48, 50, 52-55
Sekhemkhet, PYRAMID 53 46
Sekhmet, BIBLE LANDS 30 25
Seleucids, BIBLE LANDS 30 54
self-inductance, ELECTRICITY 77 35, 50
self-righting lifeboat, SHIPWRECK 72 40
Selkirk, Alexander, BOAT 36 58; SHIPWRECK 72 58
semaphores, SHIPWRECK 72 36, 37
semiconductors, ELECTRONICS 90 36-37, 52
amplifiers, ELECTRONICS 90 38
circuits, ELECTRONICS 90 53
Semitic alphabet, WRITING 48 14
Senate, ANCIENT ROME 24 16
senators, ANCIENT ROME 24 7, 8, 16, 18
Seneca, RENAISSANCE 91 32
Senkamanisken, PYRAMID 53 51
Sennacherib, King, BIBLE LANDS 30 28, 46
Sennedjsui, PYRAMID 53 25
sens, MONEY 18 53
Senusret I, PYRAMID 53 40
Senusret II, PYRAMID 53 40
Senusret III, PYRAMID 53 28, 42
Senwosret, ANCIENT EGYPT 23 12
Septimus Severus, ANCIENT ROME 24 22
sequoia, TREE 5 6, 17, 31, 44
serandite, CRYSTAL & GEM 25 23
Serapis, ANCIENT ROME 24 50
Serbia, FLAG 16 38
serfs, KNIGHT 43 6; RUSSIA 74 16-17, 21
Sergius, St., RUSSIA 74 18
Sermon on the Mount, RELIGION 68 53
Serpent Mound, ARCHAEOLOGY 56 12
serpentine, CRYSTAL & GEM 25 39, 51
serval cats, CAT 29 14, 23, 38-39; SKELETON 3 56
Seshemnufer, PYRAMID 53 24
sestertius, MONEY 18 36
Seth, ANCIENT EGYPT 23 45
Seti I, MUMMY 44 28, 33, 36, 50
sets, CINEMA 34 29, 31, 38-39
setters, DOG 32 17, 50, 51
Seurat, Georges, IMPRESSIONISM 92 58, 59; MONET 95 25, 32; VAN GOGH 96 34, 41

La Grande Jatte, MONET 95 32
sewage treatment, ECOLOGY 86 15
sewing machines, ELECTRICITY 77 39
sextants, INVENTION 27 35; SHIPWRECK 72 32; TIME & SPACE 81 13
Seychelles Islands, JUNGLE 54 9
Sforza, Lodovico, RENAISSANCE 91 38, 39
shabti figures, ANCIENT EGYPT 23 19; ARCHAEOLOGY 56 56; MUMMY 44 12, 21, 32-33; PYRAMID 53 50, 51
shadow theatre, CINEMA 34 6-7
shadows, LIGHT 75 10-11, 35
shakers, MUSIC 12 56
Shakespeare, William, AMPHIBIAN 41 48; SKELETON 3 10, 28; WITCH & WIZARD 70 17
shakuhachi, MUSIC 12 10
shalako, DESERT 51 14
shale, EARTH 83 29; SEASHORE 15 11
Shalmaneser, King, BIBLE LANDS 30 33, 38, 49
Shamans, ARCTIC & ANTARCTIC 57 39, 48, 51; EARLY PEOPLE 10 36; MEDICINE 88 7, 10-11, 13; RELIGION 68 16, 17
American Indian, NORTH AMERICAN INDIAN 60 9-11, 22-23, 54
shamanism, WITCH & WIZARD 70 8, 26, 27, 41
Shang dynasty, CHINA 55 6, 10-11, 56
Shanghai, CHINA 55 50, 52
Shapur, King of Persia, PIRATE 59 11
Shari'ah, RELIGION 68 58, 59
Sharif, Omar, CINEMA 34 56
sharks, OCEAN 62 10-11, 27-29; SHARK 40 6-7, 12-13; SKELETON 3 13, 21, 36, 41
angel, SHARK 40 17-18, 36-38
basking, SHARK 40 24, 34-35
blue, SHARK 40 53, 56-57, 62
cat, SHARK 40 6, 12, 20-21
electric signals, ELECTRICITY 77 7; SHARK 40 18-19, 29, 51
fins, SHARK 40 6, 11, 13, 40
great white, SHARK 40 28-31, 52-53
hammerhead, SHARK 40 19, 23, 42-43
jaws, SHARK 40 24-25, 30, 61
megamouth, SHARK 40 6, 44-45

predators, SHARK 40 6, 28, 42, 58
prehistoric, FOSSIL 19 13, 14, 34; PREHISTORIC LIFE 52 7, 21
reproduction, SHARK 40 10, 20-23, 58
respiration, SHARK 40 10-11, 36
senses, SHARK 40 18-19, 41, 56
"warriors of the sea", FISH 20 58-59, 60-61
whale shark, SHARK 40 6, 27, 32-34
worship, SHARK 40 46-47
Sharma, Rakesh, SPACE EXPLORATION 71 13
Sharman, Helen, SPACE EXPLORATION 71 20, 27, 29, 36
Sharp, Bartholomew, PIRATE 59 26, 40
Shaw, G. B., CINEMA 34 37
Shaw, Percy, FUTURE 100 9
shawls, COSTUME 35 7, 10, 39
shawms, MUSIC 12 12, 13, 20
Shawnee, NORTH AMERICAN INDIAN 60 20-21
Shearer, Moira, CINEMA 34 57
Shearer, Norma, CINEMA 34 62
shearwaters, ARCTIC & ANTARCTIC 57 23; BIRD 1 32
sheathbills, ARCTIC & ANTARCTIC 57 22, 23
sheaths, BIRD 1 20, 27, 58, 59
sheep, CASTLE 49 54; MAMMAL 11 10, 20, 21, 63; SKELETON 3 32, 58; VIKING 50 37, 38, 44
desert, DESERT 51 42, 43, 46, 58
farm, FARM 66 45, 51, 56, 62
shearing, FARM 66 7, 50, 52, 53
sheepdogs, DOG 32 42, 43
sheets, BOAT 36 22, 60, 63
shekels, MONEY 18 6, 24, 63
shell, CRYSTAL & GEM 25 54, 55
shell middens, ARCHAEOLOGY 56 45
shellfish, commercial, ECOLOGY 86 50
shells, ammunition, BATTLE 63 29, 32, 33, 50
shells, marine, OCEAN 62 58-59, 62-63; ROCK & MINERAL 2 14, 20, 38-39; SEASHORE 15 26-29, 62-63; SHELL 9 6-7, 18-19
collecting, SHELL 9 62-63
edible, SHELL 9 34-35
growth, SHELL 9 10-11, 32-33
in magic, WITCH & WIZARD 70 28, 51, 56, 57

as skeletons, SKELETON 3 23, 24-25, 43
Shemaah of Gibesh, BIBLE LANDS 30 46
Shepard, Ernest H., WATERCOLOUR 97 45
Shepherd, David, ELEPHANT 42 63
shepherd fishes, FISH 20 46
shepherds, FARM 66 50, 51, 56
sheriffs, CASTLE 49 48; CRIME & DETECTION 73 11, 14, 15
Sherlock Holmes, ARMS & ARMOUR 4 56
Sherwin, Frank, WATERCOLOUR 97 57
Shetland Islands, SHIPWRECK 72 30; VIKING 50 17, 38, 55
Shi Huangdi, First Emperor, CHINA 55 6, 16-17
shields, ARMS & ARMOUR 4 11, 20; BATTLE 63 6, 39; CASTLE 49 24, 27, 30, 31; KNIGHT 43 8, 44, 48
African, AFRICA 61 42, 43, 46, 62
Indian, ARMS & ARMOUR 4 32-33, 34-35
parrying, ARMS & ARMOUR 4 8-9
Roman, ANCIENT ROME 24 11, 12, 14, 30
Viking, VIKING 50 11, 12, 13, 15
shillings, MONEY 18 48, 50, 51, 55
Shimeon, BIBLE LANDS 30 39
shingles, BUILDING 58 10, 26, 27
Shining Path guerillas, SPY 67 55
Shinto, RELIGION 68 34-35
shipping lines, BOAT 36 55, 56
ships, AFRICA 61 48, 50-51; ARCHAEOLOGY 56 32-35, 51; ARCTIC & ANTARCTIC 57 8, 11; BOAT 36 6, 32, 41; FUTURE 100 26
building, ARCHAEOLOGY 56 33, 51; BOAT 36 46-47; TECHNOLOGY 89 34; VIKING 50 43
burial, ARCHAEOLOGY 56 6, 10, 26-27; VIKING 50 54-55
cargo, BOAT 36 29, 48-49, 50-51
container, BOAT 36 6, 50
merchant, BOAT 36 27, 40-41, 50
repairs, PIRATE 59 40-44
Roman, ANCIENT ROME 24 7, 60
sailing, BOAT 36 26-27

steam, BOAT 36 36-37, 48, 52, 54; PIRATE 59 58-59
trading, BOAT 36 17, 24, 25, 28
tramp, BOAT 36 48, 49, 50
treasure, PIRATE 59 36-37
Viking, VIKING 50 8-9, 24-25
warships, VIKING 50 10-11
shipwrecks, OCEAN 62 54-55; SHIPWRECK 72
air rescues, SHIPWRECK 72 9, 41
British, SHIPWRECK 72 20, 21
films, SHIPWRECK 72 59
literature, SHIPWRECK 72 13, 58, 59
locating, SHIPWRECK 72 50, 51
myths, SHIPWRECK 72 58
salvage, SHIPWRECK 72 14, 54, 55
survivors, SHIPWRECK 72 38, 39
treasures, SHIPWRECK 72 8, 13, 15, 21
shirts, COSTUME 35 21, 26, 57, 61
shisha work, DESERT 51 55
Shiva, RELIGION 68 18, 19, 21, 28
shock absorbers, CAR 21 38, 39, 54, 55
shoes, ARCHAEOLOGY 56 7, 17, 29, 34, 48; CASTLE 49 47; DANCE 99 25; MEDIEVAL LIFE 65 23, 28, 37, 55
shoemakers, MEDIEVAL LIFE 65 49, 55
sports, SPORT 8 37, 39, 41, 56
shoguns, CASTLE 49 36; FLAG 16 18-19, 52
Shona peoples, AFRICA 61 52
shooting, SPORT 8 54
shoreline, ECOLOGY 86 25, 42-43
short circuits, ELECTRICITY 77 28
short sight, LIGHT 75 11, 16, 19
shorthand, WRITING 48 57
Shostakovich, Dmitri, RUSSIA 74 48
shotguns, ARMS & ARMOUR 4 57; SPORT 8 55
shoulders, HUMAN BODY 87 15, 18, 23
shovelers, BIRD 1 15, 50
shrapnel, BATTLE 63 33
shrews, MAMMAL 11 8, 11, 38, 48
shrimpfishes, FISH 20 21
shrimps, DESERT 51 14, 16; POND & RIVER 6 57; SEASHORE 15 32, 44, 62; SHELL 9 9, 22, 44, 53
ocean, OCEAN 62 47, 58
shrouds, BOAT 36 7, 22, 23, 61; MUMMY 44 16-17
shunting, TRAIN 39 26, 35, 41, 50

shutters, BUILDING 58 48, 57
shuttlecock volva shells, SHELL 9 13
Si'a, BIBLE LANDS 30 25
siamang, GORILLA 64 30; JUNGLE 54 44-45
Siamese cats, CAT 29 52, 55, 56, 61
Siberia, ARCTIC & ANTARCTIC 57 38, 39, 48, 52; CAT 29 11, 30; RUSSIA 74 10, 11, 23; WEATHER 28 60
Kamchatka, VOLCANO 38 11, 21
native peoples, RUSSIA 74 13
Trans-Siberian Railways, RUSSIA 74 39
Sicily, ANCIENT GREECE 37 14, 27; ANCIENT ROME 24 6, 58; VOLCANO 38 7, 18, 36
mummies, MUMMY 44 60-61
sickles, CASTLE 49 52; EARLY PEOPLE 10 30; FARM 66 20, 31
sidereal time, ASTRONOMY 82 8, 13
siderite, CRYSTAL & GEM 25 20
side-scan sonar, SHIPWRECK 72 25, 50
Sidon, BIBLE LANDS 30 22
Siebe, Augustus, SHIPWRECK 72 45
siege money, MONEY 18 22, 23
sieges, BATTLE 63 32, 33, 37, 54; CASTLE 49 24-25, 26, 30; KNIGHT 43 25, 26-27
Siemens, Werner von, ELECTRICITY 77 37; TRAIN 39 38
Siemens company, ELECTRICITY 77 39
Siemens galvanometer, ELECTRONICS 90 24
Siena, RENAISSANCE 91 10-11
Sierra Leone, AFRICA 61 18, 28, 36, 37; EXPLORER 31 20
sight hounds, DOG 32 15, 40, 46-48
Signac, Paul, IMPRESSIONISM 92 58; WATERCOLOUR 97 51
signals, TRAIN 39 15, 32-35, 61
signalling lamp, SHIPWRECK 72 37
signalmen, TRAIN 39 34, 50, 56
signatures, WRITING 48 52-53
Sigurd, VIKING 50 43, 51, 57, 58
Sikhism, RELIGION 68 38-39
Sikorsky, Igor, FLYING MACHINE 22 52-53
silage, FARM 66 11, 16, 35, 45
silica, CHEMISTRY 79 24, 40, 45; CRYSTAL & GEM 25 9; ROCK & MINERAL 2 20, 42
silicates, CRYSTAL & GEM 25 14-15; EARTH 83 6, 7, 20, 44

silicon chips, ELECTRICITY 77 63; FUTURE 100 10, 52; CHEMISTRY 79 18, 23, 26, 27; EARTH 83 20
in crystals, CRYSTAL & GEM 25 8, 14, 26, 31
in humans, FUTURE 100 40
microchips, ELECTRONICS 90 54-55; TECHNOLOGY 89 54
semiconductors, ELECTRONICS 90 36-37
silk, ARCHAEOLOGY 56 29-30, 34, 51; CASTLE 49 50; CHEMISTRY 79 8; COSTUME 35 11
artificial, CHEMISTRY 79 53
Chinese, CHINA 55 22, 46-47, 57
paintings, WATERCOLOUR 97 18
trade, CHINA 55 8, 57, 58-59
Viking clothes, VIKING 50 29, 44
Silk Road, CHINA 55 8, 22, 57, 58-59; DESERT 51 62, 63; EXPLORER 31 16-17
silk route, ARCHAEOLOGY 56 29, 51
sillimanite, CRYSTAL & GEM 25 49
silt removal, SHIPWRECK 72 50
Silurian period, EVOLUTION 85 46, 60
silver, ANCIENT EGYPT 23 40; ARCHAEOLOGY 56 6-8, 26; CHEMISTRY 79 12, 15, 23, 58; VIKING 50 27, 33, 47, 49
precious, CRYSTAL & GEM 25 52, 53; ROCK & MINERAL 2 58
threads, COSTUME 35 11, 17
silver butterflies, BUTTERFLY & MOTH 7 57
Silver Ghost, CAR 21 12, 13
silver nitrate, LIGHT 75 41
silverback gorilla, GORILLA 64 34, 42-43, 44
Silver-Y Moth, BUTTERFLY & MOTH 7 51
Simon Bar Kochba, BIBLE LANDS 30 25
Simpson, Charles, COWBOY 45 35
Simpson, James, MEDICINE 88 48
Simpson Desert, DESERT 51 7, 51
Sinai, Mt., BIBLE LANDS 30 7, 38, 58, 63; RELIGION 68 42
Sinai Desert, DESERT 51 54
Sinai Peninsula, PYRAMID 53 14, 21
Sinatra, Frank, SPACE EXPLORATION 71 8
Sind Desert, DESERT 51 7, 40, 41, 61

Singer, Isaac, ELECTRICITY 77 39
singers, MEDIEVAL LIFE 65 20; DANCE 99 15, 17
Singin' in the Rain, DANCE 99 8
sinhalite, CRYSTAL & GEM 25 49
sinistral snails, SHELL 9 15
Sirius, ASTRONOMY 82 9, 60, 61
Sisley, Alfred, IMPRESSIONISM 92 17, 36, 43, 58; MONET 95 10, 20, 24, 29, 48
Autumn, Banks of the Seine, IMPRESSIONISM 92 35
and painting, IMPRESSIONISM 92 10
Saint-Martin Canal, IMPRESSIONISM 92 36
The Seine at Port-Marly: IMPRESSIONISM 92 36-37
Sistine Chapel, RENAISSANCE 91 53, 54, 56-57
sistrum, ANCIENT EGYPT 23 51
sitar, MUSIC 12 26, 41
Sitting Bull, NORTH AMERICAN INDIAN 60 31
situlá, ANCIENT EGYPT 23 30
Siva, Nataraja, DANCE 99 34, 35
Six Day War, SPY 67 58
sixpences, MONEY 18 46, 51
Skaftar, Iceland, VOLCANO 38 24, 34
Skara Brae, ARCHAEOLOGY 56 53
skates, FISH 20 9, 42, 56; SPORT 8 19
skeleton, CRIME & DETECTION 73 48, 49; EVOLUTION 85 15, 63; GORILLA 64 8-9; SKELETON 3
exoskeleton, FOSSIL 19 30
human, HUMAN BODY 87 6, 14-15, 49
skillings, MONEY 18 42, 43
skin, HUMAN BODY 87 20, 38, 50-51
skinks, DESERT 51 36; REPTILE 26 28, 29, 50, 61
skins, FARM 66 8, 48, 50, 54
Skipper butterfly, BUTTERFLY & MOTH 7 57
skipping rope, SPORT 8 43
skirting boards, BUILDING 58 55
skis, ARCTIC & ANTARCTIC 57 59
skittles, SPORT 8 57
Skopje, Yugolslavia, VOLCANO 38 46
skullcaps, WITCH & WIZARD 70 9, 17
skulls, EVOLUTION 85 8, 9, 62, 63; GORILLA 64 6, 43, 50, 63; SKELETON 3 30-31; WITCH & WIZARD 70 8, 26, 27, 30

human, **HUMAN BODY 87** 15, 23, 31 53; **SKELETON 3** 26-29
skunks, **MAMMAL 11** 9, 21; **REPTILE 26** 46
Skylab, **SPACE EXPLORATION 71** 29, 36
skyscrapers, **BUILDING 58** 36, 48; **FUTURE 100** 22-23
slapstick, **CINEMA 34** 54, 55
slate, **BUILDING 58** 17, 26, 27; **EARTH 83** 28; **ROCK & MINERAL 2** 14, 24, 25, 34
slaters, **POND & RIVER 6** 9, 12, 59
slates, **WRITING 48** 51
slavery, **BOAT 36** 28, 29; **PIRATE 59** 10, 15, 38; **VIKING 50** 26, 28
Africa, **AFRICA 61** 50-51
Greece, **ANCIENT GREECE 37** 18, 32, 33, 34
Rome, **ANCIENT ROME 24** 17, 22, 30, 39
child slaves, **ANCIENT ROME 24** 20
status, **ANCIENT ROME 24** 16, 23
Slavs, **RUSSIA 74** 8
Slayton, Donald, **SPACE EXPLORATION 71** 13
sled dogs, **DOG 32** 47, 57
sledges, **ARCTIC & ANTARCTIC 57** 58, 59; **PYRAMID 53** 37, 46; **VIKING 50** 40, 55
Sleeping Beauty, **DANCE 99** 20, 30, 31, 41
sleeping sickness, **MEDICINE 88** 30, 32
Sleipnir, **VIKING 50** 53, 58
slingers, **KNIGHT 43** 30
slings, **ARMS & ARMOUR 4** 9
slippers, **COSTUME 35** 11
slit shells, **FOSSIL 19** 60, 61
sloops, **PIRATE 59** 30, 58
sloths, **EVOLUTION 85** 14, 23, 63; **MAMMAL 11** 8, 14, 22
three-toed, **JUNGLE 54** 31
slugs, **INSECT 17** 9; **OCEAN 62** 24-25
smallpox, **MEDICINE 88** 32, 34, 43, 63
smart cards, **CRYSTAL & GEM 25** 28
smell, **HUMAN BODY 87** 46, 56-57, 59; **MAMMAL 11** 16, 24
brain, **HUMAN BODY 87** 61
senses, **HUMAN BODY 87** 50, 52
Smellie, William, **MEDICINE 88** 27
smelting, **EARLY PEOPLE 10** 42, 50; **ENERGY 76** 8, 10, 20; **TECHNOLOGY 89** 12-13
Smilodon, **CAT 29** 8,9
Smith, Billy, **CRIME & DETECTION 73** 20

Smith, William, **DINOSAUR 13** 9; **EARTH 83** 22, 26; **FOSSIL 19** 15; **EVOLUTION 85** 16, 17
smiths, **CASTLE 49** 60-61
Smithsonian Institution, **WEATHER 28** 13
smog, **WEATHER 28** 61
smoke detectors, **ELECTRONICS 90** 42
smoke signals, **BATTLE 63** 53; **ENERGY 76** 38
smoking cap, **COSTUME 35** 36, 46
smuggling, **CRIME & DETECTION 73** 27-29, 54, 56; **SPY 67** 46, 54; **WRITING 48** 61
snails, **ARCHAEOLOGY 56** 6, 46-47; **FOSSIL 19** 18, 26, 27, 61; **INSECT 17** 9; **SHELL 9** 15, 41, 58, 59
freshwater, **SHELL 9** 14, 56-57
sea, **SHELL 9** 12-14
shells, **POND & RIVER 6** 52, 53; **SHELL 9** 8, 10
snake demons, **RELIGION 68** 22
snakes, **ECOLOGY 86** 40, 49, 56, 57; **FOSSIL 19** 16, 44; **REPTILE 26** 8, 10, 13, 20; **SKELETON 3** 21, 36-37, 40; **VIKING 50** 37, 60
camouflage, **JUNGLE 54** 52; **REPTILE 26** 49
egg-eating, **REPTILE 26** 44-45
evolution, **REPTILE 26** 17, 22
feeding, **REPTILE 26** 40-41
flying, **JUNGLE 54** 55; **REPTILE 26** 27
grass, **REPTILE 26** 47
movement, **REPTILE 53**
poisonous, **REPTILE 26** 42-43
poison, **JUNGLE 54** 34, 35, 47
rat, **REPTILE 26** 22-23
reproduction, **REPTILE 26** 18-21
sea, **REPTILE 26** 20, 42
skin, **REPTILE 26** 24-25
water, **POND & RIVER 6** 40-41
see also under individual snakes
snakestones, **FOSSIL 19** 16
snapdragon vines, **DESERT 51** 16, 17
snares, **EARLY PEOPLE 10** 29; **GORILLA 64** 63
Sneferu, **ANCIENT EGYPT 23** 12; **PYRAMID 53** 14-15, 47
Snell, Willebrord, **LIGHT 75** 14
Snettisham, **ANCIENT ROME 24** 43
snipes, **BIRD 1** 35, 51; **POND & RIVER 6** 30, 31
snooker, **SPORT 8** 63
snorkelling, **OCEAN 62** 50, 53
Snow, Dr. John, **MEDICINE 88** 34

snow, **DESERT 51** 6; **WEATHER 28** 33, 40, 41, 52
snow blindness, **ARCTIC & ANTARCTIC 57** 53
snow shoes, **ARCTIC & ANTARCTIC 57** 58
snowstorms, **WEATHER 28** 54
snow leopards, **CAT 29** 10, 12, 33
Snowbirds, **FLYING MACHINE 22** 26-27
snuff boxes, **COSTUME 35** 18, 36
soap, **CHEMISTRY 79** 42, 43, 53, 62
soccer, **SPORT 8** 6-9
Société Anonyme, **MONET 95** 24
socks, **COSTUME 35** 57
Socrates, **ANCIENT GREECE 37** 47
Söderala Church, **VIKING 50** 9
sodium, **CHEMISTRY 79** 16, 18, 19, 22; **MATTER 80** 12, 18
aluminium extraction, **CHEMISTRY 79** 47
ions, **CHEMISTRY 79** 20, 21
isolation **CHEMISTRY 79** 25, 36, 46
sodium bicarbonate, **CHEMISTRY 79** 7, 63
sodium carbonate, **CHEMISTRY 79** 45, 62
sodium chloride, **CHEMISTRY 79** 20, 21, 44; **MATTER 80** 27, 32
electrolysis, **CHEMISTRY 79** 46
flame test, **MATTER 80** 32
ions, **MATTER 80** 33, 51
sodium hydroxide, **CHEMISTRY 79** 39, 46, 47
sodium lamps, **LIGHT 75** 53
softball, **SPORT 8** 25
soft-shells, crabs, **SHELL 9** 24
soil, **ARCHAEOLOGY 56** 10-11; **ECOLOGY 86** 6, 22-23, 56; **FARM 66** 12-15, 28; **LIFE 84** 16, 17, 20
composition, **DESERT 51** 8
erosion, **ECOLOGY 86** 23, 34, 63
importance, **EARTH 83** 52-53
nitrogen, **ECOLOGY 86** 21
solar clocks, **AZTEC 47** 30
solar energy, **ENERGY 76** 48, 58, 59, 61; **FUTURE 100** 13, 18, 19, 21
photosynthesis, **ENERGY 76** 50
solar panels, **SPACE EXPLORATION 71** 41, 42, 49
solar power, **ELECTRICITY 77** 45, 53; **FORCE & MOTION 78** 41; **LIGHT 75** 50-51; **WEATHER 28** 18

Solar System, **ASTRONOMY 82** 18, 36-37, 38; **EARTH 83** 6, 10, 62; **LIGHT 75** 6, 61; **SPACE EXPLORATION 71** 11, 42, 46; **TIME & SPACE 81** 10, 14-15, 28, 48
comets, **ASTRONOMY 82** 58
eclipses, **ASTRONOMY 82** 8, 31, 39
gravity, **FORCE & MOTION 78** 32-33
years, **ASTRONOMY 82** 8, 10
solar winds, **ASTRONOMY 82** 43, 51, 52, 58
solar year, **ASTRONOMY 82** 8, 10
soldiers, **ANCIENT GREECE 37** 27, 40, 54-55, 56; **MEDIEVAL LIFE 65** 9, 14, 28-29
foot, **BATTLE 63** 8-9, 15; **KNIGHT 43** 9, 30-31, 32
professional, **KNIGHT 43** 60-61, 62
wounded, **BATTLE 63** 60-61
soldos, **MONEY 18** 41
sole, **FISH 20** 24, 25, 27
solenoids, **ELECTRICITY 77** 30, 31
Solfatara, Italy, **VOLCANO 38** 26, 36, 39
Solidarity, **FLAG 16** 18
solids, **MATTER 80** 6, 7, 12-13, 18
electrolysis, **MATTER 80** 50
and molecules, **MATTER 80** 38
solutions, **MATTER 80** 7, 18, 26, 29
state of matter, **MATTER 80** 22
Solnhofen, **FOSSIL 19** 20
Solomon, **BIBLE LANDS 30** 20, 33, 40, 43; **ELEPHANT 42** 54; **RELIGION 68** 55
temple, **BIBLE LANDS 30** 21, 22
Solomon Islands, **WITCH & WIZARD 70** 56
solstices, **ASTRONOMY 82** 8, 11, 14
Solvay process, **CHEMISTRY 79** 62-63
solvents, **CHEMISTRY 79** 14, 38
chromatography, **CHEMISTRY 79** 15
industrial, **CHEMISTRY 79** 52-53
polymers, **CHEMISTRY 79** 54
Solzhenitsyn, Alexander, **RUSSIA 74** 44, 45
Somalia, **AFRICA 61** 8, 14, 18, 31; **BIBLE LANDS 30** 40; **EXPLORER 31** 8
Somerset Levels, **ARCHAEOLOGY 56** 22, 47
somites, shelly rings, **SHELL 9** 22

sonars,
 SHIPWRECK 72 25, 34, 50, 51
Song, The, **DANCE 99** 10
Song dynasty,
 CHINA 55 23, 24, 30, 32
Songhay empire,
 AFRICA 61 7, 30, 48
Sonnabend, Yolande,
 DANCE 99 50
Sonoran Desert,
 DESERT 51 6, 16, 28, 30
Sophia, Princess of Russia,
 RUSSIA 74 18, 20
Sophocles,
 ANCIENT GREECE 37 39, 61
Sorel, Agnes, **CASTLE 49** 39;
 CRYSTAL & GEM 25 35
Sorge, Richard, **SPY 67** 27, 34
sorrels, **CAT 29** 17, 25, 52
sorties, **CASTLE 49** 25, 26
Soto, Hernando de,
 EXPLORER 31 32
soul catchers, **NORTH
 AMERICAN INDIAN 60** 10
sound, **ENERGY 76** 13, 14;
 INVENTION 27 44, 45, 46
 energy, **ENERGY 76** 6, 10, 37;
 FORCE & MOTION 78 40, 41
 waves, **ELECTRICITY 77**
 58-59, 61; **ENERGY 76** 40, 41;
 FORCE & MOTION 78 49, 50,
 51; **MUSIC 12** 6, 48, 58
sound barrier, **FUTURE 100** 10
soundboard,
 MUSIC 12 27, 42, 46
sound effects,
 CINEMA 34 46-47
sound recording,
 CINEMA 34 12, 22, 23
sound track, **CINEMA 34** 23,
 46-47, 48
sous, **MONEY 18** 31, 48
Sousa, John Philip,
 MUSIC 12 25
sousaphone, **MUSIC 12** 25
South Africa, **AFRICA 61** 7, 15,
 29, 43; **MONEY 18** 23, 63;
 VOLCANO 38 39
South America, **BUILDING 58** 7,
 8, 62; **PYRAMID 53** 54;
 VOLCANO 38 10, 56
 American Indians, **ARMS &
 ARMOUR 4** 62-63
 cats, **CAT 29** 34-35, 36-37,
 40-41
 currency, **MONEY 18** 38, 57
 discovery of,
 EXPLORER 31 23-25,
 49-51, 62
 mummies,
 MUMMY 44 55
 vegetation,
 JUNGLE 54 30-31, 61, 62
 weather, **WEATHER 28** 7, 48
South Pole, **ARCTIC &
 ANTARCTIC 57** 54-55;
 EXPLORER 31 54-55

sovereigns, **MONEY 18** 47
Soviet Union, **SPACE
 EXPLORATION 71** 13, 19
Soviet Writers' Union,
 RUSSIA 74 45
Soyuz spacecraft,
 SPACE EXPLORATION 71 12,
 13, 18, 24
spa towns, **VOLCANO 38** 37
space, **SPACE EXPLORATION 71**
 10-11, 58
space exploration,
 FUTURE 100 10, 55-57, 59;
 RUSSIA 74 40, 41
 animals, **SPACE
 EXPLORATION 71** 18, 20, 21
 travellers, **SPACE
 EXPLORATION 71** 54-55
space probes, **SPACE
 EXPLORATION 71** 35, 54;
 TECHNOLOGY 89 55
 Cassini, **SPACE
 EXPLORATION 71** 44, 45
 Galileo, **SPACE
 EXPLORATION 71** 43
 Giotto, **SPACE
 EXPLORATION 71** 44
 Huygens, **SPACE
 EXPLORATION 71** 44-45
 Luna, **SPACE
 EXPLORATION 71** 18, 46
 Mariner,
 SPACE EXPLORATION 71 46
 Mars, **SPACE
 EXPLORATION 71** 35, 44, 47
 Pioneer, **SPACE
 EXPLORATION 71** 42
 Venera, **SPACE
 EXPLORATION 71** 18, 47
 Viking, **SPACE
 EXPLORATION 71** 71 47
space shuttles, **ENERGY 76** 30,
 31; **FUTURE 100** 11, 43, 54,
 57; **SPACE EXPLORATION 71**
 13, 16-17, 35, 37
space stations,
 Alpha, **SPACE
 EXPLORATION 71** 58-59
 Freedom, **SPACE
 EXPLORATION 71** 59
 Mir, **SPACE EXPLORATION 71**
 29, 30, 36-37
 Salyut, **SPACE
 EXPLORATION 71** 13, 34,
 36-37
spacecrafts,
 INVENTION 27 62, 63
Spacelab,
 SPACE EXPLORATION 71
 17, 30, 38-39
spacesuits, **SPACE
 EXPLORATION 71** 26-27, 31, 55
space-time,
 FORCE & MOTION 78 60;
 TIME & SPACE 81 34-35, 38
 black holes,
 TIME & SPACE 81 46, 47

Big Bang,
 TIME & SPACE 81 60
 curved, **TIME & SPACE 81** 10,
 41, 42
 ripples, **TIME & SPACE 81**
 44, 61
 strings, **TIME & SPACE 81**
 58, 59
spadefish, **FISH 20** 11
Spaggiari, Albert, **CRIME &
 DETECTION 73** 59
spaghettification, **TIME &
 SPACE 81** 46-47, 62
Spain, **ANCIENT ROME 24** 7, 60;
 MUSIC 12 42, 56;
 PYRAMID 53 54, 60;
 WITCH & WIZARD 70 12
 Altamira, **EARLY PEOPLE 10**
 24, 25
 castles, **CASTLE 49** 16-17
 conquest of Americas,
 AZTEC 47 62-63
 conquistadors,
 COWBOY 45 7-9, 16, 24,
 30, 38
 currency, **MONEY 18** 38, 39
 flags, **FLAG 16** 30, 36-37
 houses, **BUILDING 58** 33, 48,
 61, 62
 in Manet's paintings,
 MANET 94 18-19
 navigation, **EXPLORER 31**
 6-7, 23-25
spaniels, **DOG 32** 38, 50,
 58, 59
Spanish Armada,
 SHIPWRECK 72 22, 23, 33
Spanish cats, **CAT 29** 51
Spanish Main, **PIRATE 59**
 20-21, 22, 26
spanners, **KNIGHT 43** 63
Sparnodus, **FOSSIL 19** 34, 35
sparrowhawks, **BIRD 1** 32, 53
spars, **BOAT 36** 23
Sparta, **ANCIENT GREECE 37** 7,
 12, 56-57, 63
Spartacus,
 ANCIENT ROME 24 33
spears, **ARMS & ARMOUR 4** 9,
 13, 36; **AZTEC 47** 15, 28;
 EARLY PEOPLE 10 21, 28, 29,
 47; **KNIGHT 43** 6, 30;
 VIKING 50 14
 Bronze Age, **ARMS &
 ARMOUR 4** 10, 11
 spearheads,
 EARLY PEOPLE 10 26, 46
 Stone Age,
 ARMS & ARMOUR 4 7
special effects,
 CINEMA 34 42-43
Special Theory of Relativity,
 TIME & SPACE 81 34-35,
 39, 42
species, **EVOLUTION 85** 13, 36,
 40-41; **LIFE 84** 42, 48, 50
 animal, **LIFE 84** 53

evolution, **LIFE 84** 43
fossil, **EVOLUTION 85** 44
genus, **EVOLUTION 85** 48
natural selection,
 EVOLUTION 85 22
plants, **LIFE 84** 52
specific gravity,
 CRYSTAL & GEM 25 18
speckled wood butterflies,
 BUTTERFLY & MOTH 7 29
spectacles, **COSTUME 35** 36;
 INVENTION 27 28; **LIGHT 75**
 16, 46; **MEDIEVAL LIFE 65** 40
Spectre de la Rose, Le,
 DANCE 99 55
spectrometers, **LIGHT 75** 44
spectroscopes, **CHEMISTRY 79**
 18, 19, 32;
 CRYSTAL & GEM 25 19
spectroscopy, **CHEMISTRY 79**
 45, 59; **ELECTRICITY 77** 54;
 LIGHT 75 31, 45, 62;
 MATTER 80 32, 33, 56
spectrum, **CHEMISTRY 79** 19,
 44, 59; **ELECTRONICS 90** 14,
 34; **ENERGY 76** 40, 43, 48;
 LIGHT 75 28-29, 30, 32
 analyzer, **ELECTRONICS 90**
 15, 34, 49
 electromagnetic,
 LIGHT 75 40, 41, 63
 infrared,
 TECHNOLOGY 89 59
 spectroscope,
 CRYSTAL & GEM 25 19
speed, **FORCE & MOTION 78**
 36, 42, 54
 of flow,
 FORCE & MOTION 78 45
 of light, **FORCE & MOTION 78**
 58-59, 62
 of rotation,
 FORCE & MOTION 78 20
speedline device,
 SHIPWRECK 72 42
Speke, John Hanning,
 EXPLORER 31 46
spelling, **WRITING 48** 50
Wells, Thomas Spencer,
 MEDICINE 88 51
sperm, **LIFE 84** 38, 39
 cells, **HUMAN BODY 87** 12,
 39, 42-44
Sperry, Elmer, **FORCE &
 MOTION 78** 57
sphalerite,
 CRYSTAL & GEM 25 49
sphene, **CRYSTAL & GEM 25**
 42, 48
spheroid bone,
 SKELETON 3 29
Sphinx, **ANCIENT EGYPT 23** 11;
 PYRAMID 53 6, 18, 26-27, 63
sphygmomanometers,
 INVENTION 27 43
Spice Islands,
 EXPLORER 31 9, 20, 24, 30, 40

spices, EARLY PEOPLE 10 8, 9;
JUNGLE 54 58; PIRATE 59 47;
TREE 5 42
Spice Route,
ARCHAEOLOGY 56 50;
CHINA 55 58
spider crabs, SHELL 9 25, 55
spiders, FOSSIL 19 20, 30, 60;
INSECT 17 9; JUNGLE 54 34,
52; LIFE 84 24, 37, 39
exoskeletons,
SKELETON 3 22, 23
water, POND & RIVER 6 51
Spielberg, Steven, CINEMA 34
42, 44; PIRATE 59 62
spies, CRIME & DETECTION 73
11; SPY 67
catchers, SPY 67 41, 50, 51
espionage, SPY 67 8, 10,
38, 58
planes, SPY 67 52, 53
ring, SPY 67 41
trials, SPY 67 34, 56
spikes, SPORT 8 39
spinal cord, HUMAN BODY 87
46, 58-59, 61; SKELETON 3
39, 41
spindle shells, SHELL 9 43
spindles, EARLY PEOPLE 10 33
spine, human,
MEDICINE 88 24, 45;
SKELETON 3 20,
38-41, 63
see also vertebrae
spinel, CRYSTAL & GEM 25 19,
27, 37, 46, 57
spinning, CASTLE 49 51;
COSTUME 35 7, 8, 13, 14;
DESERT 51 58; MEDIEVAL
LIFE 65 23
early, EARLY PEOPLE 10 32, 33
evolution of,
INVENTION 27 36-37
spinning frame,
TECHNOLOGY 89 34-35
spiny boxfish, FISH 20 21
spiny spider crabs,
SKELETON 3 25
spiral, FORCE & MOTION 78
13, 54, 55
spires, BUILDING 58 36
Spitfires, FLYING MACHINE 22
25, 39
spitz dogs, DOG 32 9, 54,
57, 59
spleen, HUMAN BODY 87 32,
37, 41
spodumene,
CRYSTAL & GEM 25 49
Spondylus, FOSSIL 19 26
sponges,
ARCTIC & ANTARCTIC 57 12, 13;
EVOLUTION 85 9, 55;
OCEAN 62 10, 44, 58, 63;
PREHISTORIC LIFE 52 14, 16;
SEASHORE 15 19, 33, 43, 58
fossils of, FOSSIL 19 17, 18, 25

spores, LIFE 84 15, 20, 51, 52
sports, FUTURE 100 10;
HORSE 33 38, 44, 58-61;
RUSSIA 74 54, 55; SPORT 8
see also under individual sports
spotted rock crabs, SHELL 9 53
sprats, FISH 20 56
springs, ENERGY 76 15, 17
springtails, INSECT 17 10
spritsail, BOAT 36 14, 24, 62
spruce, TREE 5 11, 30, 31, 44
spurs, ARMS & ARMOUR 4 15,
30; HORSE 33 30, 42-44;
KNIGHT 43 8, 20, 29
jingle-bob, COWBOY 45 11,
24-25
prick, COWBOY 45 11, 24
rowels, COWBOY 45 11,
23-27, 50-53
shanks, COWBOY 45 11, 25
Sputnik, ASTRONOMY 82 34;
RUSSIA 74 50; SPACE
EXPLORATION 71 18
squalls, WEATHER 28 34
square crabs, SHELL 9 55
square dancing,
COWBOY 45 61
squash, SPORT 8 36
squash-bugs,
BUTTERFLY & MOTH 7 15
squids, ARCTIC &
ANTARCTIC 57 12, 47;
FISH 20 60; OCEAN 62 10, 32,
34, 40; SEASHORE 15 26, 38,
56; SHELL 9 18, 19
cephalopods,
FOSSIL 19 21, 28, 29
squires, CASTLE 49 43, 46;
KNIGHT 43 10-11, 28-29
squirrels, DESERT 51 31, 37;
MAMMAL 11 52, 54-55, 62;
SKELETON 3 15
flying, MAMMAL 11 29
ground MAMMAL 11 56
tree, MAMMAL 11 11
Sri Lanka, WHALE 46 59, 62;
WITCH & WIZARD 70 50
stabbing,
CRIME & DETECTION 73
9, 22
stables, FARM 66 40, 41
stadiums,
ANCIENT GREECE 37 25, 44
Stafford, Thomas, SPACE
EXPLORATION 71 13
stagecoaches, HORSE 33 48-49
Stahl, Georg, MATTER 80 30
stained glass, BUILDING 58
50-51; MEDIEVAL LIFE 65
34-35, 53
stainless steel,
FUTURE 100 9
staircases,
BUILDING 58 38-39, 54;
CASTLE 49 27
spiral, BUILDING 58 38, 39
stake, burning at, CASTLE 49 33

stalactites, CRYSTAL & GEM 25
9, 22; EARTH 83 17, 51;
ROCK & MINERAL 2 9, 22, 23
stalagmites,
ROCK & MINERAL 2, 23;
CRYSTAL & GEM 25 9;
EARTH 83 17, 51
Stalin, Joseph, RUSSIA 74
34-35, 36, 37
Stalingrad, RUSSIA 74 36
stallions, HORSE 33 12-14,
26-27
stamps, FLAG 16 45, 54, 55, 59
Stanhope, John, ANCIENT
GREECE 37 13, 61
Stanley, Henry, EXPLORER 31
46-47, 63
star rubies,
CRYSTAL & GEM 25 37, 59
star sapphire,
CRYSTAL & GEM 25 59
starboard, ship side,
BOAT 36 7, 39, 52, 61
lights, BOAT 36 52, 53
starch, LIFE 84 8, 33;
PLANT 14 14, 15
starfish, ECOLOGY 86 13, 42, 47;
INSECT 17 9; SEASHORE 15
28-29, 40-41; SHELL 9 9, 20;
SKELETON 3 25
Arctic, ARCTIC &
ANTARCTIC 57 13
fossils, FOSSIL 19 18, 19, 32
echinoderms, OCEAN 62 10,
18-19, 25, SEASHORE 15
40-41;
movement, SEASHORE 15
28-29
stargazers, FISH 20 54
Starling, Ernest,
HUMAN BODY 87 40
starlings, BIRD 1 24, 43, 61
Starr, Belle, COWBOY 45 58
Starr revolver, COWBOY 45 40
Stars and Stripes,
FLAG 16 24-25
stars, sky,
ARCTIC & ANTARCTIC 57 14,
37; ASTRONOMY 82 7,
60-61, 62; PYRAMID 53 47;
TIME & SPACE 81 7, 24,
25, 28, 41
catalogues, ASTRONOMY 82
10, 18, 28
charts, ASTRONOMY 82 6, 9
distance, TIME & SPACE 81
14, 49
hydrogen,
TIME & SPACE 81 39
neutrons,
TIME & SPACE 81 45
pulsars,
TIME & SPACE 81 56
stars, Hollywood,
CINEMA 34 18, 20-21, 24
make-up,
CINEMA 34 34-35, 42

wardrobe, CINEMA 34 30, 31,
36-37
star-shells, SHELL 9 47
staters, MONEY 18 10
static, FORCE & MOTION 78 43
static electricity,
ELECTRICITY 77 7, 9;
ENERGY 76 19, 23;
WEATHER 28 36
stations, TRAIN 39 21, 34, 48-49
Metro, TRAIN 39 57
royal, TRAIN 39 44
station-master, TRAIN 39 50
stator, ELECTRICITY 77 41
statues, MUMMY 44 10, 12, 34,
40; PYRAMID 53 9, 11
Staurikosaurus,
DINOSAUR 13 7
staurolite, CRYSTAL & GEM 25
20, 60
stays, BOAT 36 7, 22
staysails, BOAT 36 24, 35
Steadman, Philip,
PERSPECTIVE 98 43
steam, CHEMISTRY 79 7, 35, 53;
ENERGY 76 28-29, 32;
INVENTION 27 37, 55
exhaust, CHEMISTRY 79 35,
36, 37
steam clipper, SHIPWRECK 72 21
steam engines,
ENERGY 76 30, 31, 33; FORCE
& MOTION 78 20, 21, 22, 40;
INVENTION 27 32-33, 58, 59;
TECHNOLOGY 89 6, 34, 36, 42
on farms, FARM 66 10, 12,
13, 24
locomotives, TRAIN 39
12-15, 52-53
trains, TRAIN 39 10-11, 52-53
uses, TRAIN 39 6, 19, 23, 29
steamers, BOAT 36 36, 37, 38
steel, BUILDING 58 32, 36, 62;
CHEMISTRY 79 8, 40-41, 46,
47; TECHNOLOGY 89 11,
12-13, 17
alloy, TECHNOLOGY 89
10, 14
cables, TECHNOLOGY 89
22, 23
reinforced concrete,
TECHNOLOGY 89 21
stainless, TECHNOLOGY 89
15, 23, 42, 52
stilts, BUILDING 58 11, 63
steer wrestling,
COWBOY 45 62-63
Stegosaurus,
DINOSAUR 13 11, 21, 34, 35
Stein, Sir Aurel,
ARCHAEOLOGY 56 29, 51
stelae, PYRAMID 53 25, 44
Steno, Niels Stensen,
EVOLUTION 85 9;
FOSSIL 19 14
Step Pyramid, PYRAMID 53
10-13, 42

Stephens, John,
PYRAMID **53** 59
Stephenson, George,
ARCHAEOLOGY **56** 60;
INVENTION **27** 33;
TRAIN **39** 12
Stephenson, Robert,
ARCHAEOLOGY **56** 60;
TRAIN **39** 7, 12, 13, 19
steppes, RUSSIA **74** 11
stereophonic sound,
ELECTRICITY **77** 53
stereoscopes,
PERSPECTIVE **98** 45
Sterling, Ford, CINEMA **34** 54
stern, BOAT **36** 33, 49, 60, 62
rudder, BOAT **36** 35
trawling, BOAT **36** 44, 45
sternum, *see* breastbone
sternwheelers, BOAT **36** 36
stethoscopes, INVENTION **27** 42,
43; MEDICINE **88** 7,
28-29, 61
Stetson, J.B., COWBOY **45** 21
label, COWBOY **45** 20
Stevenson, Robert Louis,
PIRATE **59** 6, 60-61
stibnite, CRYSTAL & GEM **25** 20
Stichocentrus, FISH **20** 13
sties, FARM **66** 40, 42, 56
"Still Life" at the Penguin Café,
DANCE **99** 26
stingrays, FISH **20** 23, 54, 59
stirrups, CASTLE **49** 61;
COWBOY **45** 16, 23, 51, 57;
HORSE **33** 30-32, 34, 40;
KNIGHT **43** 20
stoats, ARCTIC & ANTARCTIC **57**
36; MAMMAL **11** 9, 23, 29
stock routes, COWBOY **45**
38, 56
stockings, COSTUME **35** 19, 31,
37, 56
stockmen, COWBOY **45** 20,
56-58
stockwhip, COWBOY **45** 56
Stokes, Sir George,
WEATHER **28** 18
stomach, HUMAN BODY **87** 7,
34-37, 41
stomachers, COSTUME **35** 22, 30
stomata, ECOLOGY **86** 9, 41
stone, ARCHAEOLOGY **56** 15, 34,
52-53; PYRAMID **53** 32, 34;
TECHNOLOGY **89** 10, 21, 22
architecture, BUILDING **58** 7,
16-19
carvings, BUILDING **58** 47,
49, 59
columns, BUILDING **58** 32-33
floors, BUILDING **58** 44, 45
masons, BUILDING **58** 6, 16,
17, 19; MEDIEVAL LIFE **65**
32, 52-53
memorial, VIKING **50** 57,
58-59
mould, ARCHAEOLOGY **56** 50

quarrying,
ARCHAEOLOGY **56** 50
staircases, BUILDING **58** 39
tiles, BUILDING **58** 26
tools, ARCHAEOLOGY **56** 7, 50,
59; INVENTION **27** 10-11
vaults, BUILDING **58** 34-35
Stone Age, AFRICA **61** 10;
ANCIENT EGYPT **23** 6;
EARLY PEOPLE **10** 17, 31, 32,
33; ELEPHANT **42** 10, 11, 52
weapons,
ARMS & ARMOUR **4** 6-7
stone crabs, SHELL **9** 46
stonefishes, FISH **20** 35, 54, 55
Stonehenge, ARCHAEOLOGY **56**
7; TIME & SPACE **81** 26
stopwatches, SPORT **8** 38
storks, BIRD **1** 47, 58
storms, SHIPWRECK **72** 9, 52;
WEATHER **28** 38, 44, 41, 58
Stradivarius, MUSIC **12** 30
strakes, BOAT **36** 19
strangulation, CRIME &
DETECTION **73** 9
stratification,
ARCHAEOLOGY **56** 10
stratigraphy,
ARCHAEOLOGY **56** 25, 54-55;
EARTH **83** 46, 60-61
stratosphere, EARTH **83** 11;
WEATHER **28** 7, 36
Stravinsky, Igor, DANCE **99** 44;
RUSSIA **74** 48, 49
straw, FARM **66** 22-24, 34, 43
straw hats, COSTUME **35** 46,
47, 51
straw tubularia polyps,
SHELL **9** 52
strawberries, PLANT **14** 32
string instruments,
MUSIC **12** 26-27
early, MUSIC **12** 28-29
Indian, MUSIC **12** 40-41
violin-making,
MUSIC **12** 32-33
*see also under individual
instruments*
string quartets, MUSIC **12** 30
Stringfellow, John,
INVENTION **27** 58, 59
strings,
TIME & SPACE **81** 58-59
strings, musical, MUSIC **12**
26-27, 38, 43
see also string instruments
Stroh violin, MUSIC **12** 29
Strozzi, Palla,
RENAISSANCE **91** 17
Struthiomimus,
DINOSAUR **13** 36
Stuart, Charles,
EXPLORER **31** 38
Stuart, John, EXPLORER **31** 38
Stubbs, George,
HORSE **33**
10-11; SKELETON **3** 14

studios, CINEMA **34** 21, 27,
30-31
studs, SPORT **8** 7, 13
stunts, CINEMA **34** 40-41, 42
sturgeon, FISH **20** 9, 10, 14, 30
Sturgeon, William,
ELECTRICITY **77** 28, 30
Sturt, Charles,
EXPLORER **31** 38
styluses, INVENTION **27** 18, 31,
46, 47; PERSPECTIVE **98** 17;
WRITING **48** 16, 17, 24, 30
Styracosaurus,
DINOSAUR **13** 44
Su Song, Su Sung,
CHINA **55** 22;
INVENTION **27** 23
subatomic particles,
MATTER **80** 58-59, 60
submarines,
FUTURE **100** 10; OCEAN **62**
50-51; SHIPWRECK **72** 29;
SPY **67** 52, 53
Succoth, BIBLE LANDS **30** 14
succulents, DESERT **51** 18, 19,
20-21, 36
Sudan, AFRICA **61** 10, 14, 52;
MONEY **18** 8, 63;
PYRAMID **53** 6, 44, 48
Dinka peoples,
AFRICA **61** 44, 47, 18, 46, 49
The Mahdi, AFRICA **61** 42
suede shoes,
COSTUME **35** 24, 25
Sufism, RELIGION **68** 59
sugar, CHEMISTRY **79** 35, 37, 48,
50, 60; CRYSTAL &
GEM **25** 62
Sui dynasty, CHINA **55** 7, 39
suits, COSTUME **35** 29, 50,
52, 57
Sukha, BIBLE LANDS **30** 33
sulphur, CHEMISTRY **79** 14, 20,
23, 27; CRYSTAL & GEM **25**
16, 50
copper pyrites,
CHEMISTRY **79** 47
vulcanization,
CHEMISTRY **79** 52, 54
sulphur dioxide,
CHEMISTRY **79** 6, 38, 63
sulphuric acid,
CHEMISTRY **79** 27, 36, 42, 44
fire extinguisher,
CHEMISTRY **79** 7
industry,
CHEMISTRY **79** 62, 63
Sumatra, VOLCANO **38** 57
Sumer, ARCHAEOLOGY **56** 14-15;
EARLY PEOPLE **10** 40
writing, WRITING **48** 9
sumo wrestling, SPORT **8** 48
sun, FORCE & MOTION **78** 6, 20,
25; MATTER **80** 9, 28, 56, 57;
SPACE EXPLORATION **71** 11,
39, 42; TIME & SPACE **81** 6,
9, 12, 14

astronomical units,
ASTRONOMY **82** 37
comets, ASTRONOMY **82** 58
distance, TIME & SPACE **81**
10, 12, 33, 35, 48
elements, ASTRONOMY **82** 37
energy, ENERGY **76** 48-49;
FORCE & MOTION **78** 41,
57, 63; TIME &
SPACE **81** 31
gravity, FORCE &
MOTION **78** 60, 61;
TIME & SPACE **81** 29, 42,
43, 46
mask, NORTH AMERICAN
INDIAN **60** 55
midnight sun,
ARCTIC & ANTARCTIC **57** 7
photosynthesis,
ENERGY **76** 50
and planets, FORCE &
MOTION **78** 28, 29, 32, 33
position, TIME & SPACE **81** 18
solar system,
ASTRONOMY **82** 7, 8, 38-39
spectroscopy,
ASTRONOMY **82** 30-31
sunny weather,
WEATHER **28** 16, 17, 18-19
symbols, NORTH AMERICAN
INDIAN **60** 35, 54-55
worship, PYRAMID **53** 7, 38,
47, 57
sun god, ANCIENT EGYPT **23** 24;
MUMMY **44** 11, 25
see also Ra
Sun Tzu, SPY **67** 34
Sun Zi, CHINA **55** 14
sunbirds, JUNGLE **54** 25
Sundback, Gideon,
INVENTION **27** 7
sundial shells, SHELL **9** 11, 42
sundials, INVENTION **27** 22;
LIGHT **75** 7, 10; PIRATE **59**
25; SHIPWRECK **72** 32;
WEATHER **28** 16
sunflowers, PLANT **14** 10, 21, 30
sunglasses,
COSTUME **35** 34, 36
sunset siliquas, SHELL **9** 42
sunstars, OCEAN **62** 10
sunstone,
CRYSTAL & GEM **25** 45
supercomputers,
ELECTRONICS **90** 59
"Supergun", Iraqi, SPY **67** 11
supermarkets, FUTURE **100** 11
supernatural, WITCH &
WIZARD **70** 27, 36, 38, 40
supernova, ASTRONOMY **82**
60, 61, 63
Supersaurus,
DINOSAUR **13** 12
supersonic speed,
FUTURE **100** 11, 27
superstitions, WITCH &
WIZARD **70** 17

Surcouf, Robert, **PIRATE 59** 50-51
surgeon fishes, **FISH 20** 17
acanthodian, **FISH 20** 12
surgery, **MEDICINE 88** 48-49, 50-51; **PIRATE 59** 40
ancient, **ANCIENT ROME 24** 55; **MEDICINE 88** 8, 14, 20
instruments, **MEDICINE 88** 20, 25, 26-27
keyhole, **MEDICINE 88** 52-53
Surrealism, **PERSPECTIVE 98** 58-59
surveillance, **CRIME & DETECTION 73** 38-39; **SPY 67** 44, 48-53
visual, **SPY 67** 14, 15, 48
see also bugging
surveying, **ARCHAEOLOGY 56** 12, 22-24; **INVENTION 27** 34, 35; **SHIPWRECK 72** 50, 51
Susa, **BIBLE LANDS 30** 52
suspenders, **COSTUME 35** 37
suspension, cars, **CAR 21** 31, 39, 54, 55
Sutherland Highlanders, **BATTLE 63** 16
Sutton Hoo, **ARCHAEOLOGY 56** 9-10, 26-27, 43; **CRYSTAL & GEM 25** 44
sutures, **SKELETON 3** 28
Svein Forkbeard, King, **VIKING 50** 9, 22
swallows, **BIRD 1** 44, 47
swallowtail butterflies, **BUTTERFLY & MOTH 7** 26-27, 32, 58, 59
mating, **BUTTERFLY & MOTH 7** 11
swallow-tail moths, **BUTTERFLY & MOTH 7** 43
Swammerdam, Jan, **HUMAN BODY 87** 22, 23, 32
swamps, **JUNGLE 54** 6, 9, 16, 48; **PREHISTORIC LIFE 52** 7, 26-27; **TREE 5** 18, 31
Swan Lake, **DANCE 99** 29, 41, 50, 51
Swan, Joseph, **ELECTRICITY 77** 47, 49; **INVENTION 27** 7; **LIGHT 75** 52
swans, **ARCTIC & ANTARCTIC 57** 20; **BIRD 1** 9, 20, 24, 33; **FARM 66** 60; **POND & RIVER 6** 18, 28, 29
Swanson, Gloria, **CINEMA 34** 20, 29
Swastika, **FLAG 16** 13, 29
sweat, **HUMAN BODY 87** 38, 39, 50
Sweden, **FLAG 16** 44-45; **MONEY 18** 42, 44, 45; **VIKING 50** 8, 18, 42, 56; **VOLCANO 38** 55
navy, **SHIPWRECK 72** 26
sweet oil butterflies, **BUTTERFLY & MOTH 7** 10, 17

sweet peas, **PLANT 14** 20
sweet potato hornworm moths, **BUTTERFLY & MOTH 7** 44
Swift, Jonathan, **SPACE EXPLORATION 71** 36
swifts, **BIRD 1** 14, 32, 44, 47
swim bladders, **FISH 20** 8, 9, 23
swimwear, **COSTUME 35** 34-35
swindles, **CRIME & DETECTION 73** 18, 19, 52
Swiss Railways, **TRAIN 39** 63
switches, **ELECTRICITY 77** 25, 46, 47, 56; **TECHNOLOGY 89** 33, 54
Switzerland, **BATTLE 63** 45; **FLAG 16** 32-33; **MONEY 18** 32, 62
sword fish, **FISH 20** 34, 35
swords, **ANCIENT EGYPT 23** 37; **BATTLE 63** 10, 40-41, 57; **PIRATE 59** 12, 55
Anglo-Saxon, **ARMS & ARMOUR 4** 14-15
boy's, **ARMS & ARMOUR 4** 50-51
Bronze Age, **ARMS & ARMOUR 4** 10-11
cavalry, **ARMS & ARMOUR 4** 53
early, **EARLY PEOPLE 10** 43, 46, 47, 53
fencing, **SPORT 8** 50
Indian, **ARMS & ARMOUR 4** 34
Japanese, **ARMS & ARMOUR 4** 36-37
medieval, **KNIGHT 43** 7, 8, 9, 18-19
"nimcha", **PIRATE 59** 14-15
police, **ARMS & ARMOUR 4** 54-55
types, **ARMS & ARMOUR 4** 16-17, 42-45
Viking, **VIKING 50** 7, 14, 16, 43
sycamores, **TREE 5** 16, 36, 46, 51
Sydenham, Thomas, **MEDICINE 88** 26
Sydney, **PYRAMID 53** 62
Sydney Harbour Bridge, **TRAIN 39** 22
Sylbaris, Ludger, **VOLCANO 38** 33
Symbolists, **MONET 95** 51
symplesite, **CRYSTAL & GEM 25** 19
synagogues, **RELIGION 68** 44-46
synsacrums, **SKELETON 3** 47
synthesizers, **MUSIC 12** 62, 63
synthetics, **FUTURE 100** 54
Syria, **ANCIENT GREECE 37** 8, 14; **BIBLE LANDS 30** 14, 16, 24, 52
art, **BIBLE LANDS 30** 43
desert, **BIBLE LANDS 30** 50
Szabo, Violette, **SPY 67** 31

tabby cats, **CAT 29** 6, 45, 55, 60
tabla, **MUSIC 12** 51
table tennis, **SPORT 8** 34
tabor, **MUSIC 12** 50
Täby, **VIKING 50** 40, 59
tadpoles, **AMPHIBIAN 41** 36-37
metamorphosis, **AMPHIBIAN 41** 38-39
Tagglioni, Marie, **DANCE 99** 29, 44
Taharquo, **PYRAMID 53** 50-51
Tahiti, **EXPLORER 31** 35
Tai Zu, Emperor, **CHINA 55** 50
tailplanes, **FLYING MACHINE 22** 27, 33, 40, 59
tails, **GORILLA 64** 16, 18
Tainter, Charles, **INVENTION 27** 47
Taiwan, **WHALE 46** 59
Taj Mahal, **ROCK & MINERAL 2** 27
Takhenmes, **PYRAMID 53** 47
Takla Makan, **DESERT 51** 7
Talbot, W. H. Fox, **INVENTION 27** 40
talc, **CRYSTAL & GEM 25** 18; **ROCK & MINERAL 2** 49
talismans, **WITCH & WIZARD 70** 28-31, 55
talkies, **CINEMA 34** 19, 22-23, 36
tally sticks, **INVENTION 27** 30
Talmadge, Norma, **CINEMA 34** 21
tamanduas, **MAMMAL 11** 8, 51
tamarind, **TREE 5** 42
tamarins, **GORILLA 64** 12, 14, 15; **JUNGLE 54** 31; **MAMMAL 11** 8
tambourines, **MANET 94** 18-19; **MUSIC 12** 56
tamburas, **MUSIC 12** 41
Tanagras, **ARCHAEOLOGY 56** 55
Tang dynasty, **CHINA 55** 7, 26, 28, 56
Tanganyika, Lake, **EXPLORER 31** 46-47
tango, **DANCE 99** 9, 24, 59
tankards, **PIRATE 59** 45
tankers, **BOAT 36** 48, 50
oil, **BOAT 36** 7, 50, 59
super, **BOAT 36** 39, 50
Tantrism, **RELIGION 68** 28

Tanzania, **AFRICA 61** 7, 18
tanzanite, **CRYSTAL & GEM 25** 48
Taoism, **RELIGION 68** 30, 32, 33
t'ao-ku, **MUSIC 12** 50
tapaderos, **COWBOY 45** 8, 14-15, 23
tape recoders, **ELECTRONICS 90** 38, 42; **SPY 67** 13, 18-19
tapestry, **ARMS & ARMOUR 4** 14, 15; **CASTLE 49** 38; **KNIGHT 43** 8-9
see also Bayeaux Tapestry
tapetum lucidum, **CAT 29** 16
tapeworms, **SHARK 40** 27
tapirs, **JUNGLE 54** 48; **MAMMAL 11** 10, 23, 58
tar, **BOAT 36** 10, 11, 27; **FOSSIL 19** 6, 21
tarantulas, **JUNGLE 54** 46; **SKELETON 3** 23
tarot, **BOAT 36** 10, 11, 27
tarot cards, **WITCH & WIZARD 70** 37
tarpon, **FISH 20** 15
Tarquin the Proud, **ANCIENT ROME 24** 6
tarsiers, **GORILLA 64** 6, 10, 12; **MAMMAL 11** 8
Tartaglia, Niccolò, **PERSPECTIVE 98** 35
tartan, **COSTUME 35** 41, 60
Tasman, Abel, **EXPLORER 31** 34, 63
Tasmania, **EXPLORER 31** 39; **FLAG 16** 51
Tasmanian wolves, **FOSSIL 19** 57
tassel-finned fishes, **FISH 20** 9
Tatars, **RUSSIA 74** 8, 9, 12, 13
Tatlin, Vladimir, **FLYING MACHINE 22** 7
Tatsumi, Hijikata, **DANCE 99** 43
tattoos, **AZTEC 47** 53; **DESERT 51** 59; **MUMMY 44** 49, 57, 63
Tavernier, Jean Baptiste, **CRYSTAL & GEM 25** 56
tawney coster butterflies, **BUTTERFLY & MOTH 7** 23
tax evasion, **CRIME & DETECTION 73** 25
taxes, **MEDIEVAL LIFE 65** 8-10, 26, 48
Taylor, "Buck", **COWBOY 45** 61
Taylor, Elizabeth, **CINEMA 34** 21
Taylor, Ron and Valerie, **SHARK 40** 53
Tchaikovsky, Pyotr, **DANCE 99** 50; **RUSSIA 74** 48
tea dance, **DANCE 99** 48
Teach, Edward, see Blackbeard
teals, **POND & RIVER 6** 28, 29

technology, TECHNOLOGY 89
team dancing, DANCE 99 19
teddy boys, COSTUME 35 6, 57
Teel es-Sa'idiyeh,
    BIBLE LANDS 30 18, 37,
    40, 43
tees, SPORT 8 13, 58
teeth, HUMAN BODY 87 15, 34,
    56, 57; MAMMAL 11 12-14,
    50-51; SKELETON 3 26-28,
    36-37
    development,
        HUMAN BODY 87 48-49
    feeding, MAMMAL 11 48-49
    human, EARLY PEOPLE 10
        11, 15, 23
Tel-Aviv, BIBLE LANDS 30 45
telecommunications, SPACE
    EXPLORATION 71 13, 48-49
telegraph, ELECTRICITY 77 29,
    43, 56, 58; ELECTRONICS 90
    8, 24, 28, 42, 48;
    INVENTION 27 44, 52;
    WEATHER 28 13
    cables, ELECTRICITY 77 23
    poles, ELECTRICITY 77 21
    receivers, ELECTRICITY 77
        26, 30, 31, 57
Teleilat Ghassul,
    BIBLE LANDS 30 9
teleosts, FISH 20 9, 10, 13;
    FOSSIL 19 13, 35;
    PREHISTORIC LIFE 52 18, 20
telephones, ELECTRICITY 77 27,
    30, 58; ELECTRONICS 90 6, 7,
    25; FUTURE 100 8, 9, 20, 30;
    MONEY 18 20, 21;
    TECHNOLOGY 89 48-49
    cables, ELECTRONICS 90 13
    exchanges,
        ELECTRONICS 90 38, 47
    fibre optics,
        ELECTRONICS 90 63
    invention, INVENTION 27
        44-45, 46, 52
    microprocessors,
        ELECTRONICS 90 58
    mobile, ELECTRONICS 90
        60, 63; FUTURE 100 11, 12,
        28, 53
    solar, FUTURE 100 13
    tapping, CRIME 73 38, 39;
        SPY 67 16-18, 44, 48, 50
    transducers,
        ELECTRONICS 90 42
    videophone, FUTURE 100 13,
        28, 30, 59
telescopes,
    ASTRONOMY 82 7, 23, 27, 62;
    FORCE & MOTION 78 24, 29;
    MATTER 80 10, 57;
    SHIPWRECK 72 36; TIME &
    SPACE 81 13, 15, 32, 48
    astronomical,
        TIME & SPACE 81 7
    early, BATTLE 63 24, 25;
        PIRATE 59 19, 25

refracting, LIGHT 75 20
    reflecting, LIGHT 75 21
    graphic, PERSPECTIVE 98 45
    Hubble, TIME & SPACE 81
        45, 49
    invention, ASTRONOMY 82 20,
        21, 22; INVENTION 27 28, 29
    lens, LIGHT 75 20-21
    optical, ASTRONOMY 82
        24-25, 28-29
    radio, ASTRONOMY 82 27,
        32-33, 46; TIME &
        SPACE 81 56, 61
    reflecting telescope,
        ASTRONOMY 82 21, 23,
        26, 54
    refracting telescope,
        ASTRONOMY 82 23, 24, 25
    satellite, SPACE
        EXPLORATION 71 8, 39,
        52-53
    solar, ASTRONOMY 82 27, 38
    space, ASTRONOMY 82 7, 32
television, ELECTRONICS 90 6,
    10, 45, 60; ENERGY 76 34, 35,
    41; FUTURE 100 9, 13, 33, 52;
    LIGHT 75 31, 42; SPACE
    EXPLORATION 71 48, 51
    camera, ELECTRONICS 90
        27, 49
    cathode ray tube,
        ELECTRONICS 90 26
    codes, ELECTRONICS 90 48
    colour, ELECTRONICS 90 15,
        39, 44
    future, ELECTRICITY 77 62-63
    invention, INVENTION 27 53,
        56-57, 62
    in medicine,
        TECHNOLOGY 89 57
    satellite, ELECTRONICS 90 41
telex, FUTURE 100 9
Tell, William,
    ARMS & ARMOUR 4 21;
    SPORT 8 53
Tell Dan, BIBLE LANDS 30 15
Tell Deir 'Alla, BIBLE
    LANDS 30 14
Tell el-'Ajjûl, BIBLE LANDS 30
    16, 24, 35, 43
Tell Halaf, BIBLE LANDS 30
    29, 44
tells, BIBLE LANDS 30
    14-15, 62
temperature, ECOLOGY 86 6, 41,
    42, 52; ENERGY 76 20, 21, 25,
    55; JUNGLE 54 6, 8, 62;
    LIGHT 75 40, 43;
    WEATHER 28 7, 10, 42, 49, 62
    Big Bang, ENERGY 76 62
    calorie, ENERGY 76 36
    Earth, EARTH 83 6, 40
    ocean, EARTH 83 31, 32
    thermodynamics,
        ENERGY 76 26
    weathering, EARTH 83 50
Templars, KNIGHT 43 56-57

Temple of Siva, PYRAMID 53 6
temples, ANCIENT EGYPT 23 20,
    28-29; BUILDING 58 6, 36, 53,
    57, 60; PYRAMID 53
    24-25, 38, 39, 54
    Buddhist, RELIGION 68 26, 35
    Confucian, RELIGION 68 30
    Hindu, RELIGION 68 22-23
    Jain, RELIGION 68 36-37
    Sikh, RELIGION 68 38
    Zoroastrian, RELIGION 68 41
temporal bone,
    SKELETON 3 27, 63
Ten Commandments,
    RELIGION 68 42, 44, 47
Tenayuca, PYRAMID 53 61
tench, FISH 20 18
tenders, TRAIN 39 14, 15,
    17, 18
tendons, HUMAN BODY 87 20,
    21, 23, 51
Tenniel, Sir John,
    AMPHIBIAN 41 42
tennis, SPORT 8 30-33
Tennyson, Alfred Lord,
    EVOLUTION 85 34, 35
Tenochtitlán, PYRAMID 53 60
tents, ARCTIC & ANTARCTIC 57
    49; DESERT 51 44, 45, 58-59
Teotihuacan, PYRAMID 53 54
teredo shipworms, SHELL 9 60
terminal velocity, FORCE &
    MOTION 78 30, 42
termites, ECOLOGY 86 49;
    GORILLA 64 55;
    INSECT 17 26, 53, 55, 61;
    JUNGLE 54 6, 29, 37, 39
Terra Nova, ARCTIC &
    ANTARCTIC 57 55
terracotta,
    ARCHAEOLOGY 56 55, 57;
    BUILDING 58 43
terrapins, REPTILE 26 30, 31, 37;
    SHELL 9 8, 9, 28
terriers, DOG 32 9, 38, 55
    Australian, DOG 32 12, 39,
        52, 58
terrorism,
    CRIME & DETECTION 73 29;
    SPY 67 54, 55
Tertiary period,
    EVOLUTION 85 47, 62
Tesla, Nikola, ELECTRICITY 77
    40, 41; ENERGY 76 33
testes, HUMAN BODY 87 40,
    42, 43
tetanus, MEDICINE 88 32
tetrapods, PREHISTORIC
    LIFE 52 24-25, 60
Teutonic Order, CASTLE 49 18
Tew, Thomas, PIRATE 59 34,
    36, 47
Texas, COWBOY 45 18, 23, 27,
    38-39
Texas Rangers, COWBOY 45
    42, 47
Texcoco, Lake, AZTEC 47 7

textiles,
    AFRICA 61 20-21, 26;
    ARCHAEOLOGY 56 8, 31,
    40-41; AZTEC 47 10, 42, 43,
    60; COSTUME 35 13;
    MUMMY 44 52, 54, 60, 63
    medievel, CASTLE 49 50-51
    mills, TECHNOLOGY 89 34-35
Thailand, CAT 29 53, 55;
    MONEY 18 9, 10, 63;
    WITCH & WIZARD 70 52
    court dancers,
        DANCE 99 21, 33
thalers, MONEY 18 23, 32, 33, 55
Thales, INVENTION 27 38
thallium, CHEMISTRY 79 19,
    23, 44
Thames, River, EXPLORER 31 13;
    MONET 95 48, 50-51
Thamnopora, FOSSIL 19 23
Thar Desert, DESERT 51 7, 34
thatching, BUILDING 58 26, 28,
    30-31
theatres, ANCIENT ROME 24
    36, 37, 48, 51; RUSSIA 74
    45, 52
Thebes,
    ANCIENT GREECE 37 6, 14,
    63; MUMMY 44 22, 29, 36;
    PYRAMID 53 41
thecodontians,
    DINOSAUR 13 7, 57
Thecodontosaurus,
    DINOSAUR 13 57
theft, CRIME & DETECTION 73
    16, 17, 29, 39
theodolite, INVENTION 27 34
Theory of Everything,
    TIME & SPACE 81 59
thermals, FLYING MACHINE 22
    58; WEATHER 28 24, 25, 26
thermioic valves,
    INVENTION 27 52
thermodynamics,
    ENERGY 76 20, 26-27;
    TIME & SPACE 81 21, 30-31
thermoelectricity,
    ELECTRICITY 77 52
thermoluminescence,
    ARCHAEOLOGY 56 55
thermometers,
    ELECTRONICS 90 43;
    ENERGY 76 37; FORCE &
    MOTION 78 40;
    MATTER 80 11, 16
    clinical, MEDICINE 88 28, 57
    invention, INVENTION 27 43
    thermocouple,
        ELECTRICITY 77 52, 53
    weather, WEATHER 28 11,
        12, 23, 63
thermoplastics,
    TECHNOLOGY 89 26-27
thermosphere, WEATHER 28 7
theropoda, DINOSAUR 13 24
Thesiger, Wilfred,
    DESERT 51 62

top hats

thigh bone, **HUMAN BODY 87** 15, 17, 18, 19

Thirty Years War, **BATTLE 63** 46; **CASTLE 49** 21

thistles, **PLANT 14** 29, 30, 37

Thomas, Heck, **COWBOY 45** 43

Thompson, Benjamin, **ENERGY 76** 21

Thompson, William, **EVOLUTION 85** 28, 29

Thomson, Joseph John, **MATTER 80** 48, 49; **ELECTRICITY 77** 54; **ELECTRONICS 90** 26, 27

Thomson, William, Lord Kelvin, **TIME & SPACE 81** 31

thongweed, **SEASHORE 15** 21

Thor, **VIKING 50** 7, 46, 53, 63; **WEATHER 28** 36

thornback rays, **FISH 20** 56, 57

thorns, **PLANT 14** 36, 37

thoroughbreds, **COWBOY 45** 12

Thoth, **ANCIENT EGYPT 23** 19, 24; **PYRAMID 53** 21

Thrace, **ANCIENT ROME 24** 13, 30, 33

Three Musketeers, The, **ARMS & ARMOUR 4** 42

"three wise monkeys", **GORILLA 64** 58

three-spined sticklebacks, **FISH 20** 40, 41, 43

thresher sharks, **FISH 20** 58, 61

threshing, **EARLY PEOPLE 10** 30

throat, **HUMAN BODY 87** 54, 55, 56-57

Through the Looking-Glass, **WHALE 46** 42

thrushes, **BIRD 1** 38, 39, 42, 46

thuja, **TREE 5** 31

thumbs, **SKELETON 3** 49, 63

thunder, **WEATHER 28** 36, 37

thunderbolts, **FOSSIL 19** 17

thunderstones, **FOSSIL 19** 16

Thutmose III, **PYRAMID 53** 35

Thutmose IV, **PYRAMID 53** 26, 27, 49

Thylacosmilus, **FOSSIL 19** 56

thyme, **SEASHORE 15** 17

Thyre, Queen, **VIKING 50** 60, 61

thyridid moths, **BUTTERFLY & MOTH 7** 53

thyristors, **ELECTRONICS 90** 38

Ti, **PYRAMID 53** 24

Tiahuanaco Empire, **AZTEC 47** 10, 18

tiaras, **COSTUME 35** 11

Tiber, River, **ANCIENT ROME 24** 6, 55

Tiberius, Emperor, **ANCIENT ROME 24** 8, 9; **BIBLE LANDS 30** 55

Tibet, **DANCE 99** 32; **RELIGION 68** 28-29; **WITCH & WIZARD 70** 51

tibia, **HUMAN BODY 87** 15, 18, 19

tickets, **TRAIN 39** 28, 48, 49

tidal force, **ASTRONOMY 82** 40, 45

tidal waves, see tsunamis

tides, **ASTRONOMY 82** 40, 45; **FORCE & MOTION 78** 33; **OCEAN 62** 10, 45; **SEASHORE 15** 6, 14-15, 58

spring, **SEASHORE 15** 8, 12-13, 63

tidal zones, **ECOLOGY 86** 25, 42-43

Tiepolo, Giovanni Battista, **GOYA 93** 7, 8

ties, **COSTUME 35** 37, 40, 57

Tiger Moths, **FLYING MACHINE 22** 43

tiger sharks, **FISH 20** 60

tiger's-eye, **CRYSTAL & GEM 25** 33

tigers, **CAT 29** 11, 19, 30-31; **JUNGLE 54** 47, 51; **SKELETON 3** 52, 53

white tigers, **CAT 29** 58-59

tights, **COSTUME 35** 16, 59

tigons, **CAT 29** 59

Tigris, River, **BIBLE LANDS 30** 48, 50

Tikal, **PYRAMID 53** 58, 59

tiktiri, **MUSIC 12** 13

tiles, **CASTLE 49** 14, 20, 38

floor, **BUILDING 58** 44-45

ornamental, **BUILDING 58** 61

roof, **BUILDING 58** 26-27

wall, **BUILDING 58** 42, 43

tillers, **BOAT 36** 7, 22, 33, 35, 62

timber, **TREE 5** 56, 57

see also wood

Timbuktu, **AFRICA 61** 7, 15, 48; **DESERT 51** 62; **EXPLORER 31** 19

time, **TIME & SPACE 81** 38-39

biological, **TIME & SPACE 81** 20-23

cyclic, **TIME & SPACE 81** 26

measurement, **TIME & SPACE 81** 6, 16-19, 56-57

Planck time, **TIME & SPACE 81** 56, 60, 61

Super time, **TIME & SPACE 81** 38

travel, **FUTURE 100** 57, 59; **TIME & SPACE 81** 7, 51, 62-63

timpani, **MUSIC 12** 48

tin, **ARCHAEOLOGY 56** 36, 50; **CRYSTAL & GEM 25** 24; **ROCK & MINERAL 2** 6, 57; **TECHNOLOGY 89** 11, 12, 14

tinder box, **INVENTION 27** 21

Tintoretto, **RENAISSANCE 91** 44, 47

Tir peoples, **AFRICA 61** 40

Tirthankaras, **RELIGION 68** 36, 37

Tischendorf, Constantine, **BIBLE LANDS 30** 58

tissues, **LIFE 84** 14-15

Titan, **SPACE EXPLORATION 71** 44-45

Titanic, **ARCTIC & ANTARCTIC 57** 9; **FUTURE 100** 9; **OCEAN 62** 54; **SHIPWRECK 72** 28, 29, 37, 39

titanium, **CRYSTAL & GEM 25** 32, 37; **EARTH 83** 29; **ROCK & MINERAL 2** 56; **TECHNOLOGY 89** 12, 14, 15, 57

tithes, **KNIGHT 43** 52; **MEDIEVAL LIFE 65** 9, 30

Titian, **MONET 95** 12; **RENAISSANCE 91** 44, 46-47, 48

Tito, Marshal, **FLAG 16** 38, 39

tits, **BIRD 1** 49, 52, 60, 61

Titus, **ANCIENT ROME 24** 28, 30; **BIBLE LANDS 30** 54-55, 61

Tiwal esh-Sharqi, **BIBLE LANDS 30** 11

Tiye, **ANCIENT EGYPT 23** 23

toadfishes, **FISH 20** 54

toads, **DESERT 51** 15, 16, 17, 26; **FOSSIL 19** 16, 42; **POND & RIVER 6** 12, 20, 38-39; **REPTILE 26** 8-9

African clawed, **AMPHIBIAN 41** 13, 43-44, 59

African square-marked, **AMPHIBIAN 41** 6, 20-21

Asian horned, **AMPHIBIAN 41** 20, 44

Asian tree, **AMPHIBIAN 41** 23, 42, 44

camouflage, **AMPHIBIAN 41** 14-15, 20-21

European, **AMPHIBIAN 41** 17, 19, 32, 43

food, **AMPHIBIAN 41** 6, 18-19, 39

hibernation, **AMPHIBIAN 41** 38, 43

Oriental fire-bellied, **AMPHIBIAN 41** 16, 21, 23, 26

ornate horned, **AMPHIBIAN 41** 14, 18-19, 45

reproduction, **AMPHIBIAN 41** 32, 36-37, 40

senses, **AMPHIBIAN 41** 22-23

toadstones, **FOSSIL 19** 16, 35

tobacco, **COWBOY 45** 36; **MEDICINE 88** 37, 62; **NORTH AMERICAN INDIAN 60** 23, 49

toes, **SKELETON 3** 54-55, 56-57, 62

togas, **ANCIENT ROME 24** 8, 16; **COSTUME 35** 10, 34

Tolbachik volcano, Siberia, **VOLCANO 38** 21

Tollund Man, Denmark, **EARLY PEOPLE 10** 50; **MUMMY 44** 9

Tolstoy, Leo, **RUSSIA 74** 16, 44, 45

Toltecs, **AZTEC 47** 8; **PYRAMID 53** 56, 57, 58

Tom Thumb, **SKELETON 3** 58

tomahawks, **ARMS & ARMOUR 4** 62-63

tomatoes, **PLANT 14** 55

Tombaugh, Clyde, **ASTRONOMY 82** 57

tombs, **AFRICA 61** 40; **ARCHAEOLOGY 56** 11, 20, 21, 53; **CHINA 55** 13, 16, 43, 52; **RELIGION 68** 9, 11, 31, 55

Central Americans, **EARLY PEOPLE 10** 58

Egyptian artefacts, **MUMMY 44** 14, 30-31

Neanderthal, **EARLY PEOPLE 10** 38

robbery, **MUMMY 44** 7, 12, 36-37; **PYRAMID 53** 22, 38, 40, 43

sarcophagus, **MUMMY 44** 28-29

tomography, **MEDICINE 88** 38-39

Tompion, Thomas, **INVENTION 27** 23

Tonga island, **DANCE 99** 14; **WHALE 46** 62

tongues, **HUMAN BODY 87** 34, 56-57, 59; **MAMMAL 11** 16, 19, 44-47

tools, **ARCHAEOLOGY 56** 50, 61; **BUILDING 58** 9, 18, 30; **MONEY 18** 8, 11, 52, 54; **ROCK & MINERAL 2** 28-31, 62-63; **TECHNOLOGY 89** 6, 10, 24-25

early, Aztec, **AZTEC 47** 13, 23

bronze, **EARLY PEOPLE 10** 43, 44, 47, 49

Egyptian, **ANCIENT EGYPT 23** 42-43; **PYRAMID 53** 30, 34-35, 46, 60

flint, **EARLY PEOPLE 10** 18, 19, 27, 32

iron, **EARLY PEOPLE 10** 50, 51

Roman, **ANCIENT ROME 24** 11, 26, 43

Viking, **VIKING 50** 42-43

desert, **DESERT 51** 50-51

fossils, **FOSSIL 19** 58, 59, 62, 63

inventions, **INVENTION 27** 8, 10-11

toolmaking, **EARLY PEOPLE 10** 10-11, 12-13

top hats, **COSTUME 35** 39, 46, 47

topaz, CRYSTAL & GEM 25 11, 15, 42-43; ROCK & MINERAL 2 45, 49, 54
Topkapi daggers, CRYSTAL & GEM 25 39
topknots, FISH 20 25
topography, EARTH 83 32, 36, 38, 39; ECOLOGY 86 22
topsails, BOAT 36 24, 27
topshells, SEASHORE 15 14, 26-27, 32
Torah, RELIGION 68 42-45, 47
Tornabuoni family, RENAISSANCE 91 13
tornadoes, WEATHER 28 46, 47
torpedo, FISH 20 57
Torricelli, Evangelista, FORCE & MOTION 78 44; MATTER 80 20, 21; WEATHER 28 10, 11, 52
Torrington, John, MUMMY 44 9
tortoises, DESERT 51 26; REPTILE 26 11-12, 30-31; SHELL 9 9, 28, 32, 58; SKELETON 3 23
tortoiseshell, shells, SHELL 9 8, 30, 31
tortoiseshell cats, CAT 29 16, 27, 53
torture, CASTLE 49 32
Tory, Geofroy, WRITING 48 44
totem poles NORTH AMERICAN INDIAN 60 52-53; WITCH & WIZARD 70 44
toucans, JUNGLE 54 28
Toulouse-Lautrec, Henri de, DANCE 99 58; IMPRESSIONISM 92 26; VAN GOGH 96 25, 28-29
tourism, AFRICA 61 6
tourmaline, CRYSTAL & GEM 25 6, 36, 42-43, 58
tournaments, ARMS & ARMOUR 4 25, 30-31; CASTLE 49 44, 48; KNIGHT 43 42-43; MEDIEVAL LIFE 65 27
tourneys, KNIGHT 43 43
Tower of Babel, see Babel
towers, BUILDING 58 36-37, 39; CASTLE 49 6, 10-11; KNIGHT 43 24-25
towns, ARCHAEOLOGY 56 10-12, 18-19, 22
medieval, MEDIEVAL LIFE 65 6, 7, 46,48
Toyokuni, VAN GOGH 96 37, 47
toys, RUSSIA 74 15, 51, 52; SPACE EXPLORATION 71 9, 26, 32-33; VIKING 50 30
early, ANCIENT EGYPT 23 52-53; ANCIENT ROME 24 21
trace fossils, FOSSIL 19 7
tracery, BUILDING 58 49
trachea, see windpipe

tracheotomy, MEDICINE 88 58
track events, SPORT 8 38
tractors, FARM 66 10-11, 33
trade, AFRICA 61 48-49, 51; DESERT 51 47, 63; MONEY 18 34, 35, 42, 46; VIKING 50 26-27, 36, 62
ancient, ARCHAEOLOGY 56 50-51
medieval, MEDIEVAL LIFE 65 6, 7, 44-47
traders' banners, FLAG 16 58
Trafalgar, battle of, FLAG 16 19
traffic, lights, FUTURE 100 9
problems, FUTURE 100 24, 25
trail drives, COWBOY 45 18, 38-41
trains, TRAIN 39; FUTURE 100 23, 26, 27
diesel, TRAIN 39 6, 38, 40
electric, TRAIN 39 7, 38-39, 47
express, TRAIN 39 13, 39, 41, 54
freight, TRAIN 39 26-27, 50, 61
mail, TRAIN 39 8, 36-37
passenger, TRAIN 39 28-29, 42-43
Supertrains, TRAIN 39 63
Trajan's Column, ANCIENT ROME 24 40
trances, WITCH & WIZARD 70 21, 27, 36, 37
Transamerica Pyramid, PYRAMID 53 63
transducers, ELECTRONICS 90 7, 42-43, 58
transformers, ELECTRICITY 77 25, 40, 41, 57; ELECTRONICS 90 18-19, 25, 31
distribution network, ELECTRICITY 77 44, 45
transistors, ELECTRICITY 77 63; ELECTRONICS 90 16, 29, 38-39, 62; FUTURE 100 10, 52; TECHNOLOGY 89 54
Transit of Venus, ASTRONOMY 82 28, 46
translucency, LIGHT 75 46, 47
transmitters, ELECTRICITY 77 58, 59, 60, 62; ELECTRONICS 90 13, 25, 63; INVENTION 27 52, 53; SPY 67 13, 16, 17, 19
transmutation, MATTER 80 48, 49
transplants, MEDICINE 88 54-55
transport, ARCHAEOLOGY 56 45, 60; BATTLE 63 20-21
Trans-Siberian Express, TRAIN 39 42
Trapped Person Detectors, VOLCANO 38 59
trappers, KNIGHT 43 20
traps, EARLY PEOPLE 10 29

Travolta, John, CINEMA 34 57
trawlers, BOAT 36 42, 43, 44-45
treadmills, INVENTION 27 24
treason, SPY 67 40, 41, 54
treasure, PYRAMID 53 22; VIKING 50 49, 56
buried, PIRATE 59 36
maps, PIRATE 59 60
ships, PIRATE 59 22, 36-37
underwater, OCEAN 62 54-55
Treasure Island, PIRATE 59 60-61
tree houses, JUNGLE 54 38-39
trees, AFRICA 61 20; ARCTIC & ANTARCTIC 57 8, 36; PLANT 14 61; TREE 5 6-7
bark, TREE 5 11, 22-23, 63
branches, TREE 5 9, 10, 16
canopy, JUNGLE 54 6, 12-13
emergents, JUNGLE 54 6, 8, 10-11
growth, TREE 5 14-17, 18-19
rings, ARCHAEOLOGY 56 54, 62; ECOLOGY 86 29, 45
leaves, TREE 5 28-31, 46-47
logging, JUNGLE 54 62-63
medicines, JUNGLE 54 42-43
mythology, TREE 5 6-7, 11, 38
produce, JUNGLE 54 31, 58
in rituals, JUNGLE 54 56
roots, TREE 5 14, 17, 18-19
trunk, TREE 5 6, 16, 20, 21
as weapons, JUNGLE 54 34, 38
see also under individual trees
tree-shrews, GORILLA 64 9, 10
Trelleborg, VIKING 50 15, 22-23
tremors, VOLCANO 38 46, 47, 52, 55
trenches, BATTLE 63 50, 52, 54, 55; EARTH 83 38, 39, 45; OCEAN 62 8-10, 47, 53
Très Riches Heures, Les, WATERCOLOUR 97 12-13
Trevithick, Richard, ENERGY 76 29; FORCE & MOTION 78 20; INVENTION 27 33; TRAIN 39 10
Triads, Chinese gangs, CRIME & DETECTION 73 26, 50
Triassic Period, DINOSAUR 13 56; EVOLUTION 85 46, 61; MAMMAL 11 12-13
triatomines, INSECT 17 37
tribrachidiums, FOSSIL 19 12
triceps muscle, HUMAN BODY 87 21, 22
tricolours, FLAG 16 27, 29, 31, 34
tricorne hat, COSTUME 35 28
triggerfish, FISH 20 31, 35, 38, 51
trigonometry, INVENTION 27 34
trilobite larva, INSECT 17 31
trilobites, DINOSAUR 13 56; EVOLUTION 85 26, 46, 60; FOSSIL 19 6, 12, 20, 30; PREHISTORIC LIFE 52 10-12, 16, 17, 20

trimarans, BOAT 36 60
Trinity, RELIGION 68 48, 51
triodes, ELECTRICITY 77 55, 61, 63; ELECTRONICS 90 28, 29, 38
Trionyx, FOSSIL 19 44
triple jump, SPORT 8 41
triplets, CRYSTAL & GEM 25 40, 56
tripod fish, FISH 20 33
triremes, BOAT 36 20; PIRATE 59 10-11
Tristan and Iseult, KNIGHT 43 41
Tristan, CASTLE 49 38
Trnka, Jírí, CINEMA 34 52
Trobriand Islands, JUNGLE 54 39
troika, RUSSIA 74 10, 11
Trojan War, ANCIENT GREECE 37 12-13, 55, 61
trombones, MUSIC 12 9, 12, 22, 23
Trondheim, VIKING 50 30, 32
tropical rainforests, ECOLOGY 86 7, 50, 56-57
tropics, TREE 5 12, 13, 18, 42
tropidophora snails, SHELL 9 15
troposphere, EARTH 83 10, 11; WEATHER 28 6, 7, 28
Trotsky, Leon, RUSSIA 74 31, 33-35
troubadours, MEDIEVAL LIFE 65 26, 56
trout, FISH 20 18, 36; POND & RIVER 6 26-27
Trouville, MONET 95 16-18, 38
Troy, ANCIENT GREECE 37 6, 12, 13, 61; ARCHAEOLOGY 56 14
true, WHALE 46 14, 19
trumpet, BATTLE 63 52; MEDIEVAL LIFE 65 56; MUSIC 12 9, 20, 22, 23
Moroccan, MUSIC 12 21
trumpetfish, FISH 20 34
truncheons, ARMS & ARMOUR 4 55
trunk hose, COSTUME 35 22, 23
trunkfish, FISH 20 10, 11
T'sai Lun, INVENTION 27 7
tsars, RUSSIA 74 20-23, 28, 31
T-shirts, COSTUME 35 60
tsunamis, OCEAN 62 45; VOLCANO 38 47, 56, 57, 63
tsuzumi, MUSIC 12 50
Tuareg peoples, AFRICA 61 12, 14, 23, 53; DESERT 51 13, 47, 48, 50
tuataras, FOSSIL 19 44, 60; REPTILE 26 6, 36-37, 60
tubas, MUSIC 12 9, 20, 24, 25
tuberculosis, MEDICINE 88 34, 36, 63
Tubina, FOSSIL 19 27
tugs, BOAT 36 7, 50, 51

tulips, **PLANT 14** 20, 33, 60; **TREE 5** 27, 37, 41, 47
Tull, Jethro, **FARM 66** 16, 17
Tulum, **PYRAMID 53** 59
tuna, **FISH 20** 9, 30, 52; **WHALE 46** 59
tundra, **ARCTIC & ANTARCTIC 57** 8-9, 19; **ECOLOGY 86** 7, 8 28, 29
animals, **ARCTIC & ANTARCTIC 57** 36-37
species, **ECOLOGY 86** 52, 53
tune ships, **VIKING 50** 25
tungsten, **TECHNOLOGY 89** 12, 41
tuning fork, **MUSIC 12** 6, 7
Tunisia, **BIBLE LANDS 30** 23
tunnels, **TRAIN 39** 20-21, 56, 57
Tuojiangosaurus, **DINOSAUR 13** 34-35
Tura, **PYRAMID 53** 32, 38
Tura, Cosimo, **RENAISSANCE 91** 33
turban shells, **SHELL 9** 11, 13
turbines, **ELECTRICITY 77** 42, 44, 45; **ENERGY 76** 32, 33, 47, 58; **TECHNOLOGY 89** 36, 37
turbots, **FISH 20** 25, 27, 42
turbulence, **WEATHER 28** 57
Turin Shroud, **BIBLE LANDS 30** 58; **MUMMY 44** 56
Turkana peoples, **AFRICA 61** 18, 19
Turkestan, **BIBLE LANDS 30** 52
Turkey, **BATTLE 63** 59; **CAT 29** 46, 56; **VOLCANO 38** 6, 51
ancient, **ANCIENT GREECE 37** 12, 20, 27, 52; **ANCIENT ROME 24** 51; **BIBLE LANDS 30** 10, 28
buildings, **BUILDING 58** 43, 44, 61, 62
currency, **MONEY 18** 10, 20, 40, 41
turkeys, **FARM 66** 60, 61
wild, **BIRD 1** 23, 25, 26
Turner, J. M. W., **PERSPECTIVE 98** 29, 46, 47; **WATERCOLOUR 97** 7, 28, 36-37
Rain, Steam, and Speed, **MONET 95** 50
Turpin, Dick, **ARMS & ARMOUR 4** 49; **CRIME & DETECTION 73** 14, 56; **HORSE 33** 46
turquoise, **AZTEC 47** 33, 52, 54; **CRYSTAL & GEM 25** 50, 56, 58, 61; **DESERT 51** 56; **ROCK & MINERAL 2** 52
turrets, **KNIGHT 43** 23, 24
Turritella, **FOSSIL 19** 27
turritella shells, **SHELL 9** 43
turtle crabs, **SHELL 9** 26
turtle doves, **BIRD 1** 12

turtles, **OCEAN 62** 10, 32, 38-39; **POND & RIVER 6** 41; **REPTILE 26** 21, 23, 30-33; **SEASHORE 15** 56; **SHELL 9** 8, 9, 28, 56
African helmeted, **REPTILE 26** 61
big-headed, **REPTILE 26** 62
as food, **PIRATE 59** 42
fossils, **FOSSIL 19** 44, 47
giant, **PREHISTORIC LIFE 52** 38-39; **SHELL 9** 29, 30
green, **SHELL 9** 51
hawkbill, **SHELL 9** 31, 52
leatherbacks, **SHELL 9** 29
leopard, **SHELL 9** 30
mud, **REPTILE 26** 11
Murray river, **REPTILE 26** 48
skeletons, **SKELETON 3** 21, 23
starred, **SHELL 9** 59
tushes, **ELEPHANT 42** 20
tuskers, **ELEPHANT 42** 20, 21, 33, 38
tusk shells, **SHELL 9** 18
tusks, **ARCTIC & ANTARCTIC 57** 43, 46; **ELEPHANT 42** 20-21, 32, 35; **SKELETON 3** 37
Tutankhamun, **ANCIENT EGYPT 23** 11, 36, 42, 53; **ARCHAEOLOGY 56** 11; **FUTURE 100** 9; **LIGHT 75** 7
curse, **MUMMY 44** 40-41
mask, **MUMMY 44** 7, 39
tomb, **MUMMY 44** 24, 29, 35
treasures, **ANCIENT EGYPT 23** 23; **MUMMY 44** 38-39; **PYRAMID 53** 22
Tuthmosis I, **ANCIENT EGYPT 23** 22
Tuthmosis III, **ANCIENT EGYPT 23** 25
Tuthmosis IV, **ANCIENT EGYPT 23** 11
Tutsi peoples, **DANCE 99** 22
Twain, Mark, **PYRAMID 53** 20; **VOLCANO 38** 29; **WRITING 48** 58
tweed, **COSTUME 35** 60
Twentieth Century Fox Studios, **CINEMA 34** 21
twist, **DANCE 99** 59
Tyler, Wat, **MEDIEVAL LIFE 65** 10
Tylocidaris, **FOSSIL 19** 33
Tyndale, William, **BIBLE LANDS 30** 61
Tyndall, John, **MATTER 80** 22
typecasting, **INVENTION 27** 26-27; **WRITING 48** 36-37
typefaces, **WRITING 48** 44-45
typesetting, **WRITING 48** 38-39
typewriters, **WRITING 48** 58-59
typhoid, **MEDICINE 88** 34-35, 63

typhoons, **OCEAN 62** 12; **WEATHER 28** 38, 44, 45
Tyr, **VIKING 50** 14
Tyrannosaurus rex, **DINOSAUR 13** 6, 14, 24, 39; **EVOLUTION 85** 61; **FOSSIL 19** 49, 50; **PREHISTORIC LIFE 52** 8, 34-35
Tyre, **BIBLE LANDS 30** 22, 23, 40, 43
tyres, **CAR 21** 60, 61
tzeze, **MUSIC 12** 39

U

Uccello, Paolo, **PERSPECTIVE 98** 13, 16-17; **RENAISSANCE 91** 23, 28
Udjahor, **PYRAMID 53** 45
Uganda, **AFRICA 61** 20, 22, 26, 61
Ugaritic alphabet, **WRITING 48** 14
Uji River, **CASTLE 49** 36
Ukraine, **RUSSIA 74** 12, 22, 30, 33
ulna, **SKELETON 3** 48-49, 50-51, 62
Ulster, **FLAG 16** 46
Ultrasaurus, **DINOSAUR 13** 12
ultrasound, **FORCE & MOTION 78** 51; **FUTURE 100** 34
imaging, **MEDICINE 88** 39
ultraviolet light, **ENERGY 76** 42; **LIGHT 75** 41, 43, 45; **MEDICINE 88** 35
radiation, **ASTRONOMY 82** 32, 43, 48; **ECOLOGY 86** 36
rays, **FUTURE 100** 50
Ulysses, **SHIPWRECK 72** 59
umbilical cord, **HUMAN BODY 87** 44, 45, 47

umbrella crabs, **SHELL 9** 26
umbrellas, **COSTUME 35** 19, 37
Umbundu peoples, **AFRICA 61** 60
umpires, **SPORT 8** 25, 26, 31
Unas, **PYRAMID 53** 22, 32
uncertainty principle, **TIME & SPACE 81** 52-53, 56
Uncle Sam, **FLAG 16** 25
underclothes, **COSTUME 35** 42-43, 52, 54-55
undercote, **COSTUME 35** 15
underground railways, **TRAIN 39** 38, 56-57, 58
ungulates, **MAMMAL 11** 10, 13, 14, 35
unicorns, **FOSSIL 19** 17; **HORSE 33** 7, 42; **WHALE 46** 10, 32, 36
uniforms, military, **BATTLE 63** 8-9, 16-17
Union Jack, **FLAG 16** 14, 46-47, 51
Union Pacific Railroad, **TRAIN 39** 18, 61
United Artists, **CINEMA 34** 21
United Kingdom, *see* Britain
United Nations, **FLAG 16** 19; **WHALE 46** 59
United States, **PYRAMID 53** 62, 63; **VOLCANO 38** 14-15, 35, 36
Air Force, **SPY 67** 53
Army Signals Intelligence Service, **SPY 67** 27
currency, **MONEY 18** 6, 28, 29, 48
flag, **FLAG 16** 24-25
Navy, **SHIPWRECK 72** 24; **SPY 67** 10
Naval Intelligence, **SPY 67** 37
in space, **SPACE EXPLORATION 71** 16, 19, 22-23
U-2 spy plane, **SPY 67** 39, 53
weather, **WEATHER 28** 13, 40, 52, 56
see also America
univalve shells, **SHELL 9** 12
universal indicator, **CHEMISTRY 79** 42, 43
Universal Studios, Florida, **CINEMA 34** 30
Universe, **ASTRONOMY 82** 13, 62-63; **MATTER 80** 6, 61, 62-63; **TIME & SPACE 81** 8, 9, 58
beginning, **TIME & SPACE 81** 6, 24-25, 60, 61
collapse, **TIME & SPACE 81** 63
disorder, **TIME & SPACE 81** 30, 31

Einstein, **TIME & SPACE 81** 40, 44

expanding, **TIME & SPACE 81** 43, 48

geocentric, **ASTRONOMY 82** 11, 17, 18, 19

heliocentric, **ASTRONOMY 82** 18, 19, 20

order, **TIME & SPACE 81** 27, 28-29

quantum theory, **TIME & SPACE 81** 50-51

universities, **MEDIEVAL LIFE 65** 6, 7, 40

Upanishads, **RELIGION 68** 18

Uppsala, Sweden, **VIKING 50** 52; **VOLCANO 38** 55

Ur, **BIBLE LANDS 30** 10, 28

Urals, **RUSSIA 74** 10, 13, 15, 16

uranium, **CRYSTAL & GEM 25** 47; **MATTER 80** 46-47, 54, 55

Uranus, **ASTRONOMY 82** 24, 54-55, 56

orbit, **ASTRONOMY 82** 36, 37

urethra, **HUMAN BODY 87** 38-39, 42, 43

urine, **HUMAN BODY 87** 38-39, 42; **LIFE 84** 21, 26

testing, **MEDICINE 88** 22, 29, 61

Urnes style, **VIKING 50** 36, 48

Ursa Major, **ARCTIC & ANTARCTIC 57** 37

Userkaf, **PYRAMID 53** 38, 39

USSR, *see* Russia

Utamaro, Kitagawa, **IMPRESSIONISM 92** 56

Ute peoples, **DANCE 99** 39

uterus, **HUMAN BODY 87** 44-45, 46, 48

Uxbridge, Earl of, **BATTLE 63** 60

Uxmal, **PYRAMID 53** 58

V2 rocket, **SPACE EXPLORATION 71** 15

vaccination, **MEDICINE 88** 32, 42, 63

vacuum cleaners, **INVENTION 27** 54, 55; **TECHNOLOGY 89** 40

vagina, **HUMAN BODY 87** 43, 44, 46

valency bonds, **MATTER 80** 40

Valentino, Rudolph, **CINEMA 34** 20

Valhalla, **VIKING 50** 9, 53

valiha, **MUSIC 12** 39

Valkyries, **VIKING 50** 30, 53

Valley of the Kings, **ANCIENT EGYPT 23** 18, 22-23; **MUMMY 44** 10, 36-37, 38; **PYRAMID 53** 22

valleys, **EARTH 83** 37, 39, 48-49

Valparaiso, Chile, **VOLCANO 38** 46

Valsalva, Antonio, **HUMAN BODY 87** 54, 55

valves, **ELECTRONICS 90** 29, 37; **TECHNOLOGY 89** 36, 54

Van de Graaff, Robert, **ELECTRICITY 77** 12

van Gogh, Johanna Bonger, **VAN GOGH 96** 56

van Gogh, Theo, **VAN GOGH 96** 7, 10, 48

death, **VAN GOGH 96** 61

profession, **VAN GOGH 96** 33, 59

van Gogh, Vincent, **VAN GOGH 96**

asylum, St. Remy, **VAN GOGH 96** 48-51, 57

colours, **VAN GOGH 96** 32, 38, 40, 45

etchings, **VAN GOGH 96** 52, 58

family, **VAN GOGH 96** 6, 7, 18, 56

lithographs, **VAN GOGH 96** 15, 52

paintings,
The Bedroom, **VAN GOGH 96** 44

A Cornfield with Cypresses, **VAN GOGH 96** 54-55, 57

Four Sunflowers, **VAN GOGH 96** 38

Fourteen Sunflowers, **VAN GOGH 96** 39

Irises, **VAN GOGH 96** 50-51

Night Café, **VAN GOGH 96** 42-43

Noon: Rest, **VAN GOGH 96** 52

The Potato Eaters, **VAN GOGH 96** 22-23, 43

self-portraits, **VAN GOGH 96** 29, 30, 46 49

Wheatfield with Crows, **VAN GOGH 96** 60

Vancouver, **VOLCANO 38** 14

vandium, **CRYSTAL & GEM 25** 39, 44

Vanezis, Dr. Peter, **CRIME & DETECTION 73** 49

Vangelis, **CINEMA 34** 63

Varanasi, **RELIGION 68** 20

variable stars, **ASTRONOMY 82** 61, 62

Varro, Marcus, **MEDICINE 88** 18

Vasari, Giorgio, **PERSPECTIVE 98** 14, 16; **RENAISSANCE 91** 6, 32, 48, 54

vases, **ANCIENT EGYPT 23** 7, 12, 47

vassals, **MEDIEVAL LIFE 65** 8, 24

Vatican, **RENAISSANCE 91** 52-53, 56-57

Vatican City, **FLAG 16** 32, 34

vats, papermaking, **WRITING 48** 22

vaulting, **KNIGHT 43** 24

vaults, **BUILDING 58** 34-35; **CASTLE 49** 57

Vedas, **RELIGION 68** 18, 20; **WITCH & WIZARD 70** 50

vegetables, **FARM 66** 34, 36, 37, 62

veils, **COSTUME 35** 14, 44, 47

veins, **HUMAN BODY 87** 23, 28-31; **LIFE 84** 15, 27

Velázquez, Diego, **GOYA 93** 16, 17, 57, 59; **MANET 94** 36, 38, 39, 51; **MONET 95** 48; **PERSPECTIVE 98** 34

vena cava, **HUMAN BODY 87** 6, 29, 36, 39

Venda peoples, **DANCE 99** 19, 40

Venera probe, **ASTRONOMY 82** 47; **SPACE EXPLORATION 71** 18, 47

venereal diseases, **MEDICINE 88** 42

Venericardia, **FOSSIL 19** 26

Venezuela, **FLAG 16** 55

Venice, **FLAG 16** 34; **MONET 95** 48, 49; **PIRATE 59** 14; **RENAISSANCE 91** 44-45; **VIKING 50** 18

Venn, John, **ELECTRONICS 90** 50

vent, **VOLCANO 38** 18, 20, 23, 37

Venta, La, **PYRAMID 53** 54

ventifacts, **DESERT 51** 9

ventilation shafts, **PYRAMID 53** 23, 46, 47

ventricles, **HUMAN BODY 87** 6, 28-29, 63

Ventris, Michael, **WRITING 48** 10

Venus flytrap, **PLANT 14** 40, 42-43

Venus, goddess, **ANCIENT ROME 24** 6, 51

Venus, planet, **ASTRONOMY 82** 40, 42, 46-47; **SPACE EXPLORATION 71** 18, 46, 47

asteroid belt, **ASTRONOMY 82** 58

orbit, **ASTRONOMY 82** 36, 37

phases, **ASTRONOMY 82** 20

Veracruz, **EXPLORER 31** 30

Vercingetorix, **ANCIENT ROME 24** 12

Vermeer, Jan, **PERSPECTIVE 98** 42, 43, 49

vermetids, **FOSSIL 19** 27

Verne, Jules, **FUTURE 100** 8; **INVENTION 27** 59; **SHIPWRECK 72** 59; **SPACE EXPLORATION 71** 8

Verneuil, August, **CRYSTAL & GEM 25** 27

Veronese, Paolo, **RENAISSANCE 91** 44, 45

Verrazano, Giovanni da, **EXPLORER 31** 40; **PIRATE 59** 22

Verrocchio, Andrea del, **RENAISSANCE 91** 26, 27, 36

vertebrae, **EVOLUTION 85** 15, 62; **SKELETON 3** 8, 38-41, 63

vertebrates, **AMPHIBIAN 41** 6, 10; **EVOLUTION 85** 22, 23; **LIFE 84** 22, 27, 28, 49, 53; **PREHISTORIC LIFE 52** 18-19; **SKELETON 3** 20, 40

Vesalius, Andreas, **HUMAN BODY 87** 6, 10, 11, 54; **MEDICINE 88** 24; **SKELETON 3** 28

Vespasian, Emperor, **BIBLE LANDS 30** 39, 55

Vespucci, Amerigo, **EXPLORER 31** 23

Vesta, **ANCIENT ROME 24** 52

Vestal Virgins, **ANCIENT ROME 24** 19, 52

Vesuvius, Mt., **ANCIENT ROME 24** 57; **ARCHAEOLOGY 56** 28; **MUMMY 44** 9; **ROCK & MINERAL 2** 19

eruption of, **VOLCANO 38** 21, 26-31, 63

vexilloids, **FLAG 16** 8, 18

vibrations, **FORCE & MOTION 78** 46, 48-49

Victoria, Australia, FLAG **16** 51
Victoria, Lake,
 EXPLORER **31** 46
Victoria, Queen of England,
 BATTLE **63** 59; CRYSTAL &
 GEM **25** 35; TRAIN **39** 44, 45
video, FUTURE **100** 28, 31;
 TECHNOLOGY **89** 49, 55
 conferencing, FUTURE **100** 12,
 13, 29, 59
 recorders, ELECTRONICS **90**
 10-11, 44, 60
videophones, FUTURE **100** 13,
 28, 30, 59
Viking space probes, SPACE
 EXPLORATION **71** 47
Vikings, ARCHAEOLOGY **56** 6,
 10, 17; ASTRONOMY **82** 37,
 49; KNIGHT **43** 8, 22;
 MEDIEVAL LIFE **65** 6;
 VIKING **50**
 Borre style, VIKING **50** 6
 bows and arrows,
 VIKING **50** 12, 14
 bridges, VIKING **50** 23, 40
 costumes, COSTUME **35**
 12-13, 18
 legends, VIKING **50** 50,
 52-53, 58
 magic,
 WITCH & WIZARD **70** 29
 pirates, PIRATE **59** 12-13, 50
 varangians, RUSSIA **74** 8
 Viking York, Jorvik,
 ARCHAEOLOGY **56** 6, 10,
 46, 63
 voyages, EXPLORER **31**
 12-13, 40
 weapons,
 ARMS & ARMOUR **4** 14-15
Villa Farnesina,
 PERSPECTIVE **98** 30-31
villages, MEDIEVAL LIFE **65** 10,
 11, 14, 15
villas, Roman,
 ANCIENT ROME **24** 24, 58, 59
vina, MUSIC **12** 40
Vincent of Beauvais,
 WRITING **48** 27
Vindolanda,
 ANCIENT ROME **24** 40
vines, JUNGLE **54** 20, 21
vineyards, CASTLE **49** 15,
 52, 53
Vinland, VIKING **50** 20, 21
violas, MUSIC **12** 28, 30
violet coral shells, SHELL **9** 50
violets, POND & RIVER **6** 46, 54
violins, MUSIC **12** 6, 26, 27
 family, MUSIC **12** 30-31
 making, MUSIC **12** 32-33
 Stroh, MUSIC **12** 29
violoncellos, see cellos
viols, MEDIEVAL LIFE **65** 57;
 MUSIC **12** 29
vipers, JUNGLE **54** 52;
 REPTILE **26** 20, 49

Virchow, Rudolf,
 MEDICINE **88** 30
Virgil, WITCH & WIZARD **70** 12;
 WRITING **48** 7, 42
Virgin Mary, KNIGHT **43** 52;
 RELIGION **68** 48-50
Virginia, Pirate 59 18
virtual reality, FUTURE **100** 28,
 29, 48-49
 images, LIGHT **75** 12-13, 16-17
viruses, LIFE **84** 7, 58-59, 60
 disease, LIFE **84** 28, 29
Vishnu, RELIGION **68** 18, 20-23
Visigoths, ARCHAEOLOGY **56**
 18-19
visors, KNIGHT **43** 14, 46
Vistavision, CINEMA **34**
vitamins, CHEMISTRY **79** 9, 20,
 21, 29; MEDICINE **88** 34-35
Vitruvius, ANCIENT ROME **24**
 27; PERSPECTIVE **98** 10, 35;
 RENAISSANCE **91** 30
Vivekananda, RELIGION **68** 23
viviparus snails, SHELL **9** 14
voice box, HUMAN BODY **87** 19,
 23, 25
voiceprints, CRIME &
 DETECTION **73** 50
volcanoes, ARCHAEOLOGY **56**
 9-10, 25, 28-29; EARTH **83** 37,
 44-45; PREHISTORIC LIFE **52**
 6, 10, 19; VOLCANO **38**
 ash, VOLCANO **38** 16, 58
 dormant, VOLCANO **38** 6,
 38-39
 deep-sea, OCEAN **62** 9, 23,
 45-46
 gas, VOLCANO **38** 20, 36,
 37, 44
 Kilauea, VOLCANO **38** 22,
 23, 40, 43
 Mt. El Chichón,
 VOLCANO **38** 35
 Mt. Erebus, Antarctica,
 VOLCANO **38** 11
 Mt. Etna, Sicily,
 VOLCANO **38** 7, 8, 18
 Mt. Fujiyama, Japan,
 VOLCANO **38** 6, 57, 63
 Mt. Katmai, Alaska,
 VOLCANO **38** Alaska, 35
 Mt. Krakatau, Indonesia,
 VOLCANO **38** 35, 57
 Mt. Pelée, Martinique,
 VOLCANO **38** 15, 32
 Mt. Pinatubo, Philippines,
 VOLCANO **38** 17, 35, 56
 Mt. Rainier, USA,
 VOLCANO **38** 39
 Mt. St. Helens, USA,
 VOLCANO **38** 14, 35, 39
 Mt. Tambora, Indonesia,
 VOLCANO **38** 42
 Mt. Unzen, Japan,
 VOLCANO **38** 42
 Mt. Vesuvius, Italy,
 VOLCANO **38** 21, 26-31, 63

 outer space,
 VOLCANO **38** 44, 45
 rocks,
 lava, ROCK &
 MINERAL **2** 19
 pyroclastic, ROCK &
 MINERAL **2** 10, 18
 St. Pierre, Martinique,
 VOLCANO **38** 16, 32-33
 see also lava, magma
volcanologist,
 VOLCANO **38** 21, 32, 42-43
voles, MAMMAL **11** 9, 21, 22, 23;
 PREHISTORIC LIFE **52** 59
Volga, River, VIKING **50** 18,
 19, 36
volleyball, SPORT **8** 21
Volta, Alessandro,
 CHEMISTRY **79** 46;
 ELECTRICITY **77** 16, 17, 26,
 32; HUMAN BODY **87** 58;
 INVENTION **27** 38
voltage, ENERGY **76** 32, 33,
 36, 48
voltaic cells, CHEMISTRY **79**
 25, 46
Voltaire, VOLCANO **38** 47
voltameters, ELECTRICITY **77**
 32, 33
volts, ELECTRICITY **77** 18, 19,
 25, 42
volute shells, SHELL **9** 13
voodoo, WITCH &
 WIZARD **70** 48
Voragine, Jacobus da,
 RENAISSANCE **91** 8
vortex, FORCE & MOTION **78** 54;
 WEATHER **28** 47
Vostok spacecraft,
 ASTRONOMY **82** 34; SPACE
 EXPLORATION **71** 19
Voyager spacecraft,
 ASTRONOMY **82** 50, 52, 56, 57;
 SPACE EXPLORATION **71** 11
Voysey, Charles,
 WATERCOLOUR **97** 56
vulcanisation, CHEMISTRY **79**
 52, 54; VOLCANO **38** 36
vultures, BIRD **1** 8, 52, 53;
 EAGLE **69** 8, 10, 34-35
 feeding, EAGLE **69** 28-29
Vyse, Howard,
 Pyramid 53 38

waders, BIRD **1** 33, 35, 46, 51
wadi, DESERT **51** 8, 11
waggoners, PIRATE **59** 24
Wagner, Otto,
 BUILDING **58** 59
wagons, BATTLE **63** 21;
 FARM **66** 8, 43;
 VIKING **50** 40
Wagons-Lits Company,
 TRAIN **39** 43
wagtails, BIRD **1** 32, 45, 60
Wahiba Sands, DESERT **51** 23
Wailing Wall, RELIGION **68** 42
waistcoats, COSTUME **35** 28,
 33, 41, 59
Walcott, Charles,
 PREHISTORIC LIFE **52** 14
Waler, COWBOY **45** 56
Wales, MONEY **18** 46, 62
Walker, Bill, FOSSIL **19** 50, 51
Walker, John, SPY **67** 10
Walker, Captain Samuel,
 COWBOY **45** 46
wall paintings, CASTLE **49** 22
 see also cave paintings,
 frescoes
Wall Street, FUTURE **100** 9
wallabies, MAMMAL **11** 8,
 30-31; SKELETON **3** 52, 56
Wallace, Alfred,
 EVOLUTION **85** 20, 36, 58;
 EXPLORER **31** 48-49;
 JUNGLE **54** 60, 61
walnuts, TREE **5** 28, 33, 57, 58
walruses, MAMMAL **11** 9;
 SEASHORE **15** 56;
 VIKING **50** 26;
 WHALE **46** 15, 23, 28, 42-43
 Arctic, ARCTIC &
 ANTARCTIC **57** 17, 42-43
Walsingham, Francis,
 SPY **67** 41
waltz, DANCE **99** 48, 58
wands, WITCH & WIZARD **70**
 26, 27, 48, 58
war, FUTURE **100** 8-11, 50;
 MEDIEVAL LIFE **65** 6, 7, 28,
 60; MONEY **18** 22, 23
 in Africa, AFRICA **61** 22,
 42-43, 44-47
 Franco-Prussian,
 MANET **94** 43-45
 Roman, ANCIENT
 ROME **24** 6, 7, 12, 62
 spies, SPY **67** 30-31, 56, 57

see also warriors, World War I, World War II

war dances, **Dance 99** 18, 32, 35

anti-war dances, **Dance 99** 18, 38

war hammers, **Arms & Armour 4** 3, 25

war horses, **Horse 33** 22-23, 42-45

warblefly, human, **Insect 17** 32

warblers, **Bird 1** 39, 52

Warburton, Peter, **Explorer 31** 38

warm fronts, **Weather 28** 32, 34

Warner Brothers, **Cinema 34** 21, 51

Warren, Sir Charles, **Bible Lands 30** 62; **Crime & Detection 73** 54

warriors, **Ancient Greece 37** 14, 35, 55, 57; **Dance 99** 22, 23, 28; **Early People 10** 60

Bronze Age, **Early People 10** 46-47

Iron Age, **Early People 10** 52-53

Viking, **Viking 50** 12-15, 28

Warsaw Pact, **Spy 67** 36, 39

warships, **Boat 36** 20, 21, 32, 33; **Shipwreck 72** 14, 18, 20, 22; **Viking 50** 10-11

battle ships, **Boat 36** 47

Washington, George, **Writing 48** 52

wasps, **Insect 17** 38-39, 50-51; **Jungle 54** 37, 54

jewel, **Desert 51** 22, 23

waste, **Life 84** 6, 26, 17, 27

water, **Chemistry 79** 7, 14, 20, 28; **Energy 76** 27, 35, 36; **Life 84** 16, 21, 55, 62; **Matter 80** 7, 9, 22, 23; **Technology 89** 6, 22, 62

carbonated, **Chemistry 79** 28, 29

compounds, **Chemistry 79** 18, 60

conservation, **Future 100** 20, 21

in the Earth, **Earth 83** 14-15, 26

electrolysis, **Chemistry 79** 46

energy, **Energy 76** 12, 58

"freshwater", **Ecology 86** 54-55

living processes, **Chemistry 79** 35, 50, 51

molecules, **Matter 80** 6, 18, 36

pH, **Chemistry 79** 42, 43

photosynthesis, **Life 84** 17

pollution, **Ecology 86** 15, 54, 62

power, **Invention 27** 24, 25, 37; **Matter 80** 19; **Technology 89** 34-35, 63

properties, **Earth 83** 16-17

in reactions, **Chemistry 79** 25, 34, 35, 44

water beetles, **Pond & River 6** 9, 17, 50-51

water boatmen, **Insect 17** 36, 46

water closets, **Invention 27** 54

water cycle, **Ecology 86** 14, 16-17

water hyacinths, **Jungle 54** 16; **Pond & River 6** 42

water lilies, **Plant 14** 48, 49; **Pond & River 6** 34, 42-43, 44

water measurer, **Insect 17** 49

water mills, **Force & Motion 78** 10, 20

water plantains, **Pond & River 6** 7, 15, 56, 57

water pumps, **Invention 27** 32

water spouts, **Ocean 62** 12

water striders, **Insect 17** 36

water supply, **Desert 51** 7, 14-15, 19, 22; **Farm 66** 40, 41

water vapour, **Chemistry 79** 48, 51; **Matter 80** 20, 31, 34, 58; **Weather 28** 7, 19, 22, 24

watercolours, **Watercolour 97**

abstraction, **Watercolour 97** 52, 60-61

animal studies, **Watercolour 97** 14-15

nature studies, **Watercolour 97** 16, 27, 49

nudes, **Watercolour 97** 54-55

paints, **Watercolour 97** 15, 28, 29, 37, 39

palettes, **Watercolour 97** 6, 25

portraits, **Watercolour 97** 22-25

Waterloo, battle of, **Battle 63** 19, 27, 49, 56

Waterloo Station, London, **Train 39** 49

Waterman, Edson, **Invention 27** 19

watermills, **Farm 66** 28, 29; **Medieval Life 65** 15

waterwheel, **Force & Motion 78** 10, 12

Watkins, Dudley D., **Cowboy 45** 36

Watson, James, **Evolution 85** 52, 54; **Future 100** 10; **Human Body 87** 48; **Life 84** 35; **Matter 80** 42, 43

Watson, Thomas, **Electricity 77** 58

Watt, James, **Electricity 77** 42; **Energy 76** 28, 29, 30, 36; **Force & Motion 78** 21, 41; **Perspective 98** 45

steam engine, **Invention 27** 32, 33; **Train 39** 10

wattle and daub, **Building 58** 21, 22, 23; **Medieval Life 65** 11, 16, 19; **Technology 89** 28

watts, **Electricity 77** 25, 42, 46

wave theory, **Light 75** 34-35, 36, 61

waves, electrical, **Force & Motion 78** 50-51; **Light 75** 56, 58-59, 63; **Time & Space 81** 17, 51, 52-53

electromagnetic, **Light 75** 42-43

waveform, **Music 12** 6-7

wavelengths, **Time & Space 81** 48

waves, water, **Ocean 62** 12-13, 45; **Seashore 15** 6, 8, 10, 12; **Shipwreck 72** 10; **Weather 28** 57

wax, cylinder, **Invention 27** 47

lost-wax process, **Africa 61** 54-55, 56

tablets, **Writing 48** 16, 24, 50

Wayne, John, **Cinema 34** 58; **Cowboy 45** 26, 60

weapons, **Arms & Armour 4**; **Jungle 54** 34, 38; **North American Indian 60** 6, 14, 28; **Shark 40** 46-47, 60; **Technology 89** 12, 38

African, **Africa 61** 44, 46-47

ancient, **Ancient Greece 37** 10, 54, 55; **Ancient Rome 24** 8, 11, 12; **Archaeology 56** 33, 35-38; **Early People 10** 19, 29, 51, 55

bronze, **Early People 10** 43, 46, 47, 55

flint, **Early People 10** 19, 26, 27

iron, **Early People 10** 52-53

Aztec, **Aztec 47** 15

Chinese, **China 55** 10, 14-15

in dance, **Dance 99** 18, 23, 37

desert, **Desert 51** 50-51

espionage, **Spy 67** 36-37

medieval, **Medieval Life 65** 25, 28, 29

pirate, **Pirate 59** 28-29

Russian, **Russia 74** 9, 22, 25, 32

Viking, **Viking 50** 14-15, 21, 23

see also under individual weapons

weasels, **Mammal 11** 9

weather, **Farm 66** 20, 27, 33, 35; **Ocean 62** 12-13; **Weather 28** 6, 7, 10

artificial climate, **Farm 66** 36

forecasting, **Weather 28** 8, 9, 12, 44

instruments, **Weather 28** 11, 13, 42, 46

satellites, **Space Exploration 71** 50, 51

stations, **Weather 28** 12, 15, 52, 62

weather buoys, **Shipwreck 72** 11

weather vanes, **Viking 50** 9, 60; **Weather 28** 42

weathering, **Desert 51** 6, 8, 9, 10; **Earth 83** 22, 26, 50-51; **Ecology 86** 22; **Rock & Mineral 2** 10, 11, 12-13; **Volcano 38** 38, 40

weaver birds, **Bird 1** 48, 49

weaving, **Costume 35** 7, 8, 13, 38; **Invention 27** 36-37; **North American Indian 60** 49, 57, 63; **Viking 50** 44-45

in Ancient Greece, **Ancient Greece 37** 30, 31, 40, 53

desert, **Desert 51** 58-59

primitive, **Early People 10** 32, 33, 60

Webb Ellis cup, **Sport 8** 14

wedge-sole shoes, **Costume 35** 56

Wedgwood, Josiah, **Technology 89** 34

weeds, **Ocean 62** 10, 33; **Pond & River 6** 44

control, **Farm 66** 13, 18, 19

water, **Pond & River 6** 19, 47

see also seaweeds

weevers, **Fish 20** 54

weevils, **Insect 17** 16, 30, 61

weightlessness, **Time & Space 81** 42, 43

weightlifting, **Sport 8** 44

weights, **Ancient Egypt 23** 40, 45; **Money 18** 6, 7, 19, 36

weights, dive, **Shipwreck 72** 45, 46, 47

Weinberg, Steven, **Force & Motion 78** 63

welding, **INVENTION 27** 14, 15;
  TECHNOLOGY 89 18, 19, 43
Welland, Colin, **CINEMA 34** 63
Welles, Orson, **FUTURE 100** 9
Wellington, Duke of,
  BATTLE 63 24, 27, 56, 58;
  FLAG 16 14; **GOYA 93** 42
wells, **ARCHAEOLOGY 56** 11;
  CASTLE 49 15
Wells, H. G., **FUTURE 100** 8,
  9, 57; **LIFE 84** 62
Wells, Horace, **MEDICINE 88** 48
Wells Fargo, **HORSE 33** 49
welwitschia, **DESERT 51** 18, 28
wendlertraps, **SKELETON 3** 25
Went, Frits, **LIFE 84** 25
Wentworth, William,
  EXPLORER 31 38
werewolves, **DOG 32** 23
Werner, Carl, **BIBLE LANDS 30** 7
West Indies, **EXPLORER 31**
  22-23, 30; **MONEY 18** 21
West Side Story, **DANCE 99** 14
westerns, **CINEMA 34** 18,
  31, 58-59
wet suits, **SHIPWRECK 72** 47
weta, **INSECT 17** 17, 47
wetlands, **ECOLOGY 86** 16
Weyden, Rogier van der,
  RENAISSANCE 91 20, 21, 25
whale sharks, **FISH 20** 10, 34,
  58, 61; **WHALE 46** 20
whalebones, **COSTUME 35**;
  VIKING 50 21, 30
whales, **FISH 20** 6, 28;
  OCEAN 62 36-38, 62-63;
  SEASHORE 15 56;
  SHIPWRECK 72 38, 58;
  WHALE 46
  Arctic, **ARCTIC &**
  ANTARCTIC 57 14, 17, 63
  blow-hole, **WHALE 46** 17,
  35, 37, 39
  blue, **OCEAN 62** 26;
  WHALE 46 11, 18, 20-21
  communication,
  WHALE 46 26-28, 38, 43
  endangered, **WHALE 46** 49,
  58, 62, 63
  eyes, **WHALE 46** 17, 18, 33, 34
  food, **WHALE 46** 22-23, 24, 25
  grey, **WHALE 46** 10-11, 24,
  57, 63
  humpback, **ARCTIC &**
  ANTARCTIC 57 46, 47;
  OCEAN 62 28, 38;
  WHALE 46 25, 26, 30, 60
  killer, **OCEAN 62** 27;
  WHALE 46 13, 19, 22, 34-35
  as mammals,
  MAMMAL 11 10, 20, 29, 51
  mating, **WHALE 46** 26, 28,
  29, 30
  myths, **WHALE 46** 33, 36,
  54-55
  reproduction,
  WHALE 46 28-29, 59, 60

senses, **WHALE 46** 18, 40
skeleton, **SKELETON 3** 15, 41;
  WHALE 46 12-13, 40, 45
sperm whale,
  OCEAN 62 10, 36, 40, 51;
  WHALE 46 11,
  18, 27, 39
swimming, **WHALE 46** 16,
  17, 18, 19
teeth, **WHALE 46** 8, 22-23
whaling, **BOAT 36** 30-31;
  WHALE 46 11, 21, 49-51
boats, **WHALE 46** 46, 47,
  48, 50
wheat, **EARLY PEOPLE 10** 8, 30;
  FARM 66 14, 16, 22, 26;
  PLANT 14 56-57
Wheatstone, Charles,
  ELECTRICITY 77 56;
  FORCE & MOTION 78 62;
  PERSPECTIVE 98 45;
  ELECTRONICS 90 24, 48
wheelbarrows,
  FORCE & MOTION 78 17
Wheeler, Edward L.,
  COWBOY 45 18
wheelhouse, **BOAT 36** 52
wheels, **FORCE & MOTION 78**
  7, 10-11, 30, 39;
  INVENTION 27 12-13, 24,
  25, 31; **TECHNOLOGY 89**
  32, 33, 35
  balance, **FORCE &**
  MOTION 78 22, 47
  bicycle, **FORCE &**
  MOTION 78 21, 57
  car, **CAR 21** 39, 58, 59
  machines,
  FORCE & MOTION 78 22
  momentum,
  FORCE & MOTION 78 54
  paddle, **FORCE &**
  MOTION 78 40
  pulley, **FORCE &**
  MOTION 78 18, 53
  train, **TRAIN 39** 11, 14, 15, 19
whelks, **SEASHORE 15** 30,
  48-49, 59; **SHELL 9** 14, 34
  dog, **SEASHORE 15** 14, 27, 32
whetstones,
  ROCK & MINERAL 2 31
whip scorpions,
  DESERT 51 24, 25
whippets, **DOG 32** 46, 53
whips, **PIRATE 59** 41
  "cat of nine tails",
  PIRATE 59 40
whirling dervishes,
  DANCE 99 34
whiskers, **MAMMAL 11** 16, 20,
  25; **WHALE 46** 15, 18, 23, 43
Whisky Galore,
  SHIPWRECK 72 58
Whistler, J.A.M.,
  IMPRESSIONISM 92 60, 61;
  MANET 94 23, 27;
  PERSPECTIVE 98 48

whistles, **BATTLE 63** 53;
  MUSIC 12 10, 56;
  TRAIN 39 19, 49, 51, 60
Whitbread Round the World
  Race, **BOAT 36** 60
White, Edward, **SPACE**
  EXPLORATION 71 34
White, Gilbert, **DOG 32** 54
White, John,
  NORTH AMERICAN
  INDIAN 60 9, 18
White Army, **RUSSIA 74** 32
white blood cells,
  HUMAN BODY 87 17,
  32-33, 41; **LIFE 84** 27, 28, 34
white dwarf,
  ASTRONOMY 82 60
White Ensign, **FLAG 16** 16
white flag, **FLAG 16** 14
Whittington, Dick,
  MEDIEVAL LIFE 65 48
Whittle, Sir Frank,
  FLYING MACHINE 22 36;
  FUTURE 100 9;
  TECHNOLOGY 89 37
wicketkeepers, **SPORT 8** 26
wickets, **SPORT 8** 26
wigs, **COSTUME 35** 11, 28-29, 33
  powered, **COSTUME 35** 31-32
wigwag code, **SHIPWRECK 72** 36
wigwams, **EARLY PEOPLE 10** 60;
  NORTH AMERICAN
  INDIAN 60 12, 22, 58-59
Wilberforce, William,
  AFRICA 61 51
Wild West, **CRIME &**
  DETECTION 73 11-15, 56
wildcats, **CAT 29** 10, 39, 44-45
  bobcats, **CAT 29** 10, 13, 24, 36
wildlife conservation,
  ECOLOGY 86 63
Wilkes, Sir Charles,
  EXPLORER 31 44;
  WRITING 48 36-37
William I, the Conqueror,
  King of England,
  WRITING 48 52
William of Normandy,
  BOAT 36 17; **HORSE 33** 31;
  KNIGHT 43 8-9;
  MEDIEVAL LIFE 65 7, 8;
  VIKING 50 10
William of Orange,
  FLAG 16 30
Williams, Tennessee,
  FUTURE 100 10
willows, **POND & RIVER 6** 7,
  11, 15, 21; **SPORT 8** 28;
  TREE 5 14, 26, 50, 61
Wills, John, **EXPLORER 31** 38, 63
Wills, William,
  DESERT 51 62
Wilson, Captain,
  BIBLE LANDS 30 63
Wilson, Charles, **MATTER 80** 58
Wilson, Edward, **ARCTIC &**
  ANTARCTIC 57 54, 55, 60

Wilson, Robert, **ENERGY 76** 62;
  TIME & SPACE 81 61
Wilton Diptych,
  CRYSTAL & GEM 25 50
Wimbledon, **SPORT 8** 31
winch, **SHIPWRECK 72** 43
Winchester rifles,
  ARMS & ARMOUR 4 60-61
wind, **OCEAN 62** 12-13;
  SEASHORE 15 8, 16, 17, 61;
  SHIPWRECK 72 9, 10, 11;
  WEATHER 28 13, 14
  force, **FORCE & MOTION 78**
  41, 42, 43, 50
  power, **TECHNOLOGY 89** 63
  spiralling, **FORCE &**
  MOTION 78 54, 55
wind energy, **ENERGY 76** 6, 7,
  12-13, 30
  sailing, **ENERGY 76** 9, 12, 13
  vanes, **WEATHER 28** 12, 42,
  43, 62
wind erosion, **ROCK &**
  MINERAL 2 12
wind roses, **INSECT 17** 43
wind synthesizer, **MUSIC 12** 63
windlasses,
  ARMS & ARMOUR 4 18-19
windmills, **COWBOY 45** 29;
  FORCE & MOTION 78 53;
  INVENTION 27 12, 24, 25;
  WEATHER 28 43
  early, **FARM 66** 28, 29
  energy from, **ENERGY 76** 59
windows, **BUILDING 58** 20, 28,
  48-49; **MEDIEVAL LIFE 65**
  16, 17, 33
  stained glass,
  BUILDING 58 50-51
windpipe, **HUMAN BODY 87**
  6, 19, 24-27
windscreens, **CAR 21** 24, 27,
  40-41; **FLYING MACHINE 22**
  42, 43
windsurfers, **BOAT 36** 8
wine, **ANCIENT GREECE 37** 7,
  20, 36, 48; **ANCIENT**
  ROME 24 46, 51, 59, 60;
  MEDIEVAL LIFE 65 20,
  30, 46, 54
  jars, **ANCIENT EGYPT 23** 47
wing cases, **INSECT 17** 6, 12, 13
wing-nuts, **TREE 5** 28, 40
wings, aeroplane, **FLYING**
  MACHINE 22 20-21, 26-27
wings, bird, **BIRD 1** 10, 11;
  EAGLE 69 17, 20, 21, 32;
  INSECT 17 12-13, 18, 19;
  SKELETON 3 50, 51
Winkler, Clemens,
  ELECTRONICS 90 37
Winnie-The-Pooh,
  ELEPHANT 42 51
winnowing baskets,
  DESERT 51 47
Winter Palace,
  RUSSIA 74 15, 25, 28, 30

wire, **TECHNOLOGY 89** 17
wireless, **ELECTRICITY 77** 57, 60, 62; **SHIPWRECK 72** 37
Wister, Owen, **COWBOY 45** 61
witch doctors, **EARLY PEOPLE 10** 36, 37; **WITCH & WIZARD 70** 27, 37, 39-43
witch hunts, **WITCH & WIZARD 70** 22-25, 38, 43
  burning, **WITCH & WIZARD 70** 15, 18, 22
  punishment, **WITCH & WIZARD 70** 10, 12, 13
witches, **EARLY PEOPLE 10** 36, 37; **GOYA 93** 30-31, 44, 52; **WITCH & WIZARD 70** 8-9, 10-11
  Africa, **WITCH & WIZARD 70** 27-29, 32, 58
  America, **WITCH & WIZARD 70** 24, 25, 27
  Asia, **WITCH & WIZARD 70** 10, 34, 36
  Britain, **WITCH & WIZARD 70** 32, 33, 36
  broomsticks, **WITCH & WIZARD 70** 10, 19
  fictional, **WITCH & WIZARD 70** 16, 17, 18, 19
  France, **WITCH & WIZARD 70** 13, 15, 39
  Germany, **WITCH & WIZARD 70** 13, 16, 22, 23
  Italy, **WITCH & WIZARD 70** 15, 30, 31
  Scandinavia, **WITCH & WIZARD 70** 10, 29, 36
  Spain, **WITCH & WIZARD 70** 12
  spells, **WITCH & WIZARD 70** 9, 13, 32-34
  see also witch hunts
witchetty grub, **DESERT 51** 25
Withering, William, **MEDICINE 88** 7
wizards, **WITCH & WIZARD 70** 12, 13, 15, 17
Wodaabe peoples, **DESERT 51** 48, 56
Wöhler, Friedrich, **MATTER 80** 42
wolf, **DOG 32** 15, 32, 33
Wolf, Marcus, **SPY 67** 41
Wolfe, James, **BATTLE 63** 62
wolfhounds, **DOG 32** 34, 38, 48, 49, 47
Wollaston, W. H., **INVENTION 27** 38; **MATTER 80** 15
Wolsey, Cardinal, **BUILDING 58** 41; **SPY 67** 40

wolverines, **ARCTIC & ANTARCTIC 57** 37
wolves, **ARCTIC & ANTARCTIC 57** 35, 38, 40-41; **COWBOY 45** 40; **DOG 32** 9, 12, 22-23, 40; **MAMMAL 11** 9, 43; **VIKING 50** 37, 51
womb, **HUMAN BODY 87** 44-45, 46, 48
wombats, **FOSSIL 19** 56, 57
women, **ANCIENT GREECE 37** 30-31; **CASTLE 49** 30, 46-47
  American Indians, **NORTH AMERICAN INDIAN 60** 19, 26, 32
    matrilinear society **NORTH AMERICAN INDIAN 60** 46, 49
    sacred, **NORTH AMERICAN INDIAN 60** 37
  in battle, **BATTLE 63** 12, 40, 44
  bound feet, **CHINA 55** 36, 46
  noble, **KNIGHT 43** 38-39
  Roman, **ANCIENT ROME 24** 18-19, 34, 36
    and religion, **ANCIENT ROME 24** 50, 52
    status, **ANCIENT ROME 24** 22
  Viking, **VIKING 50** 30-31, 33, 44
Wonders of the World, **PYRAMID 53** 21
wood, **ARCHAEOLOGY 56** 15, 29, 34; **BUILDING 58** 20-23; **TECHNOLOGY 89** 18, 24-25, 62; **TREE 5** 48, 56, 58, 59
  ancient times, buildings, **ARCHAEOLOGY 56** 8, 37
    in Egypt, **ANCIENT EGYPT 23** 42-43
    objects, **ARCHAEOLOGY 56** 15, 29, 35, 58
  architecture, **BUILDING 58** 6, 8-9
    balconies, **BUILDING 58** 56
    houses, **BUILDING 58** 10-11, 20-23
    roofs, **BUILDING 58** 24-25
  carving, **BUILDING 58** 54-55
  fossils, **FOSSIL 19** 6, 36, 39
wood block printing, **CHINA 55** 24, 25
wood carvings, **RUSSIA 74** 15, 50
Wood, Stanley L., **COWBOY 45** 41, 62
Woodade men, **DANCE 99** 26
woodcocks, **BIRD 1** 25, 30, 35, 59
Woodland Grayling butterflies, **BUTTERFLY & MOTH 7** 29
woodland management, **ARCHAEOLOGY 56** 12, 37, 47
woodlice, **INSECT 17** 9
woodpeckers, **BIRD 1** 13, 19, 32, 39; **DESERT 51** 30, 31

woodpigeons, **BIRD 1** 18, 52
Woodward, Sir Arthur Smith, **EARLY PEOPLE 10** 10
woodwind instruments, **MUSIC 12** 8-9, 16-17
  see also under individual instruments
woodwork, **CASTLE 49** 58-59
wool, **ARCHAEOLOGY 56** 28, 34, 45; **COSTUME 35** 7, 8; **EARLY PEOPLE 10** 32, 33; **VIKING 50** 37, 38, 44
  Llama, **AZTEC 47** 42, 44, 60, 61
  medieval, **CASTLE 49** 50-51
Woolley, Sir Leonard, **BIBLE LANDS 30** 10
woolly mammoths, **EARLY PEOPLE 10** 18, 24, 26
woolly-handed crabs, **SHELL 9** 56
word processors, **FUTURE 100** 52
World Health Organization, **MEDICINE 88** 63
World Meteorological Association, **WEATHER 28** 12
World War I, **BATTLE 63** 20, 50, 52, 63; **FLAG 16** 13, 28, 36, 39; **RUSSIA 74** 30, 39, 48
World War II, **FLAG 16** 13, 25, 57; **RUSSIA 74** 29, 34, 36, 37; **SPACE EXPLORATION 71** 15
world wide web, **FUTURE 100** 12
worms, **OCEAN 62** 10, 31, 55; **PREHISTORIC LIFE 52** 12, 14, 15, 18; **SEASHORE 15** 26, 42, 47, 59
  fan, **SEASHORE 15** 36, 37, 42
  marine, **SHELL 9** 6, 13, 43, 60
wracks, **SEASHORE 15** 12, 20-21, 33
wrasses, **FISH 20** 16, 17, 47, 50
wreck buoys, **SHIPWRECK 72** 10
wrens, **BIRD 1** 60
wrestling, **ANCIENT GREECE 37** 33, 44, 45; **KNIGHT 43** 10
Wright Brothers, **ENERGY 76** 31; **EXPLORER 31** 56; **FLYING MACHINE 22** 11, 14, 27, 52; **FUTURE 100** 8; **INVENTION 27** 58, 59
Wright, Frank Lloyd, **VOLCANO 38** 60
Wright, Joseph, **WATERCOLOUR 97** 41
writing, **ARCHAEOLOGY 56** 14-15, 40-41, 52; **AZTEC 47** 40, 41; **CHINA 55** 11, 12, 30-31; **WRITING 48**
  ancient, **ANCIENT ROME 24** 40, 41; **EARLY PEOPLE 10** 40-41, 54, 58
  implements, **INVENTION 27** 18-19

  in pyramids, **PYRAMID 53** 22, 46, 56-57, 58-59
wrought iron, **BUILDING 58** 56
Wu, King, **CHINA 55** 12
Wu Di, Emperor, **CHINA 55** 14, 18, 36
Wu Tai Chin, Larry, **SPY 67** 11
wulfenite, **CRYSTAL & GEM 25** 22, 63
Wynn, Steve, **PYRAMID 53** 63

xerography, **ELECTRICITY 77** 14
Xerxes, **ANCIENT GREECE 37** 54; **BIBLE LANDS 30** 52
Xhosa peoples, **AFRICA 61** 15
Xian Feng, Emperor, **CHINA 55** 19
X-rays, **ARCHAEOLOGY 56** 8, 40, 43; **LIGHT 75** 43, 46; **MATTER 80** 6, 46, 56; **SKELETON 3** 27, 61; **TECHNOLOGY 89** 57
  invention of, **INVENTION 27** 52, 56
  in medicine, **FUTURE 100** 34; **MEDICINE 88** 38-39, 52-53
  mummies, **MUMMY 44** 48-51
  photons, **ENERGY 76** 43
  surveillance, **CRIME & DETECTION 73** 29
  uses, **FUTURE 100** 50, 51
xylophones, **MUSIC 12** 48,55

Y Z

yachts, **Boat 36** 7, 51, 60-61
yams, **Jungle 54** 39, 42
yang qin, **Music 12** 38
Yangzi River, **China 55** 38-39
Yardley, Herbert, **Spy 67** 27
yardsticks, **Invention 27** 17
Yassi society, **Africa 61** 36
yeast, **Life 84** 19, 32, 46, 51
Yeats, W.B.,
    Witch & Wizard 70 59
Yellow River, **China 55** 38-39
yellowtail snapper, **Fish 20** 53
Yeltsin, Boris, **Russia 74** 58, 59
yen, **Money 18** 52, 53, 63
Yeo-Thomas, Tommy,
    Spy 67 56
Yermak, **Russia 74** 23
yeti, **Gorilla 64** 59
yews, **Tree 5** 23, 30, 32, 38
yin and yang, **China 55** 26, 28,
    38; **Medicine 88** 15;
    Religion 68 32, 33;
    Witch & Wizard 70 55
yoga, **Medicine 88** 44
yoghurt, **Desert 51** 46
Yom Kippur, **Religion 68** 45
Yong Le, Emperor, **China 55**
    20, 60
Yonnet, Joseph, **Cowboy 45** 54
York, **Viking 50** 26, 29
Yoruba peoples, **Africa 61** 13,
    62; **Dance 99** 35
  clothes, **Africa 61** 27
  kings, **Africa 61** 31
  myths, **Africa 61** 37
  rites, **Africa 61** 34, 41
Yosemite, Sam, **Cowboy 45** 45
Yoshida, Hiroshi,
    Elephant 42 52
Young, John, **Space**
    Exploration 71 23
Young, Thomas, **Force &**
    Motion 78 40;
    Light 75 36, 40
yuan, **Money 18** 52, 53, 63
Yuan dynasty, **China 55** 8,
    44, 48
  trade, **China 55** 58, 59
Yucatán, **Pyramid 53** 54, 56
yucca, **Desert 51** 25
Yugoslavia, **Flag 16** 38-39;
    Volcano 38 46
yurt, **Desert 51** 44
Yury, Prince of Russia,
    Russia 74 26

Zaire, **Africa 61** 34, 52, 58, 62
  currency, **Africa 61** 49
  pygmies, **Africa 61** 18-19
Zambezi, River,
    Explorer 31 47
Zambia, **Africa 61** 38;
    Volcano 38 50
Zanzibar, **Africa 61** 48
Zapf, Herman, **Writing 48** 44
Zapotecs, **Pyramid 53** 54, 55
Zarethan, **Bible Lands 30** 18
zebra butterflies,
    Butterfly & Moth 7 16
zebras, **Horse 33** 6-8, 18-19;
    Mammal 11 10, 36, 58
zebroid, **Horse 33** 18
zedonk, **Horse 33** 19
Zeiss, Carl, **Invention 27** 41
Zen, **Religion 68** 26
zenith, **Astronomy 82** 14, 60
Zeno's paradoxes,
    Time & Space 81 8, 9
zephyr blue butterflies,
    Butterfly & Moth 7 30
Zeus, **Ancient Greece 37**
    26, 44, 50, 60;
    Ancient Rome 24 50
Zhang Heng, **China 55** 22
Zhou dynasty,
    China 55 6, 12, 14
Zhukovsky, Nikolai,
    Russia 74 40
Zimbabwe,
    Africa 61 17, 52;
    Cat 29 43
  railways, **Train 39** 53
  see also Great Zimbabwe
zinc, **Chemistry 79** 17, 18, 23,
    36, 46; **Crystal & Gem 25**
    19, 46, 49, 53; **Rock &**
    Mineral 2 57;
    Technology 89 12
  alloys, **Chemistry 79** 15
Zinjirli, **Bible Lands 30** 40
zips, **Invention 27** 7
zircon, **Crystal & Gem 25** 37,
    47, 57; **Rock & Mineral 2**
    45, 54
zithers, **Music 12** 38-39
zodiac, **Astronomy 82** 7, 9, 13,
    16-17
zograscopes, **Perspective 98** 44
Zola, Emile, **Impressionism 92**
    16, 25, 32; **Manet 94** 29, 36,
    40, 56

zone, twilight,
    Ocean 62 10, 40-41
zoos, **Elephant 42** 9, 51, 63, 39;
    Gorilla 64 60, 62
  keepers, **Elephant 42** 26
  training,
    Elephant 42 41, 50
Zoroaster, **Religion 68** 40, 41
Zoroastrianism, **Religion 68**
    40-41
zorro, **Dog 32** 32, 33
Zukor, Adolph, **Cinema 34** 21
Zulu peoples, **Africa 61** 22, 26,
    43, 46; **Battle 63** 16;
    Early People 10 29
Zuni peoples,
    Desert 51 14, 47, 49, 52
Zworykin, Vladimir,
    Electricity 77 63

ird • Rock & Mineral • Skeleton • Arms & A
port • Shell • Early People • Mammal • Mus
Money • Fossil • Fish • Car • Flying Machine •
eptile • Invention • Weather • Cat • Bible La
Boat • Ancient Greece • Volcano • Train • Sh
owboy • Whale • Aztec • Writing • Castle • V
China • Archaeology • Arctic & Antarctic • B
cean • Battle • Gorilla • Medieval Life • Farm
xploration • Shipwreck • Crime & Detection
Motion • Chemistry • Matter • Time & Space •
uman Body • Medicine • Technology • Elec
lanet • Monet • Van Gogh • Watercolour • Per
Skeleton • Arms & Armour • Tree • Pond &
eople • Mammal • Music • Dinosaur • Plant •
ar • Flying Machine • Ancient Egypt • Ancie
Weather • Cat • Bible Lands • Explorer • Dog •
Volcano • Train • Shark • Amphibian • Eleph
Writing • Castle • Viking • Desert • Prehistor
rctic & Antarctic • Building • Pirate • North
Medieval Life • Farm • Spy • Religion • Eagle
Crime & Detection • Russia • Light • Energy
Time & Space • Astronomy • Earth • Life